The Ghent Altarpiece
and the Art of Jan van Eyck

The Ghent Altarpiece
and the
Art of Jan van Eyck

LOTTE BRAND PHILIP

PRINCETON, NEW JERSEY

PRINCETON UNIVERSITY PRESS

Copyright © 1971 by Princeton University Press

L.C. Card: 73-113007

ISBN: 0-691-03870-8

ISBN: 0-691-00316-5 pbk.

ALL RIGHTS RESERVED

Printed in the United States of America
by Princeton University Press, Princeton, New Jersey

This book has been composed in Linotype Granjon

First Princeton Paperback, 1980

FOR MY HUSBAND
OTTO H. FÖRSTER

PREFACE

WHEN some artists of our time insist that their creations should be called non-art or anti-art, it is understood that the concept "art" connotes those human creations which, in their elevated and venerated sublimity, are detached from all practical purpose. In the present century and in the previous one, the word "art" is generally employed for works whose sole intent is to edify the viewer aesthetically. Thus, such mediaeval or Renaissance objects as a chalice or a monstrance which were expressly created for use in Christian ritual are often called applied art. They may even be listed as "minor art," which means that they are not regarded as great art or as art proper.

But the distinction between real art and minor art is not actually valid for the earlier period. In the fifteenth century, even those works whose "greatness" is undenied today, the Ghent Altarpiece for example, were "applied art" in the sense that they were intended for a practical use in the ecclesiastical service.

Altar painting was a servant of religion. With a function outside the realm that we call art, its art-aspect was subordinate to a higher all-embracing idea. And when a complete separation (or should we say: alienation?) from a non-artistic purpose is seen as the prerequisite of great art today, it may even be this very quality which makes some of our present-day artists so violently reject "art." Perhaps the modern battle cry for non-art or anti-art hides a silent longing for a lost non-artistic purpose of the artist's work.

Today, even though artists and art historians are perfectly willing to accept the fact that an ingenious master of the fifteenth century should have created an object which was meant for practical use, it is still the former attitude, so well expressed in the axiom *l'art pour l'art*, which guides the art historian in his approach to the art works of all periods. Its continued influence is not surprising when we take into account that it was in the wake of this very trend that modern art history came into its own in the late nineteenth century, concurrent with the gradual growth of museums into educational institutions.

Some of the museum practices based on the *l'art pour l'art* attitude and rather widespread at the time seem almost barbarian to us today. The Berlin Museum, for instance, which then owned part of the paintings belonging to the Ghent Altarpiece, separated the painted fronts of these panels from their painted backs by sawing them apart. The decision to take this harsh measure (intended to facilitate the exhibition of the panels and their inspection by an art-loving public) becomes more understandable if we see the separating process as obliterating the last traces of the paintings' former ecclesiastical use and thus greatly stressing their character as "art pure and simple."

As for art history, the emphasis on this approach was compounded by the use of modern photography in research, a development which doubtless played a part in its sudden growth. Though we hear again and again that art students should work from the originals, this is a hypocritical remark at worst, while at best it is an admonition to check with the originals from time to time. The truth is that the larger part of all art historical study and writing was and is done from photographs on the scholar's desk, for this procedure is the only basis for a scrutinizing stylistic or iconographic analysis which can include the comparison of works actually located hundreds of miles apart.

Photographic reproductions, so indispensable for our scholarly activity, make every work of art, regardless of its specific character and function, appear as "art pure and simple." Aiming at the greatest clarity of detail, a photograph is normally a "close-up" reproducing the work of art in "splendid isolation." In our reproductions, therefore, even those works of a former time which have remained *in situ*, appear divorced from the natural context of their original environment and practical purpose.

It is this isolated work of art which art historians have often sought to put into a broader context by linking its form and content to modes and trends of the period which were known to them from other fields. But while it may be instructive to see art in a general framework of *Geistesgeschichte* or sociology, applied to it, as it were, artificially from without, we should not forget that for each individual work there had once existed a specific and natural "framework" quite palpable and concrete and supremely "sociological" in essence. Perhaps the simple and direct method of placing a work of art back into the very context of its own original setting and practical purpose can supply important new insights on the nature and meaning of a masterpiece.

The present study on the Ghent polyptych is an attempt to apply this method. The basic idea of my book goes back a great many years to a delightful evening when the still young but already famous Erwin Panofsky had invited his students to his apartment in the *Alte Rabenstrasse* in Hamburg. I was one of the youngest guests and completely fascinated when our teacher spontaneously started to explain his personal theory on the Ghent Altarpiece then still unpublished. Though a mere beginner and by no means familiar with all the angles of the famous art historical problem posed by the Van Eyck polyptych, my deep admiration for Panofsky's brilliant and witty discourse was mixed with a feeling of violent contradiction. Little did I suspect at that time that one day in the far future I would want to clarify in my mind the non-conscious reasons of my youthful objections, nor did I know that I would undertake the hard and time-consuming task of explaining these reasons in writing.

Anyone reading the following pages with their innumerable references to Panofsky's text will realize that my study is a tribute to a great teacher in spite of my contradicting him, or, as Panofsky himself would have said, "rather because of it."

Friends and colleagues who have helped me with one or the other detail of my study are gratefully named in the pages in question. But my thanks are also due to Harriet Anderson of Princeton University Press, who immediately took up the idea that my findings should appear as a book and carried the publication to a happy completion.

PREFACE

During the final phase of the publication work (when, due to an operation, I was unable to inspect illustrations and captions), Horst W. Janson offered his help in a most generous way, an act of friendship which is greatly appreciated. I also want to thank John Kalesh for his efficient assistance in compiling the index.

My deepest gratitude goes to my friend Elizabeth Crawford Parker whose selfless work during all stages of the manuscript—untiringly editing, typing, reshaping the text while cheerfully reassuring the author—makes the following pages her book as well as mine.

ACKNOWLEDGMENT FOR PHOTOGRAPHS

Unless listed below, the photographs in this publication were supplied by the museums, institutions, or collectors owning the works.

A. C. L., Brussels: 2, 3, 4, 5, 12, 19, 22, 32, 33, 34, 37, 39, 40, 46, 49, 53, 71, 72, 74, 81, 88, 89, 109, 122, 123, 129, 130, 132, 171, 173, 174, 184, 188, 189, 196, 202

Alinari, Florence: 36, 45, 50, 51, 77, 91, 93, 95, 99, 119, 121, 150, 181, 191, 199, 200, 209

Anderson, Rome: 11, 75, 92, 125, 175, 210

Archives Photographiques, Paris: 24

G. Bayer, Rothenburg-ob-der-Tauber: 146, 147

P. Bijtebier, Brussels: 1, 9, 56, 57, 62, 83, 107, 108, 117, 118, 139

Bulloz, Paris: 166

W. Castelli, Lübeck: 155, 157

A. Dingjan, The Hague: 158, 159, 165

A. Fréquin, The Hague: 76, 80, 110, 182

Gabinetto Fotographico Nazionale, Rome: 124

Giraudon, Paris: 21, 192

H. Hell, Reutlingen: 44

Landesdenkmalamt, Münster: 23, 148

Marburg, Marburg-Lahn: 6, 7, 8, 10, 15, 18, 30, 31, 43, 61, 103, 104, 105, 212

Mas, Barcelona: 20, 54, 204

J. Mills, Liverpool: 127

M. Moretti, Orvieto: 180

Pfauder, Dresden: 128

Rampazzi, Turin: 27, 131

Rémy, Dijon: 58, 177, 178, 185, 186

Rheinisches Bildarchiv, Cologne: 17, 152, 162, 169, 176

R. Schwerin, Jerusalem: 163

Soprintendenza alle Gallerie, Florence: 197

Staatl. Amt für Denkmalpflege, Karlsruhe: 145

W. Steinkopf, Berlin-Dahlem: 35, 134, 135, 205

After L. Bagrow, *History of Cartography*: 208

After G. Bandmann, *Kauffmann Festschrift*, 1956: 98

After E. Dhanens, *Inventaris VI*: 47

After R. de Fleury, *La Messe, V*: 65

After E. Grimme, *Aachener Goldschmiederkunst*: 96

After G. Hulin de Loo, *Heures de Milan*: 133

After Karlinger, *Gotik*: 68

After Panofsky, *Abbot Suger*: 26

After N. Pevsner, *European Architecture*: 116

After A. Ress, *Martinskirche in Landshut*: 16

After H. A. Schmid, *Grünewald*: 13

After H. Schnitzler, *Aachener Kunstblätter*, 1964: 70

After A. Springer, *Die Kunst der Altertums*: 112

After Viollet-Le-Duc, *Dictionnaire raisonné*: 25, 28, 29, 63

After J. Wilpert, *Die römischen Mosaiken*: 115

CONTENTS

CONTENTS

ILLUSTRATIONS

The Ghent Altarpiece

and the Art of Jan van Eyck

ON THE FOOTNOTES

The following abbreviations are used:

Bandmann *Fassadenprogramm* Günter Bandmann, "Ein Fassadenprogramm des 12. Jahrhunderts und seine Stellung in der christlichen Ikonographie," *Das Münster*, v, 1/2, 1952

Dhanens, Inventaris v Elisabeth Dhanens, *Sint-Baafskathedraal Gent*, Inventaris van het Kunstpatrimonium van Oostvlaanderen, v, Ghent, 1965

Dhanens, Inventaris vi Elisabeth Dhanens, *Het retabel van het Lam Gods in de Sint-Baafskathedraal te Gent*, Inventaris van het Kunstpatrimonium van Oostvlaanderen, vi, Ghent, 1965

Documenten *Jan en Hubert van Eyck. Documenten*, Utrecht, 1954

Friedländer-Veronee Max J. Friedländer, *Early Netherlandish Painting* (Engl. ed. of "*Die altniederländische Malerei*," Berlin/Leiden, 1924-1937). Comments and notes by Nicole Veronee-Verhaegen. New York, Washington, 1967f.

Panofsky 1953 Erwin Panofsky, *Early Netherlandish Painting, Its Origin and Character*, Vols. 1 and 11, Cambridge, 1953

For identification of titles referred to as *op.cit.*, see the Bibliography on pp. 227ff. If more than one publication by an author is cited, the year of publication is included in the footnotes.

CHAPTER 1

The Altarpiece Reconstructed

I. THE PRESENT INCONSISTENCIES

THE famous inscription which declares the Ghent Altarpiece to be the work of two masters, Hubert and Jan van Eyck, was first published in 1823.[1] The discovery of this text started the continuing dispute about what share each of the two artists may have had in the execution of this work.[2] No agreement on this point has ever been reached. A clear-cut division between the contribution of Hubert and that of Jan proved to be a difficult task.

This is not surprising since, although much is known about Jan's style, nothing is known about Hubert's. It is, nonetheless, dismaying. It was by the analysis of this very work—the Ghent Altarpiece—that scholars had hoped to learn something about Hubert's style through studying those portions which, in their opinion, could not possibly be attributed to Jan. However, as Max J. Friedländer has said, the style of the paintings, which at first sight looks so heterogeneous, flows together, merging the very instant one attempts to parcel out the work into areas painted by different hands.[3]

[1] This poem, which is inscribed on the four lower horizontal members of the exterior frames (Figs. 2, 3, and 49), will be discussed in detail in Chapter 2. The text was first known in a copy found in Christopher van Huerne's manuscript collection of tomb inscriptions. Shortly afterwards, the actual inscription came to light when the overpaint on the frames was removed. For a detailed history of the discovery, cf. Elisabeth Dhanens, *Het retabel van het Lam Gods in de Sint-Baafskathedraal te Gent,* Inventaris van het Kunstpatrimonium van Oostvlaanderen, VI, Ghent 1965, pp. 10f. This inventory volume on the Ghent Altarpiece was preceded by another one on the Ghent church in general, Elisabeth Dhanens, *Sint-Baafskathedraal Gent,* Inventaris van het Kunstpatrimonium van Oostvlaanderen, V, Ghent 1965. These two books will be referred to hereafter as "Dhanens, Inventaris V" and "Dhanens, Inventaris VI."

[2] For "Hubert and/or Jan van Eyck" and the enormous previous literature on this problem, cf. Erwin Panofsky, *Early Netherlandish Painting, Its Origin and Character,* Cambridge (Mass.) 1953, I, pp. 205-46 and the footnotes on pp. 441-44. Panofsky's book will hereafter be quoted as "Panofsky 1953."

[3] Max J. Friedländer, *Die altniederländische Malerei,* I, Berlin/Leiden 1924, p. 87: "(der Genter Altar), der merkwürdigerweise beim ersten Anblick vielspältig erscheint, bei jedem Versuch einer Auseinanderlegung sich wie flüssige Materie zusammenschliesst. . . ." Cf. also the text on p. 85, in which Friedländer mentions the opinion of his teacher Ludwig Scheibler. In 1894, Scheibler had warned his student Friedländer never to occupy himself with the separation of hands in the Ghent Altarpiece, since this would be a fruitless endeavor. In the New English edition of Friedländer's work, published under the title *Early Netherlandish Painting* and annotated by Nicole Veronee-Verhaegen (I, New York/Washington 1967), the two passages can be found on pages 54 and 55. This edition, whose first volume appeared after the first chapter of the present study was completed, will be cited hereafter as "Friedländer-Veronee."

This state of affairs had already prompted some impatient scholars to regard the inscription as spurious and Hubert as a myth, when a new consideration arose. A number of incongruities, not in the style of the paintings but in the compositional structure of the altarpiece as a whole, appeared to indicate a change of plan during the execution of the altarpiece. They seemed to suggest an eventful prenatal history of the work and thus to confirm the authenticity of the inscription, which tells us that the altarpiece was begun by Hubert but finished by Jan.

Professor Panofsky has pointed out these incongruities distinctly and in considerable detail.[4] While the altarpiece with wings closed presents a combination of panels which forms a relatively convincing spatial unit (Fig. 2), the twelve panels visible when the shutters are opened appear a rather motley ensemble (Fig. 1). No other altarpiece of the region and time is composed of such a peculiar accumulation of variegated panels.

The altarpiece, consisting of a stationary middle section and movable wings, is divided into a lower and an upper zone, both in the central section and in the wings. The upper level of the stationary section, portraying the three figures of the Deësis, and both levels of the wings are again vertically subdivided. But, while each of the wings thus consists of four different panels, these panels vary in size and proportion. Only those of the lower tier are of uniform size. The upper wing level consists of two wide panels showing musical angels, and two very narrow ones depicting Adam and Eve.

True, there is a functional reason for this discrepancy. Closed, the lower wings cover a single panel—the Adoration of the Lamb—and could, therefore, be evenly divided. The upper wing panels, however, have to cover a set of individual panels—the Deësis. While each of the two panels of the musical angels must cover one of the side figures of the Deësis group, Adam and Eve together must cover the central figure. The disparity in size of the upper wing panels is thus a direct consequence of the particular subdivision of the upper stationary section. However, the whole arrangement gives the impression of entangled complexity. The differences in panel size not only in the top itself, but also between top and bottom, are disturbing.

There is a further complication. On closer examination, it becomes apparent that the upper wings, when closed, do not really cover the Deësis panels. While these three central panels have straight tops, the tops of the paintings with the musical angels and with Adam and Eve are curved. Thus, closed, the altarpiece is topped by a forlorn set of six empty spandrels. This peculiar sight, seldom included in illustrations, is clearly visible in an untrimmed photograph (Fig. 3). Even when the wings are open, the six spandrels on top of the Deësis are unsettling. Their blue paint clashes with the blue of the sky that arches over the angelic musicians.[5]

[4] Panofsky 1953, I, pp. 209f.

[5] If the modern blue paint of the spandrels is based, as the Brussels Laboratory kindly informs me, on traces of an old blue color, the old blue paint of the spandrels did not match the sky color in the angel

Furthermore, this blue sky in the panels of the angels in itself seems rather strange. Why do these musicians, and they alone, appear in an open space? All the other figures in the upper zone of the altarpiece are shown in an interior setting. No transition from this interior to the open space in which the angels play or sing is provided. In addition, the indoor setting is not uniform throughout the other upper panels. Adam and Eve stand in shallow stone niches topped by stone reliefs; the three figures of the Deësis, on the other hand, are seated within deeper niches made of gleaming metal.

Stranger still is the abrupt change in the scale and perspective of the figures. Adam and Eve are not only larger than the angels and smaller than the Deësis; they are also, in contrast to all the other figures of the upper level, depicted in a decidedly realistic perspective. They and their crowning stone reliefs are the only figures seen from below. All the other representations of the upper zone are shown in the neutral perspective of an ideal vision which does not take the viewer's position into account.

The perplexing differences in shape, setting, scale, and perspective which prevail in the upper zone of the opened altarpiece are absent in the lower one, where one large landscape, populated with small figures, extends across its whole length. Although the lower level is unified in itself, it clashes oddly with the upper level, for all those figures seem giants in comparison with the ones below. Furthermore, the large figures of the upper zone stand upon a solid floor which appears to be a part of a heavy architectural structure. And since this structure hovers unsupported over the light airy landscape, the interior view of the Ghent Altarpiece looks altogether top-heavy.

It is evident, then, that the combination of panels which constitutes the main view of the polyptych lacks balance, logic, and harmony. This prompts a basic question: Why should a wealthy and influential donor, Jodocus Vijd, who had just built a number of chapels in the newly erected chevet of the Ghent church, have accepted the Ghent Altarpiece? He had certainly spent a good deal of money to obtain the services of his Duke's court painter for the huge work that was to serve as an altarpiece for the discriminating congregation of a powerful Flemish metropolis. For the modern art lover the miraculously high quality of the individual sections of the painting may compensate for the shortcomings of the whole. But no fifteenth century patron who had commissioned a work destined to serve an ecclesiastical purpose could have been satisfied with a painting so obviously incoherent as a unit.

The only explanation for the baffling appearance of the Ghent Altarpiece would

---

panels. If these blue traces should in fact be the original Eyckian finish of the spandrel area, this area cannot have been intended to belong to the blue sky. The spandrel area, in fact, was originally hardly meant to show at all. Though intended to be covered by the frame, the spandrels were certainly, nevertheless, protected during the paint process by a preliminary finish. It is, however, by no means certain that the old layer of blue paint was this original protective finish. Perhaps instead it was a sixteenth century coat applied to the spandrels after the frame was removed.

seem to be that the work has endured significant changes. Panofsky has assumed that the composition of the polyptych is the result of an emergency solution in which Jan combined in a makeshift fashion various panels started by Hubert and not originally meant to form an ensemble.[6] Such an assumption, however, does not answer our question. In fact, this explanation becomes all the more untenable when we consider the conscientious manner in which Jan worked and his strong sense of spatial logic. In his only surviving ensemble of panels, the Dresden Altarpiece, we see that this logic governed not only the composition of his individual panels but also the unit formed by those panels (Fig. 128). It is difficult to imagine Jan van Eyck delivering a work marred by manifold signs of a makeshift solution.

It is perfectly true that considerable changes are the only possible explanation for the disconcerting appearance which the work offers today. It is, however, quite improbable that these changes took place before Jan completed the work. The alternate explanation, namely, that they took place after the delivery of the altarpiece, seems more likely.[7]

II. RECONSTRUCTION OF THE UPPER LEVEL

WHEN we look at the seven panels of the upper level, the various architectural details appear, at first sight, unconnected and entirely heterogeneous. On closer examination, however, we notice that these details fall into two distinct categories. The panels of Adam and Eve show a stone architecture. The ceramic tile floor, on which the two groups of the angels are placed, also may well belong to a stone building (Fig. 4). The Deësis alone appears in a metallic setting. The niches are gold; the tiled floor is golden too. Van Eyck depicted these tiles as having been covered with coats of dark blue and dark red enamel, which left only narrow strips of the metal base, forming a network of golden lines, visible between the tiles (Fig. 5). Thus, in the upper zone of the altarpiece, we have a two-fold setting: one stone; the other, gold.

The specific meaning of the golden setting which encloses the Deësis can be determined. Indeed, it was determined some thirty years ago when Charles de Tolnay remarked

---

[6] Panofsky 1953, I, pp. 217-22. Julius S. Held, in his review, "Erwin Panofsky's *Early Netherlandish Painting, Its Origin and Character*," *The Art Bulletin*, XXXVII, 3, September, 1955, pp. 205-34, already saw "the problematic aspects" of Panofsky's theory. Held's objections, not identical with the ones stated in the present study, are found on pp. 220f of his review.

[7] The opinion that the Ghent Altarpiece was changed after its completion has been expressed before. Cf. Martin Konrad, *Meisterwerke der Skulptur in Flandern und Brabant*, Berlin 1929-34, pp. 22-28. It was Konrad who first recognized the mutilated condition of the work. The kind of mutilation that he had in mind is, however, entirely different from that which I am going to discuss in the following text. For the thesis of Konrad (in the meantime disproved by the laboratory examination of the altarpiece) cf. below note 43. Konrad's book, which came to my attention shortly before completion of this study, played no part in the genesis of my own argument. I only recently noticed that Konrad had already adduced some of the same material that appears in my discussion. Cf. below notes 13, 43, and 50.

on the striking similarity of the golden setting in the Ghent Deësis with the façades of those large, ancient reliquary shrines that are shaped like golden houses with slanting roofs.[8] Huge reliquaries of this shape formed the most treasured possessions of important churches in the region of the Meuse and the Lower Rhine. Their narrow sides always present the same traditional design: three niches framed by an arcade with the central arch rising higher than the two others. This can be seen, for example, in the Shrine of the Three Kings in Cologne (Fig. 6).[9]

In this type of reliquary shrine, the base is usually much wider than the house-shaped structure placed on it (Fig. 7). The metal floor visible in front of the Eyckian Deësis figures corresponds to the projecting base of a reliquary.[10] The similarity between Van Eyck's representation and the golden shrines goes even further. The niches behind the figures of the shrine almost always have a series of receding archivolts which are adorned with inscriptions (Fig. 8). We also find this motif in the niches behind the Deësis figures (Fig. 9). It is therefore apparent that the golden setting in the Deësis panels actually imitates a reliquary shrine. De Tolnay's brief remark about the shrines has, as far as I know, never gained any attention in later studies. Nonetheless, it provides an important clue to the comprehension of the Ghent Altarpiece.

Perhaps the kinship to the reliquary shrine, though clear enough in the present condition of the Ghent Altarpiece, was formerly even more explicit. The unattractive empty spandrels above the Deësis can hardly have been original.[11] They must have been covered

---

[8] Charles de Tolnay, *Le Retable de l'Agneau Mystique des Frères van Eyck*, Brussels 1938, p. 5, compares the figures of the Deësis in their golden setting to the sculptures of the Romanesque reliquary shrines. In his introductory paragraphs, pp. 3-4, he describes the function of these shrines as a symbolic screen behind the mensa. The inevitable conclusion (not actually drawn by De Tolnay but the basis of my following discussion) that Van Eyck had intended to imitate the appearance of a golden shrine in a representation meant to be a painted "substitute" of the ancient arrangement will prove to be of great importance for the reconstruction and interpretation of the Ghent Altarpiece.

[9] This shrine, the most precious and important one of its kind, has two stories of which only the upper one is illustrated here. The two-storied reliquary is, however, an exception. The reliquary shrines of the house type have, as a rule, one story which precisely corresponds in form to the representation by Van Eyck. Cf. our Fig. 7 and other shrines illustrated in E. Stephany, *Wunderwelt der Schreine* (ed. H. Busch and B. Lohse), Frankfort-on-the-Main 1959, pp. 5, 6, 9, 20, 22, 25, 53, 65, 77, and 79. A figure especially similar to the central figure of the Deësis in the Ghent Altarpiece occurs in the Shrine of the Virgin in Aachen. *Ibid.*, p. 56, color reproduction on the dust jacket of that book. Indeed, the jacket illustration of this book, which came to my attention shortly after its publication, gave me the idea for the present study. De Tolnay's text I did not know at that time.

[10] Even the base of the Lord's throne as it appears in the Ghent Altarpiece is reminiscent of the shrines. The low step formed by this base and carrying an inscription is similar in shape to the bases as they are found, for instance, in the Shrine of St. Heribert in Deutz. (*Ibid.*, pp. 8 and 9.) Although the inscriptions in this shrine appear not on but below the bases, the very fact that an inscription is placed on an architectural part under the figure connects the Ghent representation with the images in the shrines.

[11] Cf. note 5.

by a frame which has long been lost. The wooden moldings which today frame the four panels of the central section are modern.[12]

In the golden reliquary shrine, the gable above the three niches was traditionally filled by a design of three incomplete circles, as we can see in the Shrine of the Three Kings (Fig. 6). We can see this basic pattern even better in the reliquary of St. Anno in Siegburg, where all the figures are missing (Fig. 10). Perhaps in the Ghent Altarpiece too the design of the golden shrine was originally completed by three medallions appearing in the frame above the Deësis.

This assumption becomes very probable, in fact, when we consider Jan Gossart's free copy of the three central figures of the Ghent Altarpiece (Fig. 11).[13] This painting still shows one circle in the gable over the Deësis, with the design completed by two flanking circles in the frame. Following the ever increasing tendency in later art to represent everything in the technique of painting, most of the architectural details in the Gossart work are painted. However, in the Ghent Altarpiece, the architecture which enclosed the figures and which showed the three medallions at the top, may well have appeared in a frame that was carved.

The custom of partly carving, partly painting an architectural setting is very old. In early Netherlandish art it is derived from works of the Italian Trecento.[14] Around 1400,

[12] Cf. the chapter, "État materiel avant traitement," written by A. Philippot and R. Sneyers in Paul Coremans, *L'Agneau Mystique au Laboratoire* (Les Primitifs Flamands, III, 2), Antwerp 1953, p. 86. This book will hereafter be referred to as "Coremans, *op.cit.*"

[13] Also Konrad, *op.cit.*, p. 24, briefly mentions the Gossart painting in connection with his ideas on the Ghent Altarpiece. His vague suggestion that the top of the Ghent polyptych may have been similar to that in the free copy implies that some architectural details of the Van Eyck retable may have been lost. He supposed that part of the original paint surface was lost when the panels were trimmed in a later period. Cf. our notes 7, 43, and 50. The old frame, visible in our illustration of the Gossart painting, has recently been replaced by a more "Gothic"-looking object. Although the earlier frame may not actually have been the original one, its very "oddity" (which perhaps caused its replacement) speaks for the assumption that it must have been very close to the frame that Gossart himself had used. Older restorations on the surface of damaged paintings are usually also much closer to the original form than are our modern repairs. The old restorer often still knew the shapes of the ruinous parts. The removal of an older frame, just as the removal of an older restoration, is thus often a disadvantage.

[14] Most striking are the examples in the work of the Lorenzetti. While sometimes the architectural forms of the frame are but loosely related to the architecture shown in the painted panels, there are also instances in which the carved parts form a representational unity with the painted portions. Cf., for example, our Fig. 121 or Ambrogio's Siena Annunciation, well illustrated in Monika Cämmerer, *Die Rahmungen der toskanischen Altarbilder im Trecento*, Strasbourg 1966, plate 25 a and b. The procedure of rendering a coherent representation in the two different techniques is deeply rooted in the archaic Italian tradition. In works of the Dugento, for instance those by Coppo di Marcovaldo and his followers, we find a more ancient and outspoken version of the mixed technique. The main figures, such as those of the Madonna and Child, can be carved, while a part of the same representation, namely the throne, can be painted. This handling, heretical according to nineteenth century aesthetics, has a long afterlife lasting into the fifteenth century. In a Cologne Crucifixion, by no means inferior in quality, carved heads are attached to the painted bodies

it had already become quite popular in other European countries and was probably equally popular in the North.[15] In the fifteenth century, the new era of naturalistic representation, this mixed technique celebrated new triumphs. Through the use of this device, the artists sought to heighten the effect of tangible reality in their painting. We can see this, for instance, in Dirc Bouts' Justice pictures in Brussels: the tracery work over the doorway of a painted room is completed by the same design in the carved frame (Fig. 12).

Although the work by Bouts is not an altarpiece, there were many altarpieces in Van Eyck's time which had such frames. In Rogier van der Weyden's Granada-Miraflores retable, the carved arches of the frame complete the painted archivolts and tracery spandrels of the panels (Fig. 205). Rogier's work, however, does not have the characteristic form of a tall altarpiece with movable wings, which is the shape of the Ghent polyptych and of many other Northern retables.

The typical form of the frame in this kind of altarpiece is familiar to us from German examples of the late fifteenth century and the early sixteenth. It occurs most frequently in retables carved entirely in wood. But it can also be found in works consisting mainly, if not entirely, of painted panels, for instance, in Grünewald's famous Isenheim Altarpiece (Fig. 13). Here we can see the characteristic arrangement of the carved framework as it appears in hundreds of retables of the time.

Two areas of architectural forms crown the representation, one on top of the other. First, there is an "interior" architecture, which belongs to the shrine proper and appears immediately above the scenes. This usually consists of Gothic canopies or, as in the Grünewald Altarpiece, of architectural leaf-work. Secondly, there is an "exterior" architecture which crowns the "interior" one and forms the superstructure of the retable. A tall top of openwork tracery, it soars up in a series of canopies, statuettes, towers, and delicate finials.

This dual architectural framework is an old type and already occurs in the time of Van Eyck. In fact, it must have existed in the North at least as early as the latter half of

---

of the three figures. Illustrated in *Wallraf-Richartz-Museum der Hansestadt Köln*, 1. *Die Gemälde alt-deutscher Meister*, Cologne 1939, p. 63, no. 57. By that time, however, this version of the mixed technique had become utterly archaic. The other version, however, the one found in the Lorenzetti paintings, remains valid throughout the fifteenth century in all the great centers of art—the architectural setting of the painted representation can be partly painted, partly rendered in the carved parts of the frame.

[15] The scanty preservation of the altarpiece production of the time outside Italy makes a definite statement about this point difficult. It is difficult even to give the correct attribution of the few preserved works to specific countries. The "Carrand Diptych," for instance (cf. Grete Ring, *A Century of French Painting, 1400-1500*, New York 1949, fig. 24 and plates 1-3), a work in which the fusion of carved with painted parts is most pronounced, is sometimes ascribed to the Parisian school, sometimes regarded as Spanish. No matter to which school this work should finally turn out to belong, I do not agree with Panofsky, who feels that the fusion of painted and carved details would be "heresy" in a French work (cf. Panofsky 1953, 1, p. 82). Since the models of the French painters were Italian and the later development in the North makes profuse use of the mixed technique, I think that an arrangement as seen in the "Carrand Diptych" may have been quite orthodox in France.

the fourteenth century. In small Northern altarpieces, such as the Meran retable of 1370-72, we see an early form of this type (Fig. 14). The painted panels are crowned by carved gables and finials; the center of the retable is surmounted by a tall tower-like open tracery. Originally Broederlam's Dijon Altarpiece may also have had such a dual architectural framework whose crowning tracery is no longer preserved (Figs. 177 and 178).[16]

Since the painted panels of early Netherlandish altarpieces have usually entered public and private collections as "pictures" taken from their original context, very few painted altarpieces of the first half of the fifteenth century have come down to us in their original frames. The fragile tracery top was, of course, the first portion to be removed. We can, however, see the dual architectural top in a number of German altarpieces of the period which are still *in situ*. One, for instance, is preserved in the Tucher Altarpiece of about 1445 in the Church of Our Lady in Nürnberg.[17]

The tracery top with its towers and finials is usually best preserved in Northern altarpieces that were carved in stone, for example, the stone retable of 1424 in St. Martin in Landshut and of 1434 in the cathedral of Frankfort-on-the-Main (Figs. 15, 16, and 17). While the latter has no "interior" architectural top, it is most interesting as an example of the frame's forming a complete canopy with lateral supports rising from the ground. The framing structure surrounds and crowns the mensa so much like a real diminutive building that one can almost call it a frame and an altar ciborium combined. It is, in fact, in the fourteenth and fifteenth century altar ciboria, which occur in the North as well as in Italy, that we find painted altarpieces framed in wood but surrounded and surmounted by a stone architecture (Fig. 18).[18] Here the two parts of the dual framework actually belong to two structures with different functions: the wooden "interior" frame supports the panels; the "exterior" stone frame encloses the mensa and the altarpiece as a whole.

If the Ghent Altarpiece was originally crowned by the usual dual architecture, the roof of the golden shrine in which the Deësis appears must have been the "interior" part of it. We can visualize this "interior" architectural top of the Ghent Altarpiece on the basis of the reliquary shrines and of Gossart's free copy. Perhaps we can then also form a general idea of the lost "exterior" architecture of the Eyckian work. There is, in fact, a composition connected with the Ghent Altarpiece which may help us in this respect. I

[16] For the Meran Altarpiece, cf. *Europäische Kunst um 1400*, Vienna 1962 (catalogue of the exhibition in the Museum of Art History in Vienna), pp. 135f. For the Dijon Altarpiece, cf. Panofsky 1953, I, plate 19, and II, plates 50-51.

[17] This altarpiece, usually illustrated, like all other painted altarpieces of the time, with only part of the frame, can be seen with the tracery top in the illustration of the interior of the church in Paul Frankl, *Gothic Architecture*, Baltimore 1962, plate 118 on the left side.

[18] For stone retables in the North, cf. the article "Altarretabel" in *Reallexikon zur deutschen Kunstgeschichte*, I, Stuttgart 1937, cols. 529-64, with a list of German stone retables in col. 533. The Frankfort retable, with the Dormition of the Virgin as its subject matter, is certainly derived not only from the wall ciboria but also from the wall tomb and the wall type of the Holy Sepulcher. For the ciboria, cf. the article "Altarciborium," *ibid.*, cols. 473-83, with illustrations of works from the fourteenth and the fifteenth centuries.

refer to the famous Fountain of Life, which exists in two versions, one in Madrid (Fig. 19), the other in Oberlin, Ohio.[19]

The kinship between this painting and the Ghent Altarpiece is quite apparent. While the three-figured group at the top has a strong similarity to the Eyckian Deësis, the lamb on the altar and the garden-like ground represented below this group are reminiscent of the Adoration of the Lamb which, in the Ghent retable, appears in the panel below the Deësis (Fig. 1). In the Fountain of Life, the composition is dominated by a complex architecture. This architectural setting not only divides the composition into several horizontal layers on the two-dimensional picture surface, it also provides a perspective view since these layers gradually recede in space as the eye follows their succession from the bottom to the top.

The lowest layer forms the foreground. Here, the architecture consists of a sort of balustrade wall and flanking towers which, rising to the highest zone and crossing all the others, frame the composition on both sides. The wall appears behind the tiled floor on which the artist has placed his main representations, the fountain, and the two groups of Synagogue and Ecclesia. This wall, however, is not only the background of this scene but also serves as a retaining wall for an elevated tract of garden-like land which forms the next layer. This grassy ground is equally divided by a stream of water that springs from beneath the altar with the Lamb. Incorporated into the base of the architecture that rises behind the grassy land, the altar forms part of the uppermost zone of the painting. It belongs to the background section of the architectural arrangement. This section provides the setting for the group resembling the Deësis. Its main feature is a kind of towered pavilion which contains the throne of the Lord and crowns His figure with a large canopy adorned by an immense tracery top soaring up to a considerable height.

Two sharply contrasting opinions about this painting have recently been expressed. Professor Bruyn claims that it is the original creation of a later master who utilized Eyckian motifs, especially those of the Ghent retable, but also other motifs which occur in later Eyckian works.[20] According to him, the composition of the Fountain of Life presupposes the existence of the Ghent Altarpiece. Professor Pächt, on the other hand, maintains the traditional view that the painting reflects a lost early work by Van Eyck, similar to the

[19] The version in the Allen Memorial Art Museum at Oberlin, Ohio, is illustrated in the Bulletin of the Museum, xi, 2, Winter 1954, plate and no. 33. A detail of it is well reproduced in Josua Bruyn, *Van Eyck Problemen*, Utrecht 1957, fig. 3. Since the painting in the Prado is of finer quality than that at Oberlin but renders the Hebrew text—which is legible in the Oberlin version—as a purely decorative combination of letters, the inevitable conclusion is that neither of these two preserved versions can be the original. This original is now lost. Its composition, however, must have been identical with that of the two preserved copies. For no two copyists could have arrived independently at two paintings which so precisely agree with each each other in all the details if they had not worked from the same original. For my attribution of this lost original, cf. below note 22.

[20] Bruyn, *ibid*. Cf. especially the conclusions in the last chapter, pp. 133f.

Ghent Altarpiece but completed before it. According to Dr. Pächt, the ingenious architectural arrangement can hardly have been invented by a painter who was obviously only a copyist; it must be a design by Van Eyck.[21]

I should like to suggest that both scholars are right. I think that the painting is indeed a reflection of the Ghent Altarpiece itself, as Dr. Bruyn claims. It is an ingenious reinterpretation of the Van Eyck retable as it appeared in its entirety, complete with carved frame, tracery top, painted panels, predella, and altar table. When we see the composition of the Fountain of Life not as it develops in space but as a two-dimensional configuration on the picture plane, it gives the impression of a sumptuously framed altarpiece raised on a predella (the wall behind the fountain) and placed on a mensa (the tiled floor in the foreground). Comparing this composition with the framed Grünewald retable, we find that the two configurations are strikingly similar in structure and outline (Figs. 13 and 19). In fact, even the two lateral towers in the Fountain of Life correspond to a motif that occurs in the frames of some altarpieces of the time—the lateral posts, as we see them in the Frankfort retable of 1434 (Fig. 17). Apparently, the artist of the Fountain of Life not only has used the paintings of the Van Eyck panels but he has also translated tangible three-dimensional objects—the mensa and the carved frame—into a painted representation. Dr. Pächt also is certainly right: the architecture in the Fountain of Life reflects an invention of Van Eyck.

For his composition, the painter of the Fountain of Life has used, as it were, the entire appearance of the altar site in Ghent, shaping everything into a unified perspective image.[22] Prompted by the two new tendencies, widespread by the middle of the fifteenth century, he apparently decided, on the one hand, to represent everything through the art of painting alone, on the other, to emphasize perspective. Since he apparently retained the sequence of the zones in the original (predella, Garden of Paradise, Deësis), he had to

[21] Otto Pächt, "Panofsky's 'Early Netherlandish Painting'—II," *The Burlington Magazine,* XCVIII, 641, August, 1956, pp. 271f, and especially his review of Bruyn's book in *Kunstchronik,* XII, 9, September, 1959, p. 257.

[22] Such a perspective tour de force seems to me very characteristic of Petrus Christus, a most talented follower of Jan van Eyck and a near genius. This painter's interest in the construction of space was so preeminent that it superseded his interest in all other aspects of painting. He never bothered to invent a new basic composition or an entirely new design for a figure, or a group, or even a detail, either architectural or pictorial. Those he took readymade from his predecessors. But his architectural or landscape settings are more correctly designed than those created before him, and his objects and figures are powerful, three-dimensional forms more convincingly integrated into space than in any earlier painting. On this basis, he was able to create in his best works a new "still life" poetry of humans in their earthly surroundings. And when Pächt, in his polemics against Bruyn, calls the Fountain of Life the "original invention of an original painter" (ironically, but against his intention, quite correctly), this perfectly fits the mentality of Petrus Christus. The originality of the Fountain of Life—aside from the changing of the iconography—consists mainly in the solution of a problem in space representation. He integrated a number of pre-existing groups into a new unified spatial arrangement. Most likely the lost original of the Fountain of Life was a work of Petrus Christus.

change the figure scale in the individual zones. When the group of the three figures at the top appear very small but the lowermost groups very large, this is a change in form which resulted from the new accent placed on the lower groups in his own iconographic program. But this change worked hand in hand with his perspective reinterpretation, whereby the two groups of Synagogue and Ecclesia are foregound scenes and had to be represented in the largest scale.

Eliminating the representations of the wings as well as the adorers of the Lamb and drastically simplifying details, the painter of the Fountain of Life concentrated on capturing the impression given by the central part of the retable in Ghent. As he did with many other Eyckian motifs, he also eliminated part of the architectural setting—the golden reliquary shrine. But the other part of the architecture, namely, that which simulated stone, was apparently repeated by him fairly faithfully. The flanking towers seem to reflect the lateral posts of the Eyckian frame. The stone canopy above the figure of the Lord with its finials, statuettes, and reliefs, may have been the upper center of this frame and the huge tower the tracery top of the Ghent Altarpiece.

If this was so, the golden reliquary shrine that forms the setting of the Deësis in the Van Eyck retable was originally crowned by a towered canopy as the "exterior" architectural top of the altarpiece. Why should the golden shrine be topped by a huge tower? When we consider the meaning of the Gothic tower on the one hand, and that of the Eyckian reliquary shrine on the other, we understand the significance of such a combination.

Already in the time of Gregory of Tours, the Eucharist was carried in a receptacle that had the shape of a tower.[23] At a later time, we find towers of great height not only in the Gothic monstrances for the Host but also in the huge stone tabernacles of the Holy Sacrament which became popular in the Netherlands and in Germany during the fifteenth century. Dr. Bruyn has pertinently compared the towering architecture that crowns the figure of the Lord in the Fountain of Life to these familiar pieces of church equipment which, like an altar or a rood screen, were part of the "fixtures" of the church interior. He used the towered tabernacle in the St. Peter's Church of Louvain as an example (Fig. 22).[24]

The Fountain of Life is the representation of a Eucharistic theme, a fact which the painter made especially clear through his depiction of a large number of Holy Wafers floating in the stream of the paradisaic garden and in the basin of the fountain. The tower, therefore, is a completely natural motif to be used by the painter as the crowning symbol of his composition. In the Ghent Altarpiece, from which this painter apparently

[23] Gregory of Tours, *De Gloria Mart.*, Cap. LXXXVI, Migne, *Patrologia Latina*, LXXVII, cols. 178f. Cf. J. A. Jungmann, *Missarum Sollemnia*, Vienna 1948, II, p. 6. The English translation of the revised edition of this book, *The Mass of the Roman Rite*, New York 1955, will hereafter be cited as Jungmann, *op.cit.*

[24] Bruyn, *op.cit.*, p. 32.

13

derived his motif, the tower was a symbol no less appropriate. In the Van Eyck retable, the golden reliquary shrine, the object immediately below the towered canopy, was itself the paramount expression of the Eucharistic theme.

There is a close relationship between the receptacles of the relics and those of the Holy Wafer, since the kinship between relic and Host is, indeed, a most intimate one. As a manifestation of the union of God with man, the relics and the Holy Wafer are the most sacred objects of Christendom. The Wafer, in fact, is the mystical relic of Christ which constantly renews itself by virtue of its own miraculous power. It is the greatest of all the relics possessed by the Christian Church. There can be no doubt that the golden reliquary shrine in the Ghent Altarpiece was meant to be the receptacle for the "relic of Christ" and that, as such, it signified the Ark of the New Covenant. The Ark of the Covenant was traditionally represented as a golden casket. It is already rendered in this form in the famous Carolingian mosaic in Germigny-des-Prés. The Ark, moreover, is obviously depicted in the golden receptacle seen in the fifteenth century Annunciation miniature by Fouquet (Fig. 21). Here it now actually appears as a golden reliquary shrine. Standing in the apse of a sanctuary which signifies both the Jewish Temple and the Christian Church, the golden reliquary certainly represents the combined ideas of the Ark of the New Covenant and the Ark of the Old Covenant.[25] In the Ghent Altarpiece, also, the reliquary shrine was unquestionably meant as the Ark of the New Covenant. Because this sacred object was conceived as the receptacle for the Eucharist, it was completely appropriate for Van Eyck to crown his golden reliquary shrine with a huge tower.

The tower in the Ghent Altarpiece, being part of a carved frame, was a real three-dimensional object. As such, it would have had an even stronger similarity to the sacramental towers discussed by Dr. Bruyn than has the painted tower in the Fountain of Life. There was, indeed, a type of late mediaeval reliquary altar that was actually crowned by

[25] In the Carolingian mosaic, reproduced in A. Grabar and C. Nordenfalk, *Early Medieval Painting*, London 1957, p. 69, the holy object perhaps still signifies the Ark of the Old Covenant only. In Fouquet's miniature, however, the golden reliquary shrine clearly stands for the idea of both the Old and the New Covenant. The sanctuary in which the shrine is placed is adorned with statues of Moses and the prophets. Since on the "historical" (i.e. the narrative) level of meaning, the building thus signifies the Jewish Temple, on this level the shrine is the Ark of the Old Covenant. On the symbolical level, however, the Gothic building signifies the Christian Church. The edifice is not only the setting but also the symbol of the figure of the Virgin, who herself is the personification of the Ecclesia (cf. Panofsky's discussion of Van Eyck's Berlin Madonna in a Church, Panofsky 1953, 1, p. 145). In this symbolical context, Fouquet's golden reliquary shrine is, of course, the Ark of the New Covenant. It is the Christian Tabernacle which contains the sacred Host. That Fouquet was strongly influenced by the art of Van Eyck is well known. Clearly, the representation of the reliquary shrine as the Ark of the New Covenant, as we find it in the miniature, was derived from the Ghent Altarpiece. There too the reliquary shrine signifies the Ark of the New Covenant. The various implications of this Eyckian idea and its specific relationship to the Annunciation scene— depicted in the Ghent Altarpiece in the exterior wings—will be discussed in the iconographical part of this study.

a huge "sacramental" tower in Westphalia, a German region close to the Netherlands. Two examples are preserved in the Cathedral of Paderborn and in the Church of Our Lady in Herford (Fig. 23).[26] The Ghent Altar obviously imitated the form of these familiar reliquary altars. The chapel of the Ghent church which houses the Van Eyck polyptych by no means prohibited such a tall structure. All the chapels of the upper ambulatory are rather narrow, but all of them are of great height. The chapel in which the retable is placed today was unquestionably also its original location. A different opinion recently expressed about this point has proved to be wrong.[27] We see the height of this chapel as it compares with that of the present Ghent Altarpiece in an architectural drawing by Professor De Smidt (Fig. 47). The space is approximately three times as high as the present retable.

Because the Fountain of Life eliminates the golden shrine represented in the Ghent polyptych, we have no indication of how Van Eyck combined his representation of the metal architecture with the stone structure. Nevertheless, the concept and form of this combination are not too difficult to establish.

Golden reliquaries of the twelfth and thirteenth centuries were traditionally exhibited behind the tables of the ancient altars. To make these reliquaries visible to all worshipers, they were usually raised up high. This could be done simply by placing the sacred object

[26] While the tower crowns the relic of a miraculous tree in the altar in Herford, it was, in the Paderborn Altar, originally a house-shaped reliquary shrine above which the tower appeared. These altars, which show how strongly the Middle Ages felt the connection between relic and Host, have recently been discussed and well illustrated in Wilhelm Tack, "Der Reliquien-Hochaltar des Paderborner Domes," *Alte und neue Kunst im Erzbistum Paderborn*, VII, 1957, pp. 5-32, and in Joseph Brockmann, "Der Reliquien-Hochaltar des Paderborner Domes, ein Nachtrag," *ibid.*, XIII, 1963, pp. 27-30. Cf. also below note 29. For the connection between the cult of the relics and that of the Eucharist and the identity of the vessels used in the two cults, cf. the excellent study of Anton Ress, *Studien zur Plastik der Martinskirche in Landshut* (Verhandlungen des Historischen Vereins für Niederbayern, LXXXI), Landshut 1955, p. 18, with useful listings of the previous literature on the subject.

[27] A. P. de Schryver and R. H. Marijnissen, *De oorspronkelijke plaats van het Lam Gods-retabel* (Les Primitifs Flamands, III, 1), Antwerp 1952, have tried to prove that the Van Eyck polyptych was originally placed in the crypt directly below the chapel in which the retable is installed today. However, aside from the fact that the crypt of a church is a most unlikely place for a sumptuous retable, the chapel in the crypt is so low that the altarpiece—even in its present condition—would not fit in it when placed on a mensa of normal height. The argument of the two scholars, which is based on an incorrect interpretation of the sources and which was primarily suggested to them by a corrupt text, has already been twice refuted. Cf. J. Duverger in his article "Kopieën van het 'Lam-Gods'-retabel van Hubrecht en Jan van Eyck" in *Musées Royaux des Beaux-Arts Bruxelles Bulletin*, new series, III, 2, June, 1954, p. 51, note 2; and Dhanens, Inventaris VI, pp. 27, 38, and 101. The fact that the present chapel of the altarpiece in the upper ambulatory was the original place of the work, is not only attested by the roof bosses of this chapel and the adjoining bay but also by a number of reliable sources which mention this chapel as the place of the altarpiece. The roof bosses are discussed in Dhanens, Inventaris V, p. 56 with illustration in fig. 5.

on two rows of columns rising behind the mensa (Fig. 21).[28] We know, however, from the literary sources of a very early time that special canopied two-level structures were built to support and house the reliquaries. These enclosures, which are the predecessors of the tall sculptured or painted altarpieces of later centuries, became very frequent in the High Middle Ages.[29] Some of these imposing structures can still be seen today, although only in nineteenth century reconstructions. In the Abbey Church of St. Denis, a large number of these reliquary altars are displayed in the ambulatory (Fig. 24). Viollet-Le-Duc's drawings illustrate their basic construction (Fig. 25).[30] The sketch to the left in our illustration shows an altar in Notre-Dame in Paris; the sketch to the right is one of the St. Denis altars. The upper parts of these structures formed a canopy which enclosed and crowned the reliquaries. The lower stories formed a kind of porch. This porch, contained by the columns which carried the upper level, was usually partly hidden by the altar table and by the low metal or stone altarpieces of the time. The lower porch space was always empty and accessible, for this space served as the place where the believer could approach the relics from behind the altar, venerate them and, in some cases, even touch the bottoms of the reliquaries.[31]

There can be hardly any doubt that the upper stories of these reliquary structures provided Van Eyck with the idea for his combination of a golden with a stone architecture. In the Ghent Altarpiece, just as in these ancient structures, the golden reliquary was unquestionably put into the outer stone architecture which enclosed and crowned it. The tile floor in the paintings of the angels belonged to the stone platform. This platform was covered in the center by the golden shrine. Accordingly, the three panels of the Deësis show only the metal floor.

Since the Fountain of Life eliminates the angels and the figures of Adam and Eve which are represented in the upper story of the Ghent Altarpiece, we can hardly expect it to depict the upper stone structure in its entirety. However, the painted stone structure

[28] This method of exhibition was by no means only imagined by the fifteenth century painter. It was actually used in the Middle Ages. Cf. Joseph Braun, S.J., *Der christliche Altar in seiner geschichtlichen Entwicklung*, Munich 1924, II, pp. 556-58 and plate 340 left. Cf. also our Fig. 35.

[29] *Ibid.*, 1924, II, pp. 549f and pp. 555-72. In the latter chapter, Braun also discusses the Westphalian reliquary altars referred to above and in our note 26.

[30] For the reliquary altars in St.-Denis, cf. Jules Formigé, *L'abbaye royale de Saint-Denis*, Paris 1960, figs. 111, 112, 123 on pp. 138, 139, and 146. The reconstruction drawings are taken from E. Viollet-Le-Duc, *Dictionnaire raisonné de l'architecture française du XIe au XVIe siècle*, II, Paris 1875, p. 30, no. 9 (the Paris altar) and p. 46, no. 17 (a St. Denis altar). Aside from those placed in the ambulatory chapels, there were also other and larger reliquary altars in St. Denis. The original appearance of the *grand autel* can be seen in the painting by the Master of St. Gilles in the National Gallery in London (no. 111 in the plans in Formigé, *op.cit.*, pp. 66, 67; 108, 109, and 154, 155). The painting is illustrated in Erwin Panofsky, *Abbot Suger on the Abbey Church of St.-Denis and Its Art Treasures*, Princeton 1946, plates 9 and 10, and larger in Ring, *op.cit.*, fig. 136 (cat. no. 239).

[31] Cf. Braun, *op.cit.*, 1924, II, p. 563. Compare also the predella painting in the Altarpiece of St. Agilolphus, Cologne Cathedral. Paul Clemen, *Der Dom zu Köln*, Düsseldorf, 1937, p. 232 and fig. 168.

in the Fountain of Life, even in its greatly abbreviated shape, indicates one important feature of the upper portion in the lost Eyckian frame, namely, that it had the form of a cathedral. The basilican shape of the upper level of the reliquary structures is, in fact, well attested by a written source. We know from a seventeenth century text that one of the sacred objects found in the Abbey Church of St. Denis—Abbot Suger's famous tomb of St. Denis and his companions—showed a superstructure in the form of a diminutive basilica (Fig. 26).[32]

For more explicit information about the shape of the upper story of the Ghent framework, we must turn to another free copy—a miniature by a follower of Van Eyck in the Turin-Milan Book of Hours (Fig. 27).[33] This painting shows the Lord, clearly a copy of the central figure in the Ghent retable, enthroned in a cathedral-like pavilion made of stone. A substantial tower is cut short by the upper border of the picture. The core of the building which contains the throne of the Lord is placed on a platform and is connected by flying buttresses with two buttressing piers which freely rise from the same base. Between these piers and the core of the building, under the flying buttresses, there is an open space with a blue sky.

If the framing stone architecture of the Ghent Altarpiece was constructed on the same principle, the puzzling appearance of the seven upper panels can be explained. The core of the building, with its canopy and tower, enclosed the golden reliquary with the Deësis. The musical angels on each side were placed in an open space beneath flying buttresses. The panels of Adam and Eve were the buttressing piers.

This would explain why the angels, in contrast to all the other figures, are silhouetted against a blue sky. The curved tops of their panels would also become understandable. While straight tops would interfere with the openwork flying buttresses, the curves fit right into their lower outlines. If the panels of Adam and Eve formed the buttressing piers, not only their narrow format but their realistic perspective as well would be readily comprehensible.

Of all the figures of the seven upper panels, Adam and Eve alone are parts of the stone architecture. The others, the angels and the Deësis, are only framed by the structure; they do not form part of it. The Deësis and the angels belong to the sacred realm of the representation proper. They are thus rendered in the traditional neutral perspective with a high vanishing point as a view of an ideal divine reality.

In contrast, Adam and Eve belong to human reality. As the painted continuation of

---

[32] Our figure illustrates the reconstruction drawing found in Panofsky, *op.cit.*, 1946, pp. 172, 173, which corrects the old reconstruction by Viollet-Le-Duc, *op.cit.*, II, p. 25, no. 6. The basilican form also occurred in other reliquary structures, for instance, in the altar of St. Peter in St. Savin-sur-Gartempe. Cf. Braun, *op.cit.*, 1924, II, p. 558.

[33] The miniature belonged to that portion of the "Turin-Milan Hours" (*Très-Belles Heures de Notre Dame*) which was formerly in the Royal Library of Turin and which was destroyed by fire in 1904. Cf. Panofsky 1953, I, p. 45.

the carved frame—that is, of a three-dimensional material object—they form part of the world of material shapes in the physical environment of the spectator. The two figures simulate carved statues; they are, as it were, colored sculpture come to life. To make this point clear, Van Eyck has represented them in a perspective which takes the position of the spectator and the laws of human vision into account. In short, Adam and Eve are the only figures seen from below because they alone were actual parts of the frame.

Since the lost frame undoubtedly defined the various realms of reality quite clearly and made it obvious that the spectator is confronted with three different categories of figures corresponding to three different domains, even the variations in their scale, so disturbing to us today, would have been accepted as the definition of three different degrees of reality. As such, they would have appeared perfectly logical.[34] Surrounded by the frame now lost, the upper panels of the Ghent Altarpiece undoubtedly formed a harmonious ensemble.

We have seen that this part of the frame signified the upper level of a reliquary structure. But surely the framing architecture was not the portrayal of any specific object which actually existed in a church known to Van Eyck. As Panofsky has expressed it: "... never can a whole scenery or setting [by Van Eyck] be shown to portray a particular place."[35] All the cityscapes and church interiors painted by Van Eyck are purely imaginary combinations of a variety of forms the painter had seen and noted. The architecture of the Ghent Altarpiece, too, is such an imaginary combination. It does not reproduce one specific type of reliquary structure. On the contrary. It is obviously the combination of various types. In a very general sense, it represents a raised canopied platform on which a reliquary can be displayed.

The type of reliquary structure which we have discussed and which was constructed for the permanent display of one particular shrine behind the altar is similar only in certain respects to the framing structure of the Ghent Altarpiece. It has two levels, of which the upper one bears the reliquary and is crowned by a towered cathedral-like canopy. In other respects, however, its architecture seems to deviate from this type in which the upper platform was inaccessible and only wide enough to enclose the shrine. In the Ghent Altarpiece, the figures of the musical angels seem to indicate that the platform is accessible and

---

[34] Hermann Beenken (*Hubert und Jan van Eyck*, Munich 1941, p. 40), one of the most sensitive writers on the Ghent Altarpiece, has already interpreted the differences between the three sets of figures as signifying different realms of reality ("verschiedene Wirklichkeitsbezirke"). Beenken did not suspect that a now missing frame had once made this point perfectly clear. The Eyckian angels belong to the realm of "spirits" and are therefore smaller not only than the holy figures but also than humans. This idea was taken over by Hugo van der Goes in his Portinari Altarpiece (Fig. 209). There, the small scale of the angels is especially disturbing to a modern eye because they occupy the same landscape space as the large figures and appear in the foreground of it.

[35] Panofsky 1953, I, p. 137.

spacious enough to carry people. Indeed, the structure in the Van Eyck altarpiece has a very pronounced horizontal spread with ample space on both sides of the reliquary.

These two features, accessibility and a pronounced horizontal shape, occur either singly or together in another type of reliquary structure. In the cathedral of Arras, for instance, there was a huge reliquary-bearing structure of the fourteenth century whose platform was large, accessible, and apparently designed not only for the permanent display of certain reliquaries, but also, and above all, for the solemn demonstration of all the relics of the church to the worshipers below (Fig. 28).[36] Strong enough to carry a number of people, this canopied platform was freely suspended between two of the double columns in the choir of the church directly above the altar. It could be reached by a large staircase tower.

Another reliquary structure built to carry not only the relics but also the persons who showed them to the worshiper still exists in the apse of the upper chapel in the Sainte-Chapelle of Paris (Fig. 30). Here, the canopied platform is reached by two lateral staircase towers. These towers are reminiscent of those which flank the composition in the Fountain of Life (Fig. 19). We have seen that the two towers in this painting may reproduce the lateral posts in the frame of the Ghent Altarpiece.[37] The Paris structure corroborates this assumption. The lateral parts in the Ghent framework appear to have represented the staircase towers by which the upper platform of the structure could be reached.

In the Sainte-Chapelle, each of the two staircase towers is hidden behind an arcaded screen which connects the lower story of the structure with the side walls of the chapel. These wing-like lateral extensions of the reliquary architecture divide the area behind it (the apse of the chapel) from the rest of the building. Here now, we have the pronounced horizontal spread, a bridge-like shape similar to a rood-screen which divides the area of the clergy from that of the laity in the great cathedrals.

Actually, the relationship to the rood-screen is not an accidental one, for the rood-screen itself is a structure on which reliquaries could be exhibited. The rood-screen, or *coro*, often formed by two colonnaded arcades one behind the other with a narrow roofed space between them, is a structure much like a bridge and pronouncedly horizontal in shape (Figs. 29 and 31). The center of this structure usually enclosed the lay-altar of the church or formed the background for it. The roof of a rood-screen provided a narrow but long upper platform which was always accessible—usually by two staircase towers—and which served a variety of purposes.[38]

[36] Our drawing reproduces the reconstruction in Didron, *Annales archéologiques*, VIII, p. 180 and in *Bulletin monumental*, 87-88, 1928-29, plate after p. 396. For other reliquary structures with staircases leading to an upper platform, cf. Braun, *op.cit.*, 1924, II, p. 558 and p. 575.

[37] Cf. above, p. 12.

[38] Detailed and comprehensive discussion of the rood-screen (the *jubé* or the *Lettner*) can be found in Erika Kirchner-Doberer, *Die deutschen Lettner bis 1300*, Diss. Vienna 1946 (microfilm of typescript), an excellent study which, with the inclusion of more recent research, is to be published as a book. For the

On this stage-like podium, the reading of the scriptures took place; it also served for sermons and announcements; and, most important, it was sometimes the platform for the exhibition of reliquaries and the consecrated Host. Moreover, with the organ installed on it, it also functioned as a singers' tribune. When Van Eyck represented two groups of musical angels flanking the golden reliquary in his Ghent Altarpiece, it is clear that he did not have the inaccessible top story of the usual reliquary altar in mind; rather it was the long and accessible platform of a reliquary-bearing structure formed like a rood-screen.

III. RECONSTRUCTION OF THE LOWER LEVEL

IT may thus have been that as a support for the upper platform a porch-like edifice not unlike a rood-screen was represented in the lower frame portion of the Ghent Altarpiece. However, no architectural details are depicted in the lower paintings showing the Adoration of the Lamb in five panels. How, then, are we to visualize the specific form of the lower structure?

Our question is partly answered by a late sixteenth century copy which is in the Museum of Antwerp (Fig. 32).[39] The character of this painting is very different from that of the Fountain of Life. While the earlier painter was a near genius who lived in a time that had the highest artistic standards, the painter of the Antwerp copy was but a mediocre talent working in a period which, shortly before the early Baroque, marks a rather low point in the otherwise glorious development of Netherlandish painting. His work, moreover, was not meant to be a free reinterpretation of the Ghent Altarpiece but

---

various uses of the upper platform of this structure, cf. pp. 1-3 and also pp. 209-15 of the typescript with the *jubé* as the place for the Host and for the relics discussed on p. 211, as a singers' tribune with the organ installed on it, on pp. 4 and 210. For the possible form of the rood-screen as an open arcaded hall, cf. pp. 6, 10, 11, 16, and 20. For the tower-like staircases and their various positions, cf. p. 117. See also *idem*, the article "Lettner" in *Lexikon für Theologie und Kirche*, 2nd ed., Freiburg i. Br. 1961, pp. 987-88 and *idem*, "Der Lettner, Bedeutung und Geschichte," *Mitteilungen der Gesellschaft für vergleichende Kunstforschung*, Vienna 1956, pp. 117-22. It is the typescript which is cited hereafter as Kirchner-Doberer, *op.cit.*

[39] The copy repeats only the paintings of the interior view of the Ghent Altarpiece. The present frame is not the original one and even the present paint ground, which is canvas, may not be original, since the painting may have been transferred from wood. The identity of the copy with any of those mentioned in the sources of the sixteenth and seventeenth centuries has not been firmly established. Duverger, *op.cit.*, 1954, pp. 61f, believes that this is the copy which was in the courtroom of the town hall of Ghent at the end of the eighteenth century and which has changed hands many times since. It is obviously the copy that went to England in the early nineteenth century where it received the present English inscriptions and perhaps also the present frame. It was given to the Antwerp Museum in 1866. Cf. Konrad, *op.cit.*, pp. iv-v, and Duverger, *Het grafschrift van Hubrecht van Eyck*, Antwerp/Utrecht 1945, p. 33. The copy was dated by Konrad between 1520 and 1540, by Duverger (in his earlier study) around 1584, and (in his later one) 1625. I believe that Duverger's first dating (around 1584) is correct. Cf. below note 63 and the text belonging to it.

a copy in the proper sense of the word. It is, generally speaking, a most faithful one. Only in some respects is the arrangement of the original changed.[40]

Unlike the Eyckian original, the wings of the copy have the juxtaposed representations in the two tiers combined on single panels.[41] But the copyist added to his unified scenes some painted details which provided the separation of the parts.[42] In the lower tier, he divided the landscape in both of his double pictures by a tall architectural support. The two supports look like columns and that is what we shall call them, even though they are actually clusters of three thin column shafts (Figs. 33 and 34). The two columns are very "Eyckian" in design. Furthermore, they are strikingly similar to those smaller clustered columns which appear in the Annunciation scene of the Ghent Altarpiece (Fig. 88). Therefore, it is very likely that the copyist took them directly from the Ghent retable.[43] The individual forms of the Antwerp columns, however, are represented in a most awkward perspective. Moreover, they are both precisely the same in spite of the fact that a

[40] The most striking change is the reversal of the two wing panels on the lower right. In the Ghent polyptych, the present order with the Pilgrims following the Hermits is undoubtedly the original one. This was verified on technical grounds by the laboratory examination. Cf. Coremans, *op.cit.*, p. 119. It is also confirmed by the composition in the five lower panels of the Van Eyck retable. It is an essential point in this composition that the outermost figures in the wings, on the extreme left and right, are those which appear nearest to the eye of the spectator. On both sides, the figures gradually recede in space as they approach the center. When we draw two imaginary lines which connect the places where (on the left) the hoofs of the horses and (on the right) the feet of the figures touch the ground, we obtain two symmetrical lines rising from low outer points to higher points as they approach the center. These two symmetrical diagonal movements were certainly meant as a "perspective" device leading the eye of the spectator into the central landscape space. At the time when the Antwerp copy was painted, this rather archaic Eyckian *finesse* was no longer understood. To the taste of that period, it was the giant figure of St. Christopher who had to be the leader of the group at the right. Cf. below note 63 and the text belonging to it.

[41] It has been verified by the laboratory examination that the present separation of the wing scenes on different panels is original in the Van Eyck altarpiece. There can be no doubt that the present frames of the wings are the original moldings in which the panels were painted and that the panels are untrimmed. Cf. Coremans, *op.cit.*, p. 120. Aside from facilitating the movement of the wings in the rather narrow chapel, there was another and most decisive reason for this separation. Cf. our discussion on pp. 31f.

[42] In the upper tier, the separation between the representations of Adam and Eve and the adjacent groups of the angels is indicated by a very plain stone-colored post. The simplicity of this architectural form was probably in keeping with the design of the original frame of the copy, which was hardly as sumptuous and elaborate as the lost frame of the Eyckian original.

[43] This has already been assumed by Konrad, *op.cit.*, pp. 23f. In fact, the Antwerp copy was the basis for Konrad's theory about the present mutilated condition of the Ghent Altarpiece. Cf. above note 7. According to him, the wing representations in the Van Eyck retable were originally painted on the same panels just as the Antwerp copy shows them. He believed that the Eyckian panels had been separated by sawing them apart and that the paint surfaces that contained the two columns were lost during this procedure. The laboratory examination has shown that Konrad's conclusion is incorrect. Cf. above note 41. The discussion in the text will show that even for stylistic reasons it is improbable that the columns in the Van Eyck original could have been painted. Cf. also notes 13 and 50.

correct perspective, taking their different positions in the altarpiece into account, would have called for two different views. This definitely excludes the possibility that they were copied from columns painted by Van Eyck. Instead, these columns would seem to be the painted translations of some carved details within the original frame of the Ghent Altarpiece.

For the painter of the Fountain of Life, the translation of sculpture into painting was a challenge and the most interesting part of a self-imposed artistic problem which he took great delight in solving. For the painter of the Antwerp copy, on the other hand, the imitation of carved details in painting was an unwelcome but unavoidable task. To him, who merely wanted to imitate the impression given by the original, this meant an additional project, more difficult and time-consuming than the straight copying for which he was paid. Disinclined to do the translation work twice, he simply used the design of his one translation on both sides of his copy.[44] It is highly probable that the columns in the Antwerp copy are imitations of forms that appeared in the Ghent original in precisely the same places but as sculptured details of the frame.

If this is correct, we have a most important clue to the structural connection between the upper and the lower stories of the Ghent Altarpiece: a number of tall columns in the lower tier must have carried the upper platform. In the manner of a straight entablature, this platform was placed directly on the capitals of these supports. This construction, which eliminates the intermediate arches, corresponds to the simplest way of displaying a reliquary.[45] We can see it depicted in the Fouquet miniature (Fig. 21). In this miniature, however, and also, for that matter, in all reliquary altars in which the supports carry arches, the columns rise directly from the floor behind the mensa. This was apparently not the case for the structure shown in the Ghent Altarpiece. If we suppose that the architecture in the Ghent retable, together with the actual mensa, was meant to present the image of a reliquary altar, and if we suppose that the columns in the lower architecture of the retable resembled those in the Antwerp copy, the Eyckian columns could not have been depicted as rising from the chapel floor. The Antwerp columns are shown with their bases, and therefore in their full vertical extension. Appearing as a complete image above the mensa, they must have been meant to be part of a colonnade which was raised high above the floor of the chapel.

A reliquary altar, in which the supporting colonnade as well as the platform bearing

[44] The simple method of reversing the column design through tracing in order to obtain the correct symmetrical counterpart would have been of little help to the copyist. This method is good for a schematic architectural drawing, but it is not the solution in a naturalistic painting. In such a painting, determined not only by lines but chiefly by colors, the right side of a structure is not the mirror image of the left side. The light strikes the reversed forms from the opposite direction and creates shadow and color effects which are radically different in the two counterparts.

[45] Cf. notes 28 and 49.

the reliquary is raised, is of an altogether different type from those so far discussed. We have an example of this different type of reliquary altar in a sixteenth century drawing ascribed to the circle of Jan Gossart (Fig. 35). The huge structure seen in this drawing shows a striking resemblance to a tall altarpiece. The platform which carries the shrine is raised on a porch-like structure having two rows of columns. The porch itself is also raised and appears on a substantial pedestal which rises above the mensa. The upper reliquary platform is set directly on the capitals of the porch columns with no intervening arches.[45a] Thus, this colonnade repeats both of the features seen in the Antwerp copy. Its architecture may, therefore, be very close to what was visible in the lower part of the Ghent frame: all of the vertical parts in the lower tier of the Eyckian frame could have shown columns. The columns may have formed two rows, one behind the other, with the front row carrying the near edge of the upper platform, and the rear row the far edge. This arrangement would form a long, shallow, bridge-like porch and would thus have borne a strong resemblance to a rood-screen (Figs. 29 and 31).

To judge from the drawing of the Gossart circle (Fig. 35), the columns of the Ghent Altarpiece could have been placed on a floor that was visible. This floor would then form the top of a pedestal whose upper portion appeared above the mensa. The pedestal portion in the drawing looks very much like a predella, thereby strongly underlining the structure's similarity to a tall altarpiece. The predella of the Ghent polyptych also may very well have represented the pedestal of the reliquary structure. We have already mentioned in our discussion of the Fountain of Life that the foreground level of this composition bears a marked resemblance to a predella. The wall, which forms the background of this level, has a profile which shows a certain similarity to that of the predella in this drawing. This wall, and the groups set against it, may, in fact, imitate a representation in the Ghent Altarpiece which had depicted the pedestal of a reliquary structure.

While in the lower frame of the Ghent Altarpiece, the vertical members apparently showed the columns of a porch-like edifice, the lower horizontal members could have depicted the floor from which those columns rose and the upper ones the ceiling which they carried. It is true that if the laws of perspective were strictly observed, this ceiling would have been invisible. It is rather doubtful, however, that Van Eyck applied the rules of perspective in this particular case. He would probably have actually shown the ceiling in order to complete the representation of the framing porch.

But how did the artist manage to suggest the three-dimensional space of a porch in an object which was only a flat frame? He did this by representing a very shallow relief in which all the forms were only slightly raised but which was at the same time so cleverly designed in perspective that it gave the illusion of depth. Since the porch was empty, it

---

[45a] A similar reliquary structure can be found in a much earlier drawing by Parri Spinelli. Cf. *Old Masters Drawings from Chatsworth, a Loan Exhibition from the Devonshire Collection.* 1969-70. no. 65, pp. 33-4.

could act as a mere framework for the paintings in the panels. A glance at Desiderio da Settignano's Tabernacle in San Lorenzo in Florence shows how such a framing architecture might have looked in a relief representation (Fig. 36). Here we see how a foreshortened tile floor can be rendered in a relief and how the columns rising from this floor can be shown in two different scales to indicate the perspective diminution of the real columns.

This type of relief framework did not occur only in Italy. A similar design (without the Renaissance vault, of course) was used for the frames of early Netherlandish paintings. A foreshortened floor, with or without a tile pattern, represented on the tilted plane of the lower horizontal molding, with a number of receding columns or pilasters rising from this floor, are standard features in Netherlandish frames carved in wood. They occur, for instance, in Rogier's Granada-Miraflores Altarpiece and in Memling's Shrine of St. Ursula (Figs. 205 and 39). Designed to lead the eye gradually into the space of the painting, these framing architectural details so epitomize early Netherlandish paintings that we are used to seeing them in all the standard type frames for the Gothic pictures of the North (Fig. 38). Memling even imitated such a sculptural frame in painting. In the exterior wings of his retable of Jan Floreins, we see a shallow framing porch of this design acting as a *repoussoir* for the landscape shown behind it (Fig. 37). It is not impossible that all this ultimately stems from the Ghent Altarpiece.

Be that as it may, there can be no doubt that the lower frame in the Ghent Altarpiece showed an illusionistic relief simulating the open interior space of a porch which acted as a *repoussoir* for the five-part landscape of the Adoration of the Lamb. This same combination was later represented by Van Eyck himself through the art of painting alone. In the Rolin Madonna, foreground architecture and background landscape are rendered with the accent on the foreground. Basically, however, they present the same combination (Fig. 192).

Now we are in a position more readily to comprehend the two-level composition of Van Eyck's altarpiece. The upper level with its large figures depicted the upper tier of a reliquary structure and was a foregound representation. In the lower tier the foreground representation which formed the basis of this structure was entirely constituted by a carved relief in the frame. The five paintings of the Adoration of the Lamb, the only part of the lower zone which is preserved today, is but a background representation.

We find a similar two-tier architecture in many Netherlandish paintings of the sixteenth century. Lancelot Blondeel, an artist who was one of the restorers of the Ghent Altarpiece, created a number of panels in which this type of structure formed the painted setting of the composition.[46] We see it, for instance, in his picture in Tournai, in which

[46] One of these paintings is illustrated in Leo van Puyvelde, *La Peinture Flamande au siècle de Bosch et Brueghel*, ed. Meddens, Paris, *s.d.*, p. 162. The Tournai painting (with a new attribution to Pieter Coecke) is reproduced in a color plate on p. 329. Blondeel was not only a painter but a sculptor and an architect

the lower tier of a huge mannerist architecture is opened up to provide a view into a distant landscape (Fig. 40).

If the lower portion of the frame in the Ghent Altarpiece was an open porch, and if the five panels of the Adoration of the Lamb were a distant view seen through this porch, the last two of the seeming incongruities in the Van Eyck retable disappear. When the altarpiece was seen in its original frame, the heavy upper architecture no longer hovered strangely on top of an open landscape but was firmly supported by columns rising from a lower structure. Moreover, the small scale of the figures in the Adoration of the Lamb no longer clashed with the larger scale above. Seen as a background representation, the small size of the lower figures would appear as a perfectly logical perspective diminution.

The logic and harmony of the altarpiece unit was unquestionably greatly enhanced by a substantial predella which, as we have seen, very probably represented the pedestal of the reliquary structure in the upper framework of the retable. The predella, an object carved in its entirety, must have contained the receptacle of the actual Host. This can be concluded from the iconography of the altarpiece to be discussed in a later part of this study. No doubt this receptacle was incorporated into the body of the predella, a motif which is imitated by the painter of the Fountain of Life when he depicts his fountain as incorporated into the foreground wall (Fig. 19).

In the Fountain of Life, the representation of the fountain itself is flanked by two groups signifying Synagogue and Ecclesia. These two groups are certainly imitations of carved details which had appeared in the lost predella of the Ghent Altarpiece and which there had flanked the receptacle of the actual Host. They were reliefs of a rather small size, carved in stone and uncolored. This can be deduced from the two painted reliefs with the scenes of Cain and Abel which appear at the top of the altarpiece crowning the representations of Adam and Eve. The painted groups of Cain and Abel are so intimately connected in their iconography with the two groups of Synagogue and Ecclesia that we have every reason to believe that Van Eyck, when he painted the scenes of Cain and Abel, resumed the scale and stone color of the two actual reliefs in the predella. This too will be demonstrated in detail in a later part of this study. At this point, suffice it to state that the polyptych, raised on a predella, had an appearance similar to many retables of its type and formed a most convincing and harmonious ensemble.

If Van Eyck presented his altarpiece to Jodocus Vijd and the citizens of Ghent in a frame of this description, it is not surprising that they accepted the work with enthusiasm. The polyptych showed no incongruities. Moreover, the fifteenth century spectator, still familiar with the traditional reliquary structures, must have immediately recognized the new and brilliant idea on which the magnificent work was based.

---

as well. The restoration work on the Ghent Altarpiece, which he did together with Scorel in 1550, probably also included some repairs of the sculptural framework.

IV. THE FRAMEWORK AND ITS OPERATION

EVEN in my tentative reconstruction, the unit may look somewhat better than it does in its present condition (Fig. 41). Although it is based on features drawn from the copies, my reconstruction is necessarily conjectural in its details. Without some freely added connecting forms, the deduced elements could not be shaped into a coherent graphic representation fitting the form of the Ghent Altarpiece. The reconstruction is designed as a visual aid toward a readier understanding of the construction and the mechanism of the lost Eyckian frame. Thus, at this point, I should like to suggest that the reader refer to Figs. 41 and 42 and the Frontispiece as he reads the following section explaining the layout and operation of the complicated framework and the materials used to construct it.

The mechanical connection between the panels and their framework can be seen in the Frontispiece which shows a model of the altarpiece with wings half opened. It is impossible for the lateral portions of the architecture with their tall superstructure to have turned with the wings on hinges. We have to assume that these portions, although they enclosed the wings, did not physically belong to them. The lateral parts of the framework, in other words, were stationary. Together with the towered stationary center, they formed a large one-piece screen which will be called "the basic architecture" in the course of this discussion. While the center of this basic architecture enclosed the four panels with the Deësis and the Adoration of the Lamb and formed the towered canopy as well as the predella, its lateral portions were an empty architectural framework crowned by the flying buttresses and terminated on the sides by the two staircase towers. The movable wing panels were enclosed in rather light and narrow frames completely separate from the structure described. Surrounded by these light frames, they were hinged to the central part of the basic architecture. Such a construction, in which the movable wings are attached to the center instead of to the sides of the stationary portion, is, in principle, the same as that which is used in Lucas Moser's Tiefenbronn retable of 1431 (Figs. 43 and 44).[47]

In the Ghent Altarpiece, however, the stationary portion was not a simple picture wall but an architectural unit with empty lateral parts. These lateral parts framed and crowned the wings only when the latter were opened. In their opened position, the wings must have fitted these stationary lateral parts closely enough to give the illusion of being of one piece with them. Perhaps the narrow movable frames even snapped into the outer stationary framework when the wings were completely opened.

The Vijd chapel today, embellished with later structures added in the Baroque period, is not wide enough for the wings to open completely. Without these additions, however,

---

[47] In the Lucas Moser altarpiece the predella carries a stationary picture wall having the outline of a Gothic arch. The two side panels, as well as the predella and the tympanum, are stationary. The two central panels are movable wings, painted inside and out. Together they cover a recess containing sculpture. In other words, the two representations on the central panels are the painted exteriors of the two wings.

the chapel allowed enough space for the wings to open flush with the stationary part. There was even plenty of space for the two lateral posts of the altarpiece (the staircase towers). They probably rose directly from the base on which the mensa was placed and which may have extended over the whole width of the chapel (Fig. 47). The two towers were certainly worked, not in relief but as sculpture in the round,[48] just as was the central canopy and the tracery tower, which unquestionably crowned not only the panels of the retable but also the altar table in front of them. These lateral posts, moreover, rising not behind the mensa but in the space flanking it, must have appeared in a space level in front of the panels which corresponded to that of the projecting canopy in the center.

When the altarpiece was closed, the movable wings in their narrow frames covered (as they do today) only the painted representations of the interior view (Fig. 42). The entire superstructure—not just the uppermost part with the towered stone canopy but the roof portion of the golden shrine as well—remained fully visible above the sibyls and prophets of the Annunciation scene. This is a most important fact for the iconography of the exterior view, to be discussed in a later part of this study. With shutters closed, the carved stationary lateral portions of the basic architecture appeared as an openwork skeleton with the flying buttresses occurring above open spaces and the buttressing piers formed by solid masonry work. Such an openwork architecture is not as unusual in an altarpiece as one may think. A very similar view is offered by the fourteenth century reliquary altar in the cathedral of Arezzo (Fig. 45).[49]

The frames of the movable wings, though certainly relatively narrow, must originally have shown some carved parts which completed the design of the basic architecture. Carved details must have appeared not only on their inner faces, where their former existence is confirmed by the Antwerp copy, but also on their exteriors. The shadows painted on the floor in the Annunciation chamber can hardly have been thrown by simple wooden moldings (Figs. 2 and 81). These shadows suggest that the frames of the Annunciation

[48] Fully three-dimensional lateral posts occur not only in Italian Trecento and Quattrocento retables (Cämmerer, op.cit., plates 16a, 17, 32c and d, 33b and c, 34, 35a, c, and d) but also in the Frankfort Altar (Fig. 17). It is thus quite possible that the posts in the Ghent Altarpiece contained small figures of singing angels (as indicated in the Fountain of Life, Fig. 19), which were worked in the round. In some of these altars, the posts rise immediately from the base on which the mensa is placed in the manner of the posts of a ciborium. This is so, for instance, in the marble altarpiece by Jacobello and Pier Paolo delle Masegne (1388-1392) in San Francesco in Bologna and also in the Frankfort altar. A reflection of the Eyckian staircase towers seems to appear in Jean Bellegambe's Anchin Polyptych now in the Museum of Douai. Cf. Charles Jacques, Les peintres du moyen-âge, Paris, 1941, Plate 138 and p. 51. This work, obviously inspired by the Ghent Altarpiece, shows also the motif of the buttressing piers and the flying buttresses (in the panels of the Virgin and St. John the Baptist) very similar in position and form to those postulated for the Ghent polyptych in our reconstruction drawing.

[49] Our illustration shows the rear view of the altar with the columns supporting the shrine, which is here a stone sarcophagus. It may be noted that this arrangement with the shrine directly resting on the capitals of the columns is very similar to the porch in the lower tier of the Ghent Altarpiece as reconstructed in our study. In the front view of the Arezzo altar, the lower structure is concealed by the mensa.

scene showed impressive architectural details which belonged to the design of the chamber. There can be no doubt that the Annunciation room was originally seen through an arcade of columns similar to the one depicted in a miniature by the Limbourg brothers (Fig. 73).[50]

All of the foregoing leads to the assumption that the large two-part framework was made of two different materials: stone and wood. The basic architecture, which represents a stone structure, may have actually been made of stone. It would be logical for the central portion of the basic architecture, with its predella immediately rising from the mensa and a towered canopy crowning it, to have been made of the same material that was used for the mensa itself. The area of the stone structure between the canopy above and the predella below may have been open to provide space for the four-paneled stationary part of the altarpiece to be inserted. If this was so, the stationary wings with buttressing piers, the flying buttresses and the flanking staircase towers—that is to say, all the parts directly belonging to the basic architecture—must have been made of stone as well. Only that portion of the framework immediately enclosing the panels and constituting the altarpiece proper may have been worked in wood.

Wood, being light in weight, is far more practical than stone for the frames of movable wings. Therefore, the basic wooden moldings of the wings (which are original) may have formerly been covered by relief details made of the same material. In the center panels, the basic wooden moldings have not been preserved; but there can be no doubt that such moldings originally existed. Panels of the fifteenth century were always painted in their wooden frames. Moreover, the four central panels could hardly have been inserted in a stone edifice without intermediate wooden moldings. Here, too, this wooden framework may have been a two-shell construction with a relief of wood (or a combination of plaster with wood) covering the basic moldings. This would mean that most of the architectural details visible in the center, between the stone predella and the stone canopy, were wood carvings, including the parts which presented the top of the golden reliquary shrine and immediately crowned the altarpiece. Briefly then, while the outer framework was stone, the altarpiece itself may have been a wooden object throughout. This particular combination of stone with wood was, in fact, traditionally used for the specific category of altars to which the Ghent structure obviously belonged.

Judging from the huge canopy that extended over the panels, the Ghent structure was a wall ciborium.[51] In fourteenth and fifteenth century wall ciboria, the canopies and their four supports were always made of stone (Fig. 18); but the altarpieces which were

[50] Originally, therefore, the Ghent Annunciation had offered a view similar to that of Pietro Lorenzetti's Birth of the Virgin in the Cathedral Museum, Siena (Fig. 121), in which columns belonging to the painted interior appear as carved parts of the frame. Konrad, *op.cit.*, p. 27, had already noticed that the shadows in the Ghent Annunciation room must have been caused by objects formerly visible in the retable. However, he supposed that these representations had been painted and were lost when the panels of the Ghent Altarpiece were sawed apart. Cf. above notes 7, 13 and 43.

[51] Cf. note 18.

inserted into the stone structure were usually painted objects framed in wood. Normally these altarpieces consisted only of one stationary panel with an arched top to fit the pointed ciborium arch. Occasionally, however, the stone ciboria enclosed retables which had movable wings. There can be little doubt that Lucas Moser's Tiefenbronn Altarpiece, which is shaped like a ciborium retable and which, in fact, has movable wings, was designed to be used in a ciborium (Figs. 43 and 44).

It is obvious that the tremendous ciborium originally surrounding the Ghent Altarpiece was an exceptional structure deviating in form from the traditional stone baldachin. It did not show the simple square or oblong groundplan of the usual ciborium, in which four supports rising in the four corners carry a canopy of a corresponding shape. The two supports for carrying the rear part of the canopy certainly existed. These were the vertical members between the stationary part of the retable and the wings. Though these parts may have been made of stone, it is rather doubtful that they performed any actual carrying function. As to the two corresponding front supports, they may have been omitted altogether to facilitate the turning of the wings. In any case, the motif of expanding the structure on the sides by flying buttresses and buttressing piers does not, to my knowledge, occur in any other ciborium structure.

Certainly the side structure with the buttressing piers and the staircase towers was designed to give the spectator the illusion that additional supports for the canopy existed. But this was merely an illusion. The buttressing piers can hardly have actually functioned as a support. It is clear, therefore, that the heavy stone canopy must have been securely attached to the masonry work of the chapel wall behind it.

In the time of Van Eyck, the eastern part of the Vijd chapel immediately behind the altarpiece showed a Gothic doorway with a huge pointed arch which opened into the next chapel (Fig. 46).[52] This opening no longer exists. It is closed by a wall erected at a later time. While the lower part of the eastern wall is thus of a later date, the upper part above the arch is original. In this upper part of the wall, precisely in the location where the tracery top of the canopy must have appeared, there are four huge holes, large enough to be visible to the naked eye. It is possible that they mark the spots where the former iron rods or iron cramps had fastened the tracery work of the canopy to the chapel wall. The canopy itself must have been placed so that it directly covered the Gothic arch of the doorway. The anchoring of this canopy, therefore, must have been done in the masonry work that constitutes the moldings of the arch. Today the two sides of the arch are connected by a heavy iron rod. This rod (or one which had appeared in the same position) may have also played a role in the support of the canopy. No matter how the anchoring of the canopy was actually done, the construction must have been excellent, for it withstood the assault of the iconoclasts, to which, as we shall presently see, all the lower parts of the ciborium fell victim.

Although the rebels apparently tried to destroy the canopy by throwing stones at it,

[52] Dhanens, *Inventaris* v, p. 50.

the structure, though damaged and deprived of its fragile tracery top, did not come down completely. Parts of it, large enough to make a restoration worthwhile, stayed fixed to the wall. The Eyckian canopy (with substantial repairs of a much later time) is still visible in an oil painting of 1829 by Pierre François de Noter in the Rijksmuseum in Amsterdam (Fig. 48).

In this painting—which came to my attention long after my reconstruction of the Ghent Altarpiece had been completed and submitted in a lecture—De Noter tried to recapture the impression originally given by the chapel of Jodocus Vijd. The figures shown in his painting are represented in the costumes of the early sixteenth century. All the Baroque additions to the chapel are left out. Omitting them, the painter realized that the opened wings of the Ghent Altarpiece could be shown flush with the center. In his painting, De Noter proves to be an early but very close colleague of mine who also wanted to visualize the past.

His method of visualization consisted mainly of omitting all the objects which to his knowledge were not "Gothic." He had no ambition actually to "reconstruct" anything. Thus (by far more cautious than I), De Noter entirely refrained from making any free additions to complete the historical setting. It is absolutely clear that he did not "invent" anything, except for the figures in their sixteenth century costumes. In the Vijd chapel, whose location is correctly indicated by the stairs in the foreground, the image of the Van Eyck retable is faithfully reproduced without additions. Moreover, all the other objects in the chapel are also the faithful reproductions of works which actually existed in the Ghent church and which still exist today. Not only is the tomb which De Noter represented as the mensa of the Vijd altar a well-known work belonging to the Ghent cathedral, but the sculptured scene of the Burial of Christ shown by him in a recess of the chapel is also the reproduction of an existing piece of sculpture.[53] These important facts were pointed out to me by Dr. Dhanens, to whom I showed the photograph of the De Noter painting. It is, therefore, utterly unlikely that the artist invented the canopy depicted above the Ghent Altarpiece in his painting. The large object, which plays such a prominent role in the composition, certainly is the original Eyckian canopy which must still have existed in 1829.

The dome, which in the painting crowns the center of the canopy, is unquestionably a restoration replacing the broken tracery tower, which perhaps was even originally erected over a domical vault. The tracery ornaments in the lower parts of the canopy are certainly restorations too. As does the dome, some of these ornaments show the Mannerist style of the late sixteenth century. Others, however, seem to have been added in a still later period. Though the canopy depicted by De Noter is apparently a stone structure, the restorations may have been done in painted wood. This was the usual method of repair-

---

[53] Cf. *ibid.*, no. 231, discussed on pp. 114f with illustrations in figs. 111-14; and no. 143, discussed on pp. 99f with illustration in fig. 105.

ing mediaeval stone objects, although clearly not a very permanent one. It explains the obvious fact that the canopy was repeatedly restored.

But the canopy painted by De Noter shows a basic form which is Gothic. Furthermore, some of its details are still recognizable as fifteenth century ornaments and, most important, the statuettes, which have Gothic postures, strikingly resemble those in the canopy of the Fountain of Life (Fig. 19). The canopy by De Noter is, apart from its restorations, virtually identical with the one which I sketched in my reconstruction drawing long before I knew of the nineteenth century picture. No wonder, then, that I am inclined to regard the De Noter painting as a document which proves the basic accuracy of my reconstruction.

In De Noter's time, the huge Gothic arch belonging to the doorway in the eastern wall of the Vijd chapel was still completely covered by the Eyckian canopy. In fact, we can see in the De Noter painting that the form of the canopy precisely follows the outlines of the Gothic arch (Fig. 46). Because the arch was not visible, the painter apparently did not see any reason to represent the lateral moldings of the doorway which carry this arch. He presented the new lower part of the chapel wall as being one with the old part above the arch. De Noter, who tried, as we have seen, to omit everything in the Vijd chapel which could not have existed in Gothic times, thus missed one point: he depicted the lower chapel wall which did not exist in the Gothic period. To him this point was unimportant, but it is of importance to us.

Since there was no wall behind the panels of the altarpiece, the original mechanism of the polyptych could have been very different from the present one. With no wall obstructing them, the panels of the retable could not only have turned forward, but backward as well. The hinges which turned the panels, or at least some of them, may have been the hollow movable cylinders of the shafts of the frame columns themselves. This simple mechanical device, which is found in early Italian triptychs, occurs in some later altarpieces still existing in the church of St. Bavo in Ghent. Since the column shafts in the frame of the Van Eyck polyptych must have appeared paired or even tripled, a double movement of the panels—forward and backward—was easy to achieve. It is possible, therefore, that certain panels, swung back, could be hidden behind the structure, while others—which cannot be shown side by side today—could formerly appear juxtaposed. The angel panels, for instance, when folded over to cover the two side panels of the Deësis (the paintings of St. John and the Virgin), could be turned backward—each together with the Deësis panel it covered—and disappear, so that the two panels of Adam and Eve would then directly flank the panel of the Lord. This could only be done, of course, if the two side panels of the Deësis were also movable on hinges. The Deësis group itself as painted by Van Eyck suggests that this was formerly possible. Why should he have painted the figures on three separate panels, if the turning of the two outer ones were not originally intended?

31

There is a great variety of potential combinations of panels, all making good iconographic sense, beyond those few which are shown today. These combinations cannot be shown with the present comparatively simple apparatus but they could have been shown in the sturdier and more complex mechanism which originally turned the panels. Since in the upper tier fourteen different symmetrical views are possible, and in the lower one seven, there are ninety-eight symmetrical views which could have been achieved by such a mechanism. This is a number which coincides with that of the festivals of the ecclesiastical year. Perhaps the Ghent Altarpiece was a kind of religious miracle machine designed to offer a different view for each festival of the Church.

The retable, of course, has only four main views: first, with all the wings entirely closed; second, with all the wings entirely opened; third, with the upper wings opened while the lower ones are closed; and fourth, with the upper wings closed while the lower ones are opened. Nevertheless I am very much inclined to believe that a great many—if not all—of the ninety-four additional views were also shown. If this was the case, the fifteenth century visitors to the Vijd chapel, who, as we know, paid an entrance fee, saw quite a spectacle.[54] While the modern tourist secures with his entrance money only the right to see the beautiful panels painted by Van Eyck, the fifteenth century visitor must have obtained a far better value. Perhaps he had the exciting experience of seeing a large number of the possible views shown in close succession, thus watching a mechanical theater performance—a sort of ancient motion picture show.

The precise date for the erection of the chapel of Jodocus Vijd is unknown. But this date can certainly not be very far removed from the time when the commission for the altarpiece was given. Therefore, I strongly tend to believe that chapel, ciborium, and altarpiece were planned together. Adorned by the large architecture of the ciborium, the Vijd chapel was apparently meant to be a private cathedral within the Ghent church. This assumption—which will, in fact, be confirmed by the basic iconographic idea of the altar—is even suggested by the cathedral-like form of the ciborium itself. We can thus safely assume that the iconographic program of the altar was a most comprehensive one. Therefore, the passage in Marcus van Vaernewyck's book which tells us that the altar originally contained a picture of Hell may well be correct.[55] This sixteenth century author mentioned that the representation of Hell was a water-color painting ruined in an inept attempt to clean it and already lost in his time. No doubt, the picture of Hell was a fabric hanging used as an antependium and thus originally appeared in front of the mensa below the painted scenes of the altarpiece. In such a location the picture of Hell would have occurred in precisely the same position within the pictorial unit as does the image of Hell in the Eyckian Last Judgment in New York (Fig. 141).

[54] Cf. Coremans, *op.cit.*, no. 14 on p. 37.

[55] The text is reprinted in *Jan en Hubert van Eyck. Documenten*, Utrecht 1954, p. 21, and in Dhanens, Inventaris VI, p. 115. The former reference will hereafter be cited as Documenten.

V. DESTRUCTION OF THE FRAMEWORK

THE demolition of the large ciborium-like stone edifice was caused by the religious uproar in the second half of the sixteenth century. The loss of the carved wooden frames was an indirect result of this catastrophe. In the city of Ghent, the trouble started in 1566. In August of that year, two days before the iconoclasts began their fiercely destructive spree in the churches of Ghent, the prudent and foresighted Ghent officials hastily removed the painted panels of the altarpiece from the Vijd chapel and safely stored them in the tower.[56] It is reasonable to suppose that the movable panels were simply unhinged, the stationary ones detached, and all of them transported in their wooden frames still complete with the carved details. There was no reason for a complicated dismantling of parts. It was hoped that the framed panels could be fitted back into their stationary stone framework as soon as the trouble subsided. But it is not impossible that some of the wood carvings were already damaged during these hasty operations.

We have no direct information about the destruction of the frame. However, the sources of the time furnish us indirectly with some clues on this matter. It seems that a letter written by Provost Morillon to Cardinal Granvella in 1566 could belong to these sources, for the sculpture to which this letter refers may well be quite specifically that of the Eyckian frame. The passage in question reads as follows: "Aussi at esté saulvée la table d'Adam et Eve avec les relicques et ornementz de sorte que le dommaige n'est tourné sinon sur les imaiges qu'ilz appellen idôles. . . ."[57] This passage, which informs us of the fact that the Ghent Altarpiece was spared during the riot, mentions relics, "ornementz" and sculpture (les imaiges qu'ilz appellen idôles). Apparently, this passage has always been interpreted as referring to the relics, ornaments, and sculpture of the Ghent church in general. However, since the Van Eyck retable is the only work mentioned in the sentence, the word "avec" may well indicate that the relics and ornaments were those of the Vijd altar, and the "idôles" the sculpture of the Eyckian ciborium.

If the passage had this meaning, the Vijd altar must then have contained relics. Judging from the representations of the Eyckian polyptych, these may have been relics of St. John the Baptist and of St. John the Evangelist. Since the relics of an altar were often kept in a receptacle formed by the predella, the relics of the Vijd altar may have been placed in a compartment which was part of the same receptacle, containing the Host, which we mentioned above. If this was so, the two statues of St. John the Baptist and St. John the Evangelist painted in the exterior wings of the Ghent Altarpiece (Fig. 2) would have appeared directly above the relics of the two saints. The "ornementz" mentioned by the Provost are certainly the *ornamenta* of the altar, i.e., the sacred vessels and books used

---

[56] Marcus van Vaernewyck, *Van de beroerlicke Tijden in die Nederlanden en voornamelijk in Ghendt, 1566-1568*, Ghent University Library, Hs. G 2469, fols. 29v and 45v. Coremans, *op.cit.*, no. 13, p. 37, and Dhanens, Inventaris VI, pp. 108 and 110.

[57] Coremans, *op.cit.*, no. 13, p. 37.

33

in the celebration of the Mass. They perhaps included a valuable monstrance (Figs. 59 and 41-42). In any case, if this interpretation of the passage is essentially correct, we can conclude that the sculptural parts of the stone ciborium were broken during the riot of 1566.

It is, however, rather unlikely that the stone structure itself and its elaborate mechanism were already destroyed in the outbreak of 1566. It seems that the stone edifice was still usable and that the panels were still turned by the original mechanism even after the riot. When re-installed in the church in 1569, the altarpiece was apparently again placed in the Vijd chapel and into its original framework. The church accounts of the following years continue to record the proceeds earned from the fees visitors paid to watch the performance of the Van Eyck altarpiece being opened and closed.[58]

However, the religious riots were by no means over.[59] They broke out sporadically during the following years. Finally, in 1578, troops billeted in the crypt of the Ghent church began pillaging the building and breaking whatever came in their way.[60] Although the panels, which were in the Town Hall of Ghent at that time, were again saved, it is clear that the huge stone edifice did not survive this final outbreak. It is certain that the ciborium, as well as the Vijd chapel in which it stood, were left completely unusable; for when the paintings were brought back to the church in 1584, they were temporarily put into the chapel of Provost Viglius.[61] This was certainly only a makeshift installation, with the panels perhaps simply propped one after another against a wall. The church accounts do not list any payment for a new frame and they clearly state that no admission fee was collected during that time.[62] The Antwerp copy, which repeats only the interior representations of the panels, may have been painted in the course of this period.[63]

Although the Vijd chapel must have been cleared of its fallen debris by then, this does not mean that it was ready for normal use. The large battered fragments affixed to the floor of the chapel and to the lower parts of the walls also had to be removed. This was a difficult task requiring the work of skilled masons and apparently it was not undertaken prior to the over-all restoration of the Vijd chapel. It seems that this work, which was done gradually and with interruptions, started around 1586 and was completed by

[58] *Ibid.*, no. 14, p. 37.

[59] The church accounts of 1576-77 list the salaries of guards who were hired to prevent the iconoclasts from damaging the altarpiece. Cf. Dhanens, Inventaris VI, p. 115.

[60] Coremans, *op.cit.*, no. 15 (below), p. 37 with reference to the source.

[61] *Ibid.*, no. 16, p. 38, and Dhanens, Inventaris VI, p. 116.

[62] Coremans, *op.cit.*, no. 16 (below), p. 38.

[63] It seems possible that the panels were even actually attached to the wall, so that the exterior representations of the wings could not be inspected during their exhibition in the Viglius chapel. If this display showed (perhaps by mistake) the Hermits and Pilgrims in a reversed position, the Antwerp copyist may not have been responsible for the reversal of these panels. He may simply have repeated these panels in the order in which he saw them. This seems all the more possible, since another copy, the one in the Brussels Museum (which shows representations not taken from the Ghent Altarpiece on its exterior and which may have been painted at the same time), represents the Hermits and Pilgrims in the same reversed order.

1589.[64] We know that the chapel walls were refinished during that period. Furthermore, it is very possible that the present east wall of the chapel—which, as mentioned before, did not exist in the time of Van Eyck—was erected during those years. The new wall was to form the screen between the Vijd chapel and the next one, a division which was formerly made by the Eyckian "ciborium" and the wooden top piece of the panel frames.

During the last phase of the restoration work, the altarpiece was again installed in its original chapel, where it was newly consecrated in January 1588. We know from the church accounts that certain mason work was done for the mensa and the socle of the retable, and some work in wood for the altarpiece itself. We also know that the polyptych was placed on a new "foot," which was of wood and painted; we even learn the name of the painter, Jan Cools. No doubt, this "foot" was the predella as we still see it in the De Noter painting (Fig. 48). The predella, the wall behind the altarpiece and the restoration work in the canopy as they are seen in this nineteenth century picture, may all date from the time around 1588. Indeed, the De Noter painting, probably contrary to the artist's own intention, does not recapture the view of the Vijd chapel as it looked in the period of Van Eyck; rather it is an image of the chapel as it might have appeared in the last decade of the sixteenth century.

Except for its stationary part, the frames of the panels now merely consisted of the plain wooden moldings in which Van Eyck had painted his scenes. Reassembled without the wooden top piece and stripped of the carved wooden details, the altarpiece in its plain frame now formed a rather simple unit. The paint work done by Cools must have included the refinishing of the original wooden frames, for the removal of the architectural details would necessarily have left their surfaces damaged. As mentioned before, these carved details had unquestionably suffered. Indeed, during the repeated transportation of the panels, which took place after their first moving in 1566 and continued up to 1588, some of these details may have become so ruinous and loose that parts of the sculptural decoration were perhaps already intentionally removed (and the surface refinished) before 1588.[65] Even assuming that the wood carvings remained reasonably complete, they were now—after the destruction of the stone frame which had given them their meaning—only an accumulation of entirely incomprehensible fragments. No wonder, then, that they were discarded.

[64] Coremans, op.cit., no. 17, pp. 23 and 38, also Dhanens, Inventaris VI, p. 116.

[65] The nature and succession of the various layers of finish found on the moldings in the examination by the Laboratoire Central des Musées Royaux de Belgique, may speak for the assumption that the outer frames were finished one more time than the inner frames. Cf. Coremans, op.cit., pp. 120-22 and plate LXVII, figs. 1 and 2. Perhaps the outer frames were already refinished when the panels kept in the Ghent Town Hall were being prepared to send to England. Cf. ibid., no. 15, p. 37, and Dhanens, Inventaris VI, pp. 115f. It is to be hoped that a renewed laboratory examination will throw new light on the dates of the various layers. Such an examination may also clarify the function of the round holes, so far enigmatic, which penetrate the width of the frames. Cf. Coremans, op.cit., p. 87. Offhand, it seems to me not impossible that these were the holes for the pegs or dowels by which the inner and outer layers of the carved wooden relief originally adorning the frames were attached to the basic moldings.

CHAPTER 2

The Quatrain

I. THE QUESTION OF AUTHENTICITY

TODAY, the basic wooden frames of the wing panels, the only part of the original framework still preserved, show only a painted finish. A number of inscriptions appear in these frames, among them the dedicatory hexameters mentioned at the beginning of this study. This is a poem of four lines which occurs below the four panels with the two donors and the two statues in the exterior wings (Figs. 2, 3, and 49). They tell us the names of the donor and the artists and they give us the date of the completion of the work (1432) in a chronogram formed by those letters in the last line which are emphasized by their red color. Since the paint finish of the frames must be, at least in part, the one applied during the restoration of around 1588, one may be inclined to assume that the inscriptions date from the same period. While this may very well be so, we nevertheless have good reason to believe that the wording of the text is older.

There are two kinds of inscriptions: first, the hexameters already mentioned; and second, a number of quotations and titles which refer to the painted scenes. Since part of these quotations and titles recur verbally in the chronicle which described a pageant, based on the Ghent Altarpiece and performed in Ghent in 1458, there is every likelihood that this group of inscriptions at least is authentic.[66] If it is authentic, we can conclude that the other kind, namely the dedicatory quatrain, is authentic too, for the lettering is the same in both of these texts. Thus, even assuming that the present quatrain was painted in the late sixteenth century, it is extremely probable that the quatrain is a faithful copy of the inscription that had originally appeared in the Ghent retable.

However, it is by no means certain that the texts were actually inscribed at such a late date. For, considering their specific position within the framework, we realize that the present inscriptions may well be the original ones. All of them occur in the horizontal members of the frame. While the vertical members must, indeed, originally have been covered in their entirety by an outer shell of carved architectural details, this was not necessarily so as far as the horizontal parts are concerned. In Italian architectural frames of

---

[66] The description in the chronicle is published in J. De Baets, O.P., "De Gewijde teksten van 'het Lam Gods'," *Koninklijke Vlaamse Academie voor Taalen Letterkunde*, Verslagen en Mededelingen 1961, pp. 612f and in Dhanens, Inventaris VI, pp. 96f. De Baets gives a detailed comparison of the titles stated in the chronicle with the inscriptions that appear in the painted panels and in the frames of the Ghent Altarpiece. On this basis, it becomes perfectly clear that the frame inscriptions must be authentic.

the time (Northern ones of this specific type are not preserved), the inscriptions are almost always applied to a recessed area in the horizontal members of the framework (Fig. 121).[67] Whereas the vertical parts are completely covered by carved pilasters and columns, the horizontal ones usually show only two sculptural moldings, one above and the other below, framing the recessed horizontal strip on which the inscription is painted. The Ghent Altarpiece may have followed a similar method of covering the basic frames with carved details and of applying the painted inscriptions to recessed areas. Since that would mean that the Ghent inscriptions were painted on the basic frames, the present letters of the quatrain could very well be the original ones.[68]

II. EARLIER INTERPRETATIONS

WHETHER original or a faithful copy, the famous hexameters in any case are an authentic document. This document, the starting point of our study, names, as already mentioned, two artists—Hubert van Eyck, who began the work, and Jan, who completed it. We have seen that this statement played a prominent role in the formation of Panofsky's theory that a number of panels started by Hubert were utilized by Jan for an altarpiece which was newly planned by the latter. According to his hypothesis, the unsatisfying appearance of the polyptych is the result of this procedure. But this theory can hardly be correct. I have tried to demonstrate in this study that the reason for this lack of harmony is the present fragmentary condition of the work. Our reconstruction, it is hoped, has clarified two points: first, the altarpiece was originally a perfectly homogeneous unit with all its parts based on the same leading idea; and second, it was from the very beginning planned for the chapel of Jodocus Vijd. The fact referred to in the inscription—that the work was created by two artists who worked in succession— was, therefore, not responsible for this lack of harmony. Indeed, we are not absolutely

---

[67] Cf. Cämmerer, *op.cit.*, with numerous other examples apart from the one illustrated in our figure (plates 11a, 12, 13b, 14, 15b, 16e, 18, 25b, 29, 30, 32b and d, 33, 34, 35a and d). For the technique used in assembling frame and panels as well as frame and decorating relief parts, cf. *ibid.*, pp. 17f.

[68] This does not mean that they *must* be the original ones. There is, indeed, an observation made by De Baets which—when taken in a certain way—may rather speak for the assumption that these texts are faithful copies made in the late sixteenth century from the inscriptions of the original moldings. De Baets, *op.cit.*, pp. 549-58, has convincingly demonstrated that the two inscriptions under the figures of the Sibyls have exchanged their original places (Figs. 2 and 3). His conjecture, however, that it was Van Eyck or his learned adviser who was responsible for this error is hardly acceptable. Instead, the confusion is much more apt to be the fault of the restorer who reassembled the remaining parts of the damaged altarpiece before its new consecration in 1588. But even though this is assumed, it does not necessarily follow that the present texts are copies. We have to keep in mind that the inscriptions under the Sibyls appear on relatively small, separate boards of identical shape which could very easily have become confused during a restoration process and that not the texts but the boards themselves could have exchanged places. The error discovered by De Baets, though far from proving or disproving the originality of the texts, is in any case a valid additional proof for our assumption that there was a major alteration of the great work in the late sixteenth century.

sure what this statement in the inscription actually means. Possibly the meaning will become clear when we see it in the light of the appearance of the work.

Instead of judging the work from the quatrain, perhaps we should judge the quatrain from the work. As a matter of fact, scholars have done so in the past. They have not only, as previously discussed, judged the work on the basis of the quatrain; but conversely, their concept of the quatrain has also been determined by their view of the work itself. Those writers who were unable to discern two hands in the work have been inclined, naturally, to declare the inscription a fake. But the other writers, who accepted the polyptych as the work of two painters and the inscription as authentic, were also influenced by the specific view they held of the work itself in their interpretation and reconstruction of the quatrain.

Certainly the meaning of the text is not completely clear. It contains an abbreviated word whose interpretation is doubtful, and there are several letters that are seriously damaged. Moreover, one whole word in the inscription is illegible and another entirely missing. The interpretation and reconstruction of the poem has naturally been determined by a number of preconceived ideas. These ideas are based in part on the various authors' views on the character of the retable. However, they are also based on a story which, being very old and going back to an early sixteenth century text, has powerfully shaped the viewpoint of the interpreters. Almost all scholars believe that the quatrain tells us about two painters who were brothers. The older one, Hubert, had started the work but died shortly thereafter, so that the younger brother, Jan van Eyck, completed the task.

This story, in which Hubert's death is given as the reason for Jan's completion of the retable, has indeed influenced not only the scholars' opinions of the work itself but also their interpretations and reconstructions of the quatrain. Panofsky's discussion of the polyptych and its inscription is a case in point. He sees in the heterogeneous appearance of the retable an indication of a radical change in plan. After Hubert's death, Jan, inheriting a number of panels started by his deceased brother, used them for a newly planned polyptych to be created for his own donor. This view suggests that Hubert's panels may have been planned for different purposes and for donors other than Jodocus Vijd. Panofsky sees the quatrain in the light of this supposition. Thus, the fact that the name of Jodocus Vijd is mentioned in the inscription in connection with the name of Jan and not with that of Hubert is greatly stressed by Panofsky.[69] By no means, however, can we conclude from this text that Hubert did not work for Vijd. We cannot expect an ancient text to mention expressly all the facts which were self-evident at the time. If we deduce from the text that Hubert did not work for Vijd, we could with the same justification declare the portrait of his wife a fake or a later addition. For only Jodocus and not Elisabeth is mentioned in the inscription.

The story telling us that the two painters were brothers and that Hubert's death was the reason for Jan's completion of the work, first occurs in a text written by Don Antonio

---

[69] Panofsky 1953, I, p. 206.

de Beatis. Don Antonio was the secretary of Cardinal Luigi of Aragon. His text describes a trip to the Netherlands and other foreign countries taken by the Cardinal in 1517-18.[70] It has often been observed that this story is obviously a tale which was told in Ghent in the early sixteenth century to visitors to the Vijd chapel.

On first consideration, this story, even though it does not appear in the text of the

[70] Cf. Documenten, p. 12 and Dhanens, Inventaris VI, p. 102. The Hubert story is seen as the result of a copyist's error in a recent article published after my work on the present book was completed: A. Ampe, s.j., "De metamorfozen van het authentieke Van-Eyck-Katrijn op het Lam Gods," *Jaarboek van het Museum voor schone Kunsten*, Antwerp, 1969, pp. 7-60. In Dr. Ampe's opinion, the quatrain of the Ghent Altarpiece is a distorted text copied from a damaged poem which had once appeared on a sign-board attached to the predella. Hubert's name slipped into the present version through the misreading of the word *"expertus."* According to Dr. Ampe, traces of the original Latin quatrain can be found in a Flemish verse printed in De Heere's book of 1559-65 and in a Flemish prose passage appearing in Van Vaernewyck's text of 1568.

There is, however, no evidence that the Flemish quatrain cited by De Heere and described as visible in the Vijd chapel is a translation from the Latin. Some resemblances exist between the present Latin quatrain and the text in Van Vaernewyck. But the similarity of the latter to the poem in De Heere is slight; it consists only of the comparison of Van Eyck with the painter Apelles. As far as the Flemish poem and the Latin frame quatrain are concerned, no relationship at all is apparent. Dr. Ampe, nevertheless, sets out to demonstrate their intrinsic identity. His "proof" is achieved by a rather unusual method of reasoning.

Concentrating on the criticism of the frame quatrain, he offers two reconstructions for the ruinous and presumably distorted text. In the first he tries to regain the correct wording of the present copy; the second is meant to restore the original quatrain on the sign-board from which the present copy was supposedly derived. Though the basis of his two reconstructions is obviously the text in Van Vaernewyck, Dr. Ampe proceeds as though being led by grammatical and metrical considerations only. He modestly admits the purely conjectural nature of the choices which he had to make for the emendations of the distorted text. Through these emendations he arrives at an "original version" of the quatrain which has, to say the least, little resemblance to the verses visible on the frame today. Still stunned by the radical change in wording and meaning, the reader is then confronted with the passages in De Heere and Van Vaernewyck and expected to take them as the proof for the correctness of Dr. Ampe's reconstructions.

The slight similarities between the frame quatrain and the Flemish passage in Van Vaernewyck, which are the sole substance of Dr. Ampe's theory, do not actually prove his claim, because they can easily be explained on entirely different grounds. Two works of literature or poetry, distinct from each other and even contrasting in meaning, tend to overlap if they treat the same subject and the later author knows the work of the earlier one. This point is well demonstrated by the third quatrain on the Ghent Altarpiece which is a Latin poem composed by Maximilian de Vriendt, probably around 1600 (cf. below our notes 88-90 and the text belonging to them). De Vriendt's epigram (not mentioned by Dr. Ampe, although it, too, contains the name of Apelles) has a meaning thoroughly distinct from those of the other text here discussed. Yet De Vriendt's wording is obviously influenced by both the Latin frame quatrain as well as by the Flemish sign-board poem. It is the same dual influence which could have determined the wording of Van Vaernewyck's passage.

While the above considerations make Dr. Ampe's theory appear inconclusive, the following ones, kindly pointed out to me by Mr. William Voelkle, make this theory highly improbable. Since the Hubert story existed by 1517 and its presumed origin is the "garbled text" of the frame quatrain, the latter must have been inscribed on the retable before that time. However, as implied by Dr. Ampe himself, De Heere and Van Vaernewyck were still conversant with the correct wording and meaning of the original poem. If the original text was still known in that late a time, why, then, should the Ghent officials ruling before 1517

quatrain as we see it today, seems to be rather well-founded. If, as the poem tells us, a great painter started the work, which, however, was completed by another artist, these facts, in themselves, suggest that the first painter may have died. But in the sixteenth century there was evidently also another reason for such an assumption. According to the chronogram formed by the letters of the quatrain, the altarpiece was finished in 1432. There seemed to be proof that Hubert had died in 1426. The diary of the German humanist Hieronymus Münzer, who visited the Vijd chapel in 1495, tells us that the master of the altarpiece was buried in front of his work.[71] Thus, there must have been a tombstone in the Vijd chapel at that time which gave the name of a painter Van Eyck.

A tomb slab, supposed to be that of Hubert van Eyck, is still preserved in the Ghent church today.[72] Greatly abraded and with the inscriptions on the scrolls effaced, it shows a large and shallow rectangular recess, which at one time apparently held a brass tablet inserted into the stone. This tablet was lost when the Calvinists confiscated all the metal objects in the Ghent churches. Its text, however, is preserved for us in transcriptions.[73] This inscription, an overly long and rather trite poem harping on the *Vanitas* theme, gives the name of a painter Hubert van Eyck and his death date of 1426. Even supposing, as some scholars do, that this text is a sixteenth century fabrication composed in honor of Hubert long after the painter's death, it cannot have been a total fake. We know that a Ghent painter named Hubert van Eyck actually existed. This fact is confirmed by the entries in the Ghent accounts which mention a painter by that name several times and which show that he died in 1426.[74] Because no one in the sixteenth century would look up the city files to verify a death date for a new poem, we must assume, even when presupposing that the preserved text is late, that it was based on an original tomb inscription which was perhaps more modest but which certainly gave the same name and the same death date. Whether or not the brass tablet was original or a sixteenth century substitute, a tomb slab bearing the name of a painter Hubert and the date of 1426 must have been visible in the church at the time of Münzer's and Cardinal Luigi's visits. Therefore, it seems that the Ghent tale, whereby the altarpiece was completed by Jan because of the death of Hubert, was based on very good sources.

Because this story is the basis of all the recent reconstructions, interpretations, and

---

have approved a completely garbled version inscribed on their world-famous altarpiece? To this I may add that it is rather unlikely that they should have overlooked the name of Hubert which, according to Dr. Ampe, was the innocent invention of a copying painter. Chances are that this name meant something to the Ghentians which would indicate that the Hubert story was older than the present inscription.

[71] Documenten, p. 10, and Dhanens, Inventaris, VI, p. 102.

[72] Cf. Dhanens, Inventaris VI, pp. 19f and Fig. 47.

[73] *Ibid.*, p. 113 and Documenten, p. 19. In Duverger's book, *op.cit.*, 1945, a chapter, pp. 15-28, is devoted to a detailed discussion of the text with reference to the previous literature and polemics against the opinions of authors who regarded the poem as a creation of the sixteenth century.

[74] Dhanens, Inventaris, VI, pp. 85-88.

translations of the quatrain, all of them—though showing some minor differences—agree in their basic meaning. At this point, therefore, I simply submit the translation of the quatrain as given by Panofsky, so that the reader may obtain a general idea of the meaning of the text when reconstructed and interpreted in the traditional way.

> "The painter Hubert van Eyck, greater than whom no one was found,
>
> began (this work); and Jan, his brother, second in art,
>
> having carried through the task at the expense of Jodocus Vijd,
>
> invites you by this verse, on the sixth of May, to look at (or,
>
> > possibly, 'to protect') what has been done."

I should like to suggest that the reader compare this translation with that given by Duverger and Dhanens, which differs from Panofsky's in some respects. This comparison will show that the text in its traditional reconstruction offers certain difficulties.[75] There is, for instance, no agreement as to which subject belongs to the last predicate. Who is the person to invite the Ghentians to look at, or to take care of, the altarpiece? Is it Jan van Eyck or the donor Jodocus Vijd? While Duverger and Dhanens are certainly right in believing that the quatrain must have been composed for the donor and that it is he who acts as the dedicator of the work, the grammatical construction of the sentence does not permit us to regard the name of Vijd (which occurs in the genitive case) as the subject of the last predicate. We shall see later that this difficulty immediately disappears when the text is reconstructed in a different way.

The greatest difficulty, however, is offered by the fundamental meaning of the text which is, as mentioned before, the same in all recent interpretations. The two passages "greater than whom no one was found" and "second in art" are corresponding phrases, the first referring to Hubert, the second to Jan. This juxtaposition has caused embarrassment to generations of scholars. How can one explain why the quatrain bestows the highest praise on Hubert, while Jan is called only the "second in art"?

Jan van Eyck, a painter of widespread fame in his own time, has remained up to the present a palpable personality known by a considerable number of signed works. Hubert, on the other hand, is practically unknown to the art historian. Ancient sources that discuss famous painters and their work mention his name only in connection with the Ghent Altarpiece and describe no other work by him. Indeed, with no signed work existing and no unsigned paintings known which can safely be attributed to him, Hubert has aptly

[75] The translation given in Panofsky 1953, I, p. 206, and reproduced in our text, follows those of Hulin de Loo and Debouxhtay. Dhanens' translation (Inventaris VI, p. 12) is that of Duverger, *op.cit.*, 1945, p. 69. For the literature on the quatrain, cf. Panofsky 1953, I, note 206, 1 on p. 442. It may be noted that both in Dhanens' version as well as in Panofsky's, the first clause of the Latin text is a sentence without an object (which is freely added in the translation). As explained in my following text, this lack of an object is the result of these authors' specific view of the grammatical construction of the Latin poem. In my own interpretation of the Latin text, the first sentence has an object.

been called a name without an oeuvre.[76] Moreover, Jan was the court painter of Philip the Good, which meant that he held the most illustrious position possible for a painter of his time and region. How could Jodocus Vijd, for whom the quatrain was certainly composed, dare to rate the ability of another painter higher than that of the court painter of his Duke?

Scholars have tried to explain the unusually high praise which the quatrain gives to Hubert as a pious epitaph composed by Jan in honor of a beloved brother who died while working on the great task. But, even assuming that it was Jan who insisted on the praise, why should he have gone so far as to place his own accomplishments below those of his brother? Perhaps the two phrases, which are certainly corresponding in the traditional interpretation of the quatrain, belong in reality each to a different context. Perhaps the story on which this interpretation is based—that Jan took over after the death of Hubert— is not even correct. It may be worthwhile to examine the foundations of this ancient story more closely.

If the object that Münzer saw in the Vijd chapel in 1495 was actually the tomb of the Ghent painter Hubert who died in 1426, the fact that this artist was buried in the Vijd chapel would in itself prove that he was the master of the famous polyptych. It seems, however, that the object Münzer saw was not the tomb but only the tombstone of the Ghent painter. We have a sixteenth century description from which we can deduce the circumstances that led the Ghent officials to place this tombstone in the Vijd chapel.

In one of Van Vaernewyck's well-known books, we find a passage which tells us that a bone from Hubert's arm had been exhibited for many years in the cemetery of the Ghent church, where it was hung up enshrined in an iron receptacle.[77] Van Vaernewyck also mentions how this strange "relic" came to be displayed. In the course of the rebuilding of the church, a number of tombs had to be removed, among them that of the Ghent painter Hubert. Van Vaernewyck does not tell us the exact time when this took place, nor does he mention where these tombs had been located. But since the bone was exhibited in the churchyard, it is likely that these were cemetery tombs and that they had to be excavated when part of the old cemetery became the foundation area of the new towered west part of the church, which was gradually added to the building between 1462 and 1534.[78]

Van Vaernewyck had at one time personally seen the bone; but the "relic" had

---

[76] Otto Pächt, "Panofsky's 'Early Netherlandish Painting,'" *op.cit.*, p. 267: "In the case of the Master of Flémalle we have an *œuvre*, but no name (the Campin hypothesis has much to recommend itself, but still remains a hypothesis) and consequently few dates. In the case of Hubert we have a name but practically no *œuvre*, at least none on which agreement has been reached."

[77] Marcus van Vaernewyck, *Den Spieghel der Nederlandscher audtheyt*, Ghent 1568, fol. 119. Cf. Documenten, p. 20, and Dhanens, Inventaris VI, pp. 113f. For the tomb of Hubert, cf. also *ibid.*, p. 20.

[78] Dhanens, Inventaris V, pp. 42f.

already disappeared by the time he wrote his text. Displayed in an open cage-like receptacle, it had apparently completely disintegrated in the interim. Thus, the removal of the tomb may have taken place quite a while earlier, perhaps in the last decade of the fifteenth century, not too long before Münzer's visit to the church. It indeed is very probable that the excavation of the tomb prompted the Ghentians to place the tombstone in the Vijd chapel.[79]

When the tomb was found, almost seven decades had elapsed since the death of the master. If his family had stayed in Ghent and if he had any great-grandchildren, they would have been only too glad to believe, as everyone else apparently did, that the tomb was that of the artist who created the famous retable. Chances are, however, that this tomb had been theretofore completely forgotten.

The stone which Münzer saw in the Vijd chapel was thus not necessarily the tombstone of the master of the altarpiece. The name "Van Eyck" was a very common one, and "Hubert," being the name of a popular saint, was certainly not unique in the region. As a matter of fact we have no actual proof for the identity of the Ghent painter Hubert as the master of the Vijd retable. Well aware of this, Panofsky mentions that the only testimony which we have to this effect is the quatrain itself.[80] When we examine the wording of the quatrain without the traditional preconceptions however, we realize that this text, instead of proving this identity, is, on the contrary, quite a distinct testimony against it.

Even assuming that the high praise bestowed on Hubert was inserted in honor of a dead man, we would expect that the text should nevertheless contain a direct statement about his death. But nowhere in the inscription can such a statement be found. There is not even a cross behind his name—the least we could expect if the master Hubert had actually died before the work was completed. Even modern documents would never speak about "Mr. X and Mr. Y," if Mr. X was dead; they would refer to him as "the late Mr. X." If the artist was dead at the time the quatrain was composed, he would have been a soul in purgatory according to the belief of the period. Was it proper to mention a dead and a living artist in one breath in a dedicatory poem? Should we not expect that a pious donor (and still more so—a loving brother) would have exhorted the devout to pray for the soul of the deceased?

The Ghent story of two painters and of Jan's having finished the work of a beloved brother who died—a tale of great emotional appeal and beautifully suited for the account of a tourist guide—was evidently based on a case of mistaken identity and may have sprung up after the tomb was unearthed. It is clear that the formation of this story was

---

[79] For a tombstone firmly believed to be that of the famous master of the altarpiece, the Vijd chapel was certainly the most suitable and the most honorable place. The placing of tombstones (without the tombs) in the upper church was a custom often used in the time. Persons who had their actual tombs in the crypt had additional tombstones in the upper church. Cf. Dhanens, Inventaris VI, p. 20.

[80] Panofsky 1953, I, pp. 205-6.

only possible on the basis of a firm belief that both of the masters mentioned in the quatrain were painters. It is not difficult to understand how one arrived at such an assumption.

During the many decades that had elapsed between the commission of the altarpiece and the discovery of the tomb, the Netherlands had experienced a very important change in artistic climate which specifically concerned the evaluation of painting as an art. At the time when the Ghent retable was commissioned, the supremacy which the art of sculpture had held over painting was not as yet fully broken. Jodocus Vijd's plan for erecting an impressive sculptural tabernacle was certainly still prompted by the concept that sculpture was the nobler type of art. Before his time painting was even regarded as a minor substitute for sculpture. In Broederlam's Dijon Altarpiece, for instance, all the important parts were still carved; the paintings in the exterior wings covered a subordinate area (Figs. 177 and 178).[81] It was only gradually that this concept gave way to a higher evaluation of painting. Indeed, it was the gloriously illusionistic art of Van Eyck and that of his followers which brought about the final change, so that, by the end of the century, painting had become the queen of the arts.

The art lover around 1500 was so much under the spell of the new illusionistic paintings that he was blind to the beauty of any other kind of Northern art. The panels of the Vijd altar had acquired world fame by that time. The visitors to the Ghent church came to see the famous paintings in the "retable of Adam and Eve," and nothing else. No wonder then that Hubert, praised to the sky in the painted inscription occurring in these very paintings, was to the people of that period one of the artists who painted the panels.

And, after all, Hubert *was* called a painter in the quatrain. Was he really? The first letter of the word "*Pictor*," which seemingly designates Hubert as a painter, is as ruinous today as are the other letters of this word. Was this initial originally in fact the letter "P"? The capital "P" is similar enough to the capital "F" to be mistaken for it. If the first letter were formerly an "F," the word would have read "*Fictor*," which is very good Latin for "sculptor"; in fact, it is the best Latin word for it.

It seems, therefore, that all the foundations of the old Ghent story are rather weak. Let us now find out what the quatrain may have to tell us when seen, not in the light of this story, but in the light of the Vijd altar as reconstructed in this study.

III. THE QUATRAIN REINTERPRETED

THE ruinous letters in the otherwise reasonably well-preserved text occur at the beginning of the first and the beginning of the third line (Fig. 49). While the opening word of the first line is greatly damaged, it nevertheless is "readable." At the start of the third line, however, one word is entirely missing and a second one illegible. There, the wood of the frame was cut away when a latch was fastened to the

[81] For the sculptured interior representation of the Dijon retable, cf. *ibid.*, plate 19, which, however, shows the altarpiece without the wings, whose interiors were also carved.

shutters in order to lock them when closed.[82] The second word was damaged through the constant touching to which it was exposed when the latch was moved. In the following transliteration of the quatrain, I refrain from using any of the various reconstructions suggested for the missing or illegible parts:

> "(.ictor) Hubertus e eyck • maior quo nemo repertus
> Incepit • pondus • q(.) Johannes arte secundus
> .... Judoci Vijd prece fretus
> VersU seXta MaI • Vos CoLLoCat aCta tUerI"

Although, as already mentioned above, the first word has always been read as *Pictor* (painter), the abbreviated word *q(.)*, after *pondus* (the heavy mass or the important work), has found two interpretations. Sometimes it has been regarded as the relative pronoun *quod* (which), introducing a new clause and referring back to *pondus*. But it has usually been seen as the conjunction *que*, appended to *pondus* and meaning "and." Unlike the English "and," which precedes the word connected by the conjunction, the word *que*, in normal Latin usage, follows that word as an appendage.

In one respect both interpretations of the abbreviated word have the same effect. In both of these interpretations, the concept "work"—either as the noun *pondus* or the pronoun *quod*—is the object of the second clause. The statement that Hubert began the work is the first clause. With *Johannes* (Jan) the subject and *pondus* the object of the next clause, a predicate was naturally expected which stated that Jan completed the work. This predicate was believed to have appeared in the now damaged spot of the third line.

The oldest preserved transcription of the quatrain is found in the text of Christopher van Huerne, which was probably written at the beginning of the seventeenth century.[83] Van Huerne gives the two now missing words of the third line as *Frater perfectus*. While most art historians have accepted—at least tentatively—Van Huerne's word *frater*, indicating that Jan was the brother of Hubert; all of them unanimously rejected Van Huerne's *perfectus* as a misreading. Certainly, the combination *frater perfectus* makes no sense. One of these words must be wrong. Since the interpreters expected here a verbal form (third

---

[82] Coremans, *op.cit.*, no. 18, pp. 23, 38, and Dhanens, Inventaris VI, pp. 116f. The lock, mentioned in the church account between 1592 and 1597, seems to have been provided around 1592 or shortly after. It is probable, however, that the first word of the third line was damaged even before the insertion of this lock. Cf. *Ibid.*, p. 11.

[83] Van Huerne's text is reproduced in the famous book by Émile Renders (*Hubert van Eyck, personnage de legende*, Paris/Brussels 1933, p. 39), the author who made a valiant attempt to solve the problem of the Ghent Altarpiece by claiming that the quatrain was a forgery. Apparently, Van Huerne worked on his manuscript between 1575 and approximately 1628. According to Renders, he copied the quatrain between 1615 and 1622. Van Huerne gives the abbreviated word after *pondus* as *quod* spelled out in his transcriptions. The argument which Renders submits in his various publications is based on the opinion of the quatrain held by F. Lyna, the first to doubt the authenticity of the poem. The writings of F. Lyna are listed in Panofsky 1953, I, p. 524.

person singular of the perfect tense), they corrected Van Huerne's *perfectus* as *perfecit*, *perpessus*, or *perfunctus*.

However, none of the suggested forms rhymes with the following *fretus*, while Van Huerne's word does rhyme. At least visually. Since, evidently, Van Huerne reproduced abbreviations in full letters, as we see from his *quod* in the second line, the word *perfectus* in the quatrain may have appeared in an abbreviation looking like: *perfētus*.

Although Van Huerne's text cannot be dated precisely, it is likely that he copied the quatrain after the lock was inserted into the frame, which happened around 1592. Thus, the second word of the third line, which today is abraded but not actually missing, may have been quite intact when Van Huerne took his copy. The first word, however, was probably already covered by the lock. It is quite possible, therefore, that the lack of meaning in the combination *Frater perfectus* does not result from the incorrectness of the word *perfectus* but from the incorrectness of the word *frater*. Van Huerne's *frater* may have been a free reconstruction based on the familiar verbal tradition which had Jan as the brother of Hubert.[84]

Indeed, we do not necessarily have to expect a word in the damaged spot to say that Jan completed the work. The Latin *que* in a poem can, as my dictionary tells me, mean "and" without being appended to the connected word. In a poem, *que*, just like the English "and," can precede this word.[85] This means that the second phrase, starting "*que Johannes*" (and Jan van Eyck) may not have had *pondus* as an object, so that no predicate stating that Jan completed the work was required. Van Huerne's *perfectus*, therefore, may very well be correct. With the predicate of the sentence simply being *collocat* and the object *vos*, the text of the quatrain, after having stated that Hubert began the work, may have continued with the statement "and Jan invites you" without the intervening verbal form saying that Jan completed the work. But how did the quatrain express the absolutely imperative statement that Jan completed the altarpiece? And how do we reconstruct the missing first word in the third line?

The answers to both of these questions become apparent when we see the text in the light of the reconstructed altar. The altar consisted of two parts—a huge sculptural framework and a retable of painted panels. The text of the quatrain pointed to the two masters

---

[84] We know from the text of Don Antonio de Beatis (cf. note 70) that there was a rather old tradition in Ghent about Hubert's being the brother of Jan. Whether this tradition was true or simply a free invention is a point difficult to clarify. It is, in fact, not even certain that Hubert's surname was also "Van Eyck" (cf. note 92). In any case, the idea that he was Jan's brother was such an important part of the "Hubert story" that Van Huerne unhesitatingly used the word *Frater* without being troubled by the fact that it does not make sense in combination with the following *perfectus*.

[85] If the word *que* was used here not as an appendage but as preceding the connected clause, the period which is placed after *pondus* was not merely a decorative sign but a genuine interpunctuation mark indicating the end of the first clause. Cf. Panofsky 1953, I, note 206, 1 on p. 442.

of the work—to the sculptor and to the painter. If, as already mentioned above, the first word of the text had originally read *Fictor*, the following statement was made in the first part of the inscription: "The sculptor Hubert van Eyck, greater than whom no one was found, started the work." (The word *pondus*, quite an unusual substitute for the more current *opus*, was hardly chosen for the rhyme, as some writers have assumed. It quite pertinently expressed the specific character of the work, a retable surrounded by a "ponderous" tabernacle.) The statement that Hubert started the work and the other statement (which must have followed) that Jan completed it do not contain anything unusual. They simply refer to the traditional working procedure used for painted retables surrounded by a sculptural framework.

Today, a frame is selected after a painting is finished. In the Middle Ages, however—including the fifteenth century—the frame of a work was always the first part to be started and completed. The scenes in the panels were painted as the second part of the working procedure. This method was always observed not only in the North but in the whole of Europe, and quite independent of the specific character of the framework.[86] No matter whether the frame merely consisted of plain wooden moldings simply covered with a painted finish, or whether it consisted of carved wooden reliefs, or was a sumptuous shell made of a more precious material, it was always the frame which came first in the working procedure. Indeed, it could even happen that the frame was commissioned before the paintings were even ordered. The contract which Fra Angelico made for his famous Madonna of the Linaiuoli dates from 1433. It was signed many months after Ghiberti, in 1432, had received the commission for the marble frame for the work (Fig. 50).[87]

If Hubert carved the frame, it is not only quite natural that the inscription states that he started the work, but it also becomes perfectly clear why Jan is called *arte secundus*. Far from expressing a rating of his ability as a painter, the two words have a purely temporal meaning. Jan is called "second in art," because he was the painter of the panels.

As a matter of fact, we have a welcome confirmation for our assumption that Hubert was called a sculptor and not a painter in the quatrain of the Vijd retable. The word *fictor* (sculptor) conspicuously recurs in a later quatrain which refers to the altarpiece and which is a studied but rather brilliant piece of witty poetry, composed by the late sixteenth century poet Maximilian de Vriendt.[88] Full of very clever double meanings (some of them

[86] Cämmerer, *op.cit.*, pp. 18f. The time sequence within the working procedure is obvious even in a work by Van Eyck himself. In his St. Barbara panel in Antwerp (Fig. 130), the frame is completely finished, while the scene inserted into it shows only the preliminary drawing.

[87] John Pope-Hennessy, *Fra Angelico*, London 1952, pp. 7 and 169. This Italian work, by the way, also shows in its framework a combination of stone and wood.

[88] Victor Tourneur, "Un Second Quatrain sur l'Agneau Mystique," *Academie Royale de Belgique, Bulletin de la Classe des Lettres et des Sciences Morales et Politiques*, ser. 5, XXIX, 1943, pp. 57f, gives the Latin text of this quatrain (which he had discovered) and a French translation.

47

hitherto unnoticed), this poem shows that its author understood not only the Eyckian form but also the Eyckian iconography.[89]

> "Quos Deus ob vitium paradiso exigit, Apelles
> Eyckius hos Vytii reddidit aere patres:
> Arte modoque pari pariter concurrere visi
> Aemulus hinc, pictor, fictor et inde Deus"[90]

De Vriendt had married a lady from the Vijd family. He was not a foreign tourist who, during a short visit to the Vijd chapel, had neither the time nor the ambition to verify the actual meaning of the quatrain. De Vriendt, as the proud new member of this famous family, certainly had both. He surely studied not only the actual inscription, already damaged in his time, but also the family documents dealing with this text. Like all his contemporaries, he was only interested in the paintings.[91] But in contrast to them, he mentioned only one painter. Apparently, he was well informed about the role which Hubert had played in the enterprise.

De Vriendt's poem is a "paraphrase" on the older quatrain in a dual way. It expresses some of the familiar statements in different words, and it also gives some of the familiar words a different meaning. We should not be surprised, therefore, that the word *fictor* is used here not for a man but for God Himself. In his immediate juxtaposition of the two similar sounding words, *pictor* and *fictor*, De Vriendt obviously makes a pun on the older quatrain. Indeed, this juxtaposition gives us the clue to the reconstruction of the one word which is missing in the inscription of the Ghent Altarpiece. This word was not *Frater*, but *Pictor*. If the first word of the first line were *Fictor* and the first word of the third line were *Pictor*, the quatrain in the Vijd retable would read as follows:

> "Fictor Hubertus (e eyck) • maior quo nemo repertus
> Incepit • pondus • que Johannes arte secundus

[89] The Latin *reddidit*, for instance, can have two different meanings—it can be translated not only as "he depicted" but also as "he led back." It is with a sly wink of the eye that De Vriendt simultaneously intended both of these meanings. His second verse says both: "Van Eyck depicted these parents (Adam and Eve) for Vijd's money" and also "Van Eyck restored these parents for Vijd's money to Paradise" (from which God had expelled them). The appearance of Adam and Eve in the highest realm of Paradise, a feature of the Ghent Altarpiece which has baffled many of its interpreters, is, indeed, as we shall see in the iconographic discussion, the chief message of the retable.

[90] In a free translation (the construction of the last two lines cannot be imitated in English), the poem reads as follows:

> "The first parents, whom God had expelled from Paradise for their sin,
> Apelles Van Eyck led back (or depicted) for the money of Vijd:
> The art of the painter who tried to imitate their appearance
> here matches the art of the Sculptor God Who created their form."

[91] According to Tourneur (cf. above note 88), De Vriendt wrote this poem in the early seventeeth century, in a time, therefore, when only deplorable fragments of the sculpture were still in existence.

Pictor perfētus • Judoci Vijd prece fretus
VersU seXta MaI • Vos CoLLoCat aCta tUerI"

"The sculptor Hubert (van Eyck), greater than whom no one was found,
started the work, and Jan, the perfect painter
who followed him in art, invites you by this verse on Friday, the sixteenth of May,
at the request of Jodocus Vijd, to protect (or to behold) what has been done."[92]

Evidently, the good patron Jodocus Vijd bestowed on his two artists—his sculptor and his painter—an equal share of praise. It is the phrase *Pictor perfectus* (the perfect or accomplished painter), and not the embarrassing *arte secundus*, which corresponds to the phrase *maior quo nemo repertus*. The two words *arte secundus* correspond to the word *incepit*. They constitute the statement that Jan finished the work. It is Jan, as Panofsky and many other scholars have assumed, who invites the Ghent officials to take care of the great work. But, as correctly claimed by Duverger and Dhanens, Jan does not act on his own. The passage *Judoci Vijd prece fretus* is used here in its literal meaning (relying on the request of Jodocus Vijd).[93] It belongs to the verb *collocat*. The name of the donor is thus mentioned neither in connection with the work of Jan nor in connection with the work of Hubert, but relates to the dedication act. Because a long sculptured inscription is utterly impractical, and because in any case Hubert had finished his sculptural work

[92] The words *e eyck* (Van Eyck), which I have placed in parentheses both in the Latin text and in its translation, do not fit the structure of the hexameter. The first line scans properly only without these words. As a matter of fact, the excessive length of the first half of the line made it necessary to start the inscription much further to the left than was done in the succeeding lines (Fig. 49). In the first line and here alone, the lettering starts in a place directly below the vertical part of the frame, i.e., in an area which originally must have been covered by sculptural details. The conclusion that *e eyck* is an interpolation added by an early restorer after the sculptural frame was removed, is, therefore, almost inevitable. Such a conclusion is especially close at hand because a surname is not given after the name of Jan and was therefore not likely to have been added after Hubert's. Part of these observations were kindly communicated to me by Professor Otto H. Förster after he read my manuscript. His remarks, gratefully accepted, strengthened my suspicion that the *e eyck* is spurious. Neither Münzer nor Don Antonio (cf. above notes 70 and 71) mention the surname Van Eyck in their texts. It must be noted, however, that both writers apparently took the artist who was first named in the inscription for a painter. The words *fictor* and *pictor* appeared in corresponding places, one at the beginning of the first, the other at the beginning of the third line. Since they were similar looking, the visitors apparently took them for the same word.—For the date the sixteenth of May (instead of the usually given sixth of May), cf. Alfred Hirsch, *Repertorium für Kunstwissenschaft*, XLII, pp. 77ff.

[93] Panofsky (1953, I, note 206, 1 on p. 442), who sees this passage as relating to Jan's completion of the work, gives the free translation "at the expense of Jodocus Vijd." For this, he adduces, among others, the phrase used by De Vriendt "for Vijd's money." While there unquestionably is a relationship between the passage in De Vriendt's and the passage in Vijd's quatrain, we have to keep in mind that De Vriendt was always inclined to give to the original words a new and different meaning. Thus, rather than concluding from his quatrain that the expression *prece fretus* in the older poem meant "at the expense," we should conclude from De Vriendt's text that it did not have this meaning. It would, in fact, be rather strange for money to have been mentioned in a solemn ecclesiastical inscription.

long before, it remained up to Jan (or to one of his workshop helpers) to adorn the retable with a painted inscription. As the physical author of the inscription (which was certainly not composed by him), it is naturally Jan who speaks in this text, but he speaks at the request of the donor.

IV. WHO WAS HUBERT?

IT seems that Jodocus Vijd, when he planned the altar for his newly erected chapel, had two ideas in mind from the very start. He wanted Jan, the most illustrious painter of the day, whom he undoubtedly knew through his personal acquaintance with the Duke; but he also wanted a sumptuous sculptured tabernacle. The latter wish was prompted by a famous Italian work rather than by a Northern one. Vijd, a wealthy landowner and an ambitious member of the city government of a Flemish metropolis, was certainly a cosmopolitan. Thus, it is possible that it was the fame of Orcagna's tabernacle in Or San Michele in Florence which he wanted to match (Fig. 51).[94] But Jan van Eyck was a court painter and, unlike Orcagna, not the head of a large workshop equipped for both painting and sculpture. Therefore, Jodocus Vijd (or his painter) had to look for a sculptor who could do the carvings. It was a man named Hubert, and perhaps (but not necessarily) a relative of Jan van Eyck, who obliged them. The word *"repertus"* in the quatrain may even be revealing: the sculptor who was procured was the greatest anybody could have found.

Who was the great Hubert? We do not know this, because his work is entirely forgotten. This fact is not so surprising for a sculptor as it would have been for a painter. Whereas first rate Netherlandish painters of the time are, generally speaking, well-known to us through documents and through their works, this is not true in the case of sculptors. Even works of outstanding quality can only sometimes be attributed to particular names. Conversely, the names of sculptors known to us from the sources can seldom be related to works handed down to us. The fact that the interest of that time, and especially of the following century in the North, was concentrated on painting made the sculptors and their work fall into oblivion.

Was Hubert only a sculptor, or was he, like Hans Multscher, the head of a shop producing both sculpture and painting? We do not know this either. The only answer we

[94] For the Italian tabernacle, a ciborium altar in which the painting, by the way, is not by Orcagna, cf. Walter and Elisabeth Paatz, *Die Kirchen von Florenz*, IV, Frankfort-on-the-Main 1952, pp. 499-502. Dhanens (Inventaris VI, pp. 72f) gives a long and extremely interesting list of Italianate features in the paintings of the Ghent Altarpiece, some of them observed for the first time by Dr. Dhanens herself. The marble basin of the fountain in the Adoration of the Lamb shows details typical of a Trecento structure. It is, in fact, similar not only to the marble facings in the Florence Cathedral but also, and quite in particular, to the lower parts in Orcagna's Tabernacle. The architectural forms of the Ghent ciborium were (as far as we can deduce them from the Madrid and Oberlin versions of the Fountain of Life) generally derived from the Northern Gothic vocabulary, but the flanking towers with their marble columns have an Italianate flavor (Fig. 19).

can give is a negative one. Even assuming that Hubert was a painter as well, he was hardly identical with the Ghent painter Hubert who had died in 1426. The man who worked on the Ghent Altarpiece was alive in 1432. Since Vijd had imported his painter, he probably also imported his sculptor. Hubert may not have been an artist living in Ghent but a man who was established in a center famous for its sculpture, for instance, in Tournai. In fact, not even his first name is quite certain. We have two independent sources which give his name not as Hubert, but as Robert or Rubert.[95] If the present quatrain was a copy of around 1588 (a possibility which, as we have seen, cannot be excluded), or if it was restored even before that time, the restorer or the copyist might have reconstructed the already indistinct name as Hubert. This was the name known from the tombstone. Originally, however, the name may, in fact, have read Robert. If future research were to take up the problem of this hitherto unknown sculptor, it might be useful to keep in mind the possibility that the artist could have been named either Hubert or Robert.[96]

The style of the sculptor who created the tabernacle of the Ghent Altarpiece is completely unknown to us. The three statues of the canopy as they are visible in the De Noter painting are insufficient as a source for his style (Fig. 52).[97] They are distorted by their reproduction in a nineteenth century painting and probably by restorations applied before that time. But even if we possessed the Ghent tabernacle itself, this work of the master could only give us an approximate idea of his sculptural style, for it is most likely that Hubert had closely followed the sketches which Jan had made for the altarpiece.

[95] One of them is Don Antonio De Beatis' description (cf. note 70), in which the first master of the Ghent Altarpiece is called "de la Magna Alta decto Roberto." For the other, cf. Duverger, *op.cit.*, 1945, p. 31, note 101.

[96] We do not know whether or not Robert Campin in Tournai, to whom the oeuvre of the Master of Flémalle is usually ascribed, was a sculptor in addition to being a painter. The fact that he colored a statue apparently created in a workshop other than his own may not necessarily exclude the possibility that sculpture was also produced in his own workshop. His name "Campin" indicates a derivation from the region Kempen in which the town of "Eyck" was located. "Hij was . . . uut dat cleen stedekin Maesheijck . . . in dlant van Kempen" writes Van Vaernewyck about Jan van Eyck (Documenten, p. 24). Since, in the fifteenth century, fixed surnames did not as yet exist, a person called in one city Robert van Eyck could have been called Robert Campin in the other. Since Jan's art is closely related to the Master of Flémalle, the identity of the famous Hubert or Robert van Eyck with the famous Robert Campin does not seem to be impossible, now that we know that the first master of the Ghent Altarpiece did not die in 1426. But the consideration of this identity is, of course, a mere speculation. If future research should prove that the sculptor of the Ghent Altarpiece was in fact a citizen of Tournai (though not necessarily Robert Campin), the stopover which Jan van Eyck made in Tournai in October 1427 was perhaps to settle the contract for the sculptural work of the retable or to inspect the progress of this work. It may be interesting to compare a passage in Pächt quoted above in note 76. For another important lead to a future identification of the famous Hubert or Robert, cf. below the end of Chapter 3.

[97] But the statues of the canopy, still extant in 1829, may even be preserved somewhere today. They may again come to light and be identified. It is in order to help such a possible identification that I publish the enlarged detail of the De Noter painting.

V. JAN AND THE QUESTION OF OVER-ALL DESIGN

WE have seen that the Ghent retable was a work in which an all-embracing design was executed partly in painting, partly in sculpture. The particular character of the retable required not only that the general layout but also all the details be designed by the same master. It is most probably Jan who created this design. The donors of important sculptural works in the North preferred to have their painters do the sketches for the enterprise they planned.[98] This was so even when the work consisted entirely of sculpture. Some of the figures in the tomb monument of Emperor Maximilian in Innsbruck were designed by Albrecht Dürer, while famous men like Peter Vischer the Elder and Hans Leinberger did not consider it beneath them to execute these designs in sculpture.[99]

We even have an indirect proof for the assumption that it was Jan who designed the sculptural framework as well as the panels. The two groups of Synagogue and Ecclesia, as they appear in the Fountain of Life, and the prophets in the Adoration of the Lamb undeniably show the same style (Figs. 53 and 54). This is clear despite the fact that the two groups in the later painting are only an imitation. They imitated, as mentioned before, not a representation of a painted panel but sculptured reliefs that appeared in the predella of the altarpiece. These reliefs, therefore, had shown the same style as the painted parts. They were unquestionably done from designs created by Jan. In fact, the painter of the Fountain of Life most probably used Jan's original sketches rather than the reliefs in the retable.[100] We thus have every reason to assume that the form of the Vijd altar, designed by Jan in its entirety, was of one piece. And so was the iconography of the retable.

[98] Cf. the introductory essay "Flanders in the Fifteenth Century" in the catalogue *Flanders in the Fifteenth Century, Art and Civilization*, Detroit 1960, p. 47.

[99] Theodor Müller, *Deutsche Plastik der Renaissance*, Königstein 1963, pp. 7f and plates 36, 37 and 51.

[100] The figures in the Adoration of the Lamb are the earliest paintings in the Ghent Altarpiece. It is, therefore, not surprising that they should be similar to the groups of Synagogue and Ecclesia. These two groups in the copy go back to very early Eyckian sketches, which were made for the framework and were therefore created at a time before the paintings in the panels had even been started. It will become evident on the basis of our later discussion that this was the style of the youthful Jan van Eyck himself (not of an older master) and that it is the development of the style of Jan which we can trace in the paintings of the polyptych.

CHAPTER 3

The Iconography of the Altarpiece

I. SEEMING INCONSISTENCIES

IN the course of their analyses of the Ghent Altarpiece, other scholars have pointed out not only the seeming incongruities in the form of the work but also a number of strange and presumably meaningless features in the iconography of the retable. The interior, which at first sight seems to offer a view of Heaven and earth, actually represents the images of two Heavens, one superimposed upon the other (Fig. 1). The protagonist also is duplicated. Christ is rendered twice: below as the Lamb on the altar, and in the upper zone as a person enthroned (the crowned figure is distinctly characterized as Christ by the inscriptions in the cloth of honor).[101] Christ's dual appearance is, indeed, rather strange, especially in view of the fact that it is not Christ but the representation of God the Father which is required in the upper zone to complete the cycle of the Trinity indicated by the Dove and the Lamb in the lower zone. No wonder then that a number of scholars, among them Beenken and Panofsky, have taken the two zones for separate compositions not originally meant to form a unit.

There are, moreover, *pentimenti* in both of the zones which seemingly indicate that each was originally planned by a different painter and for a separate purpose, and that the two levels were only later adapted by Jan to form a unit. Furthermore, the apparent reduction in the height of the Lamb panel is believed to have become necessary when that panel was combined with the upper register.[102] The *pentimenti* underneath the present image of the Dove, which appears near the cut upper margin of the panel, seem to prove that the motif was an afterthought. Both Beenken and Panofsky hold that it is a later addition inserted by Van Eyck after the painter had decided to crown the Adoration of the Lamb with the three Deësis panels. Because Panofsky assumes that the Adoration scene

---

[101] The duality of heavens is mentioned in Panofsky 1953, I, p. 112 and footnote 1 on p. 444. For the identity of the Enthroned with Christ, cf. below note 156.

[102] *Ibid.*, p. 219. Panofsky's thesis was only a new version—or rather a revision—of Hermann Beenken's theory put forward in his article "Zur Entstehungsgeschichte des Genter Altares: Hubert und Jan van Eyck," *Wallraf-Richartz Jahrbuch*, new series, II/III, 1933/34, pp. 176f and repeated in his book *Hubert und Jan van Eyck*, Munich 1941. At the time of Panofsky's book, Beenken's version was already obsolete since the observations on which it was founded had been disproved by the laboratory examination of 1950-51. The basic idea of the theory is older than either Beenken's or Panofsky's versions. Cf. Panofsky 1953, I, p. 208, note 3 on p. 443.

originally had formed an independent picture of "All the Saints," an *Allerheiligenbild*, and because the motif of the Holy Ghost does not fit this theme, he calls the Dove "iconographically incongruous." In his opinion, the motif is an intrusion in the Adoration of the Lamb and a mere appendage when seen in relation to the Deësis.[103]

It is not clear, however, from Panofsky's text why he thinks Van Eyck should have finally inserted the Dove at all. Was it because the artist had intended to create a pseudo-Trinity cycle by adding the Dove to the images of the Lamb and the Enthroned? Scholars agree that the enthroned figure in the upper level is a Trinitarian representation. But it is certainly Christ Who is here depicted as the entire Trinity. Could we suppose that the figure functions as the First Person of the Trinity when seen together with the Dove and the Lamb? If this were so, the image of the Enthroned would have a strange ambiguity: in the context of the upper level, it would be the Trinity presented in the figure of Christ; but, in the additional series of the Trinitarian symbols below, it would signify God the Father only. Is it really permissible to give the motif of the Enthroned a dual interpretation which would imply a strong contradiction within the motif itself? In any case, even if one accepts this interpretation, the strange fact remains that the interior view of the Ghent Altarpiece contains a two-fold representation of the Trinity and that, in this representation, the Second and the Third Person are depicted twice, but the First Person occurs only once.

Furthermore, the interior of the polyptych shows a feature for which we have no precedent and which has never been imitated in any other work of art—Adam and Eve appear in the most exalted region of the heavens, promoted, according to Panofsky, "to a position of undeserved sublimity." Why do the first parents not rank among the personages of the Old Testament as they do in other representations of this type? Moreover, the groups of angels which appear between the Deësis and Adam and Eve are not really a valid link between the two themes. In fact, these angel groups so strongly suggest the sound of music that Panofsky believed that they were originally intended by Hubert to form the wings of an organ and that they were salvaged by Jan so that they could be fitted into the Ghent Altarpiece together with their already painted backs showing the Angel and the Virgin of the Annunciation scene (Fig. 2).[104]

This assumption is seemingly corroborated by the form of the Annunciation as it today appears in the exterior view of the polyptych. The scene, though containing only two figures, the Angel and the Annunciate, is painted on four panels. According to Panofsky, the two narrow center panels were inserted by Jan for the new arrangement.[105] Even

---

[103] *Ibid.*, pp. 215 and 218.

[104] *Ibid.*, p. 221. Panofsky's remark that the shifting of the figures of Adam and Eve to the upper level of the composition entailed "the promotion of the First Parents to a position of undeserved sublimity" is found on p. 222; the remark that they should be ranked among the personages of the Old Testament in the lower level appears on p. 214.

[105] *Ibid.*, pp. 208-9.

the location of the donors below the Annunciation scene seems rather illogical at first sight. The fact that they are depicted in the subordinate place on the exterior wings, far away from the Lamb, the center of the general devotion, has greatly astonished Max J. Friedländer. This place, rhetorically likened by Friedländer to the "fore-court of the Temple," appeared to him so unusual a location for the donors of a retable with an Adoration scene, that he was inclined to see the arrangement as an emergency solution.[106]

In the following iconographical analysis we shall see that the place of the donors is fully justified and the only logical one in the specific context of this altarpiece. Moreover, we shall realize that the two additional Annunciation panels had to have been planned from the start because they have a very important iconographical meaning, imperative not only to the context of the Annunciation scene itself but also to the context of the work as a whole. But not merely the motifs of the exterior view will become perfectly logical once we understand the iconography of the polyptych. All the features of the interior which we have mentioned as being surprising will then also fall into place and reveal a most profound meaning. It is the reconstruction of the altarpiece which opens the way to a new understanding of the theological program of the work.

II. THE HEAVENLY JERUSALEM

Enclosed in a sculptured wooden framework, itself surrounded by a tabernacle carved in stone, the altarpiece was the nucleus of a Gothic chapel (Fig. 41). Indeed, in the original arrangement, the whole Vijd chapel *was* the altarpiece, because the chapel architecture must have given the impression of being nothing other than the outermost architectural shell of the retable.

No doubt, the polyptych was originally centered in the open Gothic doorway of the east wall and thus appeared in the axis of the chapel. The present shift of the altarpiece to the right, toward the window wall, is obviously of a later date. The massive Baroque enclosure, today separating the chapel from the ambulatory, is so placed that it takes up much of the chapel space while keeping the ambulatory clear. The erection of this enclosure thus necessitated the shift of the altarpiece. Formerly, however, the huge ciborium, centered in the chapel, covering its entire east wall and reaching up into the vault with its tremendous tracery top, completely dominated the small interior (Figs. 41 and 46). It even defined the lateral chapel space as belonging to the retable, for the ciborium was extended, as we have seen, by projecting side structures crowned by turrets. Evidently, the side structure to the left originally formed the partition between ambulatory and chapel.[107] It is, therefore, perfectly clear that the ciborium took the chapel space, which is *de facto* only a fraction of a church, and redefined it as a self-contained unit.

---

[106] Friedländer, *op.cit.*, I, 1924, p. 39. In Friedländer-Veronee, I, the passage can be found on p. 32.

[107] As implied in a document dating from 1440, only a railing of wrought iron completed this partition. Cf. Dhanens, Inventaris VI, p. 95.

The idea that a mere part of a sanctuary should in itself repeat the symbolism of the total structure is quite a legitimate one. This was a traditional concept fundamentally rooted in the character of the Gothic church building. Since this character as such was determined by the idea of reflection—that is, of the reflection of the invisible structure of the City of God, the Heavenly Jerusalem, in a form comprehensible to the human senses—every sub-unit of the structure was capable of repeating this reflection.[108] The monumental architectural forms appeared again and again (in a scale more or less drastically reduced) in all the architectural parts of the edifice and even in the fixed or movable furnishings of the interior. And these parts and objects not only repeated the form of the whole but contained in themselves—like a thousand mirroring facets—the total idea of the complete whole. Keeping in mind that it was not always the monumental shape but often the diminutive one which was closer to the core of sacred meaning (whole churches were built around tiny reliquaries), it is only natural that the small structure of an ostensorium or of the chapel which contained it, should in itself embody the complete idea of the entire sanctuary.

The Vijd chapel, as a unit, is essentially an altar. This means that, as a unit, it is that particular object which is the *raison d'être* of a church structure. We have seen that the Eyckian tabernacle used the combined forms of two structures—the ancient reliquary edifice and the rood-screen—both of which could appear behind a mensa. As in any other individual structure located in a church, the form and symbolism of the church architecture were repeated in these traditional edifices. This is obvious in the reliquary structures. But it is true for the rood-screens as well. These large enclosures of the choir, with portals similar to those of the cathedral façades, symbolize, as do the façades, the entrance to the Heavenly Jerusalem.[109]

The Heavenly Jerusalem is a concept which has both a specific "historical" meaning and a broader eternal one. Described in the Apocalypse as the place to come at the end of time, it is a vision of the future. The concept, however, also has a general connotation, which is timeless. It is evident from the same text of Revelation as well as from Hebrews 12:22f that the Heavenly Jerusalem signifies the Christian Church *per se*. It is the timeless spiritual abode of the believers, especially when they are assembled for the celebration of the New Covenant, which is the Eucharistic rite. The liturgy here on earth is part of the never-ending song of praise in the City of God. Thus, the sacred events of past and future

[108] The "cosmic" character of the architectural organism of the Gothic church is discussed in Hans Sedlmayr, *Die Entstehung der Kathedrale*, Zurich 1950, chapter 20, pp. 81-83; for the trend in Gothic architecture to surround a large central form with similar but small satellite forms (*Das Umringen einer Kernform durch Trabantenformen*), cf. especially p. 89.

[109] This is obvious, for instance, from Albrecht von Scharfenberg's "Younger Titurel," which describes the architectural fantasy of the Temple of the Holy Grail with seventy-two chancels and choir-screens. Cf. Kirchner-Doberer, *op.cit.*, pp. 120f and note 378 with explanation of the passage (Droysen, verse 319-410), citation of the various editions, and further literature.

become mysteriously present in it. The earthly Church has its true home in the Heavenly Jerusalem towards which it makes its pilgrimage.[110] And since the proper locale of the earthly celebration is the Heavenly Jerusalem and the earthly church building is believed to present this locale, the character of the edifice is intrinsically eternal. Thus, all of its painted and sculptured scenes are fundamentally timeless images of things which, though present here and now, embrace also the past and the future.

It is in this sense that the sculptured and painted scenes in the Vijd tabernacle depict the Heavenly Jerusalem. Not only the exterior view of the retable, with its scenes of the past and the present, has an eternal meaning, but also the interior, which specifically depicts the apocalyptic vision of the future, is basically timeless. As for the apocalyptic meaning of this interior view, it is the two-leveled form of the ciborium which gave the artist the opportunity to make it thoroughly explicit. Heavenly Paradise was believed to consist of an upper and a lower zone, a biblical concept mirrored in the pictorial tradition.

To understand this concept, let us concentrate our attention for a moment on a much later representation. There is a Last Judgment triptych by Hieronymus Bosch, today preserved only in an engraving, which represents Paradise in the panel to the left (Fig. 55). The heavenly place consists of a celestial landscape below which shows the joys of the elect and an openwork architecture crowning it. This upper structure is a weightless vision supported by a cloud. In its lower arcades, it depicts various groups of angels and the view of the Sea of Glass, the apocalyptic symbol of God's mercy. The upper part of the edifice, also inhabited by angels, shows the enthroned figure of the Almighty represented as the Lord of Hosts and flanked by the Four Evangelists.[111]

Clearly, this two-leveled image of Paradise is based on the text of Revelation 21:1 (related to Isaiah 65:17 and 66:22), the classical description of the celestial vision in which the author tells us that he saw a new heaven and a new earth, for the first heaven

[110] Jungmann, op.cit., II, p. 135. In the Middle Ages, the Heavenly Jerusalem, far from merely connoting a final state in history (as it does according to our modern historical concept) rather signified the ultimate meaning of the present state. Cf. also J. Herwegen as quoted in Günter Bandmann, *Mittelalterliche Architektur als Bedeutungsträger*, Berlin 1951, p. 66, with detailed discussion and further literature. A more recent publication and the one that in the most comprehensive manner discusses the whole complex of concepts (the Heavenly Jerusalem, the City of God, Paradise, the Church, the Holy Virgin), their interrelationship and eventual identity, the biblical, patristic, and apocryphal texts pertaining to them and their reflection in the Roman Liturgy is Johan Chydenius, *The Typological Problem in Dante, A Study in the History of Medieval Ideas*, Helsingfors 1958, pp. 51-86 especially.

[111] The Enthroned is here depicted as the "Lord Sabaoth," a name which in the later biblical tradition signifies God's dominion in majesty and His power over the angels. The word Sabaoth, which appears inscribed on the stole of the Lord in the Ghent Altarpiece, certainly bears reference to the same idea (Fig. 56). Cf. Jungmann, op.cit., II, p. 134. As will be discussed below, even the symbols of the four Evangelists may have also appeared in the Ghent Altarpiece. For the possibility of a multitude of angels originally found in the Ghent retable, cf. below note 129.

and the first earth had passed away. The highest heaven is traditionally represented in architectural form, while the celestial abode of the elect is often depicted as a park-like garden similar to the terrestrial Eden.[112] What we see in the wing by Bosch is obviously a "heavenly sky" and a "heavenly earth," the first represented as a celestial architecture, the second as a paradisiac landscape.

The representation by Hieronymus Bosch was inspired by Van Eyck and was, no doubt, directly based on the Ghent Altarpiece. When we visualize the interior view of the Vijd retable as reconstructed in its sculptural framework it becomes obvious that this view with the paradisiac landscape below and the splendid cathedral above was the source for the wing by Bosch (Figs. 41 and 55). Knowing the Vijd altar in its original frame, Hieronymus Bosch still thoroughly understood the Eyckian idea. Unquestionably, in the Ghent Altarpiece too, the upper architecture depicted the New Heaven, the landscape below the New Earth of the Eternal Jerusalem. The duality of heavens is therefore by no means so strange as Panofsky seems to imply, but rather a most legitimate biblical idea.

In both the Van Eyck and the Bosch representations, the New Earth is the abode of the blessed. But the blessed painted by Van Eyck are of a different kind than those depicted by Bosch. The Van Eyck retable, though including, as we shall see, the idea of the Last Judgment, is not primarily a Judgment scene. Thus, the New Earth in the polyptych, although ready to receive all the elect whom the earth and the sea shall give forth at the last day, is not populated by the "average elect" as is the New Earth in the Bosch triptych. A specific kind of the elect is shown in the Van Eyck retable. There, we see the *Chorus Beatorum*, the Community of the Saints. Grouped according to their rank, they appear in the heavenly domain by virtue of their status in the celestial hierarchy. They constitute the lower stratum of the Eternal Jerusalem, an idea that is made perfectly clear by the towers of the City of God which form their symbolic background.

In the Ghent Altarpiece, the two levels of the interior view depict the lower and the upper stratum of the celestial hierarchy. The upper zone, indeed, as the crowning representation of the retable, demonstrates the fundamental idea of the entire two-leveled edifice. This idea is unrecognizable in the present fragmentary condition of the retable. In

[112] As the ecclesiastical architecture of the Middle Ages signifies Heaven, the image of Heaven in sculpture and painting can, in turn, be represented in the form of ecclesiastical architecture. Cf. Bandmann, *op.cit.*, 1951, p. 66. In the fifteenth century paintings of the Last Judgment, the place entered by the blessed is either a flower-studded landscape (Fra Angelico and Giovanni di Paolo) or a heavenly cathedral (Rogier van der Weyden and Stephan Lochner). However, if Paradise appears as the environment of those figures highest in the celestial hierarchy, it is an architectural setting which is usually favored. Not only the Virgin as the personification of the Ecclesia is depicted as surrounded by a cathedral architecture but also the Lord is traditionally shown in a celestial building. The front of a twelfth century reliquary from the Hüpsch Collection presents Christ in Majesty surrounded by the symbols of the Evangelists in a towered basilica (*Die Sammlungen des Baron von Hüpsch*, Exhibition Catalogue, Cologne 1964, no. 15, fig. 17). A similar later representation is found in Parisian book illumination (cf. Kathleen Morand, *Jean Pucelle*, Oxford 1962, plate XIV).

the present state, the combination of the Deësis with the figures of Adam and Eve seems so strange that Panofsky could only explain it as one of the results of the presumed change of plan. He felt that the First Parents should have appeared among the patriarchs in the lower zone, as we find them in the "new style" All Saints pictures (*Allerheiligenbilder*), in which Adam and Eve sometimes occur among the patriarchs.[113]

As Panofsky himself observed, the First Parents occur in the All Saints pictures only after the time of the Ghent Altarpiece.[114] It was certainly under the influence of the Van Eyck retable that Adam and Eve were introduced into the type. But their appearance in the theme is strictly speaking a hagiographical mistake, for the first couple, though liberated from Limbo together with the patriarchs, do not belong to the saintly personages Jewish or Pagan who foretold the coming of Christ or his sacrifice. And when Adam and Eve occasionally prefigure Christ and the Virgin, they are not to be seen as saintly figures. Thus, Adam and Eve do not belong in an All Saints picture at all. Except for a few examples of a popular nature which were painted under the influence of the Ghent retable, the First Parents are always absent from the theme, not only before the period of the great altarpiece but also in a later time. It is indicative that an important and knowledgeable master like Albrecht Dürer eliminated the representation of Adam and Eve in his famous *Allerheiligenbild*.[115]

Van Eyck omitted the First Parents in his Adoration of the Lamb because their inclusion among the saints would have been inaccurate from the doctrinal point of view.[116] His actual arrangement however, namely, to include them in the upper level of his altarpiece, is a most profound and theologically correct presentation. On the basis of our reconstruction, we readily understand his idea. The upper architecture consisted of a stone framework forming a central niche which, at some distance, was flanked by the buttressing piers that supported the structure. The stone niche enclosed the metal shrine which signified the "Ark of the New Covenant" (Fig. 41). Unquestionably, this Ark was meant as the *tabernaculum dei* which is described in Revelation 21:3-4, immediately after the passage which mentions the New Heaven and the New Earth. This passage tells us that the Tabernacle of God will be with man (*Ecce tabernaculum dei cum hominibus*). No doubt, the upper zone of the altarpiece depicts the sacred union of God with man as promised

---

[113] The opinion that the lower part of the Ghent Altarpiece is an All Saints picture and a detailed discussion on this point are found in Panofsky 1953, I, pp. 212-15. As far as I know, the iconography of the Ghent retable was first discussed at great length in connection with the Feast of All Saints by Rudolph Günther, *Die Bilder des Genter und Isenheimer Altars* (Studien über christliche Denkmäler, 15-16), Leipzig 1923.

[114] Panofsky 1953, I, p. 114, note 4, printed on p. 446.

[115] Erwin Panofsky, *Albrecht Dürer*, 3rd ed., Princeton 1948, II, no. 23, pp. 9-10 and fig. 172.

[116] Even the notion that the lower part of the Ghent polyptych presents an All Saints picture is, in itself, strictly speaking incorrect. Instead, one can perhaps formulate the situation as follows: the painting is directly based on the same source as is the All Saints liturgy, namely, on the text of the Apocalypse. The All Saints pictures, however, are based mainly on this liturgy.

in the Old Covenant and finally fulfilled in the New. Adam and Eve function as the representatives of mankind, whose promotion "to undeserved sublimity" through the mercy of the Lord is the idea of the New Law.

The specific form used in the Ghent Altarpiece for the architectural setting of the upper zone made it possible to express the biblical idea most precisely. The particular position of mankind was quite clearly defined. Adam and Eve, the first couple created and the first who have sinned and were redeemed from this sin when Christ delivered them from Limbo, are here shown in a role that is both modest and important. They are the buttressing piers of the sacred structure of the Christian Church, whose core encloses the golden tabernacle. Mankind serves to buttress the stone enclosure, not the tabernacle itself. This precisely corresponds to the meaning of the passage in Revelation which does not actually speak about a tabernacle of God and man but only of a tabernacle of God: "Behold the tabernacle of God is with man."

Most probably the lost stone frame was inscribed with the famous "*Ecce tabernaculum*" of Revelation 21:3, which also appears in raised letters in the frame of the small Eyckian Judgment panel in New York (Fig. 141).[117] We have a distinct indication that there was a dual set of inscriptions for each representation in the altarpiece. The figures and scenes were explained not only by painted texts appearing in the panels or the wooden parts of the frame but also by another set of inscriptions which must have adorned the outer stone frame. This can be deduced from a written source which mentions the inscriptions in the lower zone of the retable and which gives for the groups of saints not only the titles still partly preserved (*Justi Judices, Christi Milites*, and so forth), but also the biblical texts of the Beatitudes which are now totally lost together with the stone framework.[118] As for the panels of Adam and Eve, the texts still preserved today are those on the wooden framework which characterize the First Parents as those responsible for Death and Original Sin. Unquestionably, however, there had formerly been a number of other inscriptions which pertained to a mankind redeemed and expressed the reestablishment of man in written annotations to the *Ecce tabernaculum*.[119]

The union of God with man as expressed in the text from Revelation is the leading

[117] Although the paintings of the two small panels with the Crucifixion and the Last Judgment have been transferred from wood to canvas, the original Eyckian frames have been preserved. For their Latin inscriptions and the English translations thereof, cf. Harry B. Wehle and Margaretta Salinger, *The Metropolitan Museum of Art, A Catalogue of Early Flemish, Dutch and German Paintings*, New York 1947, p. 9. Another New Testament text on the Eternal Tabernacle is found in St. Paul's Epistle to the Hebrews; cf. below note 123.

[118] The chronicle already mentioned which describes the pageant performed in 1458, cf. above note 66. In De Baets, *op.cit.*, the part of the chronicle mentioning the Beatitudes appears on pp. 613-14; in Dhanens, *Inventaris* VI, on pp. 97-98. It can also be found in Documenten, pp. 8-9.

[119] For the inscriptions of the Adam and Eve panels still preserved today on the wooden moldings, cf. De Baets, *op.cit.*, pp. 576-79. These texts are taken from a passage ascribed to St. Augustine. They must originally have extended also to the frames of the other panels in the upper level (Death was brought through Eve, Life through Mary).

idea of the retable; it is the upper level of the interior view which dominates the entire work. It does so not only because of its particular position in the retable but also because of its prominent form. It is only in the upper level that the heavenly cathedral appears, and only there did the master present monumental figures which dominate the foreground. The foreground in the lower zone was the carved empty porch of the frame with sculptural columns carrying the upper cathedral. It may be interesting to note that the two-leveled edifice of the New Heaven and the New Earth was structurally as well as symbolically complete even in the foreground alone. For the lower columns were certainly twelve and they symbolized the apostles (Fig. 41).[120] They thus formed not only the functional but also the symbolic substructure of the cathedral. The five-part painting of the Adoration of the Lamb, which was seen behind these columns and which actually depicts the apostles together with the other saints as the pillars of the Church, can be taken as the "painted explanation," as it were, of the sculptured foreground columns.

However, the large vision of the Adoration of the Lamb has a meaning that considerably exceeds this scope. It contains a representation that is essential for the completion of the idea presented in the upper zone. The union of the Lord with a mankind burdened with Original Sin became possible only through the mercy of God, Who sacrificed His Son in expiation of this sin. The groups in the Adoration of the Lamb are assembled around the altar. The heavenly altar, which is described in Revelation 8:3-5, is here shown as carrying the sacrificial Lamb. It is the sacrifice of Christ, the means of mankind's Redemption, which is depicted in this vision. The scene below is, therefore, the indispensable foundation and explanation of the scene depicted above. The two levels together present the complete idea of the New Covenant. They in fact depict the act of the consummation of the New Law.

III. THE ETERNAL MASS

THIS act is rendered as a solemn celebration. Without doubt, the interior of the Ghent retable presents the Eternal Mass in the Heavenly Jerusalem, of which the earthly celebration of the New Covenant, the Eucharist as performed by the Church, is but the temporal reflection. The scenes in the Van Eyck altarpiece are clearly defined as signifying the solemn performance (Fig. 1). Christ in the upper region is crowned by the priestly tiara. By the crossed stole he is characterized as the officiating Priest (Fig. 56).[121] Both the Virgin and St. John the Baptist, who are enthroned together

---

[120] The idea (based on Ephesians 2:19-22) that the columns carrying a sacred edifice signify the apostles, or the apostles and the prophets, was widespread in the Middle Ages. Cf. Panofsky, *op.cit.*, 1946, pp. 104-5, for Abbot Suger's relating this idea to his chevet of St. Denis. Compare also Bandmann, *op.cit.*, 1951, pp. 64ff and p. 78.

[121] As far as I know, Charles de Tolnay was the first to suggest that the theme of the Eternal Mass plays an important part in the program of the Ghent Altarpiece (*op.cit.*, 1938, p. 4, cf. above note 8). For the Heavenly Sacrifice into which the earthly sacrifice is merged, cf. Jungmann, *op.cit.*, II, p. 233 and p. 233, notes 39 and 40; for the Heavenly Altar, p. 231; for the Heavenly Liturgy, pp. 127-28. For the crossed stole,

with Him, are shown as holding books and are depicted with their lips opened (Figs. 9 and 57). They sing or recite the sacred texts, the liturgy of the Eternal Mass. The tripartite throne on which the three figures are seated is comparable to the tripartite *sedilia* as it forms part of the ecclesiastical furniture in numerous Gothic churches (Fig. 58). The Virgin and St. John, thus characterized as the deacon and the subdeacon who aid the Celebrant, complete the image of the celestial rite. And so do the music-making angels who form the celestial choir. In this solemn act which celebrates the reinstatement of mankind, Adam and Eve, as mankind's representatives, stand "before the Lord."

While shown as the Celebrating Priest in the upper level, Christ is represented again in the lower one, this time as the Lamb sacrificed on the altar. Its position on a hill indicates the *levatio sacramenti*, the elevation of the Host at the consecration.[122] Like the Eucharistic celebration here on earth, the Eternal Mass re-enacts the sacrifice of Christ, Who cried out His *consummatum est* on the Cross. Christ is both the Sacrificing Priest and the Victim in the holy sacrifice. This, indeed, is the very idea of the Eucharist as celebrated by the Church and of the Lord's Supper as told in the Gospels as the first celebration of the Sacrament.[123] It was thus imperative in a representation of the Eucharist to depict Christ twice, that is, in both of his roles, as the Celebrant and as the Sacrifice.

---

cf. Joseph Braun, *Die liturgische Gewandung im Occident und Orient nach Ursprung und Entwicklung, Verwendung und Symbolik*, Freiburg i. Br. 1907, p. 588, and Percy Ernst Schramm, *Herrschaftszeichen und Staatssymbolik; Beiträge zu ihrer Geschichte vom 3. bis zum 16. Jahrhundert* (Schriften der Monumenta Germaniae historica) Stuttgart 1954-56, I, p. 28. The tiara had become the symbol of the worldly rather than of the spiritual rule of the pope during the Middle Ages. It is an extra-liturgical insigne not worn by the pope when officiating. Cf. Braun, *op.cit.*, 1907, pp. 498-508, and Schramm, *op.cit.*, II, pp. 62-68. However, in the pictorial tradition, the officiating pope can well be shown as crowned by the tiara. Cf., for instance, the Mass of St. Gregory ascribed to the Master of Flémalle, Friedländer-Veronee, II, plate 100. The tiara is the indispensable attribute of the celebrant's high office. In fact, Christ himself is depicted as crowned by the tiara when officiating in an Italian miniature showing the Communion of the Apostles. This miniature, dated 1438 and today in the Cini Collection in Venice, is ascribed to the Master of the *Vitae Imperatorum* and is illustrated in Alison Stones, "An Italian Miniature in the Gambier-Parry Collection," *The Burlington Magazine*, CXI, 790, January 1969, fig. 9 on p. 9. In the Ghent Altarpiece there is even a specific reason for the use of the tiara. It is that Christian insigne which is closest to the headgear of the Jewish high priest as described by Josephus (cf. *New Catholic Encyclopedia*, XIV, "tiara," p. 150). In a text most important for the Van Eyck Altarpiece (cf. below note 123), St. Paul discusses Christ in his office as the High Priest. There can be no doubt that the tiara as painted by Van Eyck makes reference to this idea.

[122] This interpretation is not contradicted by the meaning of the hill, which certainly signifies Mount Zion and may specifically indicate the symbolic rock on which Christ built His Church. Cf. Jungmann, *op.cit.*, II, pp. 126f.

[123] The main text for Christ's acting as the High Priest as well as the Sacrifice is St. Paul's Epistle to the Hebrews. Cf. especially Hebrews 9:11-14. Cf. Jungmann, *op.cit.*, I, pp. 179ff. Compare St. Thomas, *Summa theol.*, III, 83, 1-3: "Sacerdos gerit imaginem Christi, in cuius persona et virtute verba pronuntiat ad consecrandum. . . . Et ita quodammodo idem est sacerdos et hostia." Interestingly enough, it is the very text of Hebrews 9 which discusses the Heavenly Tabernacle, in verses 6-10. Cf. above note 117.

The two-fold depiction of Christ was, in fact, traditional in representations of the Mass. When we look, for instance, at the illustration of the Sacrament as it occurs in a German *Biblia Pauperum* written in 1414-15, we see that here too Christ's figure appears in both zones of the miniature (Fig. 60). In the lower one, He is depicted as the Man of Sorrows. This image corresponds to the Lamb on the altar as it is shown with Its Blood streaming into the chalice in Van Eyck's altarpiece (Fig. 62). Like the Lamb, the Man of Sorrows presents the suffering Christ of the Passion. He signifies the human Body of the Lord, His *corpus verum*, into which, according to Christian doctrine, the Host turns at the Transubstantiation.[124] As in the image of the Lamb, the Blood of the Man of Sorrows streams into the chalice. The seated figure of the Lord in the upper zone of the miniature corresponds to the enthroned Christ as He is rendered as the High Priest of the New Covenant in the upper level of the Ghent polyptych (Figs. 60 and 1).

It is perfectly clear that in the manuscript too the seated figure is not God the Father but God the Son. The youthful head surrounded by a cross-nymbus makes this connotation evident. It is clear, moreover, that a figure enthroned in a mandorla together with the crowned Virgin must be the Second Person of the Trinity, because this combination is a type derived from the Coronation of Mary.[125] Evidently, in the miniature as well as in the altarpiece, Christ is depicted in His two natures, above in His divine body, below in His human one, the *corpus verum* of the Sacrament. In both of these fifteenth century compositions, the two representations of Christ are connected with each other by the symbol of the Holy Ghost. In the Van Eyck retable, the appearance of the Dove over the altar has been called an intrusion and iconographically incongruous by Panofsky.[126] The motif, however, is not only correct but even essential in this context, for it signifies the oneness of Christ's two natures (Fig. 62).

The Dove of the Holy Spirit is described as descending from Heaven in the Gospel text on the Baptism of Christ (Matthew 3:16-17; Mark 1:10-11). This passage contains God's declaration that the human Christ as He lived here on earth was the true Son of the Almighty: "Thou art my beloved Son, in whom I am well pleased." The divine manifestation as described in this text consists of a visual part, the apparition of the Dove, and an audible one, the words spoken by God. Both are indicated in the miniature. The symbol of the Dove appears at the end of a scroll which connects the seated figure of the Lord with the standing one and which carries the text of the divine declaration (Fig. 60).

[124] For the concept of the Eucharistic species' turning into the human body of Christ, for the twelfth century's being the time of its origin, and for the ideas of earlier theologians on this point, cf. the concise and clear discussion in Adolf Katzenellenbogen, *The Sculptural Programs of Chartres Cathedral*, Baltimore 1959, pp. 13-14, with a wealth of literature cited in the notes.

[125] For the type of Christ and the Virgin enthroned together as the Bride and Bridegroom of Cant. 4:8 and Ps. 44:10 (45:9), and for the origin and development of the type, cf. Katzenellenbogen, *op.cit.*, pp. 56-65, with sources and previous literature cited in the notes.

[126] Cf. above note 103.

In the context of the Sacrament, this testimony to Christ's divinity is of the utmost importance. It proves the validity of Christ's sacrifice, which could only have become the means of mankind's Redemption because the suffering and dying Christ was the divine Son of God and free of Original Sin. The text of the miniature is, characteristically enough, not taken from the report in the Gospels. It is given in its original version as it occurs in the Second Psalm and as it is quoted in St. Paul's letter to the Hebrews, 1:5 and 5:5. This Epistle, which we have mentioned before, contains discussions on every point which became important in the ideological structure of the doctrine of the Church and, therefore, in the context of the Eucharistic celebration. It discusses not only the Heavenly Jerusalem, the Golden Ark and Christ's being both the Priest and the Sacrifice, but also, and in numerous passages (not all of which will be mentioned here), it describes the working of the Holy Ghost.

Christ, in His sacrifice, "offered Himself through the Holy Spirit unblemished unto God" according to St. Paul (Hebrews 9:14). The Holy Spirit, therefore, is the witness not only of Christ's divinity but also of the sacrifice. This is expressed in the next chapter of the Epistle (Hebrews 10:14-15), where the Holy Ghost is, furthermore, called the witness of the New Covenant (Hebrews 10:16). Indeed, in the Canon of the Mass, in the very climax of the sacred action, the Third Person of the Trinity is invoked as the witness of the sacrifice. In the liturgies of the East, this invocation, the *epiklesis* of the Holy Ghost, in which the Eternal Spirit is besought to descend upon the altar, was even believed in itself to effect the Transubstantiation.[127] There can be no doubt that the motif of the Dove was planned by Van Eyck from the start.[128]

While the glorious apparition of the Dove above the altar is the divine witness of Christ's sacrificial death, the groups assembled around it are the human witness of the sacrifice. The prophets and the patriarchs foretold it, the apostles and martyrs testified to it with their own blood, and others bore witness to it with their lives and actions. All of them, having come from the four corners of the New Earth to adore the Lamb, form the congregation in Christ's solemn celebration of the Eternal Mass (Fig. 62).

The center of the general devotion, the altar with the Lamb, is surrounded by kneeling angels, twelve enclosing it on the sides and displaying the *Arma Christi*, two with censers kneeling in front of it. These angelic groups correspond to those angels in the miniature who have come down from their exalted abode with tapers, censer, and holy

---

[127] Cf. Jules Corblet, *Histoire dogmatique, liturgique et archéologique du Sacrement de l'Eucharistie*, Paris 1885, I, pp. 270-73. For the role of the Holy Spirit in the Roman rite, cf. also Jungmann, *op.cit.*, I, p. 383, and II, pp. 70, 190-94, and 232-35; furthermore Yrjö Hirn, *The Sacred Shrine*, 2nd English ed., Boston 1957, pp. 114f and Günter Bandmann, "Ein Fassadenprogramm des 12. Jahrhunderts und seine Stellung in der christlichen Ikonographie," *Das Münster*, v, 1/2, 1952, p. 10. (For this article, which hereafter will be cited as Bandmann, *Fassadenprogramm*, cf. below our note 218.)

[128] Further discussion on this point will be offered below, pp. 68-70. Cf. notes 138 and 151.

water to surround the sacramental Christ (Fig. 60).[129] In the Ghent Adoration of the Lamb, the angels form an inner circle around the altar, while the apostles and prophets form, as it were, an outer half-circle around it. These two groups are shown as already kneeling at the foot of the hillock with the altar, whereas other groups are standing near it and yet others, those in the wings, are depicted as still in the process of approaching it. Clearly, the time motif is here used to clarify the position of each group within the celestial hierarchy, not to indicate a specific moment of the act. The Heavenly Mass is here represented in a comprehensive but entirely generalized image. Far from indicating specific liturgical acts in succession, the painting is an abstraction of them all, placed in an eternal location and therefore intrinsically timeless.[130]

Not only the celebrants in the upper parts of the altarpiece but also some groups in the congregation use books for the heavenly liturgy (Fig. 62). Perhaps the prophets were meant to recite the texts of their own prophecies so widely used in the readings of the earthly Mass.[131] In any case, it is quite obvious that the blessed must sing the heavenly songs which are sung to the Lamb in the Apocalypse. One of these songs, Revelation 5:12 ("Worthy is the Lamb that was slain . . .") is inscribed in the frame of the Antwerp copy (Fig. 32). It probably formed one of the texts that adorned the original frame of the Ghent Altarpiece itself. But the other songs in the Apocalypse, Revelation 15:3-4 or Revelation 5:9-10 (". . . and hast made us unto our God kings and priests; and we shall reign on the earth") would likewise be most suitable as texts for the Ghent Altarpiece. Most probably, these songs, which have the nature of Eucharistic prayers, had actually been used in the liturgy of the early Church. All of them have the character of popular hymns. And, indeed, even the modern *Agnus Dei* of the Communion Cycle of the Roman Mass is a hymn which is apportioned to the congregation.[132]

The prophets and apostles in the Ghent Altarpiece are rendered as kneeling at the sides of the altar in much the same way as the actual everyday congregation is shown in

[129] For the participation of the angelic world in the heavenly and the earthly oblation, cf. Jungmann, *op.cit.*, II, p. 234. The two groups of music-making angels in the upper part of the Ghent Altarpiece correspond to the angelic host that surrounds Christ and the Virgin in the miniature. The fact that these upper miniature groups depict the nine pseudo-Dionysian *chori* suggests the possibility that in the Ghent Altarpiece also a larger number of groups had formerly existed in the upper level. Originally, some sculpted angels may have inhabited the architecture of the frame and completed the painted assembly (cf. the empty parts in our reconstruction, Fig. 42). This assumption seems to be corroborated by the free copy of the Fountain of Life (Fig. 19), where we see various angelic groups that do not have their equivalent in the Ghent Altarpiece. Perhaps these groups were copied from the sculpture of the lost Eyckian frame. Cf. also above note 111.

[130] A more detailed discussion of the specific concepts of time and place as used in the images of the Ghent Altarpiece will be found below in Chapter 5.

[131] Jungmann, *op.cit.*, I, pp. 393ff.   [132] *Ibid.*, II, pp. 335f.

the miniature (Fig. 60). The miniature, as a representation which explains the meaning of the Eucharistic rite, depicts the normally invisible Eucharistic truth together with the earthly performance of the Sacrament. This results in an interesting fusion of the heavenly with the earthly event. The Ghent Altarpiece, in front of which the same earthly rite was performed, originally showed a similar fusion of image and reality. This is no longer obvious in the present fragmentary condition of the work. However, we have some distinct indications in the Lamb panel of the retable that such a fusion was originally intended (Fig. 62).

The half-circle formed by the prophets and the apostles encloses not only the altar with the sacrifice but also the Fountain of Life depicted below it. This is the Well of Living Water, described in Revelation 7:17 as the place to which the Lamb will lead the blessed. The water in the fountain signifies the Redemption of mankind, which is accomplished through the Lamb's sacrifice. It is the Water of Life which the Church offers to her children in the form of the Sacrament. The Sacrament, however, is offered not only to the Community of Saints but to all the believers of the Church. This idea was clearly expressed in the Ghent Altarpiece.

From the marble basin of the painted fountain we see an enchanting little course of water streaming down through the flowery meadows directly towards the actual mensa of the Vijd altar. This stream is today abruptly cut by the lower part of the modern frame. The original frame, however, must have indicated that the water poured into the central part of the predella. No doubt, the center of the predella had formed a recess which sheltered the receptacle with the Eucharistic species, an arrangement which frequently occurs in fifteenth and sixteenth century altarpieces (Fig. 61).[133] The water, in other words, was meant to turn into the actual wafer, an idea which is explicitly presented in the much

---

[133] Cf. Braun, op.cit., 1924, II, p. 349, with examples reproduced in plate 359. The Bordesholm Altarpiece of 1521 by Hans Brüggemann in the Cathedral of Schleswig, which is shown in our illustration and which prominently presents, as does the Ghent Altarpiece, Adam and Eve as tall standing figures in the upper zone, is, like the work by Van Eyck, one of the largest and most elaborate retables of the time. As attested to by its predella scenes, all of which depict Eucharistic subjects, the recess flanked by them can only have been the compartment used for the Holy Sacrament. The metal grill that covers this predella compartment in many of the altarpieces in question is sometimes a door which can be opened. It is stationary, however, when the Host recess is accessible from the back. This is the case in the Landshut Altarpiece of 1424, an early example of the type showing the recess not as yet in the predella but still in the "body" of the retable, though in the lower story (Figs. 15 and 16). The still earlier altarpiece of Meran seems to have presented this recess in its very center level (Fig. 14). This small work reveals itself as an armoire for relics when the two inner doors are opened (a view not shown in our reproduction). The tall and narrow center compartment may have sheltered the Sacrament in the midst of the surrounding relics. (The Host vessel, in this case, may have been a statue of the Virgin—cf. below note 191.) For the relic shrine as the ancestor of the Northern painted altarpiece, cf. Harald Keller, "Der Flügelaltar als Reliquienschrein," *Studien zur Geschichte der europäischen Plastik, Festschrift Theodor Müller*, Munich 1964, pp. 125-44, with the Meran Altarpiece reproduced on p. 131 with all the doors opened.

discussed painting of the Fountain of Life where we see a multitude of small hosts floating in the water of the well (Figs. 19 and 20).

It is clear that the copyist who painted the Fountain of Life has bluntly depicted a miracle which was indicated in Van Eyck's original in a most subtle way. There, the little stream of sacred water was simply shown as flowing into the recess which sheltered the ciborium, with the miracle itself left to the imagination of the believer. We have previously mentioned that the two contending groups of Synagoga and Ecclesia which flank the fountain in the copy must have also appeared in the Ghent Altarpiece. We now see that their place in the original can only have been to the left and the right of the ciborium, the vessel containing the Host (Fig. 59). In the Van Eyck retable, it was this ciborium which contained the reason for their disagreement. The two groups, in other words, must have been small scenes which adorned the predella (Fig. 41).[134]

It was this lost predella of the Ghent Altarpiece which connected the mensa with the image in the retable and which thus fused the picture of the Eternal Mass with the earthly rite as celebrated in the Vijd chapel. The fusion of actual reality with an image of the sacramental truth is here still more significant than it is in the miniature (Fig. 60). An actual living congregation physically appeared before the mensa in the Vijd chapel on which the picture of the celestial Mass was placed. With the representation of the Lamb's sacrifice shown directly at his eye level, the viewer was compelled to feel that he was a witness to this scene. He saw the sacred water, the result of the celestial sacrifice, flowing directly into the vessel from which the priest would hand him the Host. The believer thus virtually became a participant in the celestial rite.

It is this idea of the miraculous fusion of image and reality which accounts for the unusual handling of form in Van Eyck's Lamb panel. This form, differing from that in all the other panels, has often surprised art historians. In his analysis of the composition, Dvořák has already observed that the representation is clearly divided into an upper and a lower zone by a distinct demarcation line which crosses the panel horizontally from one side to the other (Fig. 62).[135] This line, almost straight on the sides and formed by the clustered heads of the foreground groups, continued toward the center in an upward curve

[134] The altarpieces of the North show not only the Wise and the Foolish Virgins as a popular two-part scene in their predellas but also the two figures of Synagoga and Ecclesia. As an example from the time of the Ghent Altarpiece, I should like to mention the Altarpiece of Boslunde (Denmark) in which the two allegorical figures flank the Salvator Mundi. Cf. Braun, *op.cit.*, 1924, II, pp. 503-4 and plate 328. Both of these opposing pairs, the Wise and Foolish Virgins as well as Ecclesia and Synagoga, point to the Last Judgment. The close connection of the Ecclesia and Synagoga groups in the Ghent Altarpiece to the idea of the final Judgment will be discussed later in this chapter.

[135] Max Dvořák, "Das Rätsel der Kunst der Brüder van Eyck," *Jahrbuch der kunsthistorischen Sammlungen des Allerhöchsten Kaiserhauses*, XXIV, 1904, pp. 161 *passim*, cf. especially the discussion starting on p. 196. In the book edition published in Munich 1925 under the same title, it starts on p. 62.

formed by the hill with the altar and the Lamb. All the forms that appear below this line are seen not primarily in space but rather as a two-dimensional configuration on the picture plane. Interestingly enough, the lower part of the composition has this two-dimensional character in spite of the fact that the forms are in themselves convincingly three-dimensional and in spite of the fact that the spatial distances between them are quite correctly represented. Dvořák and a number of other scholars took this part of the scene for an archaic representation and attributed it to an earlier master (Hubert). I would like to suggest, however, that this lower area in the Lamb panel is not genuinely archaic.

Conceived as being distinct from the background area, the composition in the foreground is one in which Van Eyck has intentionally stressed the flat pattern character of the form. The lower part, with its upper contour rising at the center and straightening at the sides, has the decided shape of a pediment. When the substantial predella still existed, the pediment-like part must have given the impression of being its crowning top piece. It must, indeed, have seemed as if it were an "intermediate gable" separating the stone mensa and its stone predella from the tall structure behind it, very much like the gable of an entrance hall would separate the image of this hall from the rest of the structure (Fig. 41).

The two most important objects within this gable-like foreground area of the Lamb panel are the altar with the Lamb and the fountain (Fig. 62). Their outspoken two-dimensionality is here used as an artistic device to achieve two important effects. Although they are not at all connected in three-dimensional space, the two motifs appear to us as a visual unit. The altar surrounded by the angels resembles a rose-like pattern fixed, as it were, to a stem formed by the golden pipe of the fountain below it. The viewer sees the two objects in their contour pattern in spite of their vigorous three-dimensionality. And since their contours are linked, he sees the two objects as closely connected in spite of their being completely disconnected in space.

This formal device has a powerful effect. Once obliged to see everything two-dimensionally, the spectator also saw the niche with the ciborium, which appeared directly below the two painted objects, in the same manner and, therefore, as linked to the painted forms. Their curious two-dimensionality stressed the connection between the three symbolic images which followed each other in the vertical axis of the retable. It connected the altar with the fountain and the fountain with the ciborium, which very probably had the shape of a monstrance (Figs. 41 and 59).[136]

---

[136] In some examples of later Northern altarpieces, we actually know that the Host vessel placed in the predella recess was a monstrance, as for instance, in the large Altarpiece of Our Lady in the German convent of Wienhausen. Cf. Horst Appuhn, "Der Auferstandene und das Heilige Blut zu Wienhausen," *Niederdeutsche Beiträge zur Kunstgeschichte*, 1, Cologne 1961, pp. 84ff, with highly interesting discussions on the relationship between Holy Wafer and relics, and descriptions of their vessels and their places in the altarpiece.

Seen above a predella which contained an actual vessel, the two painted forms of the fountain and the altar with the Lamb must have assumed the distinct character of religious objects. Like the niche with the monstrance, the two painted configurations must have appeared as though physically present in the chapel of Jodocus Vijd. And this brings us to the second reason for the curious two-dimensionality in the lower area of the Lamb panel. This device not only linked the three images together; it also expressed the mystery of their direct corporeal presence. Seen two-dimensionally, the painted images become divine signs imbued with an icon-like sanctity and directness. More than a mere illusion for the human eye, the painted forms assume an objective existence, filled, as it were, with the essence of the very thing which they depict.[137]

The meaning of the three images is clear. The sequence was meant to express the miracle of the Transubstantiation as a concrete occurrence taking place in the Vijd chapel. This miracle is commanded by the blessing hand of the Lord, Who is depicted as the Priest in the upper level of the retable. The human priest consecrating the Host is but the representative of the divine Celebrant. The Transubstantiation, however, is not directly effected through the Lord's command. The Dove of the Holy Spirit, which is shown immediately above the three images, is certainly meant to be the divine agent in the sacred act. The idea of the ancient liturgies, according to which the Holy Ghost was the power which worked the Transubstantiation, was not entirely foreign to the West. In the earlier Middle Ages, the Host was often kept in a dove-shaped ciborium. These containers were usually *suspensoria*, that is, they were hung above the altar. Suspended on a pulley, they could be lowered and raised (Figs. 63, 64, and 65). It seems that the lowering and the raising of the Eucharistic Dove was sometimes performed to emphasize the moment of the Transubstantiation.[138]

The early altar arrangements with a movable dove suspended in front of the retable must still have been known to Van Eyck. His painted dove is clearly the "modern" illusionistic reinterpretation of the old mechanical device. Since the Vijd altar in its entirety simulated, as we have seen, a venerable early altar, it is not surprising that the painter should have used in his retable a new illusionistic version of one of the paraphernalia occurring in these ancient structures.

[137] This magical quality of art, found in periods and cultures in which the sacred and the profane are not as yet fully separated, is mentioned in Bandmann, *op.cit.*, 1951, p. 79 and p. 100, note 244. It is similar to the character that mediaeval authors ascribe to the sacramental symbols, which were believed to contain and impart the very thing which they symbolize. Cf. Johan Chydenius, *The Theory of Medieval Symbolism* (Societas Scientiarum Fennica, Commentationes Humanarum Litterarum, XXVII. 2) Helsingfors 1960, pp. 24ff.

[138] For the role of the Dove in the Roman rite, cf. the literature given above in note 127. For the dove-shaped vessels and the literary sources connected with them, cf. Braun, *op.cit.*, 1924, II, pp. 574-82 and pp. 608-16. For his judgment on the latter's value, however, cf. Bandmann, *Fassadenprogramm*, note 94, with further discussion on the Dove on pp. 14-15 and 18.

THE ICONOGRAPHY OF THE ALTARPIECE

In Van Eyck's reinterpretation, an old toy-like device is turned into a most convincing image of a divine apparition. Hovering in the glorious blue sky of a paradisiac morning and surrounded by a magnificent halo of light, the Dove brings the blissful experience of a celestial reality right into the Vijd chapel. Appearing in the upper section of the panel where the forms no longer show the described icon-like character, the Dove is part of an atmospheric and infinite space. Even the altar and fountain, which had the semblance of icon-like objects when seen as motifs belonging to the predella, tend to lose this character when seen in connection with the Dove.

Since the two-dimensional effect in the lower portion of the Lamb panel is produced by "modern" illusionistic forms not basically different from the other painted representations in Van Eyck's polyptych, it was not difficult to fuse these forms with those in the rest of the painting. This fusion was ingeniously done right within the Lamb panel itself. The two background groups, though placed into a clearly three-dimensional, atmospheric, and infinite space, nevertheless complete the two-dimensional rose pattern of the foreground scene. And the Dove, though the perfect image of a supernatural apparition, belongs to the sequence of the iconic Eucharistic symbols in the middle axis of the painting.

It is not the Dove alone which appears as an intervening symbol between the divine Priest and the three Eucharistic objects. The crown, which rests at the feet of the Enthroned and which also appears in the vertical axis of the altarpiece, is placed still higher than the Dove and was certainly meant as the culmination of the series of symbols (Figs. 41 and 71). The crown too bears a relationship to an object that was used to adorn the ancient altar structures. Placed high above the mensa, it brings to mind the ancient votive crowns which, like the dove-shaped vessels, were suspended above the altar tables (Figs. 67 and 68). The meaning of the votive crown, which glorified the altar as both the bearer of the relics and the resting place of the Host, was certainly a most complex and comprehensive one.[139] And the same is true for the meaning of the crown that is represented in the Ghent Altarpiece.

While the enthroned figure of Christ is characterized as the Eternal Priest by the tiara that He wears, the crown at His feet is, of course, the symbol of His eternal kingship. The beautiful object, designating Christ as the King of Kings, complements the idea of the *sacerdotium* with that of the *regnum*. Interestingly enough, however, it is usually not the divine Christ but the sacramental Christ Who was called a "king" by the ancient authors.[140] Indeed, the crown in the Ghent Altarpiece points clearly to the sacrificed

[139] Charles Rohault de Fleury, *La Messe*, Paris 1887, v, pp. 101-15; Hirn, *op.cit.*, pp. 67ff; Schramm, *op.cit.*, I, pp. 134-36, and plate 5c; II, pp. 377-79, and plate 41; on the crowns in the Ghent Altarpiece, cf. III, pp. 996-98, and plate 115.

[140] Cf. Hirn, *op.cit.*, p. 148. The custom of crowning the receptacle of the Host seems to be based on the same idea; cf. below Chapter 4, the paragraph which precedes note 301.

Christ. The symbol is flanked by inscriptions on the thronepace which explain its mean-ing and which describe in four verses the aspects of eternal life.[141] According to the bibli-cal texts, the crown of eternal life is the reward of the martyr.[142] The symbol, therefore, seems to glorify Christ as the Martyr Supreme. Resting at the feet of a figure that obvi-ously signifies the divine Christ, the crown seems to indicate that the divine Being had a part in the passion and humiliation. It thus strengthens the connection between the figure of the Enthroned and the representations in the Lamb panel.

In any case, it is clear that the specific place of the crown is meant to be a link to the lower panels in which the community of saints is represented. The precious object at the feet of the Lord apparently symbolizes the combined crowns offered to Him by his saints. Having followed Christ in His sacrificial death, His martyrs are united with Him in eternal life. This idea is often represented in Early Christian and Carolingian works through the martyrs' offering their crowns to Christ (Figs. 69 and 70).[143] This idea is expressed in the Ghent Altarpiece in the single symbol of the crown. And, just as in the ancient representations, the motif does not concern the martyrs alone but has a much broader and more comprehensive meaning.

To be united with the Lord in eternal life is not just the prerogative of the martyr, it is the hope of every Christian. Certainly the beautiful crown in the Ghent retable sym-bolizes eternal life as the great gift to a mankind redeemed. This gift is imparted to the believer through the Sacrament over the altar. Unquestionably the crown symbolizes the purpose of the Eucharist. As the uppermost of the five object-symbols that appear in the axis of the work, and crowning the miracle of the Transubstantiation, the sumptuous diadem at the feet of the Lord epitomizes the meaning of the Mass.

The place of the crown in the very center of the Ghent tabernacle, equidistant from the sides, the top and the bottom of the structure, is certainly no mere accident. The sym-bol is the culmination point of all the ideas of the retable. All the lines of symbolic thought, those from the sides as well as those from the bottom and the top, converge in the symbol of the crown.

The crown, as explained, tops the chain of sacramental transformations shown in

[141] "VITA SINE MORTE IN CAPITE/GAUDIUM SINE MERORE A DEXTRIS" (on the left of the spectator); "JUVENTUS SINE SENECTUTE IN FRONTE/SECURITAS SINE TIMORE A SINISTRIS" (on the right). For a discussion on the possible sources for this text, cf. De Baets, *op.cit.*, pp. 595f.

[142] The Apocalypse is again the main text for this idea. Cf. Rev. 2:10, but also I Corinthians 9:25; II. Timothy 4:8; James 1:12; I. Peter 5:4; Wisdom 5:17.

[143] The engraving of 1690 shown in our reproduction presents the dome mosaic of Charlemagne's chapel in Aachen in the form which it had up to the beginning of the eighteenth century and in which Van Eyck must have seen it. With the exception of the figure which is depicted in the pluviale (as is the figure by Van Eyck) and which can only be a replacement of the twelfth or thirteenth century, the mosaic is Caro-lingian. Cf. Hermann Schnitzler, "Das Kuppelmosaik der Aachener Pfalzkapelle," *Aachener Kunstblätter*, 29, 1964, pp. 17-44 *passim*, and especially pp. 32ff.

the motifs of the lower vertical axis. The symbol, moreover, is also the culmination point of the idea expressed in the horizontal sequence in the panels of the upper level. The union of the Lord with mankind as presented in this horizontal sequence re-bestows the gift of eternal life upon man. The crown is the symbol for this. Indeed, it is obvious that the inscriptions on the thronepace must have been connected with the now lost inscriptions below the figures of Adam and Eve. We have seen that the negative statements below the first parents pointing to death, murder, and the mortality of a mankind burdened with Original Sin must have been superseded by others pointing to the glorious promise of eternal life. This promise is expressed in the crown and its paradisaic texts.[144] Finally, the magnificent crown is also the culmination point of a chain of vertical representations which started at the top of the tabernacle. And thus we come to the upper portion of the Eyckian structure so far omitted in our iconographical discussions.

It is perfectly clear from the liturgy of the Mass that the sacrifice which is performed by Christ as the High Priest of the New Covenant is being offered to God the Father.[145] True, in the miniature which we have discussed there is no figure of God the Father expressly depicted as the receiver of the sacrifice (Fig. 60). This miniature, however, is an abbreviated image in which the three divine symbols, Christ in Majesty, the Dove, and the sacramental Christ, were perfectly sufficient to express the simple didactic content of the *biblia pauperum*. The Ghent Altarpiece, in contrast, is a monumental devotional work demanding completeness. There, the figure of the Almighty had to be represented not only to perfect the scene of the Eternal Mass but also to round off the second cycle of Trinity symbols which was indicated by the Lamb and the Dove. As described at the start of this chapter, it is difficult to imagine that the Trinitarian figure of Christ enthroned should have completed this cycle. For, assuming this, the Second and Third Persons of the Trinity would have been represented twice, but the First Person only once. Fortunately, we have a very good proof that the First Person did appear in the Ghent Altarpiece in an extra figure. It is the representation of the exterior of the retable rather than the interior which furnishes us with this proof (Fig. 2).

In the scene of the Annunciation, Van Eyck used the enchanting motif of reversing the letters of the Virgin's answer to the angelic salutation so that the text appears upside down (Figs. 72 and 83). It was obviously meant to be read by one who looked down on

---

[144] Because the reinstatement of Adam and Eve and, therefore, of a mankind that is burdened by Original Sin but finally freed from it, is factually the chief idea of the entire altarpiece by Van Eyck, the title "The Retable of Adam and Eve" under which the work was known throughout the sixteenth century and later (cf. Dhanens, Inventaris VI, pp. 104, 108, 115, 116, 117 and 118) was by no means a misnomer, as Dvořák and other twentieth century authors have assumed. The ancient name fits the intrinsic meaning of the work much more precisely than does our modern "The Mystic Lamb." Cf. also above note 89. Panofsky (cf. below note 218) was right, at least in principle, in rejecting as a proof for the essential unity of the retable any interpretation that did not take the prominent position of Adam and Eve into account.

[145] Cf. Jungmann, *op.cit.*, I, pp. 379f.

the scene from high above and who would thus see the inscription from the right direction. This has already been noticed by Panofsky, who correctly interprets the motif as indicating that the Annunciate gives her answer directly to God in Heaven.[146] It is, however, not possible to believe that Van Eyck could have had God Himself in mind when he painted the answer upside down. This would have been a blasphemous thought inconceivable to an artist working in the fifteenth century. Certainly the answer of the painted figure of the Virgin was not directed toward the Almighty Himself but toward a representation of the Supreme Being. Numerous fifteenth century Annunciations show the image of God the Father occurring above the scene and usually rendered as a half-figure or as a bust. We have only to recall the Annunciation of the *Belles Heures*, in which the figure of the Almighty appears on a stone balcony on top of the Annunciation room (Fig. 73).[147]

It is evident that a bust or half-figure of God the Father must have appeared also in the Ghent Altarpiece, where it was undoubtedly shown in the upper part of the framing structure. Such a figure could have occurred either in the center medallion of the golden shrine or still higher in the stone tracery tower on a balcony similar to that in the miniature. Whether in one place or the other, according to the mechanical functioning of the altarpiece, the representation of God the Father would have been visible in both views— with wings opened or closed (Figs. 41 and 42). I am inclined to believe that the figure of the Almighty had appeared in the stone tracery, placed above the statuettes of the standing prophets, and that it was the crowning motif of the entire work (Figs. 41, 42, and 48).[148]

This would mean that there was also an upper vertical line of representations, starting in the figure of God the Father, continuing in the prophets and in the monumental painting of the Enthroned, and finally arriving at the same point as do all the other lines,

[146] Panofsky 1953, I, p. 138.

[147] Even the setting of the Annunciation itself, with the scene appearing behind columns is similar to that in the Ghent Altarpiece, which we have reconstructed with columns. Judging from the book illumination, it seems that the early Annunciations when occurring as the center of an altarpiece had often shown God the Father in the crowning part of the frame. (This is difficult to verify since the frame is usually lost.) While the crowning images as they appear in the Italian frames and in their early Northern derivatives are always painted (usually they are medallions) provided that the sculptured parts are gesso and wood (cf. Cämmerer, *op.cit.*, plate I, *passim*), they are reliefs when the frame is made of stone. God the Father, for instance, is rendered as a relief above Fra Angelico's painted Madonna of the Linaiuoli (Fig. 50). Compare also above note 87.

[148] It probably was this extremely high position of the figure of God the Father which made it barely visible to the unaided eye and accounts for the fact that fifteenth and sixteenth century visitors to the chapel had apparently never noticed it. This oversight explains why even such a knowledgeable reporter of the retable as Dürer could take the figure of Christ in Majesty for a representation of God the Father. Cf. *Albrecht Dürers schriftlicher Nachlass*, ed. Ernst Heidrich, preface by Heinrich Wölfflin, Berlin 1910, p. 90. Cf. also Dhanens, Inventaris VI, p. 103 and Documenten, p. 13. Compare note 149 below. For the identity of the Enthroned in the Ghent Altarpiece with Christ, cf. also below note 156.

namely at the crown in the center of the retable. This upper vertical chain of symbols distinctly characterizes the figure of the Enthroned as the image of the pre-existing Christ, Who is the Logos of the Fourth Gospel and Whose coming as the Messiah was predicted by the prophets. The crown of eternal life at His feet, when seen as the end of this line, refers to Christ's eternity and pre-existence, in other words, to His divine nature and His intrinsic identity with God the Father.[149]

Just as the horizontal line is continued all across the retable, so too the vertical line forms a stream of continuous meaning from the tracery top to the mensa. In the Eyckian sequence of symbols, the crown in the panel of the Enthroned is followed by the Dove, which is depicted in the Lamb panel. It seems that the painter may have considered exchanging the two symbols at a certain point in the working process. The laboratory examination of 1950-51 has revealed that Van Eyck apparently intended to replace the crown by a different motif, for the finished or nearly finished object was covered with a layer of silver foil. Curiously enough, however, it was again the image of a crown which was painted on this new base.[150] Similarly, there are also *pentimenti* in the area of the Dove. There, remnants of a glory appearing higher than the present one can be detected under the present surface.[151] The problem which caused these changes, betraying a baffling indecision, obviously arose when the Lamb panel had to be cut down. The elimination of a considerable strip of the paint surface along the upper margin had apparently destroyed the original design of the Dove. After the cutting, only a very narrow sky area was left above the city. And this may have been the reason why the painter had considered giving this narrow space to the crown and relocating the Dove in the upper panel instead. This reversed position of the symbols with the Dove above and the crown below actually occurs in an earlier mediaeval manuscript which shows a votive crown suspended from a haloed dove with spread wings (Fig. 66).

However, if he did in fact consider this exchange, Van Eyck very soon abandoned

[149] It is therefore not actually a grave mistake if the Enthroned in the Ghent Altarpiece was and is taken as the representation of the First Person of the Trinity. Cf. our previous note.

[150] For the changes in the crown, cf. Coremans, *op.cit.*, pp. 103ff and Panofsky 1953, I, pp. 228ff. The silver foil, used to insulate the old paint layer from a new one and thus to prevent a bleeding through of the former, covers not only the crown but also the inscriptions on the thronepace. The fact that this foil is covered not by a different motif but by the same crown and inscription has greatly baffled Panofsky. Cf. note 152 below.

[151] For the changes in the Dove, cf. Coremans, *op.cit.*, pp. 108ff and Panofsky 1953, I, pp. 218ff. Some older rays springing from a higher center and still visible today indicate that a glory higher than the present one had originally adorned the Lamb panel. Beenken (cf. above note 102) had assumed that this upper part of the panel had formerly shown not only the Dove but also a half-figure of God the Father connected with it, so that the iconography of the lower panels of the Ghent Altarpiece was in itself complete. Beenken's opinion that the lower panels had been intended to form a separate altarpiece was accepted by Panofsky although the latter rejected the particulars of Beenken's reconstruction of the unit's original state.

the idea. In the Ghent Altarpiece, the original sequence of the two motifs with the crown in the upper and the Dove in the lower zone was of utmost importance for the over-all context of the iconography. The crown had to appear above because, as a symbol of eternal life, it functioned not only as the nucleus of the vertical sequence of motifs but also as the center of the horizontal sequence. This horizontal sequence which relates to the Redemption of mankind, personified by Adam and Eve, is rendered in the upper level. The Dove, on the other hand, actually belongs to the lower zone. By shifting it to the panel of the Enthroned, the Dove would have lost much of its powerful symbolism as the direct agent of the Transubstantiation. No wonder then that, after an initial hesitation, the painter decided to reinstate the crown in the upper zone and actually to fit the haloed Dove into the narrow sky area of the Lamb panel by lowering the motif.[152] Only this sequence of the symbols, which we see today and which also was the original one, clearly expresses both the restoration of mankind to eternal life and the miracle of the Eucharistic transformation.

The Eucharistic transformation made the Host, which was kept in the predella, appear to be the result of the painted miracle. Indeed, without the vessel of the Holy Wafer's being actually visible in a recess above the mensa, the arrangement of the symbolic motifs in the Lamb panel would not make any sense. The altar in the Vijd chapel was unquestionably that altar in the Ghent church which served as the reserve of the Host and can be called the altar of the Sacrament.

Since the institution of the feast of *Corpus Christi* in the thirteenth century, the special worship of the consecrated wafer had steadily increased in the Catholic church. The Host, now an object of public veneration, was no longer shown merely on certain festive occasions but was permanently exhibited in the sanctuary. It was now important that the believer be always aware of its sacred presence and always able to adore it.[153] This is the meaning of the huge towered Sacrament-houses erected near the altar (Fig. 22). It is also the meaning of the new type of altar which provided a recess for the exhibition of the Host (Figs. 15, 16, and 61). Although the Ghent Altar may well have been the first, or at least one of the very first, to arrange this recess in the predella proper, generally speaking it is by no means the first of the type as such.

The famous stone altarpiece in St. Martin in Landshut, a work which we have already mentioned in the first chapter of this study, proves that this type existed before Jodocus Vijd and his painter started their ambitious enterprise in the Ghent chapel (Figs. 15 and

---

[152] It is thus by no means necessary to credit Hubert with the first state of the crown, as Panofsky does (*ibid.*, I, p. 229). Panofsky rejected the possibility that Jan could have changed his mind twice. Instead, he ascribed the first change (consisting of the elimination of the crown) to Hubert and the reinstatement of the crown to Jan.

[153] For the history of the cult of the Host, cf. the brief and excellent account in Hirn, *op.cit.*, pp. 137ff. More recent literature on the subject is listed in Ress, *op.cit.*, 1955.

16). In the Landshut Altarpiece, which is dated 1424, the niche for the Host receptacle forms the center of the lower tier of representations and occurs immediately above the predella. The receptacle, however, though visible from the front, was accessible only from the back of the structure.[154] It is not impossible that this was precisely the case in the Ghent Altarpiece. We have seen that originally no wall existed behind the Vijd altar to divide that chapel from the next one in the Ghent church. And since the huge and complex mechanism of the panels turning in their stone framework was certainly accessible from the neighboring chapel and was probably even operated from it, it is quite likely that the sacramental niche as well could be opened from the back and that the back of the Ghent Altarpiece looked rather similar to that of the German stone retable (Fig. 16).

With the observation that Van Eyck's polyptych must have been an early type of an altar of the Holy Sacrament, a new explanation for the curious cutting of the Lamb panel suggests itself. We now can understand that we do not necessarily have to assume a radical change of plan in order to explain the reduction of this panel. Instead, the cutting may have been caused by a problem which was created by the aforementioned purpose of the altar, namely that it served as the shelter for the Host and certain relics.

It is unlikely that Jodocus Vijd had the vessels for all of them expressly designed for his project or that he possessed the complete set when he commissioned his altarpiece. Chances are that he gradually acquired some relics in venerable ancient receptacles, that his negotiations proceeded slowly and were still going on when the work on the altarpiece was already fairly advanced. It was perhaps rather late when the final decisions about the relics and their vessels were reached. These objects then may have turned out to be considerably taller than expected, a most unpleasant surprise to an artist who was working on an altar structure of the type described in our reconstruction (Figs. 41 and 42).

For, while the height of the predella (which was naturally worked in a separate block) could be changed at any time, this had a devastating effect on the structure as a whole. Once the height of the predella was increased, it became necessary to raise the representations above it. Normally in such a case one would simply lift up the entire retable. In the Ghent Altarpiece, however, such a procedure was not possible. The huge heavy framework extended down to the floor and was solidly connected with the mensa. The height of the total unit was thus fixed and could not be altered after the frame was finished or near completion. With the original measurements of the total structure maintained even though the predella had become taller, Van Eyck had no choice but to cut down on the height of the Lamb panel.

This new hypothesis, no matter how near or far it may be from the actual truth, at

[154] For the Landshut Altarpiece, cf. *ibid.*, pp. 14ff *passim*. Another example of the same type (the altar in the Cathedral of Halberstadt, reproduced in Braun, *op.cit.*, II, 1924, p. 359) is mentioned *ibid.*, p. 14, note 10, with a complete listing of the previous literature on the various types of the altar of the Holy Sacrament. Cf. above notes 26 and 133.

least proves that the traditional Hubert-Jan theory is not the only possible explanation for the striking *pentimenti* in the two panels of the Lamb and the Lord. A novel task, for whose solution neither the artist nor the donor had as yet the necessary experience, could easily give rise to a number of technical problems. In the time of Van Eyck, an altarpiece providing predella recesses for the relics and the Host was a new enterprise in itself. Moreover, the illusionistic relationship between a landscape painted in one of the panels and the actual predella compartment containing the Host was a new and daring idea which, in fact, has remained unique in altar painting. This illusionistic connection was imperative for the meaning of the whole and had, of course, to be maintained even after the height of the predella was increased. It was, in other words, essential that the watercourse coming from the Fountain of Life remained completely distinct. This requirement explains why the cutting of the Lamb panel was done at the top only, a procedure which greatly diminished the space available for the Dove and which created the difficulties so evident to us through the *pentimenti*.[155]

The idea of explaining in the representations of a sacred structure the meaning of the holy vessels which were kept in it, though unique in the particular version in which it appears in the Ghent Altarpiece, was in essence not really new. We have seen that the huge golden shrine which is represented in the upper level of Van Eyck's retable signifies the Ark of the New Covenant containing, as it were, the mystic relic of Christ. Its character and function are thus intrinsically the same as those of the small monstrance which was kept in the predella recess (Fig. 59). A large heavenly vision explains the meaning of a small corporeal object. This real but unassuming object placed in the lowermost part of the retable is stressed in its importance by a striking and large theatrical artifice visible in a crowning representation. A very similar device is already found in the twelfth century.

When we recall the form that Abbot Suger gave to the tomb containing the relics of St. Denis and his companions, we see that this ancient structure was based on precisely the same idea (Fig. 26). While the actual reliquaries of the three saints were placed in the lower part of the edifice, three large empty chasses were displayed, for show, in the superstructure that crowned it. We have seen before that Van Eyck was strongly inclined to draw on the ideas of old and venerable structures for use in his altar. Here again, the Ghent retable employs a device of a time long past and turns it into a striking innovation.

While the empty, house-shaped artifices in Suger's twelfth century structure signify the reliquaries of saints, the painted golden house in the Ghent Altarpiece connotes the

[155] If, after the cutting, Van Eyck again centered the panel of the Lamb within the lower picture unit (as, in fact, the modern arrangement shows it—Fig. 1), he would have cut approximately 11 cm from the top of the panel in order to gain approximately 5½ cm below to make room for the new height of the predella. We can, indeed, see from the horizon line of the five panel unit in the lower level of the Ghent Altarpiece that the present arrangement must be the result of a *post factum* centering of the Lamb panel. The horizon line in the latter is strikingly higher than that in the wing panels. If we lowered the Lamb panel approximately 5½ cm, the unit would form an ensemble much more satisfying aesthetically.

vessel for the "relic" of Christ. The theme of the Sacrament over the altar, which dominates the interior view of the Van Eyck polyptych, is introduced and accentuated in this
giant symbol, which demonstrates that the monstrance in the predella is really the Tabernacle of the New Covenant. We have already shown that the golden shrine was visible in
both of the main views of the retable, with the wings opened as well as with the wings
closed. We can thus conclude that the sacramental theme must also extend to the exterior
view of the altarpiece. It is not immediately obvious in the exterior representations that
their theme also is the Eternal Mass (Fig. 2). But our discussion to follow will show that
a link between interior and exterior is supplied by a theme which is closely related to the
Eternal Mass and, indeed, to some extent is virtually identical with it—the Holy Wedding
of Christ with His bride, the Church.

IV. THE HOLY WEDDING

THE central representation in the upper level of the Ghent panels is a group which
is traditionally called the Deësis (Fig. 1). This designation is valid, for, as we
have seen, it actually is the figure of Christ, which here appears between the Virgin
and St. John.[156] The group, in other words, shows the same combination of figures as
we know them from many scenes of the Last Judgment. But in pose and dress the figures depicted by Van Eyck vary considerably from the triad familiar from other Judgment scenes. The Lord is not the bare-headed Christ of the Passion, seated on the rainbow
and showing His wounds as He passes sentence on the living and the dead. Nor are the
two flanking figures the kneeling and austerely dressed intercessors of mankind as we
know them from the Last Judgment.[157] Instead, each of the figures is enthroned; each is
placed in front of the golden niches of the Tabernacle of God; and each appears in festive
garb. Although their position and attire do not exclude their being meant to represent the
Judge with the two intercessors, the deviations from the familiar type certainly indicate
that this is not their only meaning.

The reason for the figures' being enthroned and so magnificently vested has already

[156] Cf. above notes 148 and 149. As can be seen from our earlier text, it is not only the initials of Christ,
systematically repeated in the brocade pattern behind the Enthroned, which identify this figure as the
Second Person of the Trinity but also the very context of the Eternal Mass. For the identification of the
Enthroned with Christ, cf. also the excellent discussion in Heinz Peters, "Die Anbetung des Lammes, ein
Beitrag zum Problem des Genter Altars," *Das Münster*, III, 3/4, March-April, 1950, pp. 68f. Among other
proofs, Peters cites various sources which show that an altarpiece of the time, according to church regula-
tions, had to present Christ as a person. For the identity of the Enthroned in the Fountain of Life (Fig. 19)
with Christ, Hans Kauffmann gives five reasons in his article, "Über 'rinascere,' 'Rinascità' und einige Stilmerkmale der Quattrocentobaukunst," *Concordia decennalis, Deutsche Italienforschungen*, Cologne 1941,
p. 140. All of these reasons are also valid for the figure in the Ghent Altarpiece. Further literature on the
problem can be found in Peters' article.

[157] Cf., for instance, the Last Judgment Altarpiece in Beaune by Rogier van der Weyden, Lochner's panel
in the Wallraf-Richartz-Museum in Cologne, or the Eyckian Last Judgment in New York (Fig. 141).

been discussed. They appear as the Priest and the two co-celebrants in the solemn rite of the Eternal Mass which takes place in front of the divine Tabernacle.[158] The group seems to encompass a number of overlapping and interconnecting meanings which focus on three key ideas. We may, in fact, see each of the three figures as the particular embodiment of one of these three ideas. Christ wearing the tiara refers to the Eternal Mass; the Baptist, as we shall presently discuss, to the Last Judgment; and the Virgin alludes to the theme of the Mystical Wedding, which is so distinctly implied in the lower panel by the sacrificial animal surrounded by the adorers, an image which points to the Wedding Feast of the Lamb (Revelation 19:7-9).

The characterization of the Virgin in this panel is alien to her appearance in the traditional Deësis group in that she is enthroned and wears an elaborate crown.[159] These two motifs are taken from a specific iconographic type, the "Triumph of the Madonna." The theme is often called the "Coronation of the Virgin," no matter whether the actual act of the crowning is shown or the already crowned Virgin as she is enthroned together with her Son after her elevation to Paradise. This, indeed, is also the theme which we found in the top zone of the German miniature which depicts the Mass (Fig. 60). In the Ghent Altarpiece also the figures of the Lord and the Virgin apparently depict both the Coronation and the Mass.

As Pia Wilhelm explains in her excellent study on the Coronation of the Virgin, the theme has a nuptial connotation.[160] The Triumph of the Madonna, who is elevated to a divine status, is here at the same time the image of a Holy Wedding. As the personification of the Church, the Mother of the Lord appears as the mystical Bride of Christ. Christian interpreters likened the bride in the Song of Solomon to the Church and the bridegroom to Christ. The figures of Christ and the Virgin as they appear in the Coronation of the Madonna depict the *sponsus* and *sponsa* of this sacred union.

Because the complex and sumptuous crown of Van Eyck's Virgin shows among other elements the striking feature of fresh flowers, there can be scarcely any doubt that it was meant as a bridal crown (Fig. 74). It is obvious that in Van Eyck's time the Virgin in the Ghent Altarpiece was taken for the representation of a bride. The upper portion of his Madonna reappears (as a reversed image) in the Prado Betrothal of the Virgin, a painting in which the nuptial meaning of the figure is beyond question (Fig. 75).[161] It

---

[158] Cf. above notes 117 and 123.

[159] It is true that the Virgin sometimes appears seated and wearing a crown in representations of the Last Judgment; for instance, in Traini's painting in Pisa. But this is an exception, not repeated, so far as I know, in Northern compositions of the time of Van Eyck.

[160] Pia Wilhelm (b. von Reutter zu Kaltenbrunn), *Die Marienkrönung am Westportal der Kathedrale von Senlis*, Doctoral Thesis, 1937, printed Hamburg 1941, cf. especially pp. 69-78.

[161] It is immaterial to our discussion whether the composition of the Prado painting preceded or followed that of the Ghent Altarpiece. In my opinion, it is by no means certain that the former, though unquestionably showing the earlier style, was actually painted before the Van Eyck retable. In any case, the crowns

seems, moreover, that the Ghentians of the early sixteenth century still took the group for a Coronation of the Virgin. For, apparently, the church guides of the time told the visitors that the altarpiece depicts the Triumph or Elevation of the Mother of God. This, most probably, was the piece of information which prompted Don Antonio's curious statement that the Van Eyck polyptych depicts the "Ascension of the Madonna."[162]

Taken by themselves, that is, without the figure of St. John the Baptist, Christ and the Virgin in the Ghent retable bear a marked similarity to Italian Trecento representations in which the two figures are enthroned together in Paradise (Figs. 77 and 78). They are also similar to the enthroned Virgin and Christ as they appear in the Netherlandish art which immediately precedes Van Eyck. A miniature by the so-called Boucicaut Master, for instance, as well as a small altarpiece in the Boymans Museum which was probably created by a Mosan painter around 1415, show figures with a greater kinship in iconographic detail to those in the Ghent Altarpiece than does the Coronation group in the German miniature of the Mass (Figs. 79, 80, and 60). In the Italian as well as in the Netherlandish examples, Christ appears as the ruler carrying the orb or the scepter. In all of them He is a crowned figure.[163]

The crown worn by Christ in these instances is the crown of a king and thus of a type similar to the crown of the Madonna who appears as His Queen. Such a crown is also depicted in the Ghent Altarpiece. While the head of Christ is there adorned by the tiara, the regal crown rests at His feet. This is the crown which corresponds to the bridal crown of the Virgin. Thus, along with its many other meanings, the crown at the throne-pace characterizes Christ as the mystical Bridegroom of the Holy Wedding.

It is not surprising that the group of the mystical Bride and Bridegroom should appear within the context of the Mass. The idea is an integral part of the body of thought

---

in both of the paintings show the form typical of bridal crowns, with their plantlike details shooting up in high vertical shafts. Cf. Schramm, op.cit., III, pp. 984-98, with examples of actual bridal crowns, many reproductions of their representations in German fifteenth century art, and a wealth of literature cited on their symbolism in poetry and folklore.

[162] Cf. Dhanens, Inventaris VI, p. 103 or Documenten, p. 12.

[163] These, in fact, are the usual features in a representation of the Virgin's Coronation. They are modified in the *Biblia Pauperum* miniature, because there the figure of the enthroned Christ had to be as similar as possible to the Man of Sorrows depicted below it. Indeed, a crown is worn by Christ in the very earliest examples of the scene. Even the feature of the Virgin and Christ surrounded and crowned by a heavenly architecture is traditional in the type. Cf. Katzenellenbogen, op.cit., figs. 44-49. If Heaven in the *Biblia Pauperum* miniature is depicted by festoons of stylized clouds, this is done in order to distinguish this upper zone from the lower part of the representation, which depicts our earth. In other examples, however, in which the theme is not Heaven and earth but rather a two-storied Heaven, we often find an architectural setting, as, for instance, in the small altarpiece in the Boymans Museum ascribed to a Mosan Master (Fig. 76). The two painted canopies which crown the figures of the Virgin and Christ in this small work show architectural forms already quite similar to the towered sculptural canopies that were used, according to our reconstruction, in the frame of the Ghent polyptych (Figs. 76, 80 and 41). Cf. below note 166.

underlying the Sacramental rite. In the Eucharistic mysterium, it is not only Christ Who offers Himself up to the Almighty; the Sacrament also includes the self-oblation of the Church. This is clearly stated by St. Augustine. As Professor Jungmann has expressed it, "Never is the Church so closely bound to her Master, never is she so completely Christ's spouse as when, together with him, she offers God this sacrifice."[164]

When we look at the triptych in the Boymans Museum in its entirety and compare it with the miniature depicting the Mass in the German *Biblia Pauperum*, we see that the small altarpiece, too, presents the idea of the Mass (Figs. 76 and 60). In the upper zone of the small triptych, the divine Christ is shown as the mystical Bridegroom of the Coronation; in the lower zone we see the human Christ, Who is the *corpus verum* of the Eucharistic rite and here also portrayed as the Man of Sorrows, although in a different type.[165] The small altarpiece, indeed, already contains the germ of the iconographic program which we find in the Ghent retable (Figs. 76 and 1). Just like the large polyptych, the small work consists of two architecturally framed zones both belonging to the same celestial building. In the small work, the heavenly structure is foiled by the ideal gold ground which still was in this early time the symbol *par excellence* of Paradise and thus of the Heavenly Jerusalem. And just as in the large polyptych, the upper zone of the Boymans retable depicts the divine, pre-existent Christ, while the lower one shows the suffering Saviour.[166]

In the Ghent Altarpiece, the form as well as the iconography of the unit have become

---

[164] Jungmann, *op.cit.*, I, p. 190 (with the text of St. Augustine quoted in note 45), and II, p. 39. Probably this Augustinian idea was chiefly responsible for the concept that Mary's *compassio* is a true sacrifice paralleling that of Christ. Otto G. von Simson has shown in his article "*Compassio* and *Co-Redemptio* in Roger van der Weyden's *Descent from the Cross*," *The Art Bulletin*, XXXV, 1953, pp. 10-16, that the idea of the Virgin's *compassio* and *co-redemptio* was familiar in theological writings and occurred as a chief motif in Rogier's famous painting in the Prado (cf. our Fig. 204). There can be no doubt that it is the consecrated Host in its essential meaning which Rogier has presented in his painting as the sacred Body taken down from the Cross. This Body, adorned as it is with the marks of the Passion and displayed as the center motif of the retable immediately above the mensa, naturally refers to the sacred rite celebrated over the mensa. It is, therefore, not only the *compassio* and the *co-redemptio* of the Virgin which is depicted in Rogier's composition but also the self-oblation of the Church during Mass.

[165] This different type of the Man of Sorrows appears in a similar form in another small work of the same region and period. The half-figure of the Christ of the Passion, shown with the wounds and supported by an angel but miraculously revived for the meditation of the believer, is the main representation in a tiny triptych made of gold and enamel (reproduced in the catalogue *Europäische Kunst um 1400*, *op.cit.*, fig. 40). This beautiful object, today in the Rijksmuseum of Amsterdam, contains a relic and was, in my opinion, perhaps formerly used as a pax. The crowning representation of this object is a Coronation of the Virgin, which, here again, appears immediately above the Man of Sorrows. The catalogue (pp. 397f) correctly describes this combination as a Eucharistic theme.

[166] The two small triptychs, the one in the Boymans Museum and the golden object in Amsterdam (cf. our previous note) indicate that a pictorial tradition favoring this very specific Eucharistic combination of scenes must have existed in the Netherlands immediately prior to the time of Van Eyck. There can be no doubt that Van Eyck in designing the Ghent Altarpiece drew from this tradition.

far more complex. A detailed illusionistic portrayal of the various sections of the heavenly realm has replaced the simple, traditional gold ground. This new complexity of form corresponds to a new and extremely intricate iconography. Basically, however, the underlying iconographic idea of the two celestial zones forming the settings for a two-fold depiction of Christ—above in His divine nature, below in His human nature—has remained the same in the Ghent Altarpiece and so has the idea of the Mystical Wedding.[167] Indeed, this idea, along with the concept of the two-fold nature of Christ, is important not only in the interior view of the altarpiece, but also in the paintings of the exterior. The Annunciation scene, which appears on the backs of the four panels that cover the Deësis when the retable is closed, can only be fully understood when seen in relation to these two ideas (Figs. 1, 2, and 81).

The Annunciation of the Ghent retable depicts God's message to the Virgin—as, for that matter, does any other representation of this subject—and, at the same time, the initial fact of mankind's Redemption, the Incarnation of God as man. The arrival of the Angel is the moment when the Virgin miraculously conceives her divine Son. The Incarnation of Christ is an eternal truth of divine Dispensation. Expressing this, a painted or sculptured scene of the Annunciation is always primarily the representation of a timeless fact of Christian doctrine.

The necessity of stressing this eternal aspect created an artistic problem in those paintings that no longer used a gold ground but gave a detailed realistic setting describing the locale and circumstances of the biblical occurrence with the intention of presenting the event as it might actually have happened. This problem in general and Van Eyck's solution of it in particular will be discussed in detail in Chapter 5. At this point, suffice it to say that Van Eyck meant to characterize his Ghent Annunciation as both a historical occurrence and a timeless truth and to mention the obvious indication of his intention.

The Annunciation is set in a box-shaped room covering all four panels and forming a foreground compartment of space. The rear wall is "perforated" to permit the view of a cityscape, which constitutes the background of the scene. This clearly is a domestic setting meant to describe the living quarters of the Virgin at the time when she received the heavenly messenger. There is a marked similarity between the Eyckian Annunciation chamber and the room depicted by the Master of Flémalle in his Mérode Altarpiece, which clearly is the simple living room of a burgher's house (Figs. 81 and 82).[168] When the

[167] While both of these ideas are perfectly distinct in the two small triptychs mentioned above, they are not immediately clear in the Ghent Altarpiece. Here, these ideas lie concealed under the extraordinary complexity that characterizes the form as well as the iconography of the great work.

[168] The fact that it is, nevertheless, intended to present a sacred place is mainly revealed through the symbolic meaning of the fixtures and the furniture of the room, details which have become the subject of numerous attempts at scholarly interpretation. For a complete list of these studies, cf. William S. Heckscher,

foreground chamber in the Ghent Annunciation is seen in this manner, the cityscape of the background certainly signifies the town of Nazareth as it appeared from the Virgin's windows. However, the scene by Van Eyck is not only or even primarily a historical occurrence coming to pass in a far-away place and at a time long since past. True, the kinship to the Mérode Annunciation, which depicts a domestic setting pure and simple, cannot be doubted. But it should not be overlooked that the chamber painted by Van Eyck varies from that of the Master of Flémalle in a considerable number of ways.

The Ghent Annunciation no longer consists solely of a foreground compartment, as does the Annunciation setting in the Mérode Altarpiece. Van Eyck's scene not only adds an elaborate background view but it connects this view with the foreground chamber through two small annex rooms which appear in the panels of the Angel and the Virgin. Inserted between foreground and background, the two intermediate space compartments are most important for our impression that Van Eyck's composition recedes in a smooth and continuous flow into the depth.[169] Since all of the rooms are obviously located high above street level and since the two annex rooms are vaulted, we have to conclude that the latter can hardly be anything other than the spaces in two slender towers adjoining the façade of the building. In the upper stories of mediaeval secular architecture, vaultings normally occur only in tower rooms.[170]

The introduction of the two tower spaces is, however, not the only feature that sets the Eyckian Annunciation apart from that of the Mérode Altarpiece. The room by Van Eyck shows an arcade of precious porphyry columns standing on magnificent bases and crowned by splendidly carved capitals. This is as ill-suited to a simple, middle-class chamber as are the two tower rooms with their elegant vaultings. Indeed, the splendor of the room was originally even more prominent than it is today, for the ornate carved columns of the lost frame behind which the chamber was seen were presented as parts of the painted room.

Despite one's first impression of simplicity, the interior shown in the foreground of the Ghent Annunciation is certainly not the modest living room of a burgher family but a regal hall belonging to a princely abode. It clearly signifies the city palace of the Queen of Heaven. Basically, therefore, the scenery in the Van Eyck Annunciation is a symbolic setting. The chamber, whose exterior would present a two-towered façade, seems to imply all of the meanings of the various architectural symbols for the Virgin which are traditionally depicted in an edifice with two towers, as, for instance, the *templum solomonis*,

---

"The Annunciation of the Mérode Altarpiece, an Iconographic Study," *Miscellanea Jozef Duverger*, Ghent 1968, pp. 37-65, with some new points of view and a wealth of valuable source material.

[169] A detailed description of the construction of Van Eyck's Annunciation room and a discussion of the possibility that this construction was based on an Italian model can be found in my recent article, "Raum und Zeit in der Verkündigung des Genter Altares," *Wallraf-Richartz-Jahrbuch*, XXIX, 1967, pp. 62ff.

[170] I owe this information to the kindness of Dr. Jürgen Paul.

the *turris davidis*, the *porta coeli*, and the *civitas dei* (Figs. 86 and 87).[171] All these symbols either directly connote or at least imply the idea of the Heavenly Jerusalem.

It is, in fact, evident that the chamber is an interior which belongs to the Heavenly Jerusalem. Characterized as a recess actually existing within the architecture of the retable, which itself signifies the heavenly place, it is clear that Van Eyck's Annunciation room has a celestial meaning. The foreground space, indeed, situated as it is above the city view in the background, belongs to the upper zone of the altarpiece. It thus certainly signifies the New Heaven. Is the townscape in the background, which is seen behind and below the foreground space, only the narrative description of the biblical Nazareth? Perhaps it has, in addition, a symbolic meaning connoting the New Earth to complete the idea of the Heavenly Jerusalem.[172]

We have one particular indication that the foreground and background of this scene are parts iconographically distinct one from another for, curiously enough, they are differentiated in their illumination. The foreground, which consists of the entire box-shaped space of the Annunciation chamber, including the arcaded rear wall, is lit from the right; the background cityscape is lit from the left. The two small intermediate space compartments are divided in their illumination between foreground and background, with the left annex space being lit from the right like the foreground, and the right one from the left like the background.

The light which comes from the right side and illumines the foreground is obviously meant to be the real daylight of the Vijd chapel, whose windows are located on the right. We clearly see this from the direction of the painted shadows which the carved columns of the now lost frame cast on the floor of the room. The foreground space is a *trompe l'œil* of an encasement for sculpture. Van Eyck has emphasized this not only through the stone-carved quality of the figures but also by making the space so low that the Angel and the Virgin could not really stand erect in it. The room is thus characterized as an actual recess in the retable and as a space physically existing in the Vijd chapel. It is only natural that such a space should be lit by the actual light source for this chapel.

The real daylight of the Vijd chapel, which is represented as illuminating the Annunciation room, was by no means considered merely a "natural" light. Being the light of a

---

[171] For the meaning of the popular representation of the Virgin surrounded by her symbols, cf. Herbert von Einem, "Die 'Menschwerdung Christ' des Isenheimer Altares" in *Kunstgeschichtliche Studien für Hans Kauffmann*, Berlin 1956, pp. 152-71 with other examples and the previous literature on the type.

[172] In the over-all view of the polyptych, the respective positions of the earthly and the heavenly level within the realm of the picture directly correspond to the supposed actual positions of these spheres; i.e. the New Earth factually appears in a low location, the New Heaven in a high one. This is different in the Annunciation scene. There, the use of perspective has reversed the actual space relationship. On the picture surface, the city view of the background appears in a rather high position although this view is obviously located far below the foreground interior. For the positions of the space levels in Early Netherlandish compositions, cf. Millard Meiss, "'Highlands' in the Lowlands," *Gazette des Beaux-Arts*, series 6, LVII, June 1961, pp. 275ff *passim*.

Gothic sanctuary, it is in itself the sacred light of the Heavenly Jerusalem and thus perfectly fitting to illumine a space which explicitly connotes this heavenly region.[173] The background, however, offered an entirely different problem. It could not possibly be characterized as a sculptural entity actually existing in the Vijd chapel. As a view into the distance, it is a painting pure and simple. Here Van Eyck found a different solution for its illumination. By using for the background a light which does not shine from the south as the natural daylight does, but which miraculously comes from the north, the painter has described his cityscape as having a supernatural illumination. A light coming from the north also occurs in another painting by Van Eyck, the small panel of the Madonna in the Church, in Berlin (Fig. 135). There it was noted and ingeniously interpreted by Panofsky as a divine phenomenon.[174] In the Ghent Annunciation also the northern light is a divine light which here indicates that the cityscape is not really a terrestrial view. It is not our old earth but the New Earth as described in Revelation. Actually, the City of God was already represented as a view through a colonnade in a very early time. A miniature in the famous Gospels of Soissons, painted around 800 to 810, depicts the New Earth in a remarkably similar fashion (Fig. 85).[175]

[173] The real light of the Vijd chapel is the *Standortlicht* according to the terminology used in Wolfgang Schöne, *Über das Licht in der Malerei*, Berlin 1954, p. 14 (no. 6). As Schöne (pp. 38 and 74f) has explained, the real light in the mediaeval cathedral—though *de facto* the natural sunlight coming through the window panes—was not conceived by mediaeval man as entering from the outside. Instead, one regarded the glowing images of the stained glass as themselves being the direct source of this light. The latter was thus a mystic light and believed to be sacred in substance.

[174] Of course, this light coming from the north is a supernatural phenomenon only when seen in counterdistinction to the natural daylight coming from the south. In my recent article on Van Eyck (cited above in note 169), I have explained that the mediaeval concept of the sacred church light (cf. our previous note) is already fused in Van Eyck's art with the more advanced idea that the actual church light is the light of nature; *op.cit.*, pp. 88f. The ambiguity caused by this fusion explains the seeming inner contradiction in the handling of light in the Ghent Annunciation. Further explanations on the complex concept which Van Eyck used in his Ghent Annunciation is found below in the beginning pages of Chapter 4 and in the text following note 250. The transitional character of this composition by Van Eyck is discussed below in Chapter 5, last section of Part I. For Panofsky's discussion of the supernatural light coming from the north, cf. Panofsky 1953, I, pp. 147f.

[175] Van Eyck's column-framed city view, though perhaps derived from a large painting rather than a miniature, most certainly goes back to an image that was already a very ancient one in Van Eyck's time. The curious feature of using the forms of capitals to constitute the bases of the window columns (a fact which has greatly intrigued Paul Frankl), was hardly inspired by models in real architecture, but originated instead in the pictorial tradition. Not only does our Carolingian miniature show this remarkable motif but there are also mosaics based on a Byzantine tradition which depict their columns as resting on capital-shaped bases. Cf., for instance, the mosaics in the dome of the Florentine Baptistery; John White, *Art and Architecture in Italy, 1250 to 1400*, Baltimore 1966, fig. 145 (A), upper row, right side. Of course, the main source of Van Eyck's city view as such may be found in the paintings by the Master of Flémalle in which the views are not of the Heavenly City. The problem will be discussed in detail below in Chapter 5. For Van Eyck's knowledge of Early Christian and Italian works of art, cf. Part VI of the present chapter and Part II of Chapter 5.

With the foreground architecture signifying the New Heaven and the cityscape below it the New Earth, the eternal aspect of the Ghent Annunciation is established. It is in the timeless ideal locale of theHeavenly Jerusalem that the Incarnation of God as man comes to pass. The choice of the particular image through which the Heavenly Jerusalem is rendered in the Ghent Annunciation, namely a city palace with a view of the city, enabled the painter to express both the eternal meaning of the scene as well as its "histori-cal" one. The chamber as a regal hall is the New Heaven, but with its household imple-ments it can readily be taken for Mary's living room. The background, illuminated by the supernatural light from the north, is the New Earth, but, as the convincing portrayal of a town, it can be seen as the biblical Nazareth.

The same dualism is found in every detail depicted in this setting. All of the objects that furnish the rooms have a two-fold meaning, a symbolical one pointing to the doctrinal content of the scene and a descriptive one giving a realistic illustration of the locale and circumstance of the Annunciation story. The symbolic meaning of realistic details in Early Netherlandish painting has been brilliantly discussed by Panofsky, who called the phe-nomenon "disguised symbolism," an expression which has since become a standard term in art history.[176] Panofsky has observed that disguised symbolism was consistently used for the first time in the work of Van Eyck. It was profusely but inconsistently employed in the earlier paintings by the Master of Flémalle, especially in the Mérode Annunciation. Our present analysis offers an explanation for this observation. In contrast to the older master, Van Eyck could fill every realistic motif in the Ghent Annunciation with a sym-bolic meaning and, conversely, could give to every theological symbol the convincing form of a *genre* detail because his setting has a two-fold character while that of the Mérode Annunciation has only one. Van Eyck's room is a "historical" chamber in which every-thing is a realistic illustration; but it is also the ideal locale of the Heavenly Jerusalem in which everything is a symbol.

This duality holds true not only for the main room but also for the small vaulted chamber behind the Madonna (Fig. 83). Of the two annex rooms, only this one is almost fully visible and replete with a number of interesting details. A low dado-like barrier clearly shows it to be closed. A dado at the corresponding place to the left is only partially visible, so that it remains uncertain whether or not it runs across the whole width of the left room. The distinctly closed room behind the Virgin is obviously meant as a kind of interior version of a *hortus conclusus* or, rather a tower of chastity, both familiar symbols of the virginity of the Madonna and both signifying her person. The very fact that this right tower room appears immediately next to the Virgin makes it clear that it is her sym-bol. There is, moreover, an additional indication that the vaulted room signifies the Madonna herself. The Virgin's answer to the Almighty, the words "*Ecce ancilla domini*" ("Behold the handmaid of the Lord") appear as a title, as it were, of this small room.

[176] Panofsky 1953, I, pp. 131-48; his short discussion of the symbolism of the Ghent Annunciation room and its furnishings is found on p. 137.

The divine light which comes from the left and which illuminates the background is also the light source for the annex room behind the Virgin. In fact, I am inclined to believe that the motif of the supernatural light from the north was invented primarily for this annex room rather than for the cityscape of the background. The theme of Christ's Incarnation is often expressed not only through the appearance of the Dove but also through the symbolism of light by means of a pencil of golden rays breaking through the window of the Annunciation chamber (Fig. 138).[177] It is clearly the Incarnation that is symbolized in Van Eyck's annex room behind the Virgin.

A stream of sunlight enters the dark little room in a most enchanting way, signifying the Godhead entering the bridal chamber (Fig. 83). We see the divine light as it strikes a glass carafe which is placed on the window seat of the room. This, apparently, is the seat of the Virgin, and set there, the vessel appears to take her place. The motif of the glass phial struck by light is a well-known symbol of Christ's immaculate conception. Occurring in numerous paintings in Van Eyck's time, the detail is a metaphor likening the light to the divine substance, the Madonna to the phial, and the miracle of her unimpaired virginity at Christ's Incarnation to the light passing through the glass without breaking it.

In Van Eyck's painting, the light not only strikes the vessel but it also paints some charming reflections on the walls of the little tower room. Those which are especially striking appear on the right side wall of this room, or, when seen in terms of surface pattern, immediately next to the Madonna. There can thus be no doubt that this motif too bears a symbolic reference to her. Judging from the shape of the window visible in the tower room, we should expect the light reflection to consist of three parts. Curiously, however, the sun spots on the wall are only two. By this contradiction to the laws of nature, Van Eyck apparently meant to demonstrate that the number of the sun spots has a symbolic meaning. These spots of light appearing near the Virgin seem to refer to the two-fold nature of Christ Who is at the same time divine and human. Indeed, it is the miraculous union of Logos and Man which is fulfilled in the mystery of the Virgin's conception.[178]

[177] This is so in Van Eyck's own Annunciation scene in Washington, while the Mérode Altarpiece by the Master of Flémalle depicts the seven symbolic rays not as coming from without but as emanating from the window itself (Fig. 84). The circular window in this earlier Annunciation originally showed an opening covered with gold, as has been proved by the laboratory examination of the Flémalle retable. Cf. William Suhr, "The Restoration of the Mérode Altarpiece," *The Metropolitan Museum of Art Bulletin*, XVI, 4, December 1957, p. 144. The two features, the gold ground as well as the rays coming from the window pane itself, are of course indications of an earlier concept. Cf. note 173.

[178] The mystical union of Christ's two natures is discussed in Pia Wilhelm, *op.cit.*, p. 8, note 18, who quotes the mediaeval hymn:

> *"Tu genetrix,*
> *In qua Deo*
> *Iunctus est homo,*
> *Deus homini."*

Perhaps the motif of the double shadows which is so characteristic of the art of the Master of Flémalle also

The symbolic spots of sunlight are thus the complement to the image of the phial. They are an integral and most important part of the total metaphor. As a direct reference to one of the leading ideas of the interior view of the altarpiece, namely to the two natures of Christ, this metaphor even by itself makes it perfectly clear that Van Eyck's Annunciation scene must have been invented together with the main view of the retable and as an introduction to it. But only after examining the symbolic details in the two central panels can we fully realize just how intimately Van Eyck's Annunciation is related to the interior view.

From the very outset of such an examination, it is obvious that the cityscape on the left and the still life on the right, which so distinctly appear as formal complements, must also be related iconographically (Figs. 88 and 89). The still life, moreover, is certainly a symbol that refers to the Virgin since it appears next to the panel in which she is depicted and, for that matter, immediately next to the annex room symbolizing the Incarnation.

The still life of a niche with laver, basin, and towel, has been interpreted by Panofsky as the "indoor substitute" for the most typical symbol of the Virgin's purity, the "Fountain of Gardens" or the "Well of Living Waters." The epithet occurs in the Song of Solomon in the usual dual poetic form of the Old Testament and is there used by the lover for his bride.[179] Since the bride in the poem is, in Christian belief, the Ecclesia, the Virgin in the Ghent Annunciation would be characterized as the embodiment of the Church by the details of the niche.

Panofsky's interpretation seems to me correct to the extent that it implies that the Virgin in the Ghent Altarpiece is the Church. The particular shape of the window rosette, which appears in the upper part of the niche, underscores the symbol's connection with this idea. The main part of this window has the form of a clover leaf with three circular sections that make an inseparable unit. This configuration apparently signifies the so-called Trinitarian Coronation of the Virgin. It is, as it were, a schematic rendering of this type which was popular in Italian Trecento and Quattrocento art, and which penetrated from there into early fifteenth century representations of the North (Fig. 90).[180]

---

refers to the dual nature of Christ. I should like to draw the reader's attention to the fact that I have revised, in one respect, my opinion on the two light reflections in the Ghent annex room since I wrote the article cited in note 169 above. The reflection is two-fold, not, as I have surmised, because it comes from a two-part window invisible to the spectator, because it is a deliberately supernaturalistic motif.

[179] Canticles 4:15. Cf. Panofsky 1953, I, p. 137.

[180] The type is described in Georg Troescher, *Burgundische Malerei, Maler und Malwerke um 1400 in Burgund, dem Berry mit der Auvergne und in Savoyen mit ihren Quellen und Ausstrahlungen*, Berlin 1966, with reproductions of four examples (figs. 10-13) on plate 5. A further example is found in the representation of Paradise from the frescoes by Giovanni da Modena (1410-20) in S. Petronio, Bologna (photo: Villani, Bologna). Perhaps the small spherical triangle below the clover-leaf window in Van Eyck's Annunciation (the only one of three triangles which is lighted and therefore clearly visible) signifies the Dove of the Holy Spirit, a representation which occasionally appears below the group.

It is not at all surprising that a reference to the Coronation (which is, as we have seen, the Mystical Wedding of the Church) should appear in the painting of an Annunciation. The union of the Lord with His Church is a theme that was discussed in theological texts in connection with Christ's Incarnation.[181] The two miracles belong together. They could both be summed up in the metaphor of the Mystical Wedding. This, indeed, is the idea behind Van Eyck's Annunciation scene. However, while Panofsky is right in assuming that the still life alludes to the Annunciate as the Ecclesia, it seems to me that his interpretation of the laver as the indoor substitute of the "Fountain of Gardens" or "Well of living Waters" is perhaps not entirely apt. For one thing, the vessel painted by Van Eyck does not contain "living" water. For another, the implements in and near the niche point so distinctly to the activity of cleansing (rather than to purity) that the idea must play a prominent part in the symbol's meaning.

Although the Song of Solomon is in fact the ultimate origin of the symbol, it is hardly its direct source. It is clearly Ephesians 5:25-27 which is the pertinent text. This passage, which certainly refers to the Song of Songs, likens the Lord's love of His Church to the love of a husband for his wife. But, in addition, the Epistle tells us that Christ, by delivering Himself up for His Church, cleanses her in a washing of water. Referring to the cleansing of Christ's congregation through Baptism and the sacrifice on the Cross, the still life symbol in the Ghent Annunciation designates the Mystical Wedding as the Redemption of mankind.[182]

We may now understand the meaning of the cityscape in the corresponding panel: the city signifies the world redeemed. While the right panel of the two narrow center ones depicts the means of Salvation, the left center one shows the result of it.[183] Since the latter mainly concerns the future (we have to keep in mind that the world was not as yet redeemed at the time of the Annunciation), its content could only be expressed by a timeless image. No wonder then that the cityscape is set apart from the foreground by a supernatural light which characterizes it as the New Earth, that is, as the world redeemed. The

[181] Pia Wilhelm, *op.cit.*, pp. 8off.

[182] It is clear from the specific pictorial context in which this same symbol of the laver with the towel appears in the Mérode Annunciation (Figs. 82 and 84) that this dual motif, rather than signifying Mary's purity, must mean the washing away of man's Original Sin. In the Flémalle Annunciation, the symbolic implements appear not near the Virgin but near the Angel and, in fact, as far as the surface pattern of the composition is concerned, immediately next to the infant Christ with the Cross, the symbol of the redeeming Sacrifice. This position makes it evident that the laver with the towel is a Marian symbol only in its secondary connotation, and that it concerns the Virgin only because, as the embodiment of the Ecclesia, she symbolizes Christ's congregation.

[183] The images in both of these small panels are Marian symbols. Not only the right one with the lavabo and the trifoil symbol of the "Trinitarian" Coronation refers to the Virgin as the sacred tool of Salvation but also the representation in the left panel. It is certainly not accidental that the New Earth is seen through a window, which is, as Carla Gottlieb kindly informs me, a major symbol of the Madonna. The pertinent texts and examples of the pictorial tradition that illustrate this point will be published in Dr. Gottlieb's forthcoming book on the window in art.

two panels in the center of the Ghent Annunciation thus present symbols of the greatest importance. By depicting the purpose of Christ's Incarnation, they demonstrate the ultimate meaning of the Annunciation scene.

The Annunciation of the Ghent Altarpiece, though actually portraying only the overture to Christ's First Coming, clearly signifies as well the idea of His Parousia when He will celebrate the Mystical Wedding with His Bride the Church. In fact, both ideas are expressed by the four figures which appear in the niches crowning the four Annunciation panels (Fig. 2). The inscriptions on the scrolls of the two prophets and the two sibyls distinctly point both to Christ's First Coming and to His future return. Although the specific wording of the texts as painted by Van Eyck makes this dual meaning evident, it becomes still more obvious when we consider the sources of these inscriptions, which have been carefully examined by J. de Baets and which, in some instances, refer to Christ's Second Coming alone.[184]

Combining the ideas of Christ's Union with His Church and of the Virgin's conception through the common denominator of the Mystical Wedding, Van Eyck has characterized the figure of the Annunciate as a bride in a two-fold sense. She is not only the Virgin bride of the miraculous Conception, but also the Church, the mystical spouse of Christ as the Trinity. Her counterpart, the mystical Bridegroom, could, of course, not be depicted as a person in an Annunciation scene. But His invisible presence is clearly indicated by the painter. The two narrow panels with the cityscape and the still life, the very panels which allude to the Mystical Wedding, show an entirely empty space in the foreground. No doubt this charming motif, which may be called a late version of the Early Christian *etimasia*, indicates that the Bridegroom's place is prepared (Figs. 91 and 92).[185]

Indeed, I am inclined to believe that these two narrow center panels in their entirety, that is, complete with frames and the tops showing the sibyls, were intended to form the symbol of the Heavenly Bridegroom. After having completed the reconstruction of the frame (which must have shown a dual level of ornate columns in this place appearing above and below a comparably ornate architrave), it occurred to me that the frame here formed a large cross (Fig. 42). This configuration repeats the traditional shape and proportion of the giant cross as it is familiar to us, especially in the Early Christian *crux gemmata*. It bears, for instance, a remarkable similarity to the cross that appears in the dome mosaic of the Arian Baptistery in Ravenna on the empty throne of Christ, that is, in precisely that place which corresponds to the two Eyckian panels showing the empty foreground (Fig. 92). Moreover, a similar cross is also found in the famous apse mosaic of S. Pudenziana in Rome, an Early Christian work of which the Ghent Annunciation is

---

[184] Cf. De Baets, *op.cit.*, pp. 543-58.

[185] In a short conversation on the problems of the Ghent Altarpiece which I had with Wolfgang Lotz many years ago, he mentioned the possibility that the empty foreground in the two narrow Annunciation panels may be a feature connected with their function of covering the image of the Lord.

also reminiscent in other respects, such as the background of the Heavenly City (Fig. 93). The cross formed by the frame could, in fact, be the symbol which would complete the image of the Trinity in the exterior view of the polyptych. The exterior in its entirety does not show any other symbol of the Second Person. It is thus possible that this cross was meant to present the Trinity, together with the Dove in the Virgin panel and the sculptured bust of God the Father in the tracery top (Fig. 42). This, by the way, would mean that in the Ghent Altarpiece the Trinity appears not just twice (in the interior view), but three times, a number which clearly conforms with the very idea of the concept.

While Christ's invisible presence in the Annunciation scene is only implied in the empty foreground and the *"crux gemmata"* of the two narrow panels, the interior of the retable actually depicts His person. We have seen that the enthroned figure in the Deësis group signifies Christ as the entire Trinity. Shown as He will look in the triumph of His Second Coming, Christ is rendered here as the mystical Bridegroom. It is this representation which is covered by the pair of narrow Annunciation panels when the altarpiece is closed. The image of the Heavenly Bridegroom thus actually exists behind these panels. The invisible presence of Christ is therefore not just "an idea" in the exterior view, but a factual physical reality. It is even likely that the image of the enthroned Christ was actually shown on certain days between the Angel and the Annunciate. This could easily be achieved by opening the narrow panels half way. There are a great many fourteenth, fifteenth, and sixteenth century Annunciations in which a representation of the Trinity appears between the Angel and the Virgin (Figs. 95 and 96).

As a result of the foregoing, it becomes almost superfluous to state that Van Eyck's use of four instead of two Annunciation panels is no proof of the assumption that the altarpiece underwent a change of plan. Rather, the arrangement is a profoundly meaningful one. There can be hardly any doubt that the interior and exterior of the work were planned together from the start and executed according to plan. The Annunciation is intimately related not only to the idea of the two natures of Christ but also to the theme of the Mystical Wedding as depicted in the interior view. As we have seen in the little Boymans' altarpiece as well as in the interior of the Ghent polyptych, the theme of the Mystical Wedding is also related to the theme of the Eternal Mass. In fact, Van Eyck even refers to this latter theme in his Annunciation of the exterior. The relationship of the Annunciation to the Eternal Mass will become apparent in the discussion to follow.

On closer examination, we have noticed that the Annunciation room does not have the distinct and exclusive character of a secular dwelling place. It is a celestial palace which is, of course, always also a sanctuary. Actually, the furnishings of the chamber have a strongly ambiguous quality, being suitable to either an ecclesiastical or a secular room. As mentioned in a recent catalogue, a laver of the form depicted in the still life of Van Eyck's narrow Annunciation panel is a liturgical object used by the priest to wash his hands before and after Mass (Figs. 89 and 97).[186] Here then, we have a distinct reference to the Mass. Indeed, the concept of this Sacrament is implied in the still life even without this formal reference. The motif clearly symbolizes the Redemption offered by the Lord "through His Church." The still life thus certainly has a Eucharistic connotation. It is not the still life alone, however, that alludes to the Eternal Mass. The two annex rooms in the panels with the Angel and the Annunciate also seem to owe their existence to the same idea (Fig. 81).

Seen as a pair, the two vaulted compartments are apparently meant as the *prothesis* and the *diaconicon*, the two ecclesiastical annex rooms that play a prominent part in Early Christian architecture (Fig. 98). While the *diaconicon* was used to receive the offerings of the congregation for the Eucharistic rite, the *prothesis* served for the preparation and storage of the Eucharistic species.[187] Although the use of these Early Christian rooms and of similar rooms in later architecture underwent some changes in the periods to follow, the Eucharistic meaning of the rooms was never completely eliminated. There can thus be no doubt that even the later Middle Ages were still familiar with the original purpose of the two chambers.

The scanty preservation of Northern altar painting in the time before Van Eyck makes it uncertain that the motif occurs in the North for the first time in the Ghent Altarpiece. No matter whether Van Eyck already found it in the tradition of his own region or was the first Northern artist to use it, the motif, as such, is Italian in origin.[188] In Italy, the two rooms appear most conspicuously in the east wall of Giotto's Arena Chapel in Padua (Fig. 99). His rooms also are vaulted and entirely empty, and each is obviously related to one of the two sections of the Annunciation scene painted in the upper part of the wall. Moreover, even the motif of light seems also to have played a part in the two rooms painted by Giotto, for the only fixture in each of them is a chandelier. A recent attempt to interpret the meaning of the two strangely empty rooms in the Arena Chapel, connects the dual motif with a variety of other ideas.[189] While I am far from denying the validity of this interpretation, I nevertheless should like to suggest that the primary meaning of the rooms is their reference to the Eucharist.

---

[186] *Flanders in the Fifteenth Century: Art and Civilization, op.cit.*, pp. 279-80, with illustration of one of the many actual objects preserved of the type. For drawing my attention to the miniature in the Utrecht manuscript, I am grateful to Mr. William Voelkle, who was kind enough, during the writing of the present book, to provide me not only with examples pertinent to my discussions but also with some useful literature.

[187] Cf. Günter Bandmann, "Über Pastophorien und verwandte Nebenräume im mittelalterlichen Kirchenbau," *Kunstgeschichtliche Studien für Hans Kauffmann*, Berlin 1956, pp. 19ff *passim*.

[188] It is well-known that pre-Eyckian painting in the North was steeped in Italian influence. For the features which Van Eyck himself had directly taken from Italian art, cf. above note 94, the end of the present chapter, and especially Parts I and II of Chapter 5 below.

[189] Ursula Schlegel, "Zum Bildprogramm der Arenakapelle," *Zeitschrift für Kunstgeschichte*, xx, 2, 1957, pp. 130ff.

As for the annex rooms in the Ghent Annunciation, the context in which they appear makes it highly probable that they too were meant to characterize the setting as a Eucharistic sanctuary. The Annunciation room is the locale for both great mysteries: The Incarnation of Christ and the Transubstantiation. These two mysteries belong together: in the Incarnation, Christ, the Logos, miraculously receives His human substance; in the Transubstantiation, the Eucharistic species miraculously turns into this substance.[190] The fusion of the two concepts is based on the body of symbolic thought surrounding the figure of the Virgin. She is believed to be the personification of the Church, which is the domicile of the Host, the Bread from Heaven. She thus is both the holy vessel for Christ's Incarnation and the receptacle for the Eucharistic species.

Certain specific subjects familiar from later mediaeval art express her decisive role in the basic mysteries of Christendom. The *Vierge ouvrante*, for instance, a statue of the Madonna which, rather than enclosing a sculpture of the Infant Christ, contains the crucified Saviour instead (sometimes as part of a Trinitarian image), is a case in point. But also some less familiar subjects, such as the statue or the painting of the praying Madonna clad in a dress studded with ears of corn, owe their existence to the idea that the Virgin is both God's Holy Acre, in which He plants His sacred grain of seed, and also the container for the Eucharistic Bread. Finally, there are some instances in which the pyxis for the actual Wafer is shaped into a small statue of the Madonna which can be opened and closed.[191]

[190] For the relationship of the Eucharist and the Incarnation of Christ as manifest in his appearance on earth (represented in the Nativity and the Adoration of the Magi), cf. the most instructive study by Ursula Nilgen, "The Epiphany and the Eucharist: On the Interpretation of Eucharistic Motifs in Mediaeval Epiphany Scenes," *The Art Bulletin*, XLIX, 4, December 1967, pp. 311-16, with the important sources and some literature pertaining to our point given in the notes (cf. especially notes 3-11) and an example of a Eucharistic altarpiece containing the Annunciation scene illustrated in fig. 3. Discussing the Dove of the Holy Spirit, Hirn, *op.cit.*, pp. 114-15, comes to the following conclusion: ". . . and just as the Holy Ghost assisted at the incarnation by which the Saviour clothed Himself in human flesh, so it was thought that the third person of the Trinity would now also effect the transformation of an earthly bread made by men into the Saviour's body." In the early fifteenth century missal Lat. 848 of the Bibl. Nat., Paris, the miniature of the Annunciation is pointedly paired with another one illustrating the Mass (Fig. 101).

[191] For the *Vierge ouvrante*, cf. *ibid.*, pp. 321f and note 8 on p. 528; for the Host shrine shaped as a statuette of the Mother of God, *ibid.*, p. 153 and Appuhn, *op.cit.*, p. 106, note 151 (with earlier literature); for the Virgin with the Ears of Corn, cf. Von Einem, *op.cit.*, 1956, p. 159. Von Einem lists the contrasting opinions of scholars, some of whom take the ears as a reference to the Eucharist while others see them as a symbolic characterization of Mary as the Lord's Acre. He enumerates these opinions as alternative interpretations without considering the possibility that it is the very combination of the seemingly opposed concepts which makes up the essence of the image. Cf. also the examples given in Louis Réau, *Iconographie de l'art chrétien*, II, Paris 1957, p. 924. The intimate connection between the two great Christian mysteries, the Incarnation and the Transubstantiation, is evident also from the fact that the diminutive image of the infant Christ can be used as a symbol of both. In the accounts of the Eucharistic miracles repeated again and again during the later Middle Ages, the consecrated Host is transformed into the likeness of a small

The strength of a concept that engendered such a wealth of images which are rather odd to the modern mind explains why the scene of the Annunciation was able to serve as the central and main representation of the Christian altar retable ever since the time of the Trecento. The Annunciation scene not only symbolizes the moment of God's becoming Man but also the mystery of the Transubstantiation which takes place over the very altar which is adorned by the sculptured or painted retable. The combination of the two concepts is obvious, for instance, in the central panel of the Mérode Altarpiece (Fig. 82). Indeed, the abundance of disguised symbolism which the Master of Flémalle has applied to this scene only fully explains itself when we realize that this was the painter's particular means to endow his simple domestic setting with the divine pathos of a Eucharistic sanctuary.

The table depicted in the center of the painting and dividing its protagonists, the Virgin and the Angel, from each other, is, of course, the Table of the Lord, i.e. a symbol of the altar. This table, as a matter of fact, is the chief symbol of the Virgin, who is often called the Heavenly Altar. The comparison, most familiar to us from the scenes in which the Virgin as the *ara coeli* appears to the Emperor Augustus, occurs in a rather early Annunciation miniature that evidently already combines the concepts of the Incarnation and the Transubstantiation (Fig. 100).[192] The dual meaning remains a determining factor in Annunciation scenes all through the Christian Middle Ages and is, indeed, still obvious

---

child. Cf. Peter Browe, *Die eucharistischen Wunder des Mittelalters*, Breslau 1938, *passim*. The image of the infant Christ offered by the priest instead of the Host can even function within the allegorical representations of an ordinary Mass. A nude Christ Child is offered, for instance, in a miniature of a late thirteenth century French missal, illustrated in S.J.P. van Dijk and J. Hazelden Walker, *The Origins of the Modern Roman Liturgy*, London 1960, plate 18. And when in fifteenth century Annunciation scenes the nude Christ Child with the Cross is shown as the symbol of the Incarnation (as it is, for instance, in the Mérode Altarpiece, cf. Fig. 84), this image is certainly intended at the same time to be the symbol of Christ's sacrifice, and thus of the Transubstantiation.

[192] My thanks are due to Mr. William Voelkle for drawing my attention to this miniature. The most famous example in Van Eyck's time of the Madonna as the *ara coeli* is found in Rogier's Bladelin Altarpiece, Panofsky 1953, II, plate 201. For the domestic table in its function as the symbol of the altar, cf. Nilgen, *op.cit.*, pp. 311ff *passim*. The table of the Mérode Annunciation constituting, as the symbol of the altar, the chief attribute of the Virgin, is shown as carrying the three objects which symbolize her virtues at the time of the Annunciation: the lilies, her purity; the book, her wisdom; and the blown-out candle, her humility. The last symbol is based on a passage in Philo which must have been well-known to the Christian writers. In his book *Who is the Heir?* (263-66, IV: "On Ecstasy"), Philo uses the image of the extinguished light when describing the entrance of the Divine Spirit into the mortal. He says that the Divinity comes as a beam that cannot be apprehended until the light of the human mind is extinguished, for "when the divine light shines, the human light sets." Cf. the excellent translation in *Loeb Classical Library*, 14, pp. 417ff. As the sanctuary of the Divine Spirit, the room of the Mérode Annunciation is a symbol of Heaven. The door on the left side of the room is, of course, the *porta coeli* (Genesis 28:17), not the *porta clausa* of Ezechiel, as has been erroneously assumed by scholars even up to the very latest studies on the altarpiece. The door is opened, not closed. Since it is not hinged to the far post of the door

in a painting as late as Grünewald's Annunciation in the Isenheim Altarpiece (Fig. 103). There, it is still clear that the Virgin is depicted as the altar, for the half-drawn altar curtains which are shown as flanking her figure, indicate that the scene, besides signifying the sacred moment of Christ's Incarnation, symbolizes the instant of the Transubstantiation as well.[193]

In the Ghent Annunciation, the two ideas are fused by means of their common denominator, the concept of the Holy Wedding, which dominates, as we have seen, the interior view of the polyptych. The specific meaning of Van Eyck's Annunciation room is determined by this dual symbolism. And it is this meaning of the room which will, in turn, lead us to a deeper understanding of the succession of views as we find them in the great altarpiece.

In fifteenth century art, the setting used to form the environment of the Madonna is very often itself a symbol of her person. For instance, the church interior or the *hortus conclusus* which sometimes surround the figure of the Virgin, are always the symbols of this figure: the Madonna is the closed garden and she herself is the Church. Naturally, Van Eyck's Annunciation chamber is the symbol of the Annunciate. The chamber, however, symbolizes her not only as the sacred vessel of Christ's Incarnation but also as the sanctuary of the Transubstantiation. True, the altar of the Holy Sacrifice is not explicitly presented in Van Eyck's Annunciation scene; but the room, shown as it is with the two annex chambers symbolizing the pastophories, is clearly designated as the sacred locale of the Eucharist.[194] It is characterized as the room for the Holy of Holies, the consecrated Host. It is, in other words, the interior of "the Sacred Shrine," of the ciborium, which is the tabernacle of the New Covenant. Indeed, the real ciborium, the tabernacle compartment of the fifteenth century Sacrament houses, are sometimes flanked by the relief figures of the Angel and the Annunciate, a sculptural decoration which links the Eucharist

---

opening but to the near one (and thus reaches in a most daring illusionistic attempt into the space of the spectator!), the door is even wide open. The Incarnation of Christ has opened the portal of Heaven to a sin-burdened mankind, whose pious hope for final Salvation is personified in the donors. Cf. also below notes 246, 296, and 339.

[193] For the curtains of the altar and their use, cf. Jungmann, *op.cit.*, II, p. 140 and p. 140, note 11. Annunciation scenes set in a sanctuary that contains an altar occur frequently in fifteenth century book illumination. Cf., for instance, Andrew Martinsdale, *Gothic Art*, New York/Washington 1967, fig. 189, and Margaret B. Freeman, "The Annunciation from a Book of Hours for Charles of France," *Metropolitan Museum of Art Bulletin*, XIX, December 1960, pp. 105ff (our Fig. 102). Far from having only a narrative meaning and from connoting exclusively the Jewish Temple, the sanctuary with the altar unquestionably points to the Eucharist.

[194] The miniature of the Adoration of the Magi from the Gospels of Bishop Bernward (Hildesheim, Cathedral Treasury, No. 18), which is illustrated in Nilgen, *op.cit.*, fig. 5, not only shows the manger of the Christ Child as an altar but also two flanking towerlike chambers which are correctly interpreted by Dr. Nilgen as the pastophories, cf. *ibid.*, p. 314.

with the Incarnation of Christ and which distinctly shows that the Sacramental recess is not only seen as the Host container but also as the symbol of the sacred womb of the Virgin (Figs. 146 and 147).[195]

By realizing that the Ghent Annunciation room represents the interior of a ciborium, we now finally understand the idea which determines the succession of views in the Ghent Altarpiece. What we see in Van Eyck's Annunciation is the interior of the golden shrine, whose exterior is presented in the main view of the retable (Figs. 41 and 42). The large golden object, the Ark of the New Covenant, is, as explained before, the receptacle of the Eucharist which is Christ's "eternal relic." It is this receptacle which we see opened in the Annunciation scene of the exterior view. It functions there as the bridal chamber, as the sacred locale of the two highest mysteries.

Normally, the interior of a house-type reliquary, which was the form used, as we have discussed, for the golden Ark shown in the Ghent Altarpiece, is always completely invisible to the believer. But, in his Ghent retable, Van Eyck has miraculously revealed the secret of this interior. We are granted a view into the inner sanctum of Heaven which, in a multitude of symbolic detail, discloses to us the whole glory of the divine promise. Including the sibyls and the prophets, who signify the ages of Paganism and Judaism and their prophecies of Christianity, the interior of the golden Ark assumes the broad and all-embracing meaning essential for the symbol of the New Covenant.

Permitted a look into the Holy of Holies, the believer kneeling in front of Van Eyck's retable has a foretaste of the visual enchantment to be expected in Paradise. Indeed, this view, painted as it is by the brush of Van Eyck, the greatest magician among pious painters, casts a spell of paradisaic bliss even on the modern spectator. To the contemporaries of Van Eyck, not as yet accustomed to a realistic portrayal of a convincingly illuminated and convincingly receding space, the glance into the enchanting room as it discloses a view of a cityscape lit by the warm glow of the sun, must have been a true miracle. The viewer looks into the inaccessible interior of the golden Ark, the New Heaven, a miraculous experience in itself. But this miracle is made still more overwhelming by the opening up of the chamber's back wall to permit the view into a delightful distance, which is the New Earth.

The New Earth of the Eternal Jerusalem, which, in the main view of the retable, is presented in the lower zone, is in the background of the Annunciation seen from above and close up. This view into the distance breaks the spatial limitations which Van Eyck has generally observed with great care in the painted settings of his altarpiece. Conceived, as we have seen, as a reliquary structure actually placed into the chapel of Jodocus Vijd,

---

[195] This idea is most distinctly expressed by William Durandus in his *Rationale divinorum officiorum* (Liber I, cap. 3, 25): "And mark well that the room in which the consecrated Hosts are enclosed betokens the glorious Virgin's body." . . . *quod capsa in qua hostiae consecratae servantur, significat corpus virginis gloriosae* . . . , ed. Leyden 1612 (Rousselet), p. 15 *verso*.

the altarpiece allowed only a restricted space. And while Van Eyck in general paid attention to this fact by using very shallow settings, he breaks not only the space limitations of the altarpiece but also those of the Vijd chapel itself in the background of the Annunciation scene. The New Earth is spiritually as well as physically a "prospect." It thus transcends the present time and place. This is the reason why a view into the distance is rendered in the Annunciation scene. It is only in this scene and in the Adoration of the Lamb that Van Eyck has depicted the New Earth.

The four lower panels of the exterior view, which show the donors and the two SS. John, though implying, as we shall see later, the idea of the New Earth, do not primarily represent this subject (Figs. 2 and 3). Van Eyck has made it perfectly clear that this setting connotes our own realm, for he has rendered the figures of the Baptist and the Evangelist as statues that could actually appear above the mensa of the Vijd chapel. The two donors who occupy the outer niches of the stone wall containing these statues, are shown as kneeling in prayer before the stone figures. The exclusion of the donors from the main representation and their depiction in this subordinate realm has led Max J. Friedländer to remark that they kneel, as it were, "in the forecourt of the Temple." Our new understanding of the iconographical context shows that this is not so. Having realized that the Annunciation room is the interior of the golden shrine, we see that Jodocus Vijd and his wife kneel immediately beneath the large reliquary. Since this is the very place where the believer traditionally venerated the sacred shrines, we now see that Van Eyck has allotted to his donors precisely the space which, according to ecclesiastical usage, is legitimately theirs.

The system which was used in the Ghent Altarpiece for the variation and alternation of views was apparently based on a carefully devised program. Already at this point in our investigation we obtain some insight into it. When all the panels of the retable are closed, we see what may be called an "open space" above and a "closed space" below (Fig. 42). The Annunciation in the upper zone is an "open space" because it depicts the opened interior of the golden shrine. The niched wall in the lower zone is a "closed space" because it is a parapet concealing the open landscape of the Adoration of the Lamb.

This system works in reverse for the main view of the retable, i.e. for the view in which all the wings are opened (Fig. 41). Then, the upper zone shows a "closed space," the inaccessible façade of the golden shrine; while the lower level is the "open space" of the landscape in the Lamb panels. A view into the distance, in other words, is provided in only one of the zones at a time: in the interior view, in the lower level and in the exterior view, in the upper level. While the system as such is clear, a full understanding of its iconographical implications can only be achieved by focusing on the third and final theme of the Van Eyck retable, namely on the theme of the Last Judgment.

V. THE LAST JUDGMENT

IN the interior view of the Ghent Altarpiece (Fig. 1), we find all the important motifs of the Second Coming of Christ as they are described in Revelation: the One Who is seated on the throne, the altar, the Lamb, and the Fountains of the Water of Life. Even the twenty-four elders who fall down before the Lord are suggested in the Adoration panel by the prophets and apostles, who are depicted as kneeling. We have already mentioned, moreover, that the crown which appears at the feet of the Enthroned may indicate, in addition to its other connotations, the combined crowns offered to the Lord by the twenty-four elders who "cast their crowns before the throne" (Fig. 70). It is also possible, furthermore, that the four apocalyptic creatures, which traditionally surround the figure of Christ in representations of His Second Coming, once appeared as a sculptural decoration in the architectural frame now lost. Since the Fountain of Life which we have been discussing shows the lion, the calf, the man, and the eagle as sculpture adorning the heavenly throne, this may well have also been the case in the Ghent Altarpiece (Fig. 19).[196]

The purpose of Christ's triumphal return is the Last Judgment. But while there can be no doubt that the Second Coming is depicted in Van Eyck's polyptych, the Judgment is not explicitly shown, at least not in its actual drama. This, however, does not exclude the possibility for the ideas of the Last Judgment to be expressed symbolically in the retable. The very fact that the scene is crowned by the Deësis group strongly suggests such an assumption. The representation of the One on the throne is here supplemented by the two intercessors for mankind who traditionally flank the Lord in scenes of the Last Judgment.

In the course of our discussion of the Virgin in the Deësis group and her importance for the theme of the Mystical Wedding, we suggested that the Baptist may embody the Judgment theme. He is, in fact, the one who characterizes the painting as a Last Judg-

---

[196] Since the iconography of the Fountain of Life is not identical with that of the Ghent Altarpiece, we are not permitted to take all the features occurring in the former for derivations from the Van Eyck polyptych. However, in the case of the symbols of the four evangelists, it is the very divergence between the two works which speaks for the appearance of these signs in the Ghent retable. The standard iconographic elements as they occur in the Romanesque and Gothic portals and in other Northern sculpture depicting Christ's Coming for the Last Judgment, are found only in the Ghent Altarpiece. Only there do the three main figures form the Deësis group, while in the Fountain of Life the figure which is seated to the left of the Lord is not the Baptist but John the Evangelist (cf. below note 210). For a sculptural Deësis group which depicts Christ as surrounded by the symbols of the evangelists, see, for instance, the choir-screen at Wechselburg to be discussed later in this study (cf. below note 205). Furthermore, it is only in the Ghent Altarpiece that we find the groups of the jurors traditionally belonging to the theme. Since the representations of the Four Beasts would thus fit the program of the Ghent Altarpiece even better than that of the Fountain of Life, it is most likely that the painter of the latter had simply translated sculptural motifs which he found in the frame of his famous model into the technique of painting.

ment. Since the Lord here appears as the Priest and the Mystical Bridegroom, He is not shown with the wounds of the Passion, which are His credentials as the Judge in the traditional Judgment scenes. It is the figure of St. John and his pointing gesture—the latter foreign to the usual Judgment representations—which bring to mind the famous words: "Behold the Lamb of God." The Baptist thus demonstrates the identity of the Enthroned with the sacrificial Lamb, i.e. with the Christ of the Passion. Replacing the motif of the wounds, the demonstration of this identity characterizes the Enthroned as the Judge. Moreover, the Baptist and his gesture also bring to mind the biblical idea expressed in Matthew 3:12 and Luke 3:17, which made him a key figure in the scenes of the Last Judgment. In these passages the Baptist directly refers to Christ as the Judge of the world.[197]

The Judgment theme is not only apparent in the upper level of the interior view but also in the lower one, which shows the assembly of the saints. The very appearance of Christ in the company of all His saints denotes the day of the Last Judgment. The saints are depicted by Van Eyck as grouped according to their rank. Though usually regarded as the intercessors for mankind, the saints of the Lord are also believed to be the judges of the human race. This idea, which occurs in I Corinthians 6:2 and in the introitus of the vigils of All Saints' Day, is clearly expressed by Honorius of Autun. In his *Elucidarium*, the question: "*Qui sunt qui judicant?*" is answered by the following enumeration: "*Apostoli, martyres, confessores, monachi, virgines.*" By grouping the saints according to their rank, Van Eyck has characterized them as the jury of the Lord.[198]

The Deësis represented in Van Eyck's retable is very often the crowning feature in the sculptural decoration of mediaeval rood-screens.[199] This is a most significant fact, for the large two-storied architecture of the lost frame of Van Eyck's retable was based, as the reader may recall, on the form of the rood-screen (Figs. 29, 31, and 41). Rood-screens served a variety of purposes which we have seen to be reflected in Van Eyck's representation. One important function we have not as yet discussed but it is essential in our present context: rood-screens were traditionally used as the setting for the courts of law. They were the locale for ecclesiastical, and sometimes even for secular, jurisdiction.[200] Because mediaeval man saw every act of justice in relation to the final verdict of the Lord, the usual theme of the sculptural programs on the rood-screens was the Last Judgment.

[197] "His winnowing fan is in His hand, and He will clean out His threshing floor, and will gather the wheat into the barn; but the chaff He will burn up with unquenchable fire."

[198] Honorius Augustodunensis, *Elucidarium*, Lib. III, Cap. XIII, ed. Migne, *Patr.Lat.*, CLXXII, col. 1166. Compare Kirchner-Doberer, *op.cit.*, p. 225, "Der Richter erscheint mit dem Kollegium der Apostel und dem Heiligenkreis der Kirche" and p. 230, "Die klassenmässige Gruppierung der Heiligen bezeichnet die Beisitzer des Jüngsten Gerichtes." Cf. also *ibid.*, p. 238.

[199] For examples of the Deësis group appearing in the rood-screens, cf. *ibid.*, pp. 37f, 58ff, 107ff, 133, 173, and 218f.

[200] Cf. *ibid.*, pp. 211ff, with sources given in notes 585, 599, 610-12.

At the arcade of the rood-screen the jury assembled and on its upper platform the judge was seated so that he could be seen from all parts of the church.[201] Thus, when the original frame of the Ghent Altarpiece was still intact and the rood-screen character of the setting in the paintings still obvious, the figure of the Enthroned appeared in the traditional place of the judge and the assembly of saints was characterized as the jury. In fact, in the original state of the Ghent Altarpiece, it was perfectly clear that the paintings were a symbolical representation of the Last Judgment and not simply because the architectural setting suggested this.

Today, all the parts of the great work are a portrayal of Paradise. Originally, however, the work must have also included a representation of Hell. Van Vaernewyck's text makes it highly probable that an image of Hell rendered in water color appeared in a fabric hanging which had served as the antependium of the altarpiece.[202] The image of Hell, a subordinate motif in a work that stresses Redemption rather than Damnation, would thus have appeared on a removable object which was perhaps shown only on certain days and in conjunction with a specific positioning of the movable panels of the retable. Covering the front of the mensa, the picture of the inferno formed the lowermost

[201] It may be useful to recall at this point that the donor of the altarpiece, Jodocus Vijd, had the honor of being one of the official jurors of his city, which indicates that in the Ghent of his time he was also a key administrator of the city government. He was the seventh juror in 1396, and had become the fourth by 1425, and the first juror in 1433, which means that he was the burgomaster. Cf. W. H. James Weale and Maurice W. Brockwell, *The Van Eycks and their Art*, London 1912, p. 58 and Dhanens, Inventaris VI, pp. 85-89. Cf. also *ibid.*, pp. 27-32, with further literature on the person of Vijd given in the footnotes.

[202] For Van Vaernewyck's passage, which was repeated by Van Mander, cf. note 55 above, and the text belonging to it. The conjecture sometimes found in art historical writings that the painting of Hell was the predella of the altarpiece is highly unlikely if we accept Van Vaernewyck's claim that the composition was painted in water color. This technique, however, is a usual one for the altar hangings and, in fact, the chief reason for the extreme scarcity of preserved examples. In one of the earliest nineteenth century essays on the altarpiece (G. F. Waagen and L. de Bast, *Notice sur le chef-d'œuvre des frères van Eyck*, Ghent 1825, p. 2, note 2), Van Vaernewyck's text was apparently taken for the description of an antependium. Since very few altar arrangements of the fourteenth and fifteenth centuries in the North have come down to us completely intact and since preserved antependia are particularly rare, it is not surprising that we have no precedent for the use of Hell either as a predella or as an antependium. By no means are we allowed to use this lack of examples as an *argumentum ex silentio* against the possibility that the antependium of the Vijd altar showed the picture of Hell. The theme of Hell occurs not only in the rood-screens (cf. Kirchner-Doberer, *op.cit.*, pp. 37, 55, 79, and 225) but also and very frequently in mediaeval and Renaissance altarpieces. That the theme had actually occurred in the Vijd altar is most probable not only because of the essential unity of the concepts of All Saints and the Last Judgment but also because the theme of Hell was imperative to the context of the Mass offered for the dead. Discussion of Requiem Masses in connection with the image of Hell are found in Ruth Feldhusen, *Ikonologische Studien zu Michelangelos Jüngstem Gericht*, Diss. Hamburg 1953 (typescript), pp. 73ff and note 120. For the Requiem, cf. *The Oxford Dictionary of the Christian Church*, London/New York/Toronto 1966, p. 1155. For the Vijd altar as intended for daily Masses of the Dead, and the Vijd chapel as the funerary chapel of the donors, cf. below note 405 and the text to which it belongs.

region of the total composition. Thus, when the image of Hell was shown, the Vijd altar must have offered a view rather similar to the small Eyckian panel in New York which depicts the Last Judgment (Figs. 41 and 141). As a matter of fact, the representation of Paradise in the two compositions have a number of features in common. Not only are the blessed rendered in diminutive scale and crowned by a huge Deësis group but the group of virgins approaching from the rear also points up the similarity between the two compositions. With both realms, Hell as well as Paradise, rendered in the Ghent Altar, the principal idea of the Last Judgment, namely the decision between these two opposites, was clearly suggested in the work.

If the antependium once covered not only the mensa but also the adjoining lateral parts of the socle zone (Fig. 41), the image of the inferno may have been flanked by side representations which showed the Resurrection of the Dead (the dead of the earth and the dead of the sea) as we see them in the background of the Last Judgment in New York (Fig. 141).[203] However, it is by no means essential actually to postulate such a scene for the Ghent Altarpiece. Like the mediaeval rood-screens—especially those in Germany— the Vijd altar offered a symbolical rather than a narrative representation of the Last Judgment.[204] The Resurrection of the Dead, though possible in this context, was not imperative for the completeness of a strictly symbolic program. Even without this scene, the meaning was clear enough, especially since a number of additional motifs made the symbolic context completely obvious.

These additional motifs come to the fore when we compare the themes in the Ghent Altarpiece with those constituting the programs of the rood-screens. Apart from the motif of the Deësis, the rood-screens have a number of other elements in common with the Ghent retable. The structure in Wechselburg, for instance, shows the representations of Cain and Abel, which also occur in Van Eyck's polyptych (Figs. 104, 105, 107-9).[205] In the Ghent retable, they appear above the figures of Adam and Eve as imitation relief adorning the framing architecture. While the first murder is depicted to the right, the

[203] The Resurrection of the Dead is a theme that would have been especially suitable for the two areas behind the mensa and flanking it, for these places may originally have been projected for the burial of Jodocus Vijd and his wife. Cf. below Chapter 5, the text to which notes 405 and 406 belong. For the Resurrection of the Dead as a theme of the rood-screens, cf. Kirchner-Doberer, *op.cit.*, p. 225.

[204] The symbolic treatment of the Last Judgment program is especially characteristic of the German rood-screens in counterdistinction to the French ones. Cf. *ibid.*, pp. 224 and 242.

[205] For a thorough discussion of the rood-screen of Wechselburg, which is one of the examples containing the Deësis group, cf. *ibid.*, pp. 102ff. The original place of the two reliefs of Cain and Abel is not certain in the greatly altered structure that exists today. For the present appearance of the work, the form it had in 1834, and for a (not generally accepted) reconstruction of its original condition, cf. Adolph Goldschmidt and L. Giese, *Die Skulpturen von Freiberg und Wechselburg* (Denkmäler der deutschen Kunst, II. Sektion Plastik), Berlin 1924, plates 52, 53, and fig. 9 in the text. The Deësis group with the symbols of the Evangelists is illustrated on plate 65.

motive for this murder, the sacrifice of Cain and Abel, is shown on the left side. It is clear that the two scenes emphasize Original Sin and the need for mankind's Redemption. In addition, however, they have a more strictly symbolical meaning.

The representations in Wechselburg, which contrast the three-quarter-length figure of Abel with the lamb to that of Cain with the sheaf and club, may shed light on this particular connotation. With Abel placed on the left—the good side in a Last Judgment—and Cain with his murderous club on the right—the sinister side when seen from the viewpoint of the Judge—it is clear that Abel is aligned with the elect and Cain with the damned. Although both reliefs in the Ghent Altarpiece show the two sons of the first parents, the distinction between a good and an evil side is nonetheless obvious. One figure is dominant each time: Abel in the left-hand representation, Cain in the right-hand one. Even this distribution of emphasis suggests that the left relief was intended to represent the good scene and the right relief the evil one. But it is the specific symbolism of the two events which makes this connotation certain.

The image of Abel sacrificing the lamb is a time-honored prefiguration not only of Christ's sacrifice on the Cross but also of the Eucharist, in which the Church celebrates this sacrifice.[206] While the relief on the left thus refers to the Church, the murder scene to the right is a symbol of the Synagogue. In theological writing, the murder of Abel by the hand of Cain is compared to the crucifixion of Christ by the Jews.[207] A Netherlandish fifteenth century painting with a temple scene in which the murder of Abel adorns a "Jewish altarpiece" demonstrates that this murder could be used as a general symbol of Judaism (Fig. 110).[208] There can be no doubt that in the rood-screen, as well as in the Ghent Altarpiece, the pair of scenes was meant to set Ecclesia against Synagoga as the good against the evil force.

While Ecclesia and Synagoga are presented in Wechselburg in their Old Testament prefigurations, they occur in other rood-screens in their usual form, namely, as two contesting allegorical females.[209] These two figures signify not only Judaism's rejection and

---

[206] The duality of meaning has been evident in the theme since Early Christian times. It is obvious, for instance, in the choir mosaic of San Vitale in Ravenna, reproduced in Wolfgang Fritz Volbach, *Early Christian Art*, New York, s.d., plate 160. For the Eucharistic meaning of the Wechselburg reliefs, cf. Kirchner-Doberer, *op.cit.*, pp. 109f.

[207] *Ibid.*, p. 219, with Walafrid Strabo adduced as a source in note 622. *Glossa Ordinaria*, Lib. Genes., Cap. IV, verse 8-12, J. P. Migne, P.L. CXIII, cols. 98-99.

[208] Knowledge of this most striking example I owe to the kind information of a "non-art historian" but most attentive visitor of museums, the poet Jan Swan. The miniature in an English Psalter (Fig. 106) is further evidence for the fact that the identification of Cain with the evil Jew was quite natural to the European Middle Ages. This book illumination, in which the profile of Cain is unmistakably intended to be the caricature of a Jewish face, is discussed in Pearl F. Braude, " 'Cokel in oure Clene Corn': Some Implications of Cain's Sacrifice," *Gesta*, VII, 1968, pp. 15-28, a useful essay with listings of the earlier literature.

[209] For instance, in the rood-screen of the west choir in the Cathedral of Mainz, and, according to Kirchner-Doberer, to be postulated for the original programs in Gelnhausen and the west choir of Naumburg Cathedral. Cf. *op.cit.*, pp. 58-64, and p. 235.

Christianity's acceptance of Christ's sacrifice, but also the Lord's rejection of the Synagogue and His acceptance of the Church. At Christ's sacrificial death, Judaism with her animal sacrifices collapses under the Cross, and from then on it is the Church alone who is entitled to celebrate the true sacrifice. The Lord's rejection of Synagoga and His acceptance of Ecclesia is the basis for the appearance of the two figures in the context of the Last Judgment. Ecclesia is the *figura* of the elect, Synagoga the *figura* of the doomed.[210]

The intimate connection of the symbolism of Cain and Abel with that of Synagoga and Ecclesia immediately brings our reconstruction of the Ghent Altarpiece to mind. With the free copy of the Fountain of Life as the basis, we reconstructed the predella of the polyptych as showing the Eucharistic niche in the center and the two groups of Ecclesia

[210] For Synagoga being rejected under the Cross, cf., for instance, Ludolf of Saxony, *Vita Christi*, ed. Bertrand Etienne, 1497, Part I, Cap. LIII. The theme of Ecclesia and Synagoga is treated in Bruyn, *op.cit.*, pp. 13-18, with listings of previous literature. For their appearance in the context of the Last Judgment (Portal of Amiens, Paten of Wilten), cf. Kirchner-Doberer, *op.cit.*, pp. 225 and 235, and Louis Réau, *op.cit.*, II, p. 744. A most striking fifteenth century example for the Church and the Synagogue as the *figurae* of the elect and the damned is found in the predella of the altarpiece in Boslunde, already mentioned above in note 134. A most informative book on Ecclesia and Synagoga came to my attention after this book was in proof: Wolfgang Seiferth, *Synagoge und Kirche im Mittelalter*, Munich 1964.

The form of the predella in the Ghent Altarpiece, as it is indicated in my reconstruction drawings (Figs. 41 and 42), implies that the master who painted the original of the Fountain of Life (Fig. 19) must have added in his version a number of extra figures on the extreme left and on the extreme right of the Eyckian Ecclesia and Synagoga groups respectively. There is, indeed, evidence that this later painter added three corner figures each time. In the case of the Ecclesia group, at least two of these three added figures have been regarded as the donors of the composition. Cf. Friedrich Winkler, "Die Stifter des Lebensbrunnens und andere Van-Eyck-Fragen," *Pantheon*, IV, 5, May 1931, pp. 188-92. The portrait character of these painted persons is, in fact, striking. However, far from depicting donors (donors, if added at all, must have appeared in a wing panel of the original Fountain of Life), the two kneeling figures that had attracted Winkler's attention owe their portrait character to a very different circumstance. Their faces were obviously copied from the portrait-like faces in the Ghent Altarpiece appearing in parts other than the predella.

The elderly man wearing the thorny twig emblem as a necklace has a face that reflects one of the faces in the Confessor group of the Lamb panel. I am referring to the left foreground figure of a miter-crowned bishop in this group, which is best reproduced in Beenken, *op.cit.*, 1941, fig. 37. The pseudo-portrait in Berlin (cf. Winkler, *op.cit.*, 1931, p. 191 and Friedländer-Veronee, I, plate 50 B) is a copy after this same Eyckian face in the Ghent Altarpiece, which may very well have been a portrait. As for the more youthful figure kneeling beside the elderly man in the Fountain of Life, it unquestionably is a reflection of the young horseman in the nearest foreground of the panel of the Knights (Figs. 174 and 189). For the young heroes in this panel as possible portraits, cf. below Chapter 5, the paragraph to which note 373 belongs. For the possibility that Philip and Isabella were the donors, see below note 301.

When the painter of the Fountain of Life changed the Eyckian figure of the Baptist to John the Evangelist in his composition, this change may have been the result of the particular stress which he placed on the contest between Ecclesia and Synagoga (Fig. 19). As discussed in Kirchner-Doberer, *op.cit.*, p. 221, note 626, John the Evangelist was traditionally paired with the figure of the Synagogue. It is true that the Evangelist in the Fountain of Life is characterized as the writer of the Apocalypse. But his appearance can hardly have been caused by the Apocalyptic context of the painting, as Panofsky 1953, I, p. 216 proposed. The Apocalyptic ideas in the Fountain of Life are no stronger, more explicit, or more complete than they are in the Ghent Altarpiece.

and Synagoga at the sides (Figs. 19 and 41). Unquestionably this pair of scenes in the predella corresponded to the pair with Cain and Abel at the top of the painted panels. Both showing small-sized figures, the two pairs were apparently meant as sculptural decorations of the framework. But while the scenes with Cain and Abel are imitation reliefs rendered in the technique of painting, the two groups in the predella may very well have been actual stone carvings.

By means of these four relief representations at the top and the bottom of the altarpiece, the scenes in Van Eyck's retable were distinctly placed into the focus of the Judgment theme. Both of them point to the damned and the elect. In the upper pair, in which Salvation and Perdition are presented in Old Testament prefigurations, the *figurae* of both the damned and the elect still appear in both of the scenes. Cain and Abel are the symbols of the two-fold possibility of the human race with the sharp separation between the wheat and the chaff not as yet clearly expressed. This more explicit statement is reserved for the predella. It is the New and not the Old Law which brings about the final Judgment. A glance at the assembly of Synagogue as it appears in the Fountain of Life convinces us that its turbulence (which matches the violence of the first murder) symbolizes not only Synagogue's rejection of the Eucharist and her being rejected by the Lord, but also the despair of the damned at the Last Judgment (Fig. 54).

There can be no doubt that the two predella reliefs in their strong emotional impact replaced the drama of the separation of the elect from the doomed as it appears in traditional Judgment scenes. Van Eyck's presentation is in no way inferior to the usual portrayal of the separation so far as emotional appeal is concerned; as a particular solution within the specific context of the Ghent Altarpiece, it is by far superior to it. The symbolic rendition has a tremendous advantage over the narrative one. The reader may already have noticed that both pairs of relief, Synagoga and Ecclesia as well as Cain and Abel, not only refer to the theme of the Last Judgment but also symbolize the themes of the Eternal Mass and the Mystical Wedding of the Church.[211] It is, indeed, in these framing reliefs

[211] For the Eucharistic connotation of the scenes of Cain and Abel, cf. above note 206 and the text belonging to it. As to the representation of Ecclesia and Synagoga, the Eucharistic reference to the theme has always been its chief meaning, which is automatically connected, of course, with the idea of the Sacred Wedding, in which Ecclesia is the bride of Christ. Pointing to the Church as the only rightful celebrant of the true sacrifice, which is the Eucharist, the two groups of Ecclesia and Synagoga most pertinently flank the wafer-carrying water in the painting of the Fountain of Life (Fig. 19). The Eucharistic meaning of the two groups is, in fact, my chief reason for placing them in my reconstruction to the left and the right of the Host compartment in the predella of the Ghent retable (Figs. 41 and 42). As is evident from the Bordesholm altarpiece (Fig. 61), cf. above note 133, the predella scenes flanking the Host compartment were selected for their Eucharistic connotation. It may be interesting in this context to point again to the much discussed miniature in the German *Biblia Pauperum* (Fig. 60). There the two figures of Synagoga and Ecclesia are enclosed in two of the surrounding roundels, and they appear (just as I have postulated for the Ghent Altarpiece) at the lower left and right of the main action. Since this action in the miniature is explicitly the celebration of the Eucharist, there can be no doubt about the meaning of the two figures.

that it becomes clearly apparent how intimately the three themes of the altarpiece are related and interwoven. It is only for our understanding of the iconography of the work that the ideas had to be separated in an analysis. In the painted work none of the three is separated from either of the two others. They are a solid unit, for, in mediaeval belief, the whole course of divine and human history is directed toward the Last Judgment.

With the groups of saints in the Adoration panels, the Judgment theme takes a specific turn which is most important for the over-all organization of the altarpiece. Aside from being the jury, the saints have still another connotation within this theme. We know from the chronicle which describes the pageant of 1458, and which has already been mentioned twice in our study, that there was a group of inscriptions on the altarpiece which designated the saints as the symbols of the Beatitudes pronounced by Christ in the Sermon on the Mount (Matthew 5:3-10).[212] Since these inscriptions apparently had appeared on the sculptural part of the frame now lost, none is visible today. As a matter of fact, the authenticity of that passage in the chronicle which refers to the Beatitudes has even been doubted on occasion.[213] These doubts, however, are entirely unjustified not only because the chronicle is an early and generally speaking a reliable source but mainly because we also find the Beatitudes in the program of the rood-screens, which supplied, as we have seen, the iconographical basis for many other motifs in the Ghent Altarpiece. In the not very well preserved sculptures of the rood-screen in Magdeburg, the Beatitudes appear as a number of allegorical female figures, each standing full length and furnished with her biblical inscription.[214]

The chronicle, which has been handed down to us in two manuscript copies, links the titles of the groups with the Beatitudes. The Latin titles classifying the saints according to their rank have been partly preserved in the altarpiece. In the frame inscriptions of the shutters we can still see that the four groups in the wings had been designated as the Judges, the Knights, the Hermits, and the Pilgrims. The text of the chronicle, which attempts to give both series of classifications complete, fails in so doing. Indeed, it is obviously slightly corrupted. This has caused some embarrassment to scholars and was perhaps

---

The connection between the Eucharist and the Last Judgment, which is based on biblical passages, belongs, in fact, to the leading concepts of the Christian rite. One of the texts is John 6:53-58, where the promise of eternal life through the partaking in the divine food is coupled with a threat of eternal damnation to those who reject this food. The other passage is I Corinthians 11: 29, where we read: "A man must examine himself first, and then eat of the bread and drink of the cup; *he is eating and drinking damnation to himself if he eats and drinks unworthily. . . .*"

[212] Cf. above note 118.

[213] While the text of Panofsky 1953, I (p. 209, note 2, printed on p. 444), is noncommittal on this point, De Baets clearly states that he takes the Beatitude inscriptions as they appear in the chronicle for a later invention. Cf. De Baets, *op.cit.*, pp. 570-71.

[214] Discussed in Kirchner-Doberer, *op.cit.*, p. 156. For reproductions and earlier literature, cf. *ibid.*, note 474.

even one of the reasons why the authenticity of this passage has been doubted altogether. But keeping in mind that there are ten groups of saints and only eight Beatitudes, and that the model for the present manuscripts was perhaps not very clearly arranged, we can readily understand the confusion. Fortunately, however, the mistakes are so transparent that the original linking can easily be reconstructed.

In the middle panel, the three groups on the right side were combined with the Beatitudes in the following manner: the Apostles—"Blessed are the poor in spirit" (Matthew 5:3); the Martyrs—". . . they which are persecuted for righteousness' sake" (Matthew 5:10); the Virgins—". . . the pure in heart" (Matthew 5:8). The three groups to the left were linked with the Beatitudes thus: the Prophets—". . . they that mourn" (Matthew 5:4); the Patriarchs—". . . they which hunger and thirst after righteousness" (Matthew 5:6); the Confessors—". . . the peacemakers" (Matthew 5:9). The Judges and the Knights in the left wings were linked to the Beatitude concerning the "merciful" (Matthew 5:7); and the Hermits and the Pilgrims in the right shutters are ". . . the meek" (Matthew 5:5).[215]

The striking logic of this linking confirms that it must have been part of the original program of the great altarpiece. The saints, then, presenting the Beatitudes symbolize those human virtues that Christ declares to be the ones that predestined a mortal to enter Paradise. Clearly, the groups in Van Eyck's Adoration of the Lamb not only depict the saints; they also present the *figurae* of all the elect. The painting thus directly addresses the devout who are assembled in the Vijd chapel. It offers them a demonstration, so to

[215] The linking in the chronicle (for which the reader may look up one of the three publications given above in note 118) starts with the groups appearing on the viewer's left in the Ghent Altarpiece. While the first two groups on that side, the Confessors and the Patriarchs, are correctly linked to the corresponding Beatitudes (the first pertaining to the "peacemakers," the other to those "thirsting after righteousness"), the writer of the chronicle missed the Beatitude text for the third group. This text, "blessed are they that mourn," is, indeed, completely missing in the manuscript, a mistake which reduces the eight pronouncements of Christ to seven. The Prophets, who unquestionably belonged originally to the omitted passage, are linked to the text on the "merciful" instead, though the latter was certainly intended for the Judges and the Knights. The reason for the confusion is rather obvious. Chances are that all the Beatitude inscriptions, those for the wing groups as well as those for the central panel, had originally appeared together in the lower part of the stone frame immediately beneath the panel of the Lamb. (Those parts of the inscriptions meant for the groups in the wings were probably distinctly shifted to a side position.) With such an accumulation of all the passages in the center frame, a viewer might well have been inclined to connect all of them with the central groups. The writer of the chronicle apparently made this error which, in conjunction with the complete omission of one of the Beatitude texts, caused further confusion on the right side. There he has managed to link the three first groups correctly. Having done so, however, he found himself with a remaining fourth Beatitude. This text, "blessed are the meek," should have been connected, of course, with the Hermits and the Pilgrims. However, having left the Judges and the Knights without any Beatitude inscriptions, the writer was naturally reluctant to allot such a biblical text to the Hermits and the Pilgrims. The strange solution he found for his predicament, namely to connect the "left-over" Beatitude with the Angels, was evidently the chief reason for De Baets' doubting the Eyckian origin of the Beatitude texts altogether.

speak, of those qualities that they must possess in order to enter Paradise. In such a demonstration, all levels of fifteenth century society had, of course, to be included. It is this idea that determined the particular selection of the groups in the Adoration of the Lamb, which are rather comprehensive in their portrayal of the social strata. In the panels of the wings, we find the proud and mighty to the left so strikingly contrasted with the modest and poor to the right, because it was imperative to show that both the powerless and the powerful, provided they are worthy, have a chance to be counted among the elect.[216]

This direct appeal to the viewer eminently suits the over-all character of the five lower paintings, indeed of the entire altarpiece. We mentioned earlier that the Adoration of the Lamb corresponds to the Annunciation in that these two scenes are the only representations to offer an "open view" in the Ghent retable. Whereas the chamber of the Annunciation is the normally invisible interior of the golden Ark of the Covenant, the landscape in the Adoration is the normally invisible choir of the lower sanctuary. The governing idea was here provided by the rood-screen, which formed a barrier between the choir and the area of the layman in the mediaeval churches. The exterior view of the altarpiece with the two statues and the donors shows the rear area of the imaginary church as completely closed (Fig. 42). But in the interior view, the obstacle is miraculously removed (Fig. 41). The rood-screen is now shown as an open-work skeleton through which the believer can see the enchantments of Paradise.[217] The view offered to him is not that of an architectural choir but the enrapturing infinity of a garden-like terrain in nature. This is the true image of the New Earth, of which the choir of a man-made church is but the temporal metaphor. Like the city prospect in the Annunciation scene, the distant view in the Adoration of the Lamb breaks the spatial limitations of the Vijd chapel. With his eyes drawn into the freedom of an unlimited distance, the beholder experiences a visual foretaste of eternal bliss.

This, however, is not the only feature which this landscape has in common with the Annunciation scene. Another and most important motif can be found in both of these representations. The curious motif of the empty porch constituted by the frame and forming the foreground of the Adoration of the Lamb has remained unexplained up to now

---

[216] For the titles preserved in the wings and their obvious reference to social groups, cf. Panofsky 1953, I, p. 217 and p. 217, note 1 (printed on p. 447) and especially De Baets, *op.cit.*, pp. 565-71. Strictly speaking, neither the Pilgrims nor the Judges can be counted among the Saints of the Church. But instead of taking this strange fact as additional grounds for doubting the unity of the present program, one should have concluded that the lower paintings of the altarpiece do not form an All Saints picture. In fact, while chiefly showing the saints of the Church, the idea gradually weakens at the two sides of the composition, so that the last groups (though each of them shows a particularly strong connection with the preceding one which *does* present saints) in reality belong to the community of the average blessed. The latter, though not explicitly depicted, are nevertheless, as we shall presently see, alluded to in the Ghent retable. Therefore, the inclusion of the Judges and the Knights was a most brilliant way to form a necessary transition.

[217] Even in the real rood-screens, the tendency to create open arcades with a freer view into the choir had increased by the end of the Gothic period. Cf. Kirchner-Doberer, *op.cit.*, p. 6.

(Fig. 41). The meaning of the motif now becomes clear: it obviously corresponds to the empty foreground in the two center panels of the Annunciation (Fig. 42). We have seen that this empty space in the Annunciation panels symbolizes the promise of Christ's Second Coming. The empty foreground space in the Adoration of the Lamb has a related meaning and one that even more directly concerns the viewer. The promise in the Annunciation scene is fulfilled in the interior of the altarpiece: Christ has come. He can be seen in the glory of His Second Coming above the image of the landscape of the blessed. But the elect are yet to come.

The empty foreground space, which the frame must have originally formed in front of the wing scenes with the distinguished elect, had expressed the idea that the more average elect are the next to come and that their place is already prepared. The idea of the empty place in Paradise prepared for the blessed is, as such, traditional. It appears in Early Christian mosaics where not only the throne of the Lord is shown as being empty but also the seats for the elect, who are to join Him in the paradisial locale (Figs. 91 and 92). But compared with the Early Christian representation of this idea, Van Eyck's realistic rendering strikes a new chord. Displaying the empty place in front of an enchanting, convincingly real landscape just at the eye level of the believer, he invites the spectator, as it were, not simply to observe but to enter the scene. The empty foreground hall as the image of the place where the blessed are to assemble is a serious admonition and a beautiful promise for the congregation in the Ghent church.

VI. THE CHRISTIAN UNIVERSE

THE Ghent Altarpiece was a unit of perfect harmony based on the most subtle correspondences of form and idea. The opinion that the polyptych is a work of complete iconographic and stylistic unity is also held by Günter Bandmann, who has expressed this view in an article which was published in 1952 but came to my attention only after the completion of the present chapter.[218] It is in Professor Bandmann's important study that the reader will find a convincing demonstration of the connection between Van Eyck's altarpiece and Early Christian art. While my own observations on this point are merely hints based on intuition, Bandmann has adduced solid evidence for this connection. In fact, his opinion regarding the essential unity of the Eyckian work is founded on his recognition that this work with its two-leveled representation clearly repeats the traditional program of Early Christian apse mosaics.

The interior view of the Ghent Altarpiece closely resembles the apse representation formerly adorning the old basilica of St. Peter in Rome, and handed down to us in a copy

---

[218] By a happy coincidence, the existence of Professor Bandmann's study came to my attention in the course of a correspondence with him on another matter. Unfortunately I had failed to read it during my research for the present book. Nor had I noticed that his article was mentioned (and sternly rejected) in Panofsky 1953, I, p. 207, note 7 (printed on p. 443). I have cited it as "Bandmann, *Fassadenprogramm*" (cf. above note 127).

(Fig. 115). There we see not only the two-storied representation, but also the dual depiction of Christ, Who appears in the upper level as a human figure enthroned (Christ pre-existent) and in the lower as the Lamb (Christ the Sacrifice). There, too, just as in the altarpiece, the blessed of all nations are marching toward the Lamb. In the mosaic, however, they are not rendered in human form but are themselves depicted as lambs. But the setting of their procession is similarly characterized as the paradisial New Earth with trees, flowers and the many-towered city of the New Jerusalem.[219]

The representation of the dove as the Holy Spirit, which is, as we have seen, so important in the Ghent Altarpiece, can also be found in Early Christian apse mosaics. There too, the dove connects the upper and lower levels of the composition, linking the figure of the pre-existing Christ with that of the sacrificial Christ shown as the Lamb. According to the reconstruction, the dove must have appeared in the apse mosaic of St. Felix in Nola and also in the basilica of the Lateran in Rome.[220] It is still visible in the drawing made after the apse representation of S. Pudenziana before the present baldachin covered its lower part (Fig. 94). Even the Eyckian Fountain of Life is apparently based on the symbolic water which appears in many of the mosaics in the lower part of the representation. Four streams springing from the hill of the Lamb occur in the Nola composition and the mosaic of the Lateran basilica actually shows the motif of the watercourse as a fountain of life combined with the figures of drinking animals.

This combination is best known to the art historian from a number of Carolingian miniatures (Fig. 111). It is, indeed, not impossible that the fountain in the Ghent Altarpiece was a detail mainly inspired by early mediaeval book illumination. But this does not mean that the miniatures were the source of Van Eyck's total composition as well. The basis of the Eyckian program was undoubtedly his direct contact with the old monumental art. It is true that this art was still alive in the North in Carolingian times, as the dome mosaic of the famous palace chapel in Aix-la-Chapelle proves.[221] But quite apart from the fact that the original program of this dome mosaic was no longer intact in Van Eyck's time, it is rather unlikely that the painter's inspiration was the Carolingian art of the North.

No doubt it was instead the Christian antiquity itself which had influenced the great fifteenth century painter. We have to keep in mind that the realistic settings of Jan's scenes were intended to suggest the historical surrounding of Christ's own time. Thus, to Van Eyck, the art of the Christian antiquity must have appeared as a most desirable "authentic" source for it. While Jan's ancient architecture looks Romanesque to us and was unques-

---

[219] For the relationship of the program in the Ghent Altarpiece to those of the apse mosaics, cf. Bandmann, *Fassadenprogramm*, p. 17 *passim*, with additional Early Christian works illustrated in figs. 5-14.

[220] *Ibid.*, figs. 5, 6, and 7. For Bandmann's and other authors' discussions of the motif, cf. above notes 127, 138, and 151.

[221] Cf. above note 143.

tionably derived, at least in part, from Romanesque forms, we nevertheless have indications that the painter must have imitated Early Christian architecture as well. There is one architectural motif which appears again and again in Van Eyck's interiors but occurs, so far as I know, neither in Gothic and Romanesque buildings nor in any Carolingian edifice. I refer to the strange combination of a free-standing marble column with a slim and rather high cubiform base which raises the column as though on a pedestal. The motif, used for instance in the Dresden triptych and the Van der Paele Madonna, is obviously antique (Figs. 128 and 139). It is especially characteristic of the buildings of the Constantinian era.[222] Apparently, this combination had occurred in the side aisle arcade of the Lateran basilica in Rome as well as in some of the Early Christian churches in Palestine (Figs. 116 and 114). The strong possibility of Jan's having traveled to one or both of these places will be discussed in Chapter 5 of this study. At this point, suffice it to say that the connection between Eyckian and Constantinian art, so brilliantly pointed out by Bandmann, was most probably based on the painter's direct knowledge of the latter.

Following the programs of the great Early Christian apse mosaics, the Ghent Altarpiece clearly reveals its high purpose. The retable demonstrates its position as the most important image in the most sacred part of a sanctuary. Though replacing, so to speak, an ancient mosaic decoration, the Ghent polyptych does not actually imitate this decoration, or rather, it does not imitate the mosaic alone. We have seen that the frame of the altarpiece simulated a sculptural reliquary structure, in other words an object placed in the apse of a church and thus in front of the apse mosaic. A renewed glance at Dughet's fresco of the Lateran basilica reveals how in Van Eyck's time the mosaic-decorated apse wall

[222] The motif, which is best known from the Arch of Constantine in Rome (with engaged socles), does not occur, so far as I know, in Italian Renaissance architecture before the second half of the fifteenth century. It is thus not possible that Jan took it from the Italian art of his time. There is, of course, always the possibility that Jan became acquainted with this motif not through actual buildings but through paintings presenting architecture. Compare above note 175. Roman wall paintings very often show high socles for their columns (for instance those in the House of Livia) or place their columns on dado-like parapets as does Jan van Eyck. But even a contact with the pictorial tradition of antiquity would presuppose Jan's travel to a country where examples of this tradition could still be seen. The fascination of Early Netherlandish painters with Roman wall painting is evident in an interesting dedication miniature in Ms. fr. no. 2985 of the Bibliothèque Nationale (Fig. 113). This miniature, which appears in a book treating a contemporary "Odyssey," is obviously based on an example of the famous antique Odyssey cycle which must have existed in many copies but is today preserved only in the wall paintings from a house on the Esquiline and now in the Vatican Collection (Fig. 112). In a comparison of the wall paintings with the miniature, special attention should be paid to the very similar manner in which a continuous landscape is seen behind framing foreground columns, to the formations of the rocks, and to the treatment of the sea and the ships (especially in the scene of the Lestrigonians). It may also be instructive to compare these antique wall paintings with the column-framed Eyckian landscape as it appears in the Antwerp copy of the Ghent Altarpiece (Figs. 33 and 34). In the much discussed porch motif which Jan used in the lower zone of the interior view of his polyptych, the painter obviously imitated antique architectural elements. These elements, by the way, could often be found in Early Christian mosaics too. Cf. Fig. 91.

must have foiled the huge, two-level, Gothic reliquary altar which was set in front of this wall (Fig. 116). Clearly the Ghent Altarpiece was intended to convey the ideas of both. Even the unusual form of the Vijd retable, which shows a paradisaic view behind an open-work architecture, repeats the basic arrangement as it once existed in the apse of the Roman basilica.[223]

But the program of the Ghent polyptych far exceeds the Early Christian programs in scope and intricacy. Our reconstruction and iconogaphic analysis of the altarpiece has revealed its universal character. Showing Paradise above, Hell below, and including as the representatives of our earth the real congregation in the Vijd chapel, the Eyckian program was intended to mirror the Christian universe complete. With a multitude of themes intricately wrought into one, the work in fact aimed at duplicating the total scope of a Gothic cathedral rather than merely repeating the apse representation of a Constantinian church. Indeed, the three themes comprised in the total program of the polyptych—the Eternal Mass, the Mystical Wedding, and the Last Judgment—present, as it were, the combined ideas of all three sets of portals in Chartres Cathedral, fusing the programs of Chartres West, North, and South into a single unit.[224]

This all-embracing scope is, of course, the direct consequence of the fact that the altar structure as a whole signifies the Heavenly Jerusalem, a meaning which enables the work to be the equivalent, as it were, of the large church building. This meaning also explains the seemingly incongruous placement of unmatching numbers of panels, which was shown at the beginning of our study to be the basis for the recent theory concerning a change of plan. Obviously the arrangement was designed to allow a specific number of representations in each of the two major views (Figs. 1 and 2). When the polyptych is opened, we have seven panels above and five below; when it is closed, we see three levels of representations: four below with the donors and their saints, four in the Annunciation of the central level, and four under the crowning arches showing the sibyls and the prophets. It can hardly be a coincidence that these subjects total twelve in each case. A numerical symbolism was certainly intended here. Its meaning, in fact, is quite obvious if one recalls the famous passage on the City of God which provided the numerical basis for the construction of the abbey church of St. Denis and which was extensively quoted by Abbot

---

[223] It has already been conjectured by Bandmann (*Fassadenprogramm*, p. 18) that the Gothic altarpiece may have come to replace the Early Christian apse mosaic in the course of the evolution. But even as a phenomenon within a general development following this trend, the Ghent Altarpiece was most certainly a special case in that it deliberately imitated the arrangement of an ancient apse. The Gothic two-storied reliquary structure of the Lateran basilica which we see in the Dughet mural is preserved in the present church but not in its original place. It is discussed and reproduced in Braun, *op.cit.*, 1924, II, p. 260 and plate 169. Perhaps this altar structure in the Lateran Church—in addition to the Northern reliquary edifices (St. Denis; Sainte Chapelle in Paris) and to the Northern ciborium altars—had helped Jan in crystallizing his ideas for the basic form of his Ghent Altarpiece.

[224] Cf. Katzenellenbogen, *op.cit.*, plates 2, 43, and 64.

Suger in his famous description of his building.[225] According to Ephesians 2:20, the structure of the Heavenly City is made up of Christ as the cornerstone, along with the prophets and His apostles. No doubt, in the Ghent Altarpiece, the twelve representations on the exterior of the wings presented the prophets, the twelve panels seen in the interior the apostles. Christ, the cornerstone, is, of course, each time embodied in the stone mensa.

Ideas familiar from the construction of a church edifice are here used for the construction of an altarpiece. Like a Gothic cathedral building, the Vijd altar is replete with representations. In the Gothic churches, the regions singled out to be adorned with figures and scenes were always the portal zones. The most lavish sculptural decorations were concentrated at the entrances to the nave and to the transept, and on the rood-screen, which is the entrance to the choir. A profusion of embellishments was applied to these portal zones because each was regarded as a sacred threshold which led to a realm of increased holiness. The Ghent Altarpiece simulates such a threshold zone. It leads to an illusionary realm of heavenly bliss. Behind a structure, partly sculptured, partly painted, the believer sees a representation of Paradise more "real" and more convincing than the symbolic architecture of a Gothic cathedral choir could offer. The edifice erected in the Vijd chapel though itself simulating the Heavenly Cathedral, was thus at the same time only a threshold zone: not the structure itself but the views behind it formed the celestial realm in the purest sense. As the image not only of the Heavenly Jerusalem but also of its "imitation," the Gothic cathedral, the Ghent edifice was both the heavenly region itself and the threshold leading to it. It is this intrinsic dualism which accounts for the most complex interlinking of different realms of reality in the paintings and which explains why the scenes appear partly in and partly behind the structure.[226]

Only through the ingenious fusion of architecture, sculpture, and painting could the materialization of this ambitious concept be achieved. As a result of this fusion a tremendous range of ideas was expressed in a relatively small area of space and in a relatively subordinate part of the church. It was, however, not this combination alone which made a work of such an enormous scope possible within the narrow spatial limits. The fact that a new type of painting was used, an art able to add a vast and convincing illusionary distance to the work, was also of the greatest importance.[227] Moreover, there is a third basis for

[225] Cf. above note 120. As far as I know, it has never been observed before that the subjects are twelve in the interior and also twelve in the exterior view of the altarpiece and that this dual appearance of the sacred number must have a symbolic reason. As long as scholars took the work as not completed according to a predetermined plan, this observation would, indeed, have been without meaning. The numerical symbolism in the over-all organization of subjects was observed and kindly brought to my attention by Jan Swan.

[226] This duality has an important effect on the formal treatment of the painted scenes, a phenomenon which will be discussed below in the first pages of Chapter 4.

[227] The interrelation between the new form and the new iconography in the Eyckian work will be discussed below in the first pages of Chapter 5.

this immense range, namely an entirely new use of the time factor. By the turning of the panels within an elaborate mechanism, a large program could successively unfold in a single limited area of space.

We have seen that, in contrast to the present usage, a large variety of differing views had originally been exhibited in the Ghent Altarpiece. The views were changed, as the reader may recall, not only from time to time to fit the different feasts of the ecclesiastical year, but also in a more rapid succession when a special performance was presented to a tourist or to the inhabitants of the city. The retable, in other words, could offer a kind of mechanical mystery show. Our iconographic analysis now furnishes us with further insights into the nature of this performance. The program of the Annunciation scene contains the most revealing clues to its operation in this respect. As a scene with a two-leveled iconography which signifies not only Christ's Incarnation but also His Sacred Wedding with the Church, the Annunciation had, no doubt, a dual function within the show. Presenting the initial fact of the story of man's Redemption, the scene was certainly the beginning of the performance. It was, however, also its climactic end. Revealing the interior of the golden Ark which contained the highest mystery of Christianity, the Annunciation scene would disclose its total impact only when seen after the closed Ark with the Deësis figures had previously been shown. When, after fully opening the entire retable, the upper wings were closed again, a renewed climax of the performance was reached. At that point, both of the "open views" were shown together: the Adoration of the Lamb which is the solemn celebration of the Eternal Mass, and the Annunciation scene which, as the Sacred Wedding of the Church, shows the reason for this celebration.[228] After that, the lower wings had only to be closed in order again to arrive at the starting point of the performance.

No doubt, the Ghent panels were designed for a cyclic movement analogous to the working of the cosmos. The motion returns to its own beginning; it is really without start or ending and clearly intended for infinite repetition. Keeping in mind that to effect the complicated movement of the individual panels even by hand would have required quite an elaborate mechanism, the question soon suggests itself of whether the turning of the panels was not perhaps actually done mechanically. Is it not possible that the movement was automatic, and could operate by itself once the mechanism was set at a special position?

In principle, we have to answer this question in the affirmative. It is quite possible for the panels to have been operated by a kind of clockwork. We have only to recall the outspoken predilection which the Middle Ages had for the automaton.[229] The vogue of

[228] The combination of these two "open views" was, of course, important also because it presented the two main facts of Christian doctrine—Christ's Incarnation and His sacrificial death—at the same time.
[229] Cf. Alfred Chapuis and Edouard Gélis, *Le monde des automates*, Paris 1928, I, especially chapter v,

the large astronomical clock, which can be traced back to the fourteenth century in such impressive structures as the work by Giovanni Dondi (1364) or the earliest clock in Strasbourg (1354), came to a first flowering in the fifteenth century with the immense automata in the churches of Prague, Danzig, and Lübeck.[230] These early self-operating machines included not only moving figurines but the appealing feature of a chime-work. While the huge wheels of the clocks were usually entirely or at least partly hidden, their movement was revealed to the onlooker by the motion of figures which could be seen and by the melodies which could be heard. The clocks, in other words, brought forth music. And this is a point which seems to be of utmost importance for the Ghent Altarpiece.

It was not only chime music which could be produced mechanically; wind instruments, as for instance, the pipe valves of mechanical organs, could also be operated by automata.[231] Thus, the assumption that the miracle machine of Jodocus Vijd had provided an automated concert is close at hand. It becomes all the more likely when we consider the prominence given to the musicians in the Ghent retable (Figs. 1, 117, and 118). Clearly these two groups of musical angels try very hard to convince us, not that we hear a sound which is not actually there, but rather that a sound which we really hear is produced by their instruments and their voices. Panofsky, in his great sensitivity not only for the visual arts but also for music, seemed to have sensed this point when he suggested that the angel panels may have originally been the wings of an organ. Although I do not accept his theory of which this suggestion is a part, I, too, believe that the structure to which these panels belonged produced music.[232] But I think that this work was the Ghent Altar itself. A large clock-work installed within the sturdy structure behind the polyptych may not

---

vi, and vii, and Alfred Chapuis and Edmond Droz, *Automata*, London 1958. It is interesting to note that the taste for automatic operation included—in a manner which may seem rather sacrilegious to a modern mind—holy objects and religious representations, such as the figures of the crucified Christ and the crucified thieves. (Donatello's early crucifix in S. Croce in Florence, though perhaps not operated automatically, obviously belonged to the same category of "articulated Christ figures," cf. H. W. Janson, *The Sculpture of Donatello*, Princeton 1963, p. 9.) There is even an altarpiece (dating from the Baroque) whose parts were moved by machinery. The trend, however, was most prominent, of course, in the secular decoration used in court festivals, and was particularly striking in the feasts of the Burgundian Dukes, where such mechanical marvels as living birds flying from the mouth of a dragon conquered by Hercules formed part of the attractions. Cf. Johan Huizinga, *The Waning of the Middle Ages*, London 1952, p. 232. Prof. Hanna Deinhard was kind enough to bring this example to my attention.

[230] Cf. Ernst Bassermann-Jordan, *Die Geschichte der Räderuhr*, Frankfort-on-the-Main 1905, pp. 13-28; Alfred Ungerer, *Les horloges d'edifices*, Paris 1926; Chapuis and Gélis, *op.cit.*, 1, pp. 115f; and Alfred Ungerer, *Les horloges astronomiques et monumentales les plus remarquables de l'Antiquité jusqu' à nos jours*, Strasbourg 1931.

[231] Cf. Constantin Schneider, "Die Musikstücke des Orgelwerkes im mechanischen Theater zu Hellbrunn," *Mitteilungen der Gesellschaft für Salzburger Landeskunde*, LXII, 1927, pp. 169-75, and Joh. Ev. Engl, *Das Hornwerk auf Hohensalzburg, dessen Geschichte und Musikstücke*, 2nd ed., Salzburg 1909.

[232] Panofsky 1953, 1, p. 221. Cf. above the text belonging to note 104.

only have operated the panels but may also have produced a melody which started or came to a particularly impressive passage as the upper wings of the retable were opened.[233]

This final conjecture as to the original form of the Vijd altar will perhaps always remain an hypothesis. For there is no chance that the postulated clock-work will ever be found. Made of copper or brass, it was certainly confiscated and melted down together with all the other metal objects in all the churches in Ghent in 1578. Since the stone framework which enclosed the machine had in any case been demolished in the previous riots, there would have been no reason to spare this particular piece.[234] But while we cannot hope ever to recover the interesting old machine, our theory about it may help further research on the Ghent Altarpiece in one respect. It may lead us to learn more about the famous man whose name was mentioned together with Jan in the original inscription. We have seen that this artist must have been a sculptor. Now we may further suppose that he was also an ingenious mechanic and inventor, a forerunner, as it were, of Leonardo and Grünewald. Information as to his identity might perhaps be found on the basis of this conjecture. No doubt, in his time, his fame was greater by far than that of Jan. His honorarium, too, may have considerably exceeded that which was granted to the painter. No wonder then that Jodocus Vijd, in his inscription, mentioned the name of this artist first and gave him the greatest praise.

[233] It seems that De Bast (without, of course, thinking of mechanical music) had a similar idea when he wrote: "Dans les premiers temps, les volets s'ouvraient pendant la cérémonie de la messe, usage qui devint incommode par la suite, lorsqu'on plaça sur les autels des cierges, des fleurs et d'autres ornements, ce qui n'a eu lieu généralement qu'au xvme siècle, les miniatures des livres de prières de ce temps, peuvent à cet égard, servir ce renseignement." Waagen and De Bast, *op.cit.*, p. 3, end of note 2. If, as De Bast apparently takes for granted, the retable was opened during Mass, it was at that point that the believer saw the music-making angels and received the impression of heavenly melodies.

[234] Cf. above notes 56-62 and the text belonging to them. For the document telling us about the confiscating of all the metal work, cf. Coremans, *op.cit.*, no. 15, p. 37.

CHAPTER 4

Towards Criteria for Judging Eyckian Works

I. THE QUESTION OF CHRONOLOGY

OUR reconstruction not only clarifies the iconography of the Ghent Altarpiece, it also provides the key to an understanding of the basic form of the paintings. A curious ambiguity in some of the figures and scenes explains itself when we realize that they belonged to a sculptural structure which was meant to form a threshold zone between the real space of the Vijd chapel and an imagined space behind it. The paintings were inserted into a frame which was a sculptured three-dimensional object. This object acted as a screen between the real architecture and the imagined chancel of the imagined heavenly cathedral into which the chapel of Jodocus Vijd had been transformed by an illusionistic art. A distinction is made between the figures and scenes presented as directly enclosed in the screen and those meant to appear behind it.[235] The former, intended as part of a sculptured church object, automatically turned into a sort of simulated sculpture.

This transformation is obvious where the painted figures are stone-colored as, for instance, in the reliefs above Adam and Eve or the statues of the two SS. John (Figs. 107, 108, and 2). But even the colored figures placed in the shallow niches of the structure assume the appearance of sculpture at least in their position and attitude. This impression is most distinct in the figures of Adam and Eve, which belong to the outer stone structure and whose material existence in the space of the spectator is stressed by the view from below

[235] The first category is composed of those representations which are either part of the framing structure or are enclosed in the structure. The second category comprises the scenes that provide a view into the distance. As far as the second category is concerned, it consists simply of the entire five-part Adoration of the Lamb and the background of the Annunciation scene. The first category, however, with its two subdivisions is made up of rather diversified elements. The first subdivision consists of the group of Ecclesia and Synagoga, the scenes of Cain and Abel, and the statutes of the two SS. John, all of which belong directly and physically to the stone structure. But it also consists of Adam and Eve and the donors, who belong to it although less literally. The second subdivision is composed on the one hand of the Angels, who are placed directly in the structure, and on the other hand of the Deësis group and the Annunciation figures, who are placed in it because they belong to a sacred object enclosed in it. Cf. Chapter I, Part II (the texts following note 33 and note 46), Chapter 3, Part IV (the text following note 168 and the end of that part) and Part V (the text following note 205 and especially the text which belongs to note 226).

from which they are depicted. Yet, the Deësis figures in the niches of the golden shrine, although belonging to a more remote and more sacred realm, also bear a certain resemblance to sculpture. This quality is quite consistent with their placement on the façade of a house-shaped reliquary, a holy object which is normally adorned with statues (Figs. 41 and 6). The sculptural character is especially striking in those figures that appear as "busts." Above the Angel and the Virgin of the Annunciation scene, we see two niches, each of which encloses the upper torso of a prophet. The space of the niches denies the possibility that the lower parts of their bodies exist but are merely concealed; the two figures can only be half-length statues which have miraculously come to life (Fig. 2).

Even the Angel and the Virgin along with the entire foreground of Van Eyck's Annunciation, although occupying a larger and much deeper space than that of any of the various niches, are conceived as being enclosed in the sculptural screen. The space and the figures, therefore, have a sculptural character (Fig. 81). We mentioned in the previous chapter that this foreground space in the Annunciation has the look of a relic or sculpture compartment in a piece of ecclesiastical furniture. The space is rendered as a real recess materially appearing in the stone structure.[236] It is because they are in this place that the Angel and the Annunciate have the quality of stone carving. This is the reason for their sparse coloring and the closed heavy forms of their drapery, and also for their scale, which makes them unable to stand erect in the low-ceilinged Annunciation room.

At the same time, these two figures—and, for that matter, all the other foreground figures which are rendered in full color—are not just "sculpture" but living persons as well. The foreground space in the Annunciation is not only a recess for statues; it is also a human domicile. The *trompe l'œil* does not really turn the figures into stone carving. Rather, it heightens the impression of their immediate physical presence, without diminishing the effect of real life. As described before, the back wall of their box-shaped recess is perforated to permit a glance at the infinite space behind it. The atmospheric distance of the sunlit cityscape convinces us that we see a living scene, not merely a sculptural shrine. It is, however, not the infinite space of the background alone which transforms the shrine into a chamber and the protagonists into living persons. Van Eyck's lifelike treatment of visual forms prevents us from taking them for a mere imitation of statues.

In fact, the painter has quite particularly stressed such nonsculptural values as a breathing human skin or a mass of hair which, constituted as it is by myriads of dainty filaments, is a noncompact form loosened by countless air-filled interstices and brought

---

[236] This impression remains prominent despite the city view in the rear, which expands the picture space to an endless distance. Interestingly enough, there is also a foreground window in the Ghent Annunciation. Appearing in the right side wall near the Madonna, it certainly functions as her symbol (the Virgin is the *fenestra coeli*, compare above note 183). But Van Eyck, in his brilliant penetration of the problems in spatial concepts, left the foreground window without a view, thus preserving for the area the character of a boxlike shrine.

to vibrant life by the sparkle of a living light. He depicts the presence of the Deity in the glowing pools of light cast by the sun on the walls of a human habitation. Views as enchanting as our physical eye can experience here on earth are used to present a spiritual truth. Up to the time of Van Eyck the grand forms of ecclesiastical architecture and ecclesiastical sculpture were thought to be the most suitable expression of divine reality. Now a different form for it was found in the new art of illusionistic painting. Though Van Eyck must have felt that his art could surpass the accomplishments of the two great, time-honored media, he still disguised his painted images as the tangible shapes of architecture and sculpture. His new art could do even that. Indeed, the new medium is so powerful that Van Eyck's painted figures are perfectly convincing in spite of their ambiguous character resulting from the painter's two-fold intent.

The nature and origin of the two contrasting trends which brought about the described ambiguity of form can be clearly determined. The Vijd altarpiece as reconstructed in our study shows us how and where each trend dominates the composition and demonstrates why it is only in the foreground that we see the effects of both. The trend which transforms the images into sculpture has its origin in the foreground; that which creates paintings pure and simple works from the rear. Since it is the foreground which is closest to the sculptural frame and the tangible reality of the chapel architecture, the foreground elements, conceived as belonging to these materially real forms, assume the aspect of sculpture. In the background, however, a purely imagined visionary world opens to the spectator. We are there presented with the "natural" reality of Paradise, rather than with its symbolization in sacred arts.[237] When the "real" reality of the background penetrates even the foreground forms, it there fuses with the counter force which tends to convert the forms into sculpture.

With the artistic concepts underlying the paintings of the Ghent Altar seen in a new light, a new answer may now be found to the old question concerning the historical position of the work within the evolution of Northern altar painting in general and within the development of Van Eyck's art in particular. The Ghent retable is the earliest Eyckian work to show a written date. The dates that appear on Van Eyck's panels cover only the short span of time between the years 1432 and 1439. But the sources that mention his working as a full-fledged painter start with the year 1422. Thus, in addition to our knowledge that he became court painter to Philip the Good in 1425, we also know that Jan must have been a master by 1422. No wonder then that, instead of fitting his undated works into the narrow limits between 1432 and 1439, scholars have attempted to distribute them over the whole time from 1422 to 1441 (the year of his death). Influenced by the early

[237] For Van Eyck's combined portrayal of Paradise as it really is and Paradise as it appears in ecclesiastical architecture, cf. above the text belonging to note 22.

birth date which Van Mander gave to Jan, they have even included a period before 1422 in the Eyckian chronology.

With regard to the Ghent Altarpiece, this procedure has accorded the great work a position neither particularly outstanding in the career of the painter nor especially significant for his artistic development. Followed as well as preceded by works which are not very different from it, the great polyptych seemed to be just another example of Van Eyck's illusionistic art. However, it is by no means certain that this view is correct. Its validity becomes all the more doubtful when we look at the criteria usually employed in recent chronological attempts. Far from considering the specific artistic objectives which occupied painters between 1420 and 1440, scholars still took their criteria from historical insights made in decades long past and now become obsolete.[238]

The position which the Ghent Altarpiece holds within the Eyckian oeuvre may not be quite so unimportant as the present chronologies imply. Although the phenomenon is not generally recognized in art history, in fifteenth century painting especially in the North, the fact is that, in general, it is almost exclusively from the work of an artist's late period that we have the examples which have been handed down to us.[239] Obsessed with the modern curiosity concerning the early creations of great masters—a trend which often promotes a mediocre school work to the undeserved status of a youthful product of the master himself—we tend to forget that a late and characteristic work of a famous painter always had the best chance for survival. Theoretically, therefore, it is quite possible for the preserved undated work of Jan to belong in its entirety to the last decade of the master's life. If it actually does belong there, it must at once radically change our view of the position and significance of the Ghent Altarpiece within the Eyckian oeuvre. In the following discussion, the reader should keep in mind that the objective is by no means to set a new chronology which neatly places each undated work into a specific time compartment. My

[238] A detailed knowledge of the general direction of a development, i.e. of the specific trends and aspirations of a time, is the irremissible prerequisite for establishing the chronology of the undated works created by an artist of the period. Where our apprehension of the first decades of the fifteenth century is as hazy as it is, the all too simplified view resulting from our superficial knowledge may be misleading when applied to the work of an individual artist. We shall presently see that the usual procedure, which is simply to date an Eyckian work according to its presumed similarity or dissimilarity with the forms of the International Style—a method which has led to gross errors—should have been discarded after the discovery of the work of the Master of Flémalle.

[239] In the North, our possession of a "complete œuvre" of a master starts with Dürer; and even Dürer is an exception in his particular period. Nevertheless, it is still a trend most prominent in modern art history to insist on a "complete œuvre" (as we have it for Rubens or Rembrandt) at all costs and even in a time during which works are only sparingly preserved. The results of this wishful thinking, the beautifully complete lists of the works of fifteenth century masters, are still readily and generally accepted. But they are often incorrect, as are especially those long catalogues of early works which sometimes consist chiefly of mediocre copies.

aim is both more modest and more general. I want simply to test the material for basic criteria which allow us to place a work before or after the Ghent Altarpiece.

The very fact that the paintings of the Ghent Altar were inserted into a sculptural screen and were themselves meant to imitate sculpture may indicate that they are earlier than almost all of the other compositions signed by or attributed to Jan. None of his other paintings has a pseudo-sculptural character or is enclosed in a sculptural frame. True, the particular form of the Ghent Altarpiece was the result of a specific solution to a unique problem posed by Jodocus Vijd's commission. But we have to bear in mind that the very uniqueness of this solution was not simply the automatic consequence of the problems posed. It was the choice of the artist's creative mind.

A work of art is rooted in the sum total of similar artistic solutions of a previous time as they were known and accepted by the artist. It presents the artist's adaptation of these solutions to his specific task and transforms them according to his personal artistic creed. In the hands of a very great master this process often results in a work of exciting novelty which then, for its part, becomes the basis of later art productions by the artist himself or by others. Three factors, therefore, are involved in determining the position of a certain work of art within the historical development of the artist and his time: the setting forth of the previous artistic solutions; the description of the nature and degree of their adaptation in the work under examination; and the recognition of later solutions based on this work.

When attempting such an examination in the Ghent Altarpiece, which is composed of many diverse parts, we have to select that portion which gives the greatest promise of being revealing in all three respects. This kind of study can be successful only in a composition that can be compared with earlier and later works of the same type. The part of the Ghent Altarpiece which immediately suggests itself for such a comparative analysis is the Annunciation scene of the exterior view (Fig. 81).

II. THE APPLICATION OF CRITERIA

BECAUSE the art production of the time has come down to us through only a few fortuitously preserved examples, we naturally are familiar with only an infinitely small segment of the works that were known to Van Eyck. Nevertheless, one point is clear, namely that the basic type of altarpiece composition as we find it in the Ghent Annunciation already existed in Italy before the middle of the fourteenth century. Once we realize that Van Eyck's scene appeared behind an architectural screen-work constituted by the columns of a sculptural frame, we immediately see the close connection between the Netherlandish composition and an early Italian prototype as handed down to us in Pietro Lorenzetti's Birth of the Virgin in Siena (Fig. 121).

The artistic concepts underlying the Italian work may fruitfully be compared with the Ghent Annunciation, which was completed precisely ninety years later. In each a box-shaped foreground interior is rendered with the sculptural frame acting as its exterior view. That the interior in the older work consists of two sections is a difference of no great importance because here too the major section at least is shown as continuing behind the frame. As soon as one sees that the Ghent Annunciation was the direct heir of this early type of representation, one can understand the reason for the correction which Van Eyck made in the architecture of his Annunciation setting. The earlier design, which was sacrificed during the correction, is visible in the infra-red photographs published in 1953 (Figs. 122 and 123).[240]

In front of the ceiling beams along the upper margin of Van Eyck's Annunciation chamber, the painter had originally depicted a row of six free-hanging tracery arches which framed the scene with forms matching those that were used for the same purpose in the lower tier above the figures of the donor and the two SS. John (Fig. 2). Complementing the framing arches below by a matching motif above, Van Eyck had certainly heightened the unity of the exterior view of his polyptych. However, at the same time, he had inadvertently fallen victim to an error in spatial logic, for the stone framework as shown in the Ghent retable is not actually the front of the interior visible behind it. This interior is the inside of the golden reliquary. And when the stone architecture appeared nevertheless as though being its façade, this was because of the reliquary's being so tightly fitted into the outer structure. Van Eyck's use of the old pictorial type as we find it in the Lorenzetti work no doubt made the notion that the sculptural frame is the façade of the chamber so compelling to him that he momentarily forgot that his own construction was not really identical with that of the traditional type. To retain the spatial distinction between the stone framework and the interior of the golden shrine, Van Eyck then had to eliminate the six arches in the Annunciation scene.[241]

When we compare the work by Lorenzetti with the even earlier painting of the same subject in Giotto's Padua frescos, we see that the altarpiece looks like an enlarged detail of the older scene (Fig. 119). Giotto's Birth of the Virgin still shows an entire house; Lorenzetti restricts his representation to two rooms, but he still continues to show an architectural entity which claims to be complete with the frame now having the role of the façade (Fig. 121). Two features particularly characterize his representation: the interiors shown in the foreground appear in their full extension; and they are presented as though they were the only rooms in the house. These two qualities are reminiscent of the small-scale reproduction of a building as it may be seen in a doll house. The gold ground shown

[240] Coremans, *op.cit.*, pp. 119f and plate LXII.

[241] Since the six arches—which must have matched the corresponding forms below—were certainly stone-colored and could thus have belonged only to the outer stone structure framing the altarpiece, they would have had to be visible not only in the Annunciation scene but also in the Deësis panels. There, however, these arches would have been completely superfluous from the compositional point of view and, in fact, a rather disturbing element. This, perhaps, was the main reason why Jan finally eliminated the motif.

in the window openings of the foreground indicates an ideal space outside the rooms and further adds to the impression that the painting is the portrayal of a small-scale model rather than that of a segment of a real house.

Here, then, we have the germ of the Eyckian concept that the foreground is a recess for sculpture. Indeed, even the extension of this foreground space into a realm distinctly different in character can already be found in the Lorenzetti work. Behind the vestibule depicted in the left section we see delightful architectural details obviously meant as the inner courtyard of the house. The architecture of the background has a door and several window openings. These apertures do not show a gold ground but are filled instead with a black paint that may have originally been dark blue. The same color also appears in some of the openings of the main room. For instance, it fills the diamond shape of the window to the left which faces toward the courtyard and it also appears in the doorway to the right. Clearly, this is an archaic attempt to add a different dimension to the space of the foreground box which, by means of the gold ground and the meticulously complete rendering of each room, suggests a sacred compartment materially existing behind the frame.

In Lorenzetti's altarpiece, no view of a street or a garden, or even the image of clouds, appears in any of the window or door openings. There is an absolute void behind all the parts of the structure depicted. The pictorial space, therefore, is conceived as extending no farther than the areas actually filled by the various elements of the representation. It, in other words, does not extend beyond the factually visible forms. True, the courtyard is a somewhat fragmentary view whose continuation in nonvisible parts of the painting is implied. But we are dealing here with background forms which are overlapped by those of the foreground. The foreground itself is rendered in full view and part of it covers the "missing" background section. The idea governing the composition, therefore, is that of the intrinsic completeness of a "representation" which appears in the void of a "non-representation." This archaic concept will in the following discussion be called the "concept of limited space."

A characteristic feature often found in the painted foreground of works based on this concept is perhaps worth mentioning at this point. Even in the foreground, some minor parts can be omitted at the borders. These parts are concealed by the picture frame, which is regarded as the foremost form and the foregound proper. In the Lorenzetti altarpiece, we best see this phenomenon on the right side of the triptych. A small portion of the right side wall as well as of the figure of the gift-carrying woman is cut off by the frame. Under no circumstances are we to read this feature as an indication that the foreground space extends beyond the painted room. In other words, by no means should we imagine an adjoining chamber with a door leading to the one we see. The gift-carrying couple has obviously entered the room not through such an imagined door but through the door which is visible in the back wall.

Interestingly enough, a similar overlapping of the foreground space by the frame is found in the Ghent Annunciation (Fig. 81). On the right side, the wall and some furniture elements, as well as a book and the window, are slightly cut by the frame. In the Van Eyck painting, too, this slight overlapping of the foreground is no serious impairment to the completeness of the view. The foreground space is fundamentally still the same complete and limited expanse that we find in the Lorenzetti retable. Floor, ceiling, and side walls of Van Eyck's Annunciation room are fully visible and are terminated in front by a frame characterized as materially belonging to the painted representation and thus functioning as the foreground proper. The very fact that the small window on the right is overlapped by the frame has freed the painter from the obligation to show any kind of view through it and thus has added to the impression of limited space.

Van Eyck, of course, has introduced important modifications in his use of the old concept of limited space. Some of these changes must already have existed in the art production of his own region and time, which, though firmly based on the Italian heritage, had developed many innovations in the concept of pictorial space as well as in the observation and imitation of nature. A few paintings ascribed to Malouel and one enchanting work by Broederlam indicate that a Netherlandish altarpiece production of exquisite quality must have existed in the time before and around 1400.[242] While this production is now almost totally lost, book illumination of the time tells us much about the nature and degree of the transformation which the type under discussion had undergone by the beginning of the fifteenth century. The art of the so-called Master of the Boucicaut Hours and his atelier is particularly revealing for the use and modification of this type in the North.

A miniature of the Boucicaut Master's workshop showing the Madonna with a female donor presents an early attempt to depict an unlimited distance behind the open rear wall of the foreground space (Fig. 120). An imposing colonnade replaces this wall in its full extension revealing a "distance" constituted by some charming garden elements. We now have a background with a landscape, which means that the setting is no longer surrounded by a void as it is in the Lorenzetti painting.[243] However, the viewer is not completely convinced that the scenery extends into infinite space. The garden elements do not really have the character of an atmospheric view.[244] Rather, they give the appearance of

[242] For the original existence of a magnificent pre-Eyckian altarpiece production in the Netherlands as concluded from the written sources and a few remaining examples, cf. Friedländer-Veronee, I, Introduction, pp. 19-23.

[243] Not only the rear openings of the room shown in the miniature but also its side openings reveal a blue sky or landscape elements. The location of these details corresponds precisely to the various areas of gold ground seen through the windows in the Lorenzetti painting. In the course of the development, the gold ground—which is "non-representation"—has been reinterpreted, as it were, to form a secondary category of "representation."

[244] However, in other miniatures of the time, especially in those by the Boucicaut Master himself, rather convincing atmospheric views are already found. Cf., for instance, Panofsky 1953, II, plate 27.

a tapestry hung at the rear of the room thus limiting its space and keeping it the traditional "doll house," but one in which the back wall has been replaced, as it were, by a representation.

Several valiant attempts by the miniaturist to secure the continuation of the foreground space into that of the background and to demonstrate that both are parts of the same infinite picture reality remain without effect. Cleverly he shows the landscape elements not only in the rear but also in the door opening in the right wall. But the device is unsuccessful because the figure of the angel conceals the lower part of the doorway view, which is crucial to our being convinced that we see a real garden. Another of his attempts to demonstrate the continuation of space also fails. The artist tried to establish a link between foreground and background by placing a flowerpot on the window sill. But since he set the object on the inside of the sill and in front of the columns, he was still unable to counteract the tapestry character of the landscape. Not unless he had placed the object on the outside of the sill, that is on a part which projects into the open space behind, could we gain the unmistakable impression that the background is a real landscape.

This new principle was applied successfully, however, in the Joseph wing of the Mérode Altarpiece (Fig. 82). Between the foreground space and the background the Master of Flémalle inserted a small shelf holding a mousetrap. The unit reaches from the interior outward and makes it absolutely impossible for the spectator to interpret the window view as the rear wall of the box-shaped room. The shelf with the mousetrap, although only a small motif, is entirely sufficient to create the impression of a genuine spatial continuity between the foreground and the background of the setting.

The master's penetrating observation of nature and his ability to capture it in art was, of course, the major reason for his successful representation of continuous and infinite space. His interest in fashioning every detail of his painting into a true likeness of nature had, however, a rather disconcerting side effect on the totality of his image. At this early stage of the new realism, the painter approached his work on the basis of his piecemeal observation and imitation of nature. The forms thus recorded were later fitted together but without the use of a model for the whole. This procedure resulted in a rather awkward fragmentation of his objects and figures. In the two standing figures on the right in the Frankfort painting of the "Good Thief," the process is especially pronounced (Fig. 126). Here we see a marked fragmentation not only of the figures as a whole but of each individual form as well. Even a single face or hand is segmented. In his intense concentration on the details the master constantly shifted the angle from which he observed them, so that each individual part is seen from a different viewpoint.

In his search for new and more convincing forms, the master abandoned the over-all patterns traditionally used for figures in specific poses or actions, which had assumed particularly beautiful rhythmical configurations during the period of the International Style.

Forgoing these traditional over-all patterns without inventing new ones, the Master of Flémalle has often sacrificed a basic uniformity in his shapes. It is therefore not surprising that the master was also rather insensitive to the effects wrought by the use of heterogeneous methods in the construction of space. The Mérode triptych shows an ensemble of three settings apparently derived from three diverse traditional types. Differing radically in perspective, these settings combined form a rather artificial unit (Fig. 82). Adjusted to each other with obvious effort, their combination was meant to imbue the scenes with a certain unity of time and place.

Taken as a whole, the unit shows a curious similarity to the much older retable by Lorenzetti (Fig. 121).[245] In the Mérode Altarpiece, too, a box-like foreground space runs parallel to the picture plane in all three panels. In both triptychs, all three sections of the foreground belong to the same house, and the frame (not preserved in the Mérode Altarpiece) acts as the front of the building. In both, the setting of the panel to the left is a forecourt. In the Flémalle Altarpiece, it is only in the left wing and in the Joseph panel that there is shown a view into the distance which gives a suggestion of a space not directly belonging to the chambers of the house. The central composition with the Annunciation scene presents the traditional "doll house" with no explicit extension of the space into the distance. All five sides of the box which form the Annunciation chamber are fully visible and are terminated in front by the frame, which is distinctly conceived as the material boundary of the room and which thus functions as the actual front of the two side walls which separate this room from the forecourt and from Joseph's shop.[246]

[245] In both cases there is a house with a forecourt distributed in the proportions of three-to-one on the available picture area. But, whereas Lorenzetti's house consists of one large continuous room with a vestibule annexed to it (a type ultimately derived from Giotto and used by Lorenzetti also in his Last Supper of San Francesco in Assisi), the Mérode Altarpiece shows two separate rooms with a garden court added to them. This latter pattern, which now is a unit of three parts and thus most suitable for use in a triptych, presupposes, as it were, two successive adaptations of the same Italian type. As a first step, the type was used (in reversed order) to form the unit of the Annunciation room with Joseph's workshop annexed to it. Then, as a second step, the unit of the Annunciation room with the workshop—now taken as a whole—was, for its part, provided with a forecourt. This procedure by the Master of Flémalle seems to presuppose that the Lorenzetti type was absorbed in Northern art long before it was used in the Mérode Altarpiece. The unit of the Annunciation room with the workshop was apparently derived from a Northern work that had already employed the Lorenzetti type. But the addition of the garden court to this unit may have been due to a renewed influence from the same type now transmitted in a more "modern" version.

[246] The vertical parts of the retable's original frame now lost had thus apparently shown architectural motifs representing the front of the house. The architecture, however, may have mainly consisted of Gothic bundle piers (as we find them, for instance, in the frame of Rogier's altarpiece illustrated in Fig. 205), instead of resting on the heavy columns of the Lorenzetti retable (Fig. 121). But in any case, the architectural frame of the Mérode triptych must have clarified the design of the doorway leading from the garden court of the donor panel into the Annunciation room. The lost frame had certainly made it obvious that the door itself was hinged to the post nearer to the spectator, that is, to the pier indicated by the vertical part of the frame. Cf. above note 192.

The painter's original plan for a gold ground behind the window openings of the Annunciation room logically follows from his use of this archaic concept.[247] There are two different concepts employed in the Flémalle triptych: one of strictly limited space placed against a gold ground; the other of a foreground with extensions into distant views. This two-fold concept of a pictorial space is still derived from the old duality which we have seen in the Lorenzetti painting (Fig. 121). There, the ideal realm of a surrounding gold ground contrasted with the dark void of a different outside "space": the not represented space of the surrounding nature. In the Mérode Altarpiece, this "natural" space is now actually depicted and most effectively characterized as an infinite extension into the distance. A middle panel with a gold ground would have seriously clashed with the other two representations. No wonder then that the gold was eventually replaced by a blue sky. Nevertheless, in spite of its present window view of a blue sky with clouds, the Mérode Annunciation is distinctly based on the concept of "limited space."

This concept still persists in Van Eyck's Ghent Annunciation (Fig. 81). There too the Annunciaton chamber is clearly the traditional foreground box now reinterpreted by the painter in realistic terms as a recess containing sculpture. We now, indeed, can understand that the curious ambiguity of the Eyckian image as described at the beginning of this chapter is rooted in the tradition. The "sculptural" foreground section is derived from the box-shaped recess placed against the ideal gold ground; the background showing "painting pure and simple" is the natural space, which is indicated as a "void" in the Lorenzetti painting and presented in later works as a landscape or a city view.

Van Eyck's ingenious manner of fusing the two realms brings about a new unity in the art of painting. The foreground box is no longer simply "foiled" by the background view as it still is in the Boucicaut miniature; it is really opened at the rear. On the other hand, more like the Boucicaut representation, it is this entire box which is opened and not just the sides of the composition as in the Mérode Altarpiece. At the same time, the greatest attention is now paid to the smooth and gradual transition of the foreground space into the background.

In contrast to the Master of Flémalle, who inserted only the small motif of the shelf with the mousetrap as a link between the foreground and the background in the Joseph wing of his Mérode Altarpiece, Van Eyck has introduced an entire intermediate space level for this purpose. Two complete annex rooms appear between the Annunciation chamber and the distant view. Parts of this view are visible through the arcade of the main chamber while others are seen through the Gothic windows of the annex rooms, and the viewer has no doubt that he is confronted with a continuous and uniform space in the Annunciation by Van Eyck.

The device of showing parts of the same view through differently located openings

---

[247] For the gold ground originally covering the window openings, cf. the literature cited above in note 177.

was, as such, traditional in the North, for it was already used in the Boucicaut miniature which we have described (Fig. 120). But in the art of Van Eyck this device becomes truly effective because the distance is now seen through openings which occur in walls that run parallel one to another. I have suggested in a recent article that this particular form of the device may have been derived from the art of Jan's Italian contemporaries since we already find it around 1425 in Donatello's famous relief of the Feast of Herod (Fig. 125). Moreover, Van Eyck's new and methodical handling of perspective may also point to his acquaintance with the latest Italian art of his time.[248]

By contrast, the Mérode Annunciation betrays a pronounced inconsistency in its perspective construction. The older painter even vacillated between presenting his forms in a three-dimensional space or as a surface configuration on the picture plane, a problem which remains to be discussed in a later part of our study. Van Eyck, on the other hand, made a clear decision in favor of three-dimensional space. His new method of perspective construction allowed him to depict such a space in a most convincing manner. His system of perspective is not yet based on the scientific principle of directing all the orthogonals of the interior space towards a single vanishing point. There are still two "vanishing areas" used, one for the upper and one for the lower lines of his composition.[249] But nonetheless we have here for the first time in the North a methodical approach to the problem of perspective based on a preconceived system consistently followed by the artist. This method is well able to convey the impression of a uniform space.

Van Eyck's new systematic construction unifies the composition to a certain degree, but it does not bring about a perfect homogeneity of the space. Although striking when compared with the earlier Annunciation, the uniformity in Van Eyck's representation is actually only a relative one. The painter had not completely abandoned thinking in terms of segments when he designed his Ghent composition.[250] The space in this Annunciation

[248] Cf. above note 169. For the Italian influence on the art of Van Eyck, compare also above notes 94, 175 and the text belonging to note 188.

[249] The literature on the Eyckian method of perspective is given in my article cited above in note 169. For additional literature on perspective, cf. Carl Goldstein, "Studies in Seventeenth Century French Art Theory and Ceiling Painting," *The Art Bulletin*, XLVII, 2, June 1965, especially notes 83 and 89.

[250] Even in his later works Van Eyck never totally abandoned thinking in segments, either as far as his space construction is concerned or in his figure design. Remnants of this archaic way of thinking are still noticeable, for instance, in the Madonna of the Canon Van der Paele where the upper part of the figure of St. George appears in a picture plane which is much nearer to our eye than the one in which the legs of the saint are depicted (Fig. 139). When we become aware of the persistence of this ancient trend in the art of the great painter, our doubts as to the authenticity of such a marvelous composition as the small St. Francis receiving the Stigmata should be dispelled. These doubts were apparently mainly based on the obvious inconsistencies in the design of the kneeling saint, whose feet are shown in a rather distant space while his torso is much nearer to the spectator's eye. Cf. Panofsky 1953, I, p. 192 and II, plate 139. It is not the perfect but the relative unity in space construction and figure design which makes an Eyckian painting so convincingly real to us.

scene is not as yet really continuous; it does not present an uninterrupted expanse from the foremost region to the farthest distance. The space clearly develops in successive stages. Three levels—foreground, annex rooms, and cityscape—running parallel to the panel plane, constitute the total space. The basic distinction between these levels is emphasized by their illumination with the direction of their light changing, as we have discussed, from one level to the other.[251] The duality in the handling of light corresponds to that in the spatial concept which vacillates between infinite and limited space. Indeed, the very use of a limited foreground space, rendered as a recess materially existing behind the frame and physically terminated by it, betrays the essential dependence of the Ghent Annunciation on the earlier concepts.

An essentially unlimited interior space that is conceived as only a segment of an infinite picture reality is the achievement of a later time. In the remarkably advanced representation of Van Eyck's small altarpiece in Dresden, we see that kind of infinite space (Fig. 128). There, the frame limits and articulates our vision of the picture but it does not form the physical boundary of its space; neither in front nor on the sides does the frame materially terminate the depicted room. The inner perpendicular members of the frame, which form the front of the painted sidewalls in the Mérode Altarpiece, do not act in this capacity in the Dresden triptych. In the Dresden work, the three-aisled space of a basilica is the common setting for all three panels. The representation of these aisles is not restricted to the wings (as are the lateral scenes in the Mérode Altarpiece); it also appears in part in the central panel. In the Dresden work, furthermore, the panel cuts the space of the composition above and below in a manner which implies the forward extension of the space toward the viewer.

The foreground interiors of the Mérode Altarpiece and the Ghent Annunciation contain only as much space as one can see. The frame forms the material boundary of this space and, as such, it is an integral part of the painted representation. In the Dresden Altarpiece, on the other hand, there is far more space than is actually visible. The frame is in no sense a part of the representation itself but is a totally separate independent object which coincides in its three parts, as if by chance, with the three portions of space represented behind it. Fundamentally, then, the frame is now only the optical device through which one sees several segments of an infinite and continuous picture world. For the first time, we have a genuine pictorial microcosm which shares with the macrocosm of actual reality the qualities of being infinite and continuous.

But this microcosm is essentially distinct from the macrocosm of the real world and is a self-sustaining entity. The concrete connection of the picture world with the real world, as we still find it in the *trompe l'œil* of Van Eyck's Ghent Annunciation, is no longer necessary for the illusion of reality. This illusion now lies completely within the

[251] Cf. above Chapter 3, Part IV, the text preceding note 173.

painting itself. Through his contemplation of the picture, the spectator becomes detached from his own material visual surroundings and is transported into the pictorial realm created by the artist.

Through this entirely new concept the space in the Dresden triptych is both infinite and genuinely homogeneous. No longer does the painter conquer the space step by step in separate levels which gradually recede into the distance. The back wall of the building in the Dresden painting is closed. Now it can be closed, because the infinity of its space does not depend on a distant landscape or city view shown in the background. Its frame cuts the representation of the aisle of the basilica in such a way that we are permitted to see only a segment of it. The unlimited continuation of the picture space toward the sides and toward the front is thereby convincingly implied. The essential differentiation between a limited foreground space and an infinite background has been abolished; the fundamental segmentation of the total space has come to an end. Indeed, the new cohesiveness of the setting is underlined by the uniform illumination of the scene. The light is now consistently depicted as entering only through the various windows on the left of the basilica. This new homogeneous illumination used in a cohesive space brings the uniformity of the setting to perfection.

III. THE "CANONICAL" OEUVRE OF JAN

THE newly discovered date of 1437 on the Dresden Altarpiece totally contradicts the very early dating which many scholars had attached to the small work before its inscription was known. But the inscribed date is unquestionably authentic.[252] The small retable has to be later than the Ghent Altarpiece because of its much more advanced concept of space. The uniformity of the space and the homogeneity of its perspective and light further confirm the late date. Our present analysis has furnished us with a general notion of the direction which Jan's development must have taken, and gives us two important basic criteria for determining the approximate time in which an Eyckian work was created. In order to decide on the relative date of such a work we have to recognize the concept of space on which it is based—limited or infinite—and we have to evaluate the relative coherence of the elements in the composition—its setting, perspective, and light.

---

[252] Panofsky, 1953, I, p. 184. For the newly found date, cf. Henner Menz, "Zur Freilegung einer Inschrift auf dem Eyck-Altar der Dresdener Gemäldegalerie," *Jahrbuch 1959, Staatliche Kunstsammlungen Dresden,* pp. 28-29. Even after the discovery of the inscription, Panofsky still insisted on the correctness of his early dating of the Dresden triptych, claiming the unreliability of the inscribed date. When Jacqueline Folie, "Les œuvres authentifiées des primitifs Flamands," *Bulletin de l'Institut royal du Patrimoine artistique,* VI, 1963, pp. 195-96 gives a rather unfavorable report on the orthography and the form of the letters in that inscription, this judgment is not based on her own examination of the text but on information personally given to her by Panofsky. I am deeply grateful to Miss Folie not only for informing me on this point but also for her outstandingly efficient help liberally offered to me when I examined the X rays of the Ghent Altarpiece and checked the files of the Brussels Institute for material pertinent to the problems treated in the present study.

These criteria are very different from those hitherto used to establish an Eyckian chronology. It may, therefore, be instructive at this point to scrutinize the former criteria in order to understand how a work like the Dresden triptych could have been thought to be earlier than the Ghent Altarpiece.

A painting is usually attributed to the early period of Van Eyck for two reasons that are closely related. Since both have become part of what may be called our reservoir of subconscious art historical knowledge, they are not always expressly stated. One is the similarity of a work to the creations of the International Style; the other concerns its small scale which, in combination with a certain dainty explicitness of form, is thought to show a relationship to the art of book illumination.

The first reason has to do with the tendency of scholars to consider Eyckian art in the light of a development of European painting which is conceived, in an all too general and oversimplified manner, as an evolution from the poetic abstract linearism of the International Style to a new illusionistic realism. Jan's art is seen as directly derived from the former. This view seemed all the more natural because Van Mander had set the birth date for Hubert at approximately 1366 and that for Jan a number of years after this date. If one went on the assumption that Jan was Hubert's brother, Van Mander's information could only mean that the younger painter was born toward the end of the seventies, at the latest.[253] Consequently, any work by Jan in which the forms seemed to indicate a strong similarity to those of the International Style was dated earlier than others that less conspicuously show this relationship.

Curiously enough, the notion that Jan's art directly followed from the International Style was not modified even after the discovery of the work of the Master of Flémalle. The strong indication that this master was much older than Van Eyck (probably by a full generation) and the realization that even the earliest known paintings of this older master had outgrown the International Style, should have prompted at least a rethinking of the premises for forming an opinion concerning Jan's development. In fact, chances are that the very early birth date give to Jan by Van Mander is not even approximately right. A statement by Van Vaernewyk on this matter is far more likely to be correct. According to him, Van Eyck was a very young man when he died in 1441.[254] Therefore,

[253] Karel van Mander, *Het Leven der Doorluchtige Nederlandsche en eenige Hoogduitsche Schilders* (*Het Schilder-Boek*), ed. Haarlem and Alkmaar 1604, Amsterdam 1618. In the edition of Jacobus de Jongh, Amsterdam 1764, the passage appears in Vol. I, pp. 13-14: "en Joannes eenige jaren later geboren." In the English edition by Constant van de Wall, *Dutch and Flemish Painters*, New York 1936, p. 4, the translation of the text as "many years later" is not precise. It should read "a few years later."

[254] Marcus van Vaernewyck, *Den Spiegel der Nederlandscher audtheyt*, Ghent 1568 (completed 1561, amended 1565), fol. cxvii-cxix; ed. of 1829, ii, pp. 202-9: "Joannes is ionc overleden/ hadde hy noch moghen leuen hy hadde lichtelick alle Schilders der weerelt te bouen ghehaen." Cf. Dhanens, Inventaris vi, p. 115, and Documenten, p. 21. This information was taken from the ode by Lukas de Heere, a poem placed in

if Jan did not receive his training until the second decade of the fifteenth century, and doubtless at one of the great art centers, the International Style would no longer really have been the prime source of his art. Thus, when certain features of this style occur in some of his paintings, they may well represent a reintroduction of the older forms rather than a direct continuation of them.

The sporadic reappearance of characteristic features of an older style is a phenomenon occurring in many periods of art for many different reasons.[255] In the fifteenth century, traditional forms were often reused to heighten the sacredness of a painted image. Van Eyck, however, apparently employed elements of the International Style in order to counteract the typical form fragmentation which dominated the most advanced art of his time, such as that reflected in the work of the Master of Flémalle. Therefore, if the obvious similarities to the International Style in Eyckian works do not testify to the genuine archaic character of these works but are due instead to a deliberate re-use of older forms, their appearance would not necessarily have to be restricted to the earlier part of Van Eyck's career.

The second traditional criterium for the chronology of the Eyckian oeuvre is, in my opinion, as fallible as the first one. It stems from the dual assumption that fifteenth century altarpainting has its origin in book illumination and that Jan was an illuminator in his youth. The supposition that the young Jan van Eyck was a miniaturist is based on a particular interpretation of a passage which is found in a sixteenth century Italian letter. However, this information has to be treated with caution for, aside from a question as to the accuracy of this interpretation of the text, the essential reliability of a late and foreign source is always somewhat doubtful.[256] But, even assuming that the interpretation is correct and that the source is reliable, the small size of an Eyckian form or its similarity

---

the Vijd chapel in July 1559 and containing the following line about Jan: "Dese blomme zeer vrough vande weerelt schiet." Cf. *ibid.*, p. 36, and Dhanens, Inventaris VI, p. 107. Van Mander rejects this information. The problem of the date of Jan's birth will be treated in detail below in Chapter 5.

[255] Sometimes a historicizing purpose dictated the choice of an older form. When the statue of the Madonna painted in the left wing of the Werl Altarpiece (Panofsky 1953, II, plate 97) shows the style of the fourteenth century or when the gold retable in Lochner's Presentation in the Temple in Darmstadt (Otto H. Förster, *Stefan Lochner*, Frankfort-on-the-Main 1938, pp. 24 and 53) is rendered in an early version of the International Style, the painters have used an archaic mode in order to demonstrate that the art works they included in their scenes are "antiques." The very fact, however, that such an endeavor was possible in the fifteenth century is evidence of the new ability to recognize and imitate an earlier style. Even an entire painting could be deliberately based on the forms of a venerable old model. Cf., for instance, the two Madonnas illustrated in Panofsky 1953, I, plate 26. This historicizing trend, which was, as we have seen, the determining factor in Van Eyck's imitation of an ancient golden reliquary shrine in his Deësis panels of the Ghent Altarpiece, is discussed in my doctoral thesis (Freiburg i. Br.) Lotte Brand, *Stephan Lochners Hochaltar von St. Katharinen zu Köln*, printed in Hamburg 1938, Excursus II, pp. 70-72.

[256] Pietro Summonte (1463-1526), *Lettera a Marcantonio Michiel*. The passage occurs in a letter of March 20, 1524. Documenten, p. 15. For the evaluation of the information, cf. Friedländer-Veronee, I, p. 47.

to the detailed treatment in book illumination cannot safely be used as a criterium for the early date of an Eyckian work. Two of the smallest paintings by the hand of Jan (his panel of St. Barbara and the Madonna at the Fountain, both in Antwerp, Figs. 129 and 130) bear very late dates. Moreover, one of them, the panel with St. Barbara, shows a treatment especially similar to book illumination and closely related to some of the famous miniatures that are ascribed to Van Eyck in the so-called Turin-Milan Book of Hours (Figs. 131 and 132).[257]

Some scholars assert that these miniatures were created as early as the second decade of the fifteenth century.[258] This claim depends, of course, on an early birth date for Jan. But there was also another and very important reason for this early dating of the miniatures. In fact, this other reason is the second basis for the "book illumination criterion" mentioned above.

Art history, almost generally, has accepted the belief that fifteenth century altar painting in the Netherlands was, on the whole, derived from book illumination. The creation of miniatures is, in other words, regarded as the older art, which had developed to a mature beauty at a time when altar painting was still at the beginning of its evolution. Essentially this assumption originates from Dvořák's ingenious analysis of the sources of Eyckian art.[259] Ever since this scholar successfully proved that the new art did not fall from the sky but was derived instead from a previous artistic production, early book illumination—which he used as his proof—has stood in the limelight of art historical attention as the source for the new realistic art.

[257] The relaxed and spontaneous behavior of the figures walking casually together in a landscape and forming a number of small loose groups, is identical in both examples. Even the treatment of the drapery folds, which run in rather thin and straight vertical lines, is similar in both. It is, furthermore, characteristic of both representations that they occasionally show a figure in a quick and unexpected little movement. In the St. Barbara panel, the young man walking next to the noble lady suddenly turns his head toward her to emphasize a point made by him in the conversation. In the *bas-de-page* is shown in the center a deacon who is looking down automatically as the priest dips his *aspergillum* into the holy water. The casual downward movement strikes us as so admirably natural because it plunges the little face into deep shadow thus revealing that the churchyard lies in the bright light of the noontime sun. Perhaps it was the mature Van Eyck himself who had here completed a page otherwise painted by his workshop help. If not, the artist who added this part must have used a drawing by the mature Jan van Eyck. The St. Barbara panel itself is, in my opinion, only a drawing. Since the frame of this monochrome little work is carefully finished, Panofsky believes that Van Eyck had intended the panel to remain in the present state (Panofsky 1953, I, p. 185). But, as we have seen in Chapter I, it was the practice of the time to finish the frame first. It thus seems to me that the panel is actually only the underdrawing of a work that has remained unfinished.

[258] For the reasons given for this early dating and their lack of validity, cf. below Excursus I.

[259] Cf. above note 135. While neither Dvořák nor Friedländer actually denied the possibility that the Eyckian art was derived from a great pre-Eyckian altarpiece production today lost (cf. above note 242), a remark in Friedländer's book paved the way for the present misleading stress on book illumination as the factual and sole source of the new type of painting. In Friedländer-Veronee, I, p. 22, we find the following remark: "Even though the remaining evidence is full of gaps, it seems plausible to look on Netherlandish panel painting as having its roots in the art of illumination that preceded it."

There is, in fact, very little other material handed down to us from the earlier time which could serve as the basis for a scholarly investigation.[260] In the present state of preservation, book illumination outnumbers altar painting to an extent that the latter constitutes only an infinitesimal portion of the total production of known painting. It is an error, however, to believe that the present state of preservation truthfully reflects the original situation. The notion that early book illumination overwhelmingly outweighed contemporary altar painting in number and importance is obviously wrong.

We have to keep in mind that fourteenth century altar painting had already assumed a position of great importance not only in Italy but in Germany as well. A large production of altar retables has been handed down to us from these other countries of Europe. The very few altar paintings preserved from the Netherlandish production before 1400 compare so favorably in quality with the foreign examples of the same period that there is no reason to suppose an inferiority in Netherlandish altar painters. Malouel and Broederlam are certainly giants when compared with the Cologne masters of the time or with Konrad von Soest.[261] That they were not the only Netherlandish painters of their period and that their own few preserved panels are only a fraction of a large altarpiece production is attested to by the entries in Netherlandish inventories which mention numerous artists entirely unknown to us and a great wealth of works which we have never seen.[262]

But is it possible to suppose that a large and important altarpiece production is lost in the Netherlands alone, while being substantially preserved in other countries? Is it possible to suppose such a loss when the book illumination of the same region has been preserved? What can be the reason for the elimination of one branch of art, in one country only? The answer is very simple: a historical catastrophe limited to the Netherlands which affected altar painting, without disturbing the preservation of book illumination.

[260] The scattered works illustrated in Panofsky 1953, II, in plates 11, 12, 43, 46-57, 70, and 79, differ considerably from one another in character with even the provenance of the individual piece not certain in every case. And while the connection between the Eyckian art and the miniatures of the Limbourg brothers and the Boucicaut Master on the one hand and with the panels of the Master of Flémalle, on the other, is more or less clear, there is no palpable link between the last-named master's art and the miniatures. The scanty preservation of early panels makes the historical context of the various branches of the tradition extremely difficult to judge. It was in fact only recently, through the discovery of the Entombment Altarpiece now in the Collection of Count Seilern, that something which may be called a link between the art of the Master of Flémalle and the style of Melchior Broederlam made its appearance (cf. *ibid.*, plates 51 and 85).

[261] In addition to the evidence given through the comparison of the actually preserved works, we also have a source attesting to the impressively high quality of the Flemish panels. "There is a remarkable statement in an existing document, to the effect that Philip (the Bold) had altars made on the model of those he had seen in Flanders. This hints at the superiority of Flemish altarpieces and shows how ready the Burgundian sovereigns were to exploit the creative resources open to them with this increment in territory." Friedländer-Veronee, I, p. 21.

[262] Troescher, in his new book, *op.cit.*, stresses this fact on several occasions.

The very art which we have been discussing, the new realistic and illusionistic painting of the Netherlands, caused the loss of the previous production. Quite specifically the art of Rogier van der Weyden and his followers was most likely to have been indirectly responsible for the destruction of the older works. The new art with its magic power of visual persuasion had become a new and effective religious tool. The invisible mysteries of the Holy Sacrament celebrated over the altar were revealed in visible form to the eye of the believer in the retable adorning this altar. After this new art had come into existence, rather quickly all the altar paintings of the past became obsolete. The older works were now unsatisfactory not only as objects of aesthetic enjoyment but even as religious instruments. No longer could they serve the spiritual enlightenment of the worshiper as effectively as the newer ones.

From the middle of the century on, a large number of painters well-trained in the new art were asked to fill innumerable commissions not only for retables to be placed into newly built chapels and churches but also for paintings intended to replace older altarpieces. The latter now gradually disappeared into the sacristies and basements. And, like most man-made objects no longer under the loving care and protection of man, they gradually disintegrated and were eventually discarded.[263]

If an important Netherlandish altarpiece production had existed before and around 1400, we would no longer need to summon the book illumination of the time as the prime source of the new realistic art. I am far from suggesting that book illumination should be completely discounted as an influence on altar painting. The influence was certainly mutual. Basically, however, in my opinion, it was always the large and not the small art which stood at the giving end in the relationship.[264] In any case, the traditional silent

---

[263] It is no mere coincidence that the few panels preserved are, with only minor exceptions, rather small works. Most of these tiny panels must have been in the private collections of princes, where the items were regarded as precious *objets d'art* and as such escaped destruction.

[264] In the Netherlandish art of the later fifteenth and sixteenth centuries, i.e. in an era from which a considerable part of the altarpiece production is preserved, the dependency of book illumination on the large-scale art is absolutely clear. Scholars have always regarded this fact as a result of a general decline of manuscript painting which went hand in hand with the rise of the printed book. Although this view is not entirely without grounds, the relationship of altar painting and book illumination had by no means as radically changed as one is inclined to believe. In early times too the miniature painter in search of models was unquestioably scrutinizing the altarpiece production. There are a number of miniatures in the Turin-Milan Hours whose dependency on large compositions has never been doubted. The famous Crucifixion, for instance, has always been accepted as the small-scale reflection of a large Eyckian work now lost (Panofsky 1953, II, plate 156; cf. Millard Meiss, *op.cit.*, p. 281, and idem, "Jan van Eyck and the Italian Renaissance," *Venezia e l'Europa, Atti del XVIII Congresso Internazionale di Storia dell'Arte* [1955], Venice 1956, pp. 64-68). Therefore, when Panofsky (1953, I, p. 141) did his utmost to disprove the widely held opinion that the sweet but insipid little *bas-de-page* which shows the Holy Virgins with the Mystic Lamb (*ibid.*, II, plate 159) is the reflection rather than the forerunner of the Ghent Altarpiece, his effort is

assumption that fifteenth century painting in the Netherlands developed from a diminutive size to a large scale and from fragile configurations to monumental forms is certainly incorrect. The large and the small have coexisted during the entire Trecento—we have only to think of Duccio's Maestà. Likewise, monumental Giottesque compositions were created at a time when rather dainty calligraphic forms were also in vogue.[265] Thus, when we observe the same polarity in the art of Jan van Eyck, it is not permissible to separate the two poles and to see one as the beginning, and the other as the end, of an evolutionary line. The similarity or dissimilarity to book illumination cannot be used as a criterion for the chronology of Eyckian works.

The traditional early dating for the Dresden triptych had originally been based on the treatment of forms which, in typical miniature fashion, shows a wealth of minute details on a minimum of panel surface (Fig. 128). Perhaps scholars were reminded also of the International Style by the rather flimsy figure of the donor. His stiff, tiny, doll-like hands, moreover, seemed to show the awkwardness of an early work. When Panofsky accepted the traditional dating, he submitted additional reasons for it which, however, were only a new version of ones previously given. The freedom and exuberance of form that he observed in the little work appeared to Panofsky as early, as being related to the style of the Boucicaut miniatures, and as opposed to a stony monumentality he noted in some later paintings by Van Eyck.[266]

All this, however, has very little to do with the vital artistic problems of the time which were the compelling force behind the evolution. A new illusionistic art was able simultaneously to present such opposites as freedom and rigidity, minuteness and monumentality, or a surface of glittering life together with austere stony shapes. True, these are pairs of contrasting qualities, but they are not the poles of the development. Neither the general evolution of painting nor the personal art of Van Eyck starts out from one to proceed to the opposite of these trends.

Once we acknowledge that the traditionally used criteria are far from being the real clues to Jan's development, we are free to eliminate a number of suspicious candidates from the list of works usually believed to predate the Ghent Altarpiece. The foregoing discussion of the reconstruction and iconography of the Ghent polyptych in itself suggests

---

understandable only on the basis of his firm belief that Jan's *juvenilia* can be found among the miniatures of the famous book. Cf. our Excursus I below.

[265] A work of ethereal quality showing complicated and melodious swinging curves, the large Annunciation retable by Simone Martini and Lippo Memmi was created in the same year (1333) as was Bernardo Daddi's small Bigallo triptych, whose closed simplified outlines give to his forms that power of grandeur which would have been perfectly suitable for a work of monumental size. Cf. White, *op.cit.*, 1966, plates 102 (B) and 117.

[266] Panofsky 1953, I, pp. 182f.

a revision of the dating of one particular work, namely of the Madonna in a Church in Berlin.

When we noted in the previous chapter that some sections of the Ghent Annunciation show a divine light miraculously coming from the north, we mentioned that Panofsky had already observed the same phenomenon in the small Berlin panel (Fig. 135).[267] Indeed, the light in this small painting is similar to that in the large one in another important respect. It not only shares with the Ghent Annunciation the supernatural direction of the light, but also the motif of the two-fold sun reflection, which appears on the floor in the Berlin composition and on the wall near the Madonna in the representation in Ghent (Figs. 72, 81, and 83). The artist obviously intended the identical metaphor in both paintings. It is important in the context of this metaphor that he show the supernatural direction of the light together with the two natures of Christ miraculously joined at the moment of the Virgin's conception.[268]

It is utterly improbable that this pictorial metaphor was invented *ad hoc* for the painting in Berlin. The symbolism of light was not traditional in representations of the Madonna and Child but it was in Annunciation scenes. In numerous earlier paintings of this subject, the Mérode Annunciation among them, we see a pencil of golden rays which, as a divine emanation, enter the chamber of the Annunciate (Fig. 84). The metaphor invented by Van Eyck is but a more explicit and a more illusionistic version of a motif that had occurred all along in representations of the Annunciation, and thus was no doubt created for an Annunciation painting. The possibility that the metaphor had first appeared in another Annunciation now lost, which had been created before the Ghent Altarpiece, can safely be excluded. We have seen in the previous chapter that the idea of the two natures of Christ is intimately bound to the unique over-all iconography of the Ghent Altarpiece. It is thus only natural to assume that the elaborate pictorial metaphor was specifically invented for the Annunciation of the great polyptych.

While this observation gives us a platform from which to postulate for the Berlin Madonna a date after the Ghent Altarpiece, let us reconsider for a moment the reasons for the traditional early dating of the small panel (Fig. 135). It was because of the strikingly unrealistic scale relationship between the huge figure of the Madonna and the small church architecture surrounding it that early scholars had regarded the Berlin panel as "archaic" and as pre-dating the Ghent Altarpiece. This early dating was not revised even after Panofsky had given the correct interpretation of the curious discrepancy in scale and had explained why this feature is not genuinely archaic. He pointed out that the figure of the Virgin connotes the Church. It is thus "not so much a human being, scaled to a real structure, as an embodiment in human form of the same spiritual force or entity that

---

[267] Cf. above note 174, and the text belonging to it.

[268] Cf. above note 178, and the text belonging to it.

is expressed, in architectural terms, in the basilica enshrining her."[269] Van Eyck, according to Panofsky, here follows an age-old tradition both in idea and in form.

Although his brilliant insight had removed the original basis for the early dating of the panel, this dating itself was none the less upheld. The miniature-like character of the painting together with its obvious similarity to works of the International Style made the early date continue to seem reasonable. Thus, we have here a situation comparable to that of the Dresden Altarpiece, to which, by the way, in its freedom and exuberance of form, the Berlin panel bears a marked resemblance.

However, as previously explained, none of these remarkable qualities require an early place for the two paintings within the development of Eyckian art. We have shown that specific features of the International Style can occur throughout the entire oeuvre of the painter. Indeed, it is the standing female figure quite in particular which often retains its traditional form, while other elements (sometimes in the same painting) assume more "modern" shapes.[270] Nevertheless, it is certainly true that the figure of the Virgin in the Berlin panel shows a pronounced similarity to the International Style. The pleasing s-curve which determines the over-all shape of her body and the swinging uninterrupted rhythm of calligraphic lines which determine the borders of her drapery heighten this effect beyond what we find in other works by Van Eyck. But does this have to mean that this is a genuinely archaic feature? Certainly not. Such a pronounced emphasis on a traditional form was designed to serve the same purpose as the unrealistic scale relationship between the figure and the architecture: it was meant to enhance the sacredness of the image.

We obtain valid insights into the comparative date of the Berlin panel only when we examine the treatment of space and of light. The space here is a completely unified one. Rather than receding in separate consecutive levels, it flows through the interior in an utterly convincing continuity. True, a foreground portion remains separated from the rest of the space by the choir screen in the rear and the nave arcade to the left of the figure. However, both of these barriers are perforated by openings which permit views into the areas beyond them, and the foreground section in itself extends fairly far into the distance. Moreover, the two barriers, which are obviously intended to enclose and thereby empha-size the figures of the Virgin and the Child, function only in the lower part of the com-position. The upper region is marked by the uninterrupted flow of the clerestory windows and the vaults from the nearest foreground to the distant chancel behind the choir screen.

Despite the enclosure of the figures by the walls to the left and in the rear, we do not receive the impression of a limited space. On the contrary, the feeling of an unlimited microcosmic world is clear and unambiguous. This impression is due to the many views

[269] Panofsky 1953, I, p. 145.
[270] For the tendency of the female figure in particular to be cast in traditional form while other subjects are treated in a more advanced manner, cf. Otto Kurz, "A Fishing Party at the Court of William VI, Count of Holland, Zeeland and Hainault," *Oud-Holland*, 71, 1956, p. 128, with reference to earlier literature.

through the various arcades as well as to the fact that these arcades are incomplete. Having them cut, seemingly at random, by the picture frame (which is not a representation of the exterior view of the nave), the artist implies the continuation of the pictorial space beyond the portions that we see.

The continuity and infinity of the picture space is underlined by a beautifully uniform light which comes from the left in all the parts of the painting and is characterized as entering the interior only through its own windows or doors. The miraculous light from the north, which was used in the Ghent Annunciation only in the background and in the right annex room, is now the illumination of the entire picture space. This light in the Ghent composition was a "background light" and as such was the illumination of what I have called that part of the representation which is "painting pure and simple." In the Berlin Madonna, every portion of the representation is "painting pure and simple." We are no longer confronted with an essentially compartmentalized picture space, but with a perfectly unified image. And this image is now illumined by a perfectly unified light. This new homogeneity combined with the powerful suggestion of unlimited space makes it absolutely certain that the panel was created after the Ghent Altarpiece.

The figure in the Berlin painting is a fully stereometric form convincingly placed in three-dimensional space. This impression of a mass in space is not impaired by the s-curve of the body nor is it diminished by the swinging lines of the drapery. Compared with the angel and the Annunciate in the Ghent composition, who show the "more advanced" angular folds, the Berlin figure appears more, rather than less, three-dimensional and more, rather than less, perfectly integrated in the surrounding space (Fig. 81). Indeed, the calligraphic curves of the drapery borders are cleverly used in the Berlin panel to emphasize the roundness of the figure, encircling, as they do, the body of the Virgin like a rope slung around a column.

The traditional pattern not only enhances the three-dimensionality of the Berlin figure, it also gives to the over-all shape of the Madonna a beautifully unified form. The unification of the figure stands out more clearly in a comparison with the Frankfort Madonna of the Master of Flémalle (Figs. 135 and 136). There, the drapery shows the "modern" angularity; but the figure is a mosaic of basically unconnected parts which aggravate rather than complement each other and which in the end produce a flattened pattern rather than a three-dimensional whole. The comparison with the Flémalle painting distinctly demonstrates that the Van Eyck representation is by far the more developed work.[271] Van Eyck's is a classic example of a traditional pattern employed to great advantage within the context of a representation based on a most advanced artistic concept.

[271] The background of the Flémalle Madonna is obviously only the ancient gold ground reinterpreted as the brocade pattern of a cloth of honor. The very fact that we neither see the object from which the fabric is suspended nor are informed as to the manner in which the cloth meets the grassy ground, proves that the brocade background is but a device to terminate the picture space. This is a far cry from Van Eyck's careful treatment of a figure's surroundings and differs intrinsically even from his Antwerp Madonna where a similar motif is used (Fig. 129).

When we exclude the Dresden triptych and the Berlin Madonna from those Eyckian works that are usually believed to predate the Ghent Altarpiece, a third painting, namely the Washington Annunciation, is automatically also eliminated from the list (Fig. 138).[272] In the Washington panel too, we have a picture space and a picture light of mature uniformity. The pictorial space is by no means essentially limited through the box-shape of the interior. To the contrary, its construction, with the view radically cut by the frame, is very advanced. This cutting most effectively includes the viewer in the depicted room.

The perfectly uniform picture light in this panel is shown as coming from the right side, which is the south. It is thus the natural sunlight which is consistently used to illumine the interior. And when the divine light, through which the Dove of the Holy Spirit enters this room, is here depicted in the traditional golden rays, this is not an archaism but a brilliant reworking of an old motif. In a painting in which the total illumination of the space is seen to be the natural light of the sun, a contrasting divine light which enters the space from another direction could only be rendered in a stylized idealistic form.

The lovely *repoussoir* in the right foreground, a pillow-covered taboret and some stems of lilies, is depicted as seen from above, a device which establishes the nearness of these objects to the spectator's eye. However, even though the two objects draw the eye of the viewer into the picture space, they create, at the same time, a significant distance between him and the two holy figures. These two figures, though they both stand in what may be called the middle plane of the space, do not actually occupy precisely the same plane. The angel, almost in profile and on a line with the left wall of the sanctuary is somewhat nearer to the viewer than is the Madonna who is parallel to the rear wall and is seen in front view. In their specific positions, the two figures form a "corner," as it were, similar to the one formed behind them by the two walls of the surrounding architecture. The taboret of the *repoussoir*, set at an oblique angle, points toward this corner and into the space between the two figures.

A marked distance between the viewer and the chief figures has also been established in the Dresden triptych, where the Madonna and her Child sit far back in the chancel part of the basilica. The small altarpiece also shows a spatial construction which is distinctly intended to give the impression of including the spectator. But the particular use of the *repoussoir* in the Washington panel is new. When we visualize the configuration formed by the foreground objects and the two figures on the mosaic floor, we realize that their ground plan is an isosceles triangle whose vertex points to the viewer. Obviously, the painter has deliberately arranged this ground plan configuration to produce a new illusionistic effect. He beautifully succeeded. The striking novelty of his idea argues strongly

---

[272] Not all scholars writing on Van Eyck have placed the Washington Annunciation before the Ghent Altarpiece. Ludwig Baldass, *Jan van Eyck*, New York 1952, p. 278, for instance, dates the panel between 1432 and 1435. His catalogue (pp. 272-91) includes a most convenient listing of the opinions of other scholars on the dates of Van Eyck's undated paintings.

for the assumption that the Washington Annunciation was painted still later than the Dresden Altarpiece.

IV. THE CONTESTED WORKS OF JAN

WITH all three of these paintings put at a later date, it would seem that the entire uncontested oeuvre of Jan preserved today actually is, as we speculated toward the start of this chapter, later than the Ghent Altarpiece. There remains in the early category, however, what might be called the "contested" Eyckian works which are not only thought to be earlier than the Ghent Altarpiece but have sometimes actually been placed as far back as the second decade of the fifteenth century. These are a group of highly contro-versial panel paintings and miniatures often totally different from one another in com-position and style. Several of these works are sometimes given to "Hubert" or are regarded as the *juvenilia* of Jan. Other scholars have occasionally considered a few of them to be by the hand of a follower but based on an early Eyckian invention.

Granted that the character of all of these works is different from the "canonical" Eyckian oeuvre, their being different may not always have a chronological reason. Two examples from this group bear to one another a marked similarity that has often been recognized in art historical literature, namely the so-called Turin-Milan Hours and the Crucifixion and Last Judgment in New York (Figs. 27, 131, 133, and 140, 141).

For the purposes of this study, we must confine ourselves to only a few observations concerning the difficult problems posed by the enchanting illuminations in the famous Book of Hours. First of all, it must be said that the Eyckian portion of the book is obvi-ously the result of a joint effort from the Van Eyck workshop. In itself the heterogeneous character of this collection of "Eyckian" miniatures makes it quite improbable that any one of the small compositions was invented for this book. It is more likely that this series is based on a vast collection of Eyckian and other models which had accumulated in the workshop and which included some rather divergent examples—even stemming from different periods, early and late.

There is no doubt that many hands were involved. Any attempt, however, to separate these hands seems futile to me, based on the scant evidence we have available. Moreover, there is always the theoretical possibility that illuminations done by the same hand may look different one from another, while others painted by different artists may look alike. In the first case one painter used two models of different types; in the second, two artists followed models of the same type.

In my opinion, one cannot assume that all or most of the miniatures attributed by Hulin de Loo to "Hand G" and by Baldass to the "Chief Master" were painted by Jan van Eyck.[273] Certainly the large scenes so often ascribed to him are not his. Indeed, it is

---

[273] Georges Hulin de Loo, *Heures de Milan*, Brussels and Paris 1911. Hulin was one of the very few scholars who had not only studied those portions of the book that are preserved today but also the part

by no means certain that Jan himself painted any part of the book. It seems to me that Jan restricted his activity, if any, to one or the other historiated initial or *bas-de-page*. It is possible that of all the miniatures only a few of these small scenes could have been expressly invented for an illuminated book. And it is precisely this group which closely resembles the mature style of Van Eyck as we see it in the Barbara panel.[274] Thus, in my view, it is hardly possible for the work on the miniatures to predate the middle of the 1430's, at the earliest. We may even one day find that the activity of the workshop as reflected in the Hours took place at a time when its founder was no longer alive.[275]

The two panels in New York with the Crucifixion and the Last Judgment, which are usually seen in connection with these miniatures, are, in my opinion, unquestionably originals by Jan van Eyck. Panofsky, who as a scholar living in the United States had the constant opportunity to study the panels in the original, also had no doubt that they are by the hand of Jan.[276] But they may, nevertheless, postdate the Ghent Altarpiece, as we have postulated for the miniatures. Since, at the same time, they quite obviously occupy an isolated position separate from the so-called "canonical" work, a closer examination of them may be most promising in the context of our particular study. Perhaps the two compositions in New York can help us more precisely to define the nature of the new achievements by which the Ghent Altarpiece becomes the spearhead of the great last decade of Van Eyck's career.

The two small panels with the Crucifixion and the Last Judgment were frequently referred to in the course of our discussion of the reconstruction and the iconography of the Ghent Altarpiece.[277] The idea of the Last Judgment was presented in the Vijd Altar when the wings were opened and the antependium with the picture of Hell was on display (Figs. 41, 141). The small panel of the Last Judgment in New York has no elements

---

that was destroyed by the fire of 1904. His basic classification of the entire miniature material of the Hours according to separate "hands" is followed by many scholars and was accepted even by those who objected to his particular attribution of the various groups to Hubert, Jan, or "workshop." For Baldass' and Panofsky's discussion of the miniatures, cf. our Excursus I.

[274] Cf. above note 257, and the text belonging to it. The unusual assumption that the master should have painted only some marginal details rather than reserving the large scenes for himself is based on the following considerations. As the head of an enterprise which had no particular attraction for him, Jan may have distributed the entire work among his workshop helpers. These painters, however, may have returned the book with some minor blanks where suitable models were missing. These blanks the master may have filled with elements of his own invention in order to complete the work.

[275] Since the book includes a number of miniatures which look "Flémallesque" but are obviously painted by an artist already belonging to the generation of Petrus Christus (cf., for instance, Panofsky 1953, II, fig. 289 on plate 156), there is a strong possibility that the entire Eyckian portion of the book was an enterprise of the establishment which had taken over Jan's workshop after the master's death.

[276] Cf. *ibid.*, I, pp. 238f and II, the caption for plate 166.

[277] Cf. above notes 117 and 203, and the texts belonging to them.

which are similar to the forms in the Ghent retable. Still, the idea of composing a Last Judgment with a Paradise, an Earth, and a Hell, which follow each other in vertical succession, is the same in both works.[278] Furthermore, we pointed out that as a whole the Vijd altar was a huge tabernacle which housed the consecrated Host. Indeed, the over-all shape of this structure must even have had the look of an enormous monstrance, especially when the retable shutters were opened (Fig. 59).[279] Again, the small Last Judgment in New York contains the same idea, this time expressed through the over-all shape of the painted configuration on the surface of the panel.

Paradise, which appears in the upper section as a large solid form with a kind of "opening" in the center, is connected with the skeleton in the lower part by the figure of the archangel Michael. This unit forms a large "pseudo-foreground" configuration set against a background landscape, with the land and the sea giving forth their dead depicted below the horizon line. This "pseudo-foreground" configuration strikingly resembles a monstrance: Paradise forms the receptacle for the Host (the "opening" being the place for the Wafer to be inserted); the figure of the archangel constitutes the stem with the *nodus*; and the skeleton acts as the foot of the object (Figs. 141, 59, and 143).

A monstrance, a small object for the display of the Host, may be called a tabernacle, just as is any other large or small receptacle for the Eucharistic species. Since the inscription in the frame of this small Last Judgment panel includes the famous passage from Revelation "*Ecce tabernaculum . . . ,*" there can be no doubt of the painter's intention actually to conjure up in the mind of the spectator the image of a monstrance on the panel surface. Dr. Heinz Peters in Berlin, who noticed the image of the monstrance in the New York panel at approximately the same time that I did several years ago, has recently published his important observations on the New York wings. In an attempt to end the controversy as to whether these wings belonged to a triptych or were always just a diptych,

[278] Panofsky 1953, I, p. 238, points to the composition's deviation from the customary division according to left and right with the elect appearing to the right, the doomed to the left of Christ. However, the division according to above and below as rendered in the Last Judgment in New York is not as unusual as his text seems to imply. This vertical distribution occurs, for instance, in Lanfranco and Filippolo de' Veris' magnificent but sadly ruined fresco on the outer south wall of Santa Maria dei Ghirli at Campione (Italy, Lake Lugano), which is dated 1400, M. Salmi, *La pittura e la miniatura gotica in Lombardia* (Storia di Milano), VI, 1956, and in the French breviary of 1412 in the Walters Art Gallery, Baltimore (ms. W. 300), cf. *The International Style, the Arts of Europe around 1400*, Baltimore 1962, pp. 67f and plate LIV.

[279] In the fifteenth century, the shape of the monstrance, which is a vessel very often appearing as the attribute of the figure of Ecclesia (cf. below note 297) is frequently, and sometimes in a rather unexpected context, used as a symbolic pattern. For instance, the stone wall tabernacle in the church of Gernsbach (Germany, Black Forest), instead of being the usual little house crowned by a tracery tower has been given the form of a tower ostensory with the receptacle resting on a chalice-like stem and foot. Our reproduction (Fig. 145), which shows the tabernacle in the present ruined condition and which fails to indicate the full width of the upper part, gives only a rather faint idea of the original over-all shape of the structure.

Dr. Peters suggested that the two shutters had originally been the doors of a tabernacle.[280] I enthusiastically agree with him on this point. However, I disagree with his silent assumption that it was not possible for a central representation to have occurred on the ecclesiastical object to which the New York shutters belonged. Even the wooden casement of the wall tabernacle in Rothenburg, which we discussed earlier, has not only painted doors but a back wall as well, which was originally covered with painted representations (Figs. 146 and 147).[281] House-shaped tabernacles with all their inner walls as well as their doors covered with representations had already occurred in a much earlier time, as we can see in the thirteenth century example of the Metropolitan Museum (Fig. 144).

If a center representation between Van Eyck's Crucifixion and his Last Judgment originally did adorn the back wall of a wooden box, it would explain why the nineteenth century owner of the shutters was apparently never able to get possession of the original middle part, for only the shutters of the box could be easily detached and sold.[282] More than a decade ago, I discovered the composition which, in my opinion, could very well have stood between the Crucifixion and the Last Judgment in New York. It is the Resurrection scene by Pieter Bruegel the Elder, a beautiful drawing reproduced in a famous print (Fig. 149). I believe that this scene, though not a perfectly faithful copy, could reflect Van Eyck's composition in its main elements and perhaps even in many of its details.[283]

---

[280] Heinz Peters, "Zum New Yorker 'Diptych' der 'Hand G'," *Festschrift Kauffmann, Munuscula Discipulorum*, Berlin 1968, pp. 235-46.

[281] The paint surface, which shows the remnants of several layers of later overpainting, is extremely ruinous on the inner faces of the doors; in fact it is in an advanced state of flaking off. The back wall shows the traces of having been stripped down to the raw wood with a strong alkaline solution, apparently because there this flaking condition was still more advanced.

[282] Count Tatistcheff, who was the Russian ambassador in Vienna and owned the two paintings in the 1840's, told a rather dubious story to Johann David Passavant in 1841 about the lost central panel. This story, according to which the central panel showed an Adoration of the Magi that had been stolen from him by a servant, has found quite a convincing negative evaluation in Panofsky 1953, I, pp. 237f. Cf. also Wehle and Salinger, *op.cit.*, pp. 2ff. In fact, the Berlin drawing of the Adoration of the Magi (Fig. 134), which is often thought to reflect the composition of this lost center panel, not only makes a nonsensical iconographic unit when combined with the New York panels but also shows a style worlds removed from that of the supposed wings. The stylistic clash between the drawing and the New York wings is even stronger than Panofsky has supposed. In my opinion, these compositions are separated by at least twenty years of stylistic development. It is the derivative style of the miniatures in the Turin-Milan Hours which—in its indiscriminate fusion of the old and the new—has blurred our view for the historical succession of forms. Cf. our Excursus I.

[283] The engraving and the drawing are discussed in F. Grossmann, "The Drawings of Pieter Bruegel the Elder in the Museum Boymans and Some Problems of Attribution," published in Dutch translation in *Bulletin Museum Boymans Rotterdam*, Part V, 2, July 1954, pp. 54-63, with illustrations. A larger reproduction of the drawing is found in *idem, Breugel, The Paintings*, London 1955, Figs. 30 and 31. The steeply

Bruegel's predilection for the art of Van Eyck, attested to by his frequent sketches of Eyckian scenes, is well known.[284] Bruegel probably took this particular composition of Van Eyck in order to use it in an altar triptych in which the Resurrection scene was to constitute, as was customary in Crucifixions, the righthand wing of the unit. This may have been the reason why Bruegel reversed the composition, which is now seen only in the print in its original sequence, namely with the dark opening of the cave to the left as the beginning of the story and the glorious sunrise to the right as the end.[285] Seen in this direction, the Resurrection is a perfect center piece between the two New York compositions (Fig. 153). Not only does it show the direct continuation of the steeply sloping, rocky foreground terrain as we see it in the Crucifixion; it also forms a beautiful bridge between the high horizon line in the Crucifixion and the much lower one in the Last Judgment. With the high rock of the tomb on the left and the low background landscape on the right, the Resurrection alleviates the compositional clash which is strongly felt when the two New York panels are immediately juxtaposed.[286]

A Resurrection is the ideal center piece between a Crucifixion and a Last Judgment not only from the viewpoint of the narrative sequence but also for symbolical considerations. The profound religious significance of Christ's rising from His tomb as the promise of the believer's own resurrection makes this theme suitable to form a strong climax, even between two so enormously important events as the Sacrifice of the Saviour and His Judgment of the world. But it is the particular iconographical type used in Bruegel's Resurrection which so greatly strengthens the likelihood that this very composition originally linked the two scenes in New York.

---

rising ground, the specific pattern of the rocks that are strewn over the terrain, and the style of the drapery betray an early model. The cascading folds of Christ's mantle, which fall richly and softly around the figure in spite of their basically angular form, are typically Eyckian. Their zigzag pattern, in particular, precisely conforms with the drapery of the fainting Madonna in the New York Crucifixion (Figs. 149 and 168). It is, however, obvious that Bruegel did not imitate his early model without making considerable changes. He evidently "corrected" it with the aid of forms derived from Titian and Tintoretto. While the mantle of the rising Christ is certainly Eyckian, the position and the gesture of the figure were unquestionably taken from an Italian sixteenth century work. Compare Tintoretto's The Healing of the Lame by St. Augustine in the Museo Civico of Vicenza, reproduced in *Wallraf-Richartz-Jahrbuch*, XXIX, 1967, p. 117.

[284] Cf. Friedrich Winkler, "Die Wiener Kreuztragung," *Nederlands Kunsthistorisch Jaarboek*, IX, 1958, pp. 83-108, an article in which a number of important drawings showing Eyckian designs are attributed to Bruegel the Elder. I am inclined to add to this group the drawing after the Annunciation Angel of the Ghent Altarpiece, Berlin-Dahlem, Kupferstichkabinett, Friedländer-Veronee, I, plate 67E.

[285] For a discussion of the relation of Christ and especially the risen Christ to the sun and the sun god, cf. Hubert Schrade, *Ikonographie der christlichen Kunst*, I, *Die Auferstehung Christi*, Berlin/Leipzig 1932, pp. 39ff. A most sensitive description of the Bruegel composition is found in *ibid.*, p. 332, note 4. For the rising sun as a motif used in a Resurrection scene belonging to the Eyckian art, cf. Panofsky 1953, I, p. 231.

[286] It is this compositional clash, together with the high and narrow format of the two New York paintings, which argues most strongly against Panofsky's conjecture that they had originally formed a diptych. Cf. *ibid.*, p. 238.

The depiction of the tomb of Christ as a cave and the rendering of the resurrected Christ as a figure elevated in the air are both Italian features taken from the art of the Trecento.[287] Since each of them begins to appear in the Netherlands immediately after Van Eyck and long before the time of Bruegel, it is more than likely that a master of the "Founder Generation" was the one who introduced them into Northern art.[288] The representation of Christ raised into the air fills the upper portion of the Resurrection scene with an image as powerful as the heavenly configuration of the Last Judgment panel, if not more so. In each instance, the upper part of the composition is linked to the lower one through the figure of an angel. The wings of the angel in the Resurrection are raised to indicate Salvation; those of the archangel in the Last Judgment point downwards toward the image of Damnation.

This idea of Hell and Perdition, depicted as it is here in a decidedly cavelike form, would, indeed, be beautifully foreshadowed by the dark cave tomb of the preceding image if the center of the Eyckian unit had actually been a Resurrection of the Bruegel type. The frame inscription of the two panels, which explains the main pictorial elements of the paintings, provides the strongest reason for this assumption. A representation of the tomb of the Saviour appears neither in the Crucifixion nor in the Last Judgment. Nevertheless, the inscription includes the famous passage taken from Isaiah concerning the grave of Christ.[289] It is, therefore, highly probable that an image of this tomb had originally occurred in a connected representation.

However, it is not the tomb alone whose presence in the Eyckian unit is suggested by the existing New York panels. The Crucifixion panel points to yet another motif, namely to that of the sun, which must have originally occurred in this unit. The New York Crucifixion depicts only the moon, whereas the symbols of both the moon and the sun traditionally appear in a Calvary scene.[290] The strength of this tradition would indi-

---

[287] In Italy, numerous fourteenth and early fifteenth century paintings show one of these two features. Several compositions depict Christ as a figure miraculously raised above his sarcophagus, among them the Resurrection in Andrea da Firenze's murals in the Spanish Chapel of Santa Maria Novella (Fig. 150). There are also many representations in which the sepulcher is rendered as a rock tomb with the figure of Christ placed in front of its opening. In the panel by Andrea di Bartolo, for instance, we see the Lord in His new body walking towards us from this cave (Fig. 151). His figure, however, is raised into the air in Sano di Pietro's Resurrection, which already combines the two features that we find in the Bruegel composition (Fig. 152). On these specific types in the Italian development and also on the Northern types following them (cf. our Excursus II), compare the article by Pia Wilhelm, "Auferstehung Christi," *Lexikon der christlichen Ikonographie*, Freiburg i. Br. 1968, Letter e, Cols. 215-16.

[288] For the new type of Christ's Resurrection as found in the altarpieces of Bruges and in other Northern works around and before 1500, cf. our Excursus II.

[289] Isaiah 53:6-9, 12; cf. Wehle and Salinger, *op.cit.*, p. 9.

[290] The three-quarter disc of a silvery moon appears in the sky of Van Eyck's Crucifixion in the same way as the moon disc can often actually be observed in nature on a very bright day. Placed near the right border of the scene next to the face of the crucified evildoer, who is characterized as the "Bad Thief" by

cate that since the sun is missing in the Crucifixion, the symbol must have occurred in another portion of the unit no longer preserved. The Bruegel composition very beautifully fulfills this postulate: it presents the rising sun as the symbol of the rebirth of Christ.[291]

Finally, there is one other iconographic element which powerfully links this Resurrection with the two wings in New York. This is the huge stone which so boldly stands in the very center of the entire composition and provides a resting place for the angel. It is a fact well-known from the traditional form of ancient Palestinian tombs and from the Gospel texts themselves that the stone which closed Christ's grave must have been round. In Christian art, however, the round shape of the stone as seen in the Bruegel composition, is not merely unusual: as far as I know, it is absolutely unique.[292] The use of this exceptional round shape clearly implies that a very important symbolical meaning directly connected to this roundness was intended by this specific representation of Christ's Resurrection.

---

his turning his head away from Christ, the moon disc is certainly a negative symbol implying the idea of the unbelieving Synagogue (Figs. 140 and 167). While the sun and the moon originally signified Christ and his Church (cf. Katzenellenbogen, *op.cit.*, note 86 on p. 132), the two symbols, traditionally appearing in Crucifixion scenes on the side of Ecclesia and Synagoga respectively, came to assume a meaning corresponding to the symbolism of the latter two. In both Memling's and David's Crucifixion panels the sun and moon are depicted in the sky as opposing symbols to the left and the right of Christ (Figs. 155 and 158).

[291] The Bruges altarpieces (cf. our Excursus II), though not using the Resurrection as the center scene as I suppose it for the Eyckian unit, do show the rising sun in the Resurrection in spite of the previous appearance of the sun symbol in the middle panel (Fig. 157). Apparently the rising sun was a detail of such a compelling power and beauty in the lost Van Eyck Resurrection that the Bruges followers of Van Eyck were anxious to adopt it. The full glory of the Eyckian idea is more apparent in Bruegel's composition (Fig. 149), which not only reflects the Resurrection by Van Eyck more completely than do the earlier paintings of the Bruges masters but in a manner less swayed by an influence from Rogier's art. In further study of the Bruegel scene, we notice that the group of holy women approaching the tomb and depicted immediately near the rising sun function as the first representatives of the victorious New Law in contrast to the dark cave, the burnt-out fire and the hostile guards, which symbolize the Old Law now defeated. For the sun symbol, cf. also above note 285.

[292] For the round stone in a preserved Palestinian tomb, cf. L. H. Vincent, *Jérusalem de l'Ancien Testament*, I, Paris 1954, Plate LXXXIII. The round shape of the stone is implied in Matthew 28:2 (". . . an angel of the Lord . . . rolled back the stone"), in Mark 16:3 and in Luke 24:2. Since the appearance of Christ's tomb in the pictorial tradition was not based on the site as it must have looked in Christ's time but on the Constantinian monument, which did not have a rolling door, the motif of the round stone never really found its way into Christian representations. Not even the depiction of the cave tomb, which became more frequent in Italian and Northern Renaissance art, ever included a round stone. The stone that is nearest in shape to the one represented by Bruegel (and reappearing in the numerous painted imitations of the Bruegel engraving or the Bruegel drawing) is found in a Patinir painting in Philadelphia (cf. Robert A. Koch, *Joachim Patinir*, Princeton 1968, fig. 24). This painting, obviously based on the Resurrections of the Bruges tradition and perhaps even making use of a drawing after the lost Eyckian scene, nevertheless fails to depict the stone as actually round. The shape of the object looks instead as though it is a roughly hewn, imperfect rectangle.

The slab which closed Christ's tomb was believed to be the stone of unction and, as such, assumes a Eucharistic connotation.[293] The stone on which the sacrificed body of the Saviour was annointed is, of course, symbolized by the mensa of the Christian altar. The altar, that is to say the table of the Lord, is traditionally represented as a disguised symbol in numerous biblical scenes, among them the Annunciation and the Adoration of the Magi.[294] Concealed as the image of a piece of domestic furniture in early Netherlandish art, the table of the Lord is often depicted as round, or at least roundish, in shape.[295] This round form immediately calls to mind the Eucharistic species, the consecrated Wafer. The stone in the Bruegel Resurrection which is so strikingly similar in shape to a huge Host, was certainly also meant as a Eucharistic symbol.

With this last observation, our discussion returns to the strange monstrance-like form seen in the Last Judgment panel. It seems that we are here dealing with two separate instances of the same type of symbolism.[296] Clearly in the original Eyckian unit, these two

[293] Cf. Mary Anne Graeve, "The Stone of Unction in Caravaggio's Painting for the Chiesa Nuova," *The Art Bulletin*, XL, 3, September 1958, p. 229.

[294] Cf. above note 192.

[295] The majority of the examples adduced by Nilgen, *op.cit.*, shows a round shape, cf. *ibid.*, figs. 8, 13, 14, 15, 18, 19 and 20. Though the table in the Mérode Annunciation, as well as that in the other Annunciation scenes belonging to the same type (as, for instance, the small Brussels panel and the numerous small reliefs, cf. Friedländer-Veronee, II, plate 80; *The Metropolitan Museum of Art Bulletin*, December 1957, p. 124; and *Studien zur Geschichte der europäischen Plastik, Festschrift Theodor Müller*, Munich 1965, p. 161), is not perfectly round since it actually shows sixteen angles, it is at least roundish in its general impression. This form seems to hint at the round shape of the Host or, more precisely perhaps, at the round shape of the paten carrying the Host.

[296] Cf. above note 280, and the paragraph in the text to which it belongs. The huge monstrance formed by the design of the Last Judgment wing when taken as an abstract pattern and also the huge Host formed by the roundish shape of the stone in the Resurrection belong to a type of "disguised symbolism" other than the one discussed by Panofsky as typical of Early Netherlandish art (cf. Panofsky 1953, I, Chapter v). While in the usual type analyzed by Panofsky an object can have two meanings (one narrative and the other symbolic), in the other type not considered by him, one and the same painted form can be successively seen, first as one and then as another object. This latter type, which is the basis of the ever popular puzzle picture game called *Vexier-Bild* in German, is discussed in my article "The *Peddler* by Hieronymus Bosch, a Study in Detection," *Nederlands Kunsthistorisch Jaarboek*, IX, 1958, p. 72. The *Vexier-Bild* type, however, is rather problematic, because we can never be completely certain that the painter had factually intended both of the objects which our eye is able to detect in a painted shape.

Nevertheless, it seems to me that this type, too, was traditional in Early Netherlandish art, since it had apparently already occurred in the Mérode Altarpiece by the Master of Flémalle (Fig. 82). In the Annunciation scene, the lower part of the Virgin's figure is covered by a drapery that is depicted in sharply angular folds. Though intended to be radically three-dimensional when acting as a drapery, this configuration appears rather flat to our eye at first glance, forming a two-dimensional star pattern which centers around a bright spot just below the right hand of the figure. The star shape is all the more distinct because the dress and the mantle of the Madonna which together form it are both rendered in the same red color, a uniformity rather unusual in Early Netherlandish painting.

In my opinion, the star was deliberately formed by the artist and was intended to symbolize Christ, "the

huge symbolical forms were meant to be seen together. With the round shape in the center symbolizing the Eucharist, the monstrance in the right shutter would signify Ecclesia, i.e., the Christian Church as an institution which is regarded as the sacred receptacle of Christ's sacrificed body.[297]

The connection of these two ideas leads to a third which would seem logically to complete the three-part image. A symbol of Synagogue, i.e., of the opposing Judaism, must have appeared in the left wing in order to complete the traditional metaphor of the Eucharistic Christ between Ecclesia and Synagoga. And indeed, if we look at Van Eyck's Crucifixion with this possibility in mind, we see emerging from the Calvary scene a huge symbolic configuration which corresponds in its elevated position and large size to the monstrance symbol in the Last Judgment.

The corresponding symbol in the Crucifixion scene is formed by the very unusual configuration of the three crosses. We notice that the crosses in this image are topped by similar horizontal bars, all three of which occur in the same horizontal level, without that for the Saviour being raised, as is customary, to a higher position. While the vertical posts of the crosses rise freely and separately toward the sky, their lower parts are connected to each other by the mass of the figures on the hill. The huge form made by the three vertically rising elements, connected at the bottom but topped by three separate cross bars, is the shape of the Hebrew letter "Shin." Well-known to the Christians of the time, this letter occurs in numerous altar paintings where its specific meaning may vary from case to case (Figs. 161 and 162).[298] Its general meaning, however, always stays the same: it is used as a symbol of Judaism. To the Christian of the period, the letter "Shin" was the most

---

star that rises out of Jacob" (Numbers 24:17). Indeed, the unborn Christ Child Who is sometimes depicted on the body of the Virgin in the scene of the Visitation, is usually surrounded by a radiating star (cf., for instance, the carved relief figures on the wooden church door of Irrsdorf, 1408—*Europäische Kunst um 1400, op.cit.*, No. 411, pp. 358f). If the star formed by the drapery of the Mérode Annunciate was actually meant to symbolize the unborn Christ, this symbolic configuration which appears immediately next to the blown-out candle would form the necessary complement to the latter symbol. "When the divine light shines, the human light sets." Cf. above note 192.

[297] The monstrance as an attribute of Ecclesia appears, for instance, in the Burgos Triptych of the Passion by the Master of the Godelieve Legend (reproduced in E. Haverkamp Begemann, "De Meester van de Godelieve-Legende, een Brugs schilder uit het einde van de XVᵉ eeuw," *Miscellanea Erwin Panofsky, Musées Royaux des Beaux-Arts Bruxelles Bulletin*, Nos. 1-3, 1955, fig. 2, p. 188).

[298] In the painting by the Master of Schloss Lichtenstein, this letter, adorning as it does the Golden Gate, most probably simply means "gate," which in Hebrew is *sha-ar*. Indeed, the single letter "Shin" actually stands for the word *sha-ar* in normal usage according to the traditional Hebrew abbreviations. I am most grateful to Dr. Guido Schoenberger for having explained this connotation to me. It is not impossible that the same meaning was attached to the symbolic letter as it appears in Van Eyck's Calvary scene. For, if connoting "gate," the letter in the panel could point to the well-known concept of Christ's Crucifixion as the gate to Salvation. It is probable, however, that a more general meaning of the symbol, presently to be explained in our text and in addition unquestionably attached to the symbol in the Crucifixion scene, would be its primary connotation in any case.

familar Hebrew letter not only because it is the most elaborate and decorative form among the letters of the Hebrew alphabet, but also because it was the sign which he could see on the doors of the Jewish population of his own town. As the initial of the word *Schaddai* (the Almighty), it belonged to the visibly displayed part of the text in the *mesusa*, the little parchment scroll which, according to Jewish law, had to be fastened to the right door post of every Jewish dwelling place (Fig. 163).

Without doubt, the huge letter in Van Eyck's Crucifixion panel was meant to be the symbol of Synagoga. Together with the symbol of the Host and that of the monstrance, it formed the traditional metaphor of the Eucharist between Synagoga and Ecclesia (Fig. 154). This symbolism was, of course, beautifully appropriate for the representations on a cabinet in which the Eucharistic species was actually to be kept. In fact, it is the specific practical function of the two panels in New York as the doors of this cabinet which explains why here, contrary to their location in altarpieces and miniatures, the symbol of Synagogue appears to the left and that of Ecclesia to the right.

Ecclesia normally appears on the left and Synagoga on the right, because the representations are not conceived of as being seen from the viewpoint of the spectator but rather from the viewpoint of Christ, Who is represented between the two symbols. Seen from the viewpoint of the figure of Christ, Ecclesia belongs on the right, i.e., the "good side," while Synagoga occupies the "sinister side." In a cabinet enclosing the receptacle with the Holy Wafer, the situation is somewhat different. Though the painted figure of Christ may have occurred on its back wall, in this setting it is not primarily this painted figure which is the representative of the Saviour. In a tabernacle cabinet, the Holy Wafer itself which is the real embodiment of the God-Man is the foremost representative of the Lord. Since this wafer could be turned to face the painted representations—in the same way that the priest or other believers turn to face these images—the traditional places of Ecclesia and Synagoga could be reversed. The reversed position of the symbols in the Eyckian work is required by the historical sequence in which the Crucifixion has to precede the Last Judgment. In an altar painting, this reversal would be an error, but here in a cabinet for the Host the arrangement becomes not only legitimate but profoundly meaningful.

On one specific level of meaning, the panel of the Crucifixion is the "Synagogue wing" of the Eyckian work. This idea explains the unusual stress which the painter has placed on the figures of the wicked and sneering Jews depicted below the cross as the executioners and enemies of Christ. Van Eyck's Jewish figures are all the more horribly impressive as their faces are not coarsely deformed caricatures but believable portrayals of Jewish types whose features are distorted by the evil emotions of a scoffing contempt (Fig. 167).[299] The pronounced emphasis on the wicked triumph of the Jews, so obviously shown

---

[299] It is, however, not only the enemies of Christ who are depicted around the Cross. Not even the crowd on the right which immediately surrounds the Bad Thief, shows exclusively evil people. For it is on that side that the Good Centurion is portrayed at the moment of his conversion (the figure seen from the rear

as the torturers of Christ in the New York panel, suggests that it may not have been just the "normal" consecrated Host which was kept in the cabinet which the Eyckian painting adorned. It may have been a very special example of a consecrated Wafer.

In 1433, Pope Eugene IV gave to Philip the Good, the ducal employer of Jan van Eyck, the important gift of a miraculously bleeding Host. According to mediaeval sources, a bleeding Host and its miracles are recorded time and again ever since the veneration of the *Corpus Christi* became a significant part of the religious life in the thirteenth century. A stereotype story is connected with this miracle-working relic. The Host was acquired at one point by evil Jews who sought to torture and destroy it. In their efforts to do so, they pierced the Host, and it was said to have bled.[300] I believe that it is very likely that the two New York wings were the doors of the wooden tabernacle which Philip had commissioned his court painter to decorate for the valuable relic he had received from the hands of the Holy Father.

We can well imagine the great esteem in which Philip held his miraculous Host. We know that his Duchess Isabella ordered a new monstrance for it in 1454, which was a larger and more magnificent object than the original receptacle. Isabella's new monstrance, which was adorned with the crown of Louis XII, was repeatedly portrayed in book illumination. Our earlier cited illustration of a fifteenth-century monstrance is one of the miniatures illustrating this receptacle (Fig. 143).[301]

---

with both hands raised). Thus, Panofsky's rejection of Musper's highly interesting portrait identification of the rider in the ermine-trimmed coat as Philip the Good is by no means valid. Cf. Panofsky 1953, I, p. 238, note 2, printed on p. 454. Panofsky based his view on the observation that it was not possible for the presumed portrait to appear in the midst of Christ's enemies. Cf. below our note 313. I am, indeed, inclined not only to accept Musper's hypothesis (cf. T. Musper, *Untersuchungen zu Rogier van der Weyden und Jan van Eyck*, Stuttgart 1948, p. 86) but to add to it a second conjectural identification. If the rider with the characteristic headgear and the ermine-trimmed coat is Philip (compare our Fig. 185), the aged man in the small cap who appears on his right side (our left) may be the Pope. The reader will easily gather from the ensuing text how such a possibility could have occurred to me. For Julius Held's suggestion that the female figure in the lower right-hand corner is the Duchess Isabella, cf. below note 363.

[300] Peter Browe, *op.cit., passim*, and especially p. 56, note 53, and p. 157. Compare also the catalogue *La Sainte-Chapelle de Dijon, Siège de l'Ordre de la Toison d'Or*, Dijon 1962, pp. 35, 36, 37 and plates III, IV, V, and VII; in addition, Otto Pächt, "René d'Anjou et les Van Eyck," *Cahiers de l'association internationale des études françaises*, 1956, pp. 41-51, with an earlier date (erroneously?) given for the Pope's gift.

[301] The monstrance is depicted with the same basic parts but with entirely different, greatly elongated, proportions in a Baroque antependium (cf. *La Sainte-Chapelle de Dijon, op.cit.*, no. 106, p. 48 and plate VII). The miraculous Host itself, likewise rather often represented, was impressed with a design of Christ showing His wounds while enthroned as the Judge on the rainbow, an image to which the corresponding detail in Van Eyck's Last Judgment in New York bears a conspicuous resemblance (Figs. 141 and 142). The mention of the year 1454 prompts a conjecture that might be briefly noted at this point. The much discussed painting of the Fountain of Life, whose original I believe to be by Petrus Christus, shows a style that would beautifully conform to this date (Fig. 19). Since two copies are still in existence, the composition must have been a famous work rather frequently imitated in its own time. It may, therefore, have adorned a sanctuary

The style of Van Eyck's two shutters now in New York is unquestionably much earlier than the year 1454. But do the two wings really predate this year by more than a quarter of a century as scholars have often assumed? Although the panels are usually either attributed to Hubert or given to Jan as an early work, in actual fact they may not predate the Ghent Altarpiece. Perhaps after all we can accept the year 1433 as the *terminus ante quem non*. Once freed from the idea that the miniature-like character of a work must necessarily speak for an extremely early date, we realize that a number of elements in these panels bear a conspicuous similarity not only to details in Jan's Adoration of the Lamb but even to the Rolin Madonna, a work which no recent author has believed to predate the Ghent retable.[302] The drapery design of the small figures (take, for instance, the mantle of the Madonna in the Crucifixion panel) is not really very different from the pattern of the long dainty folds which characterize the garb of the Rolin Madonna. Moreover, there is nothing quite so similar to the head of this Madonna as the sweet youthful face of St. Michael in the Judgment panel in New York (Figs. 192 and 170). Finally, the distant snow-capped mountains in the Crucifixion wing find their closest relatives in the landscape background of the Rolin panel. But what of its concept of space, which has proved to be so revealing for the chronology of other Eyckian works?

If our reconstruction of the tabernacle with the Resurrection as the back wall is correct, all three scenes would have been depicted as set into the same continuous landscape. The horizon line of the common setting, however, sharply drops on the right side (Fig. 153). True, the difference in the horizon height would be partially concealed by the rock tomb in the center which hides the horizon on the left and makes its low position on the right side less noticeable. However, the very fact that the height of this line varies from one section to the other would in itself be revealing for the concept of space here used. Clearly, this lack of uniformity betrays a space construction still rather early in the development of Early Netherlandish painting. But is it necessarily earlier than that in the Ghent Altarpiece?

We can be assured that this is not so, for the large polyptych shows precisely the same broken horizon line in the five panels with the Adoration of the Lamb (Fig. 1). There we see a very high horizon in the two left hand panels with the Judges and the Knights and also in the middle part with the mystic Lamb. It is, however, exceptionally low in the panel at the extreme right which shows the giant St. Christopher with the Pilgrims. In addition, the way in which the painter conceals this sharp drop is exactly the same as that

---

of major importance. The subject matter of the composition with Synagoga and Ecclesia is so compatible with the theme of the miraculous Host that the painting may, indeed, have been the altarpiece for the very chapel in which Philip kept his famous relic. Although Bruyn, *op.cit.*, pp. 42f and 54f, discusses the Fountain of Life in connection with the well-known mediaeval miracles of the bleeding Host and treats the occurrence in Segovia of around 1410 at great length, he does not mention the famous relic of Philip the Good.

[302] For the dates affixed by the various writers to this undated work, cf. Baldass, *op.cit.*, p. 278.

which we have assumed for the other work. The intermediate panel of the Hermits, repeating the rock composition of the left side, so skillfully hides the height of the horizon line that the unnaturalness of the low horizon in the panel of the Pilgrims could escape the attention of scholars.

True, the landscape with the broken horizon line may have been invented several years before the completion of the great work. But the very fact that Jan retained this feature shows that he was rather insensitive to its lack of logic even at the time when he finished the work. It seems that by 1432 a unified horizon line was not as yet the rule in Netherlandish landscapes. Because of the fragmentary preservation of the altarpiece production of the time, it is impossible to determine how long after the completion of the Ghent retable this curious feature persisted in the Netherlandish landscapes; chances are that the archaic method remained in use for quite some time afterwards. A Flémallesque work which is perhaps later than the Vijd polyptych still presents the horizon line at differing heights within one and the same panel (Fig. 175).[303] In any case, it is safe at least to state than Van Eyck's Crucifixion and Last Judgment do not necessarily have to be earlier than the Ghent Altarpiece; in fact, it is even possible for them to be later than the Ghent polyptych. A closer comparison of the landscape in the New York Crucifixion and the one in the Adoration of the Lamb may perhaps shed further light on this question.

It is certainly more difficult to specify the concept of space in a landscape painting than it is in the representation of an interior. While the walls of a room can be used to define the foreground of a composition as the limited space of a shrine, a landscape is an unlimited space almost by definition. In any event, the elements of a landscape cannot quite so easily be used as a device to limit the picture space. In considering this matter, we have to keep in mind that the landscape foreground in early fifteenth century paintings is essentially still the old ground line of the preceding two-dimensional art. This line has now been extended, so to speak, into the depth of the picture so as to form a ground plane on which the figures can stand. In these early paintings, however, the plane, like the line, is still simply cut at either side by the frame, without this cutting necessarily indicating a continuation of the picture space beyond the lateral framing limits. The early outdoor setting, though not usually expressly limited on the sides, is normally closed in the rear. The early painter sometimes uses a fabric hanging, sometimes a wall-like device to close the scene in the back and to create a neutral foil against which to silhouette his figures. In

---

[303] Cf. above note 161. As Dr. Charles Minot so kindly pointed out to me, the Betrothal of the Virgin in the Prado depicts St. Joseph in a type radically different from the one otherwise consistently used by the Master of Flémalle and well-known from the Nativity in Dijon (reproduced in Panofsky 1953, ii, plate 88). While Dr. Minot is inclined to believe that this divergence speaks against the Master's authorship of the Prado painting altogether, in my opinion it speaks at least against an early date for the composition. It is obviously Rogier's type of St. Joseph that was an influence in the Prado Betrothal, thus excluding the painting's having an early date. Compare also below note 344.

so doing, he establishes what could be called a "modern replacement" of the old gold ground.[304]

The four wings in the Ghent Adoration of the Lamb also use the "back wall device" (Fig. 1). The four groups depicted in these wings are set against a barrier of grass and shrubbery-covered rocks, which rise to a considerable height so that we see the distant background elements only through the spaces between them. On the right side of this five-panel composition, in the shutter of the Pilgrims, the rocks stop short to open up a large view toward a faraway, level terrain whose especially low horizon has already been noted. In the corresponding Judges panel to the left, however, the rock wall has been extended to form a most interesting spatial device (Fig. 173).

A somewhat lower rock formation is placed obliquely in the picture space in the manner of a side wall. Meeting the rear rock at an angle, it forms a corner which encloses the group of the horsemen. Clearly, this strange phenomenon of the rocks indicates the artist's desire to characterize this outdoor space as a limited expanse. The side rocks have the same function as an interior side wall. Moreover, it is clear that the limitation of the space is the sole function of these rocks for, taken as a landscape motif, they are indeed a rather unrealistic element. They restrict the movement of the horses in this panel in such an "uncomfortable" way that the spectator may well wonder how the riders shown in the rear could ever have managed to guide their mounts into that narrow crevice.

The enclosing device of the rocks in the Ghent panel is, of course, an outspokenly archaic feature. We find a similar device in other early paintings having an outdoor setting. For instance, in the small Frankfort panel of a Garden of Paradise, it takes the form of a low crenelated wall (Fig. 172). There too, the wall forms a corner which encloses only the left side of the scene. The wall corner in the Frankfort painting and the rock corner in the Ghent Altarpiece are both space symbols used for emphasis. They are meant to set off the foreground space from the other parts of the image, as a proofreader's mark sets off a certain line from the rest of the page. The fabricated corner, though appearing on only one side, is nevertheless quite sufficient to be completely effective. In the Ghent Altarpiece, the rock corner distinguishes the foreground from the background in the same way that the box-shaped room of the Annunciation sets off the primary space from the secondary one in the distance (Fig. 81).

The rocks in the rear of the wing panels in the Adoration of the Lamb are the outdoor equivalent, as it were, of the perforated back wall in the Annunciation scene. They

---

[304] For an example of a cloth hanging used in this function as late as in the work of the Master of Flémalle, cf. above note 271. In the early miniatures we often find the rock wall device used to foil the foreground figures. Cf., for instance, the Flight into Egypt of the Brussels Hours (reproduced in *ibid.*, II, fig. 44 on plate 19), the similar representation in the same scene by Broederlam (Fig. 178), or the foiling rock wall in the Berlin drawing of the Adoration of the Magi (Fig. 134).

too are interrupted by intervals which permit an intermittent distant view. These rock walls are not continued into the center panel with the mystic Lamb (Fig. 62). There, the foreground groups are silhouetted against two soft grassy mounds, which are low enough to allow an unhampered view of a vast middle plane. However, the pronounced spaciousness of the central terrain is strangely contradicted by the design of the lateral foreground groups, which consist of figures densely compressed in space and acting as though the rock barrier of the wings was in effect still continued behind them.

This impression persists even though the foreground in the center panel actually is a huge continuous expanse reaching rather far into the distance uninterrupted by any tall material barrier.[305] In one immense stretch this foreground recedes to an area quite close to the upper border of the panel, where it is crowned by a narrow background strip showing the Holy City in an additional landscape in very small scale.

The Crucifixion also shows a vast foreground expanse topped by a narrow strip with a background cityscape (Fig. 140). It is interesting to compare the manner in which the foreground is joined to the narrow background strip in the two representations. In the panel of the mystic Lamb, these background elements look as though they hover on top of the large foreground expanse (Fig. 62). In the Crucifixion, however, a rather similar background gives the convincing impression that it exists behind the foreground space. This is so because in his New York composition the painter has used a specific artistic device which was first described by Millard Meiss as the "plateau type" of space.[306]

The hill in the Crucifixion is not only shown as rising steeply in front of the spectator, it is also characterized as falling steeply into an area not visible to him. The hill is silhouetted against the narrow horizontal form of a soft shrubbery-studded mound but is obviously widely separated from the latter in space. Between the Crucifixion hill and the mound, there is a rather deep ravine of considerable breadth. The large distance between the two elevations is indicated by the radical diminution in the scale of the elements on the mound, where a miniscule rider on a tiny white horse is shown galloping up the slope. The procedure of dividing two hills by a valley of considerable width is repeated behind the mound. The background with its cityscape and its snow-capped mountains is again set apart from the mound by a large dell.

Thus, rather than the steadily rising terrain of the Adoration of the Lamb, the landscape in the Crucifixion is composed of a number of successive hills alternating with deep valleys. Only the tops of these hills are visible in the center of the painting. Showing forms progressively diminished in scale, they lead our eye smoothly and convincingly into the distance. The painter has thereby avoided the disturbing impression, which is given in the

---

[305] For the compression of the foreground space as an important aesthetic device, cf. above Chapter 3, the text following note 135.

[306] Cited above in note 172.

Adoration of the Lamb, of a terrain that still rises in its entirety together with the picture plane.

There is, moreover, still another artistic device in the New York panel which helps immensely to counteract the impression that the rising terrain is connected with the rising picture surface. In the Lamb panel, only the background with its trees and buildings is directly silhouetted against the sky, while no foreground or middle distance details are tall enough to cross the horizon. In the New York Calvary, however, we see details of the middle ground crossing the horizon and rising to a considerable height. The three tall poles of the crosses, which are large elements comparatively near to the spectator's eye, are silhouetted against the sky. Forming in a sense a lacework screen behind the foreground area and providing four openings through which we see the background details, the arrangement of the crosses convinces the spectator that he is confronted with the genuine depth of a continuous space and forces him to forget the existence of the picture surface. The screen of the crosses beautifully divides the space, not horizontally or vertically, but orthogonally, that is to say, it cuts the extension into depth of the space, thereby powerfully emphasizing the existence of this extension.[307]

This orthogonal division of space heightens the spectator's awareness of the beautiful echelon of space levels which we have described and which follow each other in depth—one softly fusing into the next—from the nearest foreground into the farthest distance. By introducing a number of strong diagonal movements in the foreground of his scene, the painter has expressly avoided the all too prominent horizontal division of the picture plane which is so very characteristic of the Adoration of the Lamb. In the Adoration panel, there is essentially only a series of horizontally extending surface levels reaching from the bottom to the top. With all the figures on all these levels silhouetted only against the ground, this ground becomes a kind of foil which flattens the entire composition.

These are not the only archaic features that are avoided in the New York Crucifixion. In his Calvary scene, Van Eyck does not attempt to characterize the foreground as a limited space either by the use of the rock corner or by the compression of the foreground groups. Quite to the contrary, he made the greatest effort in the Crucifixion to indicate

---

[307] Though the crosses are silhouetted against the gold ground in older two-dimensional painting, they are by no means always set against the sky in the more developed fifteenth century compositions. When the mountainous terrain and the cityscape of the background achieve an explicitness as elements extending in a broad three-dimensional sweep into the distance and cover part of the panel surface previously taken up by the gold ground, the crosses, having kept their original position, have "sunk," so to speak, into these background forms. Cf., for instance, the Crucifixion attributed to Lodewijk Allyncbrood, Collection Bauzá, Madrid (J. Duverger, "Brugse Schilders ten tijde van Jan van Eyck," *Miscellanea Erwin Panofsky*, p. 97, fig. 4) or the painting by Giovanni Boccati, Collection Count Cini, Venice (Meiss, *op.cit.*, 1961, fig. 44). Merging with the background details in these representations, the crosses are not employed as a space-dividing device in the same manner as they were used by Van Eyck.

that the foreground picture space continues beyond that portion which is visible to the spectator. He depicted many of the figures which appear near the left and right borders of the painting in strongly fragmented views. The horseman on the right side seen from the back and appearing near the two little soldiers who walk alongside him up the hill, is a particularly good example of the painter's method. This rider and his horse are virtually cut in two, with the larger and more important part of both figures concealed by the frame. This motif forces the spectator to imagine that the figures and the space which surrounds them do continue beyond that portion actually shown in the painting.

It is, however, not only the fragmentation of the marginal figures which indicates that Van Eyck has here used a very advanced concept of space. The treatment of the groups that surround the three crosses also attests to this more mature concept (Figs. 140 and 167). A striking effect is achieved in these groups by the same device of liberal overlapping and fragmentation of form which we have observed at the panel borders. The group under the crosses form an inextricable network of shapes in which sudden drastic changes of scale play an important part.[308] We never see a neutral background foil in the spaces between two forms. These spaces are always filled with the radically fragmented shapes of other figures or other horses. The forms popping up behind others are sometimes comparatively large in scale, sometimes comparatively small, depending on their distance from the elements in front of them. They also consist of a range in sizes of fragments from large to small. Since the painter has depicted varying distances between the components of the crowd, we sometimes see between two of them merely a fraction of a face, sometimes the whole cuirassed torso of a soldier.

The process of showing new forms in the space between two figures is repeated again and again in progressively more distant levels as our eye follows up the slope of the Crucifixion hill. We constantly see new forms, including the tops of those figures which have been moving up the hill from the far side and are about to reach its apex. Indeed, the process of continually showing new forms behind still others is repeated *ad infinitum*.[309] It is this phrase which holds the clue to the intrinsic nature of Van Eyck's spatial concept in this painting. The concept of infinite space has here reached a point of maturity far

---

[308] These sudden and radical changes in scale were recognized as an important spatial device by many of Van Eyck's followers, who attempted to imitate it. However, when the imitators did not grasp the rules of perspective diminution which formed the basis of Jan's procedure, the scale changes in their paintings, lacking any system, are completely arbitrary and do not achieve the desired effect. One can best observe this failure in the paintings of Jan's most devoted German follower, formerly believed to have the name "Pfenning" and now identified as Conrad Laib, cf. Alfred Stange, *Deutsche Malerei Der Gotik*, x, *Salzburg, Bayern, Tirol in der Zeit von 1400 bis 1500*, Munich/Berlin 1960, figs. 47 and 48. Even such a late and excellent Netherlandish painter as Gerard David is not always correct in his choice of scale when using the Eyckian device. Cf. the illustrations in the article by Davies cited in our Excursus II.

[309] This observation conforms with Panofsky's brilliant discussion of the character of the Eyckian art (Panofsky 1953, I, pp. 181f). In his explanation of the relationship between the infinitely small and the infinitely large in the form of Van Eyck, he uses the infinitesimal calculus as a comparison.

beyond that in the Ghent Altarpiece. In the Adoration of the Lamb, it is not only the foreground groups which seem strangely compressed and spaceless. Even the small groups in the background appear equally stiff and motionless when compared with the Crucifixion groups (Figs. 167 and 171).[310]

The crowd in the Crucifixion indeed gives us the impression that it is actually moving. This most astonishing kinetic effect is the consequence not only of Van Eyck's brilliant way of overlapping and fragmenting his forms, but also of the ample space which surrounds each figure. The spectator knows that a form in the rear can become visible in full only if an overlapping shape were to move out of the way. Since this possibility is strongly suggested by the airiness and variety of the group, the observer quite spontaneously sees the crowd as though it were in motion. The fluctuating movement of a non-idealized, anonymous mass of figures gives the scene the momentary quality which is so characteristic of the modern photographic snapshot. Indeed, the New York Crucifixion may well have been the work in which the passage of time and the intrinsically infinite picture space—two very modern and closely allied concepts—materialized for the first time in art. In any case, the presence of these advanced features quite conclusively demonstrates that this panel does in fact postdate the Ghent Altarpiece.

V. PURPOSE VERSUS DATE IN AN EYCKIAN WORK

Even though we may decide that the two panels from the Metropolitan Museum belong to the post-Ghentian period of Van Eyck, it is still impossible to overlook the striking difference between the two wings and the rest of his oeuvre. When we try to detect the reason for the undeniable difference, the old explanation of the miniature-like character of the New York panels again comes to mind. But to state that the compositions look like miniatures is saying both too much and not enough: there are panel paintings by Van Eyck which are far smaller in size than the New York shutters and yet do not possess the specific character of these two wings; on the other hand, very few miniatures ascribed to Van Eyck or his followers have a composition similar to our two panels.[311]

---

[310] Although some scholars, such as Dvořák and Panofsky, see in the background groups a freer and more advanced style, others hold the opposite view. Beenken, for instance, struck by the stiffness of the distant groups, believes that it is the background portion of the painting which, as the more archaic part, should be attributed to Hubert (Beenken, *op.cit.*, 1941, p. 36).

[311] In the better known of the two Calvary scenes in the Turin-Milan Hours (Panofsky 1953, II, fig. 290 on plate 156), the Cross between the Virgin and St. John is rendered as a large devotional group isolated in an otherwise empty foreground. In its restriction of the narrative to the background, it is a type entirely different from the New York Crucifixion. In addition to the miniatures that show a few large figures as the protagonists of their scenes, the Hour Book also contains a number of other types. One of them presents a landscape that is populated merely by small *staffage* figures (a type apparently created by singling out a part of the landscape background from a large painting); another type (often also used as a *bas-de-page*) silhouettes a larger number of small figures against the sky of a low horizon landscape (cf. for instance, our Fig. 131). Even the last type, which, like the New York Calvary, actually shows a landscape with a

Which qualities, then, account for the extraordinary character of the Crucifixion and the Last Judgment in New York?

While all the other Eyckian works show representations with a monumental foreground in which one or at most a few figures are depicted in large scale and function as the protagonists of the compositions, the two panels in New York present a great number of tiny figures almost evenly distributed over a large area of the available picture surface. We have here an exceptional situation in which Van Eyck has rejected his usual "showcase" arrangement by which a few saintly individuals hieratically present themselves for the devotion of the believer. In the New York Crucifixion, the events are depicted as happening at some distance from the spectator (Fig. 140). The considerable separation allows the painter to give almost equal stress to each of his groups. There is no marked difference in scale between the foremost figures at the bottom and the foreground figures at the top of the hill. The sloping terrain makes it clear that the eye of the spectator is not much farther away from the upper section than it is from the lower section of the representation. The steeply rising hill is obviously used as a realistic justification for the almost uniform scale of the groups and their even distribution over the panel area. This method, far from being an archaic feature or something specific to miniature, is a narrative device still employed more than a century later in many panel paintings by Pieter Bruegel the Elder to facilitate the presentation of the various activities of a large number of people.

The crowded Calvary scene is a traditional Trecento type familiar to the North long before the period of Van Eyck.[312] Jan, however, omitted the conventional features familiar to the type. All the symbols which are usually employed to designate the religious significance of the scene do not appear in the New York Crucifixion: no halos surround the heads of Christ and the saints; nor are these figures distinguished from the others by an enlarged ideal scale. Supernatural elements are completely eliminated. The sky which tops the scene shows some enchanting white clouds but not the usual angels and devils which populate other Crucifixion scenes. Nothing contradicts the viewer's impression that he is witnessing an ordinary execution.

---

high horizon and a densely populated foreground, still bears only a superficial similarity to the Metropolitan Museum panel. The miniature whose character comes closest to the latter is the Betrayal of Christ (*ibid.*, II, fig. 298 on plate 163). But even this scene differs essentially from the New York Crucifixion. In contrast to the panel, the miniature avoids the rising foreground and divides the picture area almost evenly between a level foreground and a rising background, the extent of whose distance is seen in the central opening between two lateral slopes.

[312] Cf. E. Roth, *Der volkreiche Kalvarienberg in Literatur und Kunst des Spätmittelalters*, Berlin 1958, also Meiss, *op.cit.*, 1961, figs. 11, 14, 22, 27, 33, 34, 38, 39, 41, 44. For the Northern type immediately preceding that of Van Eyck, cf. the large and the small Calvaries in the Wallraf-Richartz Museum, Cologne, which are both apparently derived from the Netherlandish pre-Eyckian tradition now lost. For the large one, cf. our Fig. 169; the small one is reproduced in *Wallraf-Richartz-Museum Köln, Führer durch die Gemäldegalerie*, Cologne 1957, fig. 6.

The crowd behaves precisely as a group of soldiers, officials, and serfs would act at a public event which is a welcome interruption of their daily routine. It is even difficult to recognize some of the characters that are mentioned in the Gospel text and are usually presented in this type of a Crucifixion. The man piercing the side of Christ who bears the apocryphal name of Longinus, the other with the sponge of vinegar, and the converted centurion, though actually depicted in Van Eyck's painting, somehow disappear in the fluctuating forms of the crowd.[313] The holy mourners, the Virgin and St. John surrounded by six saintly women, are found in the lower zone placed apart from the crowd as they are pictured in the Gospel (Fig. 168).[314] But this group does not address the spectator in the usual fashion of so many other Crucifixion scenes. The figures do not invite him to share in their grief. To them, the observer is but a stranger whom they disregard entirely. It is even difficult for us to locate the mother of the Saviour in this group, for her figure is so unobtrusive that it needs the shining white headdress of the woman behind her to lead our eye to the place where she collapses in her agony. The Virgin's figure is but a mass of dark blue drapery which almost entirely hides her hands and even her face in the moment of her breakdown. Thus even the important group of holy mourners shares in the general anonymity of the crowd, and it is this very quality which makes the group of the mourners so ineffably human and so overwhelmingly touching.

The same is true for the figure of the Crucified. Accentuated only by the perfectly natural feature of His high position on the central cross, Van Eyck has deliberately presented the Saviour of the world as the rather appalling image of a blood-soiled body tortured to death. Distinctly characterized as a typical Levantine, far from the idealized Christ-type of Northern art, the Crucified towers over the scene as nothing other than the gruesome image of creatural misery. If the observer did not know from the pictorial tradition that a figure represented in this position is the Son of the Almighty, he could never gather such knowledge from the scene painted by Van Eyck. The painter depicts a historical reality completely unglorified and entirely unsentimental. This is the Crucifixion as a contemporary of Christ might have seen it as a chance witness.[315]

[313] Panofsky's observation (cf. above note 299) that the right side of the painting shows only the enemies of Christ is apparently due to his having overlooked the centurion, who is represented on that side. Van Eyck did not (as some other painters do) identify this figure with that of Longinus who pierced the side of Christ.

[314] Matthew 27:55; Mark 15:40; Luke 8:2,3. (Only John 19:25, describes the women as standing beside the Cross.) The group is thus very often placed in a separate picture level below the three crosses, where it functions as a separate center of devotion. In the large Cologne Crucifixion already mentioned above in note 312, we have a good example of the type as it looked in the pre-Eyckian era (Fig. 169).

[315] It is interesting to note that the viewer of the Van Eyck Calvary sees the scene as it would be seen by a mounted spectator rather than by a pedestrian. In conjunction with the many other indications previously discussed, this feature also strongly argues against the possibility that the painting was used as an altar retable. The obvious implication of a princely donor watching the scene from his horse was perhaps connected with the presumed portraits discussed above in note 299. Both of the figures discussed are depicted

What we see in both panels are scenes as they could be observed in real life. The Last Judgment is shown in this same vein, as the realistic portrayal of a future occurrence in which the divine becomes visible (Fig. 141). In connection with the unconventional representation of the Crucifixion, the Last Judgment painted on the companion panel takes on a specific new shade of meaning. The sudden and clear manifestation of the supernatural on the last day is particularly awe-inspiring when seen side by side with the stark image of our own ordinary world as it appears in the other wing. The Last Judgment is thus the consequence of the divine occurrences which lie unseen behind our own worldly reality. And our own ordinary world is the setting in the Judgment panel too. The apparition of the heavenly Judge with His heavenly jury in the celestial Paradise and the simultaneous exposure of the horrible chasm of the inferno are dramatically set against the image of our own earth seen in the frightening uproar of the last day.

This is not merely the same old earth that we see in the Crucifixion scene, it is the exact same portion of this earth. Undoubtedly, both scenes are meant to take place in the earthly city of Jerusalem.[316] According to mediaeval and even to some modern belief, the Last Judgment will occur in the sacred city of the Old and New Testament. The background view in the Crucifixion panel is clearly the earthly Jerusalem. Herod's temple is prominently shown (Fig. 167).[317] With this building and other Herodian structures, for

---

as riders. If one of them actually is the effigy of Philip the Good, and if at the same time Philip is also assumed to be the spectator of the panel, this "duplication of the donor" is not as unusual as it may at first seem to the modern mind. In many works of the Middle Ages and the Renaissance, we find the portrait of the owner, who is sometimes even the sole spectator of the work. This usage is common in altarpieces, even in those that adorned private sanctuaries. Moreover, it is most striking in book illumination. The initial showing the portrait of Jeanne d'Évreux in the Annunciation page of her hour book now in the Cloisters, New York (James J. Rorimer, *The Hours of Jeanne d'Évreux*, New York 1957, plate 3) appears in a volume of such tiny size that the page was hardly ever looked at by anyone other than the owner herself. The famous Camera degli Sposi in Mantua, painted by Mantegna for the Gonzaga family and showing their portraits, indicates that this practice extended to secular works as well.

[316] The third scene, too, namely the Resurrection, claimed to be the center representation of the unit, must have shown a part of the same city of Jerusalem. Cf. the background details of Bruegel's composition (Fig. 149). It seems, indeed, as though the Crucifixion and the lost Resurrection had both been meant to show the same continuous terrain which had formed in the well-known traditional manner the unified setting of two successive historical events. Cf. Fig. 175.

[317] In Van Eyck's depiction of the Jewish Temple, it is interesting to note how much the design of the Moslem sanctuary, which often functions as the model for this portrayal, has been changed. This sanctuary, the Mosque of Omar, usually called the Dome of the Rock and occupying the site of the Jewish Temple since the seventh century, was built on a centralized plan showing a raised core topped by a rather high dome. Up to the sixteenth century, the design of this Moslem sanctuary was traditionally used in Christian art to illustrate the Jewish Temple—even the earliest of the three sanctuaries, which was built by King Solomon. Cf., for instance, Elisabeth Geck, *Bernhard von Breydenbach, Die Reise ins Heilige Land*, Wiesbaden 1961, folding plate 1. For the various Jewish temples successively built on the same site, cf. Irene Lande-Nash, *3000 Jahre Jerusalem*, Tübingen 1964, pp. 26ff. For the design of the Dome of the Rock, functioning as the Jewish Temple in the art of the immediate circle of Van Eyck, cf. the painting of the

instance the fortress Antonia, depicted among an array of quite ordinary houses, the view shows a marked contrast to that of the Adoration of the Lamb, where the city is an idealized dream image composed of fantastic buildings and unquestionably meant to be the Heavenly Jerusalem of the divine promise.

The setting in the Ghent Altarpiece is the Heavenly Jerusalem; that of the New York panels is the earthly city of Jerusalem. It is this basic distinction in locale between the two works which accounts for the many and outspoken differences and gives the impression that they are "worlds apart." We are, in fact, faced with two worlds. Set in the earthly realm, the scenes in the New York wings have a tenor very different from that of the large polyptych where the action takes place in a celestial domain. The Heavenly Jerusalem is an ideal place which lifts the scenes of the Ghent Altarpiece into the hieratic atmosphere of a divine immobility. The earthly Jerusalem, on the other hand, calls for a mode of representation which, no matter whether it reproduces the past or the future, is much more akin to forms similar to those that are normally visible to mortal man.

In the small New York panels, we could almost speak of their "photographic" truth had the artist not injected into them an element designed to counteract their all too natural mode of expression. The two monumental signs of the monstrance and the Hebrew letter, which the painter seems to have indicated in the outlines of the two compositions, provide the scenes with the supernatural component imperative in every religious representation of that period. The two huge signs formed by the many tiny elements of the ordinary world indicate the system of divine preordination which exists behind the natural shapes. These signs become visible to the viewer if his glance remains on the surface of the panels without actually entering into the scenes. In other words, he sees them when his attention is not as yet focused on the worldly narrative meaning of the forms.[318]

To the modern secular-minded spectator who hardly notices the large signs, the two scenes offer an enticingly natural view. There is a great freedom in the representation not only of human motion but also of human emotion. Panofsky, who remarked on the

---

Three Marys at the Tomb in the Museum Boymans-Van Beuningen, Rotterdam (Fig. 182). This design was altered in the New York Calvary by adding buttressing piers to the structure, by enlarging its core, and by flattening the dome. In short, the structure was brought back, so to speak, to the more imaginary appearance of the Temple as it had been rendered in Broederlam's Annunciation scene (Fig. 177). These alterations by Van Eyck prove that the artist was consciously depicting a "reconstruction" of the Temple as it may have looked at Christ's time. By rendering an imaginary building rather than the actually existing one, Van Eyck proved his highly developed sense of "history."

[318] The symbols become visible when the compositions are viewed as abstract forms or, better, as flat iconic shapes. In other words, they reveal their meaning when they are seen with the eyes of the old-fashioned devout rather than with those of the modern connoisseur of realistic imagery. For the idea that the star in the Mérode Altarpiece is in the same category as these symbols, compare above note 296. For the icon-like mode deliberately used as an artistic device in Van Eyck's Adoration of the Lamb, cf. Chapter 3, Part III, the text following note 135.

contrast between this free expression and the stony rigidity in other works by Van Eyck, was inclined to see the two modes as stages in the Eyckian evolution. To him, the freely expressive form charged with the drama of the event belonged to Jan's early period, whereas the immobility and monumentality of a composition was a sign to him of a more mature phase of the Eyckian art.[319]

We have to make a distinction between the freedom of the movement in space in a work by Van Eyck and his free portrayal of human emotion. The former can indeed be explained on the basis of the Eyckian development. We have seen that the figures' free motion in space presupposes an advanced spatial concept. Rather than indicating an early stage in the artist's development, it requires a date after the Ghent Altarpiece. The expression of vivid emotion, on the other hand, has nothing to do with a specific place of the work in the evolution of Eyckian art. It is the direct consequence of the painter's choice of setting. The free expression of emotion is the natural corollary of the earthliness of the place of action.

Human emotion is a concept intimately connected with life on earth. According to mediaeval belief, the Fall of Man which deprived humanity of the gift of immortality, also divested him of his original serene balance of mind. The appearance of the four temperaments was one of the unfortunate results of Original Sin. The world has been ruled by human passions ever since.[320] Thus, when Van Eyck gives free expression to the grief of the mourners and to the sneering hate of the enemies of Christ in his Crucifixion scene, he does so because this scene takes place in the earthly world of the historical Jerusalem.

When the Heavenly Jerusalem is the setting of his scenes, the painter has to refrain from this manner of representation. Instead, the atmosphere is of a hieratic immobility with the figures shown in serene repose. The lack of drama and feeling in the art of Van Eyck has often been remarked upon not only with surprise but sometimes even with reproach.[321] This soberness, however, is based on a profound logic. In the Heavenly Jerusalem, Original Sin has finally been abolished. Having regained its former immortality, mankind has now re-entered a stage of serene composure. Any outburst of human temperament of either a positive or a negative sort in a celestial scene would have no place.

---

[319] Cf. Panofsky 1953, I, the end of Section II, p. 182, and also the following Section III, pp. 182-94 containing Panofsky's chronology of Jan van Eyck's altarpieces.

[320] In the twelfth century writings of Hildegard of Bingen, who was influenced by Late Classical and Early Christian cosmological concepts, we find the idea that in Adam's initial paradisial state the four elements and the four humors were fused in a harmonious balance, but that this harmony was disturbed through the Fall of Man, which thus became the origin of the human temperaments. Cf. Hans Liebeschütz, *Das allegorische Weltbild der Heiligen Hildegard von Bingen* (Studien der Bibliothek Warburg, XVI), Leipzig/Berlin 1930, pp. 124-32.

[321] "Utterly devoid of religious feeling," says Weale about the figure of St. George in the Madonna of Canon George van der Paele (Fig. 139). "Seldom has a subject which lends itself to spiritual emotion been so undramatically, so unspiritually, treated," says C. Phillips about the Washington Annunciation, going so far as to call the work "spiritually and physically ugly" (Fig. 138). Cf. Weale and Brockwell, *op.cit.*, pp. 101 and 122.

When scholars speak of the lack of drama and emotion as a characteristic feature in the paintings of Jan, this generalization is a perfectly legitimate one. The Heavenly Jerusalem is the setting not only for the Ghent Altarpiece but also for almost all the other known works by the master. There are, in fact, a number of Eyckian paintings in which the very splendor of the setting has always suggested a celestial interpretation, and in which, indeed, Panofsky has already seen a portrayal of the Heavenly Jerusalem.[322] To him, however, this concept of the celestial city was limited in meaning to the paradisaic abode which the believer hopes to enter after his death. But the term includes the much broader connotation of the institution of the Christian Church which comprises past, present, and future. Disregarding this wider meaning, Panofsky confined his interpretation of the Heavenly Jerusalem to only a certain type of a non-narrative representation. In so doing, however, he failed to see the full importance of the theme for Eyckian art.

As previously explained, the Heavenly Jerusalem can function just as well in a narrative scene such as the Ghent Annunciation. Moreover, since the celestial locale consists of the New Heaven and the New Earth—the first depicted as an architecture, the second as a landscape or garden—the Heavenly Jerusalem can be shown as an interior setting as well as an exterior one. In the work of Van Eyck, the sacred palace of the New Heaven assumes many different shapes and guises. It takes the form of a church in the Berlin Madonna (Fig. 135), a royal chapel in the Van der Paele Madonna (Fig. 139), and a temple in the Washington Annunciation (Fig. 138); it is a city palace in the Ghent Annunciation (Fig. 81), a fortress in the Rolin Madonna (Fig. 192), the throne room of a palace in the Lucca Madonna (Fig. 137), and a palace porch in the Madonna of Jan Vos (Fig. 203); in the Dresden Madonna, it is a basilica which is both a royal palace and a church (Fig. 128). In the St. Barbara panel in Antwerp, the landscape in the foreground is the New Earth and the tower behind her the New Heaven, while the Madonna at the Fountain presents the Garden of Paradise as the *hortus conclusus* (Figs. 130 and 129). No matter whether an indoor or an outdoor setting, or a combination of the two, the scene of action is always the Heavenly Jerusalem.

Of all of these paintings, only the Ghent Altarpiece is still found in its original place and, almost up to modern times, serving its original purpose. Nonetheless, we can assume with a high degree of probability that the original function of all of them was as either stationary or portable altarpieces.[323] And when we realize at this point that only the New York wings had apparently served a different purpose and that they are also the only ones not to portray the Heavenly Jerusalem, a very interesting idea then suggests itself. In the

[322] In the Dresden Triptych, the Rolin Madonna, and the Madonna of George van der Paele, the setting has already been recognized as connoting a celestial domain. Cf. Panofsky 1953, I, pp. 139f. In fact, the setting of the Van der Paele Madonna is actually meant, in my opinion, to depict the Holy Sepulcher Rotunda in Jerusalem. Cf. our Figs. 139 and 114.

[323] In Peters, *op.cit.*, 1968, pp. 240f, the comparative scales of a number of Eyckian works are discussed, with a most instructive drawing on p. 241 and an interesting attempt to conclude the purpose of a work from its size.

New York Crucifixion and Last Judgment, the painter was able to select the earthly Jerusalem as a setting and to indulge in the free realism of a historical narrative with many small figures only because the two wings were not the parts of an altar retable. In other words, their unique character, wrongly called "miniature-like," is simply their quality of "not being an altarpiece," which means their quality of "not being a devotional image proper."

Conversely, the setting of the Heavenly Jerusalem with its monumental foreground of one or at most a few figures in serene composure is obviously an idea specifically devised for the Christian altar retable. This compositional characteristic, which recurs throughout the canonical Eyckian oeuvre, was perhaps first developed for the Ghent Altarpiece. Unquestionably the use of the Heavenly Jerusalem as a setting was of specific importance for altar painting and for altar painting alone. The predominance of this idea in the later work of Van Eyck indicates that it represented a patent solution to an important problem posed by the altar painting of the time. To understand the nature of this problem and the special role which the Ghent Altarpiece played in its solution, we have to direct our attention to the development of the painted altar retable in the North.

CHAPTER 5

The Ghent Altarpiece
in Northern Altar Painting

I. ALTAR PAINTING AND THE HEAVENLY JERUSALEM

THE painting of an altar retable had to suggest to the believer the factual presence of the depicted figures and scenes in the sanctuary that surrounded him. It is this task that distinguishes altar painting from other types of painted representations. While book illumination as well as stained glass, murals, or the painted adornments of a reliquary or tabernacle compartment fundamentally remained a sacred decor, the painting placed on an altar became one of the main devotional images of the church. It, therefore, had to present the holy personages and scenes as at the same time more hieratic and more immediately real.[324]

On the basis of its intimate connection with the Eucharistic rite the altar image acquired this singular quality. The postulate that it must characterize its representations as actually present in the sanctuary in which the altarpiece was placed followed from its function as the direct illustration of the Sacramental act. According to Catholic belief, the sacred stories of Salvation turn into a living reality during the celebration of the Eucharist. No matter whether the events told in these stories are of the biblical past or of the future, they are immediately present in the chapel or church in which the sacred rite is being performed. It is this miraculous but invisible presence of the holy persons and their stories which is made visible in the paintings of an altarpiece.

In the early fourteenth century, the style of Northern painting had developed into a form that was rather favorable for the characterization of the painted figures as materially existing in the space of the surrounding sanctuary. The famous Cologne Annunciation of around 1325 is a good example of the type (Fig. 176).[325] The two large figures

---

[324] Before the time when an altarpiece was used to adorn the mensa, a precious golden statuette or certain other valuable containers which enclosed relics had been placed upon the altar table. Statues like Sainte Foy of Conques were reliquaries and had their place on the altar. These statues and receptacles were revered for their great sanctity not only for their contents but also in themselves. A good measure of the devotion dedicated to them was inherited, in a sense, by their successor, the altar retable, whose images had to equal them not only in sanctity but also in their "tangible" presence. For the Northern altarpiece as the follower of the wooden *armoire* for relics, cf. Keller, *op.cit., passim.*

[325] It is preserved together with one other panel of the same size which depicts Christ's Presentation in

are only schematically modeled and are set as rather flat shapes upon the gold-covered panel surface. This gold ground has almost completely lost the spatial quality which it had formerly possessed as a heritage of Late Antiquity. It is now primarily only a sacred coating meant to enhance the holiness of the wooden board, which is the base of the representation. But the gold ground not only characterizes the panel as sacred, it also stresses the fact that it is a tangible object which physically exists in the sanctuary.

Placed on the surface of this gold-covered object, the two figures of the Annunciation assume the quality of a material, objective reality. This impression is especially distinct because the scene lacks its own pictorial setting. With the location of the story indicated by only a tiny elevation of rocky ground visible between the two figures, the scenery is limited to a mere suggestion of the barest essentials. Fundamentally, the figures have no space of their own in which to exist. Existing as material shapes upon the golden panel surface, their space remains virtually identical with the real space surrounding the spectator.

The basic identity of the pictorial with the real space was a great advantage for the altar painting of the time. It not only secured the actual existence of the painted figures in front of the believer, but it also imbued these figures with a pervading holiness. For the real space, to which the gold-covered retable and its representations is so strongly characterized as belonging, is a holy space. The Christian sanctuary, no matter whether it is a chapel, a church, or a huge cathedral, is believed to signify the Heavenly Jerusalem.

This meaning of the sanctuary space has previously been discussed.[326] Far from being merely a symbol of the celestial city, the building was believed to establish the factual reality of the heavenly structure here on earth. Mediaeval man, therefore, quite naturally regarded each part of the church architecture as being filled with a pervasive holiness which was conceived as an objective, magically effective quality. It is not so difficult to understand that the statues and reliefs which were part of the stone body of the building were thought of as sharing this quality of the architecture. But the concept applies as well to every part of the church furnishings, including any painted representation. It was of particular importance with regard to the altar image. As the crowning part of the altar table over which the Eucharist was celebrated and as the illustration of the Eucharistic mystery, the image of the altarpiece had to present the figures and scenes as directly present in front of the devout. This direct presence was secured by the identity of the pictorial with the real space. Since the church building was believed to establish the immediate presence of the Heavenly Jerusalem here on earth, a painting, when characterized as an actual part of the building, automatically gained the quality of a sacred immediate presence.

---

the Temple. It is highly probable that the two panels had originally formed the wings of an altarpiece showing a shrine with sculpture in the center. Cf. the guide: *Wallraf-Richartz-Museum Köln, op.cit.,* 1957, p. 22. The proposed unit would have been similar in appearance and scale to the Harvestehude Altar by Master Bertram; cf. *Katalog der alten Meister der Hamburger Kunsthalle,* Hamburg 1956, p. 31.

[326] Cf. above notes 109 and 110 and the paragraphs of Chapter 3 which belong to them.

We have seen in an earlier chapter that the stories of Salvation have an eternal as well as an historical aspect. They are the biblical events of a sacred past and the eternal truths of Christian doctrine. The eternal aspect is paramount in paintings like the Cologne Annunciation. The scene's realm of existence, still identical with the sanctuary space of the surrounding architecture, is the ideal timeless domain of the Heavenly Jerusalem. In paintings in which the scene has this supertemporal character, no problem was as yet posed in the physical joining of the painted figures and objects to the sacred picture base, the altar panel. However, the instant that the biblical scene appeared in its own setting and thus in a time and place specifically belonging to the historical event, the painter was confronted with a difficult task. The biblical place and time had to be reconciled with the surrounding church space and the present time, for only in so doing could the artist characterize his scene as a timeless doctrinal truth immediately present in the sanctuary space surrounding the worshiper.

In the Dijon Altarpiece of the late fourteenth century, Melchior Broederlam depicted four scenes from the childhood of Christ in an elaborate and complex setting designating a particular time and place for each of the biblical events (Figs. 177 and 178). This manner of representation permitted the believer to immerse himself in the sacred scenes in an act of mystical identification with the holy persons who are depicted. This new manner of representation, for which the art of the Italian Trecento had provided the basic artistic means, transported the spectator in each of the scenes into a different remote place and a different remote time.[327]

Having shown his stories in settings that were carefully described in their historical

[327] It is well known that it was the art of the brothers Lorenzetti in particular which influenced the Broederlam altarpiece. For the church interior of the Presentation scene, Ambrogio Lorenzetti's Presentation of Christ has often been cited as a model. Cf. Panofsky 1953, 1, plate 8. However, the essential difference between the Northern and the Italian work has less often been emphasized. Broederlam, though working half a century after the time of the Lorenzetti, had not even arrived at the evolutionary stage in space construction which characterizes the compositions of the two Italian painters. While in the Italian retables, the boundaries of the depicted interiors coincide more or less precisely with the boundaries of the panel, so that the pictorial space becomes a simulated recess behind the picture frame, the architectural structure to which Broederlam's temple interior belongs is still placed as a unit on the wide area of the two-dimensional picture surface. The concept that underlies Lorenzetti's composition is an essential awareness of the difference between the pictorial and the actual space. This concept, inherited by the South from Roman Antiquity, had never been entirely lost in the art of the region. Fully revived in Italy in the period around 1300, this concept soon supplanted the "Byzantine" mode, which is still so very prominent in Broederlam's representation. It was the absence of the Antique tradition which made Northern painting in a much more direct and "corporeal" manner part of the surrounding sanctuary and subjected its image to the power of this architectural whole. The subjection was all the more radical because the "architectural whole" in the North (which was the Gothic cathedral) had risen to a symbolic glory never achieved or even attempted in Italy. For the intense observation of the natural light in Northern paintings as possibly inspired by the light symbolism of the Gothic cathedral, cf. my article in the *Wallraf-Richartz-Jahrbuch, op.cit.*, p. 99 and notes 49 and 50, and also below note 390.

detail, the artist had, nevertheless, also to invest his representations with the timeless "here and now" necessary to bring out their character as an eternal truth of Christian doctrine. He solved his dual task by placing the four events in a common landscape space, spread like a low relief over the panel surface which he had covered with the traditional gold ground. This artistic device beautifully assures the material existence of the scenes on the sacred picture base and thus their factual presence in the space of the consecrated sanctuary. Both their eternal as well as their historical aspect are thus made clear. They are individual scenes each occurring in their own historical space and time; but they also present the ideal unity of eternal events which happen in the timeless place of the Heavenly Jerusalem, that is to say, of the sanctuary surrounding them.

The joining of a representation which is already clearly three-dimensional to the surface of an altar panel has the effect of transforming the painted scene into a layer of relief. This impression is understandable when we recognize the basic difference between painting and sculpture. The three-dimensionality of a painting is a quality pertaining to a purely imagined pictorial space. A piece of sculpture, however, even when characterized as surrounded by its own scenic space, always has a three-dimensionality in the real space which surrounds both the art object and the spectator. It is, by the way, this material three-dimensionality tying the work to the material space of the consecrated sanctuary which accounts for the preference for sculpture as a cult image during this period.

The relief character of a painted image as we see it in Broederlam's panels is something of an effort for the modern eye. But since in late fourteenth century representations the panel surface is still clearly acknowledged as a materially existing plane, it is possible even for the modern spectator to see this relief character and yet be able readily to accept Broederlam's scenes as "almost natural." This is not so in the later Mérode Altarpiece by the Master of Flémalle (Fig. 82). There, the factual existence of the painted board is already denied, at least in principle. No longer is the picture plane partly covered by a gold ground which stresses the solidity of the surface. Instead, the historically descriptive scenes cover the entire area with a blue sky now included as the logical continuation of their description. Taken as a whole, the three paintings of the triptych certainly present what may be called a perspective image, i.e., an image that is no longer conceived as appearing on the surface of the picture board but rather as existing behind this plane, the board now disregarded as a solid opaque object and considered, as it were, as transparent.[328]

When, in spite of this rather advanced representation in the Mérode Altarpiece, we find in the center panel of the Annunciation the surprising survival of an older concept rather similar to that of Broederlam, the effect is somewhat confusing to a modern viewer. The strange way in which figures and objects appear in the space of the Annunciation

[328] Cf. Panofsky 1953, I, pp. 3ff. For this concept, which underlies all the later methodically constructed perspective images, cf. also the literature cited above in note 249.

chamber has often been remarked upon.[329] This representation not only lacks a basic sta-
bility, it is essentially unconvincing as a perspective image. It is not just that the table and
the bench look as though they are sliding down toward the spectator, all four of the large
foreground forms, the furniture and also the two figures, appear as flat, compressed shapes
in spite of their vigorous modeling.

While the tilted effect of the furniture is simply due to the high vantage point which
is applied to them but not to the two neighboring figures, the scene's essential lack of
spatial conviction is the result of a still more serious antagonism between two concepts.
Seen as a whole, the box-shaped Annunciation room is a well-constructed perspective interior. One side of this "box," however, namely the trapezoid area which serves as a floor,
has an entirely non-perspective character. On closer examination, we notice that this trapezoid, though acting as the floor, is not really the ground plane on which the two figures
and the two pieces of furniture stand. The area is actually only the two-dimensional foil
against which the four shapes are silhouetted and which encloses them almost entirely,
with only the lilies and the upper portion of the figure of the angel projecting above. The
artist has joined his four basic shapes to the trapezoid area of the floor in the same manner
in which Broederlam attaches his large landscape scenery with its buildings to the gold
ground. The trapezoid area, in other words, is used by the later master as a replacement
for the gold ground. I have analyzed the curious outlining process by which the Master
of Flémalle affixed his forms to the trapezoid in an article recently published.[330] In the
present study, I should merely like to state that this process makes the two Annunciation
figures appear physically present in a way that is rather disconcerting to a modern eye.
These figures are modeled and lighted in an extremely lifelike manner and are surrounded
by forms characterized in the same realistic illumination and modeling. And yet, nonetheless, they have no space of their own in which to exist. Set right on the panel surface,
these two figures literally exist in the space of the spectator, a phenomenon which to the
present-day viewer is an almost unnerving invasion of his normal sphere of visual experience. For the Master of Flémalle, however, this was precisely the means to define his scene
as magically present and thus to establish its sacred character as an eternal truth of Christian doctrine.

In the center representation of his triptych, liturgically the most important, the artist
apparently still felt compelled to connect the pictorial with the real space. But why did
the Master of Flémalle find it necessary to use the ancient device while Jan van Eyck, in
his rather similar Annunciation of the Ghent Altarpiece, was evidently able to do without
it? The answer lies in the character of the setting: while the space in the Mérode Annun-

[329] Analysis of the phenomenon which is penetrating but not fully convincing in all of its details is given
in *ibid.*, I, pp. 165-67.
[330] Cf. above note 169.

ciation is depicted as the living room of a burgher family, thus describing an "historical" surrounding pure and simple, the setting in the Van Eyck Annunciation, which connotes the Heavenly Jerusalem, is primarily an eternal place no longer in need of an artificial sanctification.

In Jan's Annunciation, the concept of the Heavenly City is an intrinsic part of the iconography of the scene (Fig. 81).[331] Since formerly this concept was embodied only in the edifice surrounding the representation, up until the time of the Ghent Altarpiece, a painted scene, conceived as being part of this edifice, had been sanctified, so to speak, from the outside. Now, the celestial idea is drawn right into the image itself and forms the very foundation of the painted composition. Here shown in the guise of a royal palace, the new type of setting enabled the artist to characterize his Annunciation room as a heavenly place without sacrificing the details of the Virgin's domestic surroundings. Thus, a vivid description of the historical event could be combined with an image that is basically the hieratic declaration of a doctrinal truth, without disrupting the artistic unity of the painting. No longer does Van Eyck have to attach part of the image to the panel surface in order to establish the sanctity of the scene. Used as the setting, the Heavenly Jerusalem beautifully reconciles the historical with the eternal time without the need to stress the material connection between painted representation and surrounding sanctuary space.

Because the former "external" sanctification of the image has now been replaced by an "internal" one, a free development of the new illusionistic art has been made possible. No longer is it necessary to attach the painted forms to the panel surface and thus to reject the use of perspective construction in certain parts of the composition. The method of perspective can now rule the entire image. In so doing, it turns the representation into a fully three-dimensional, optically convincing view which now appears in its entirety as though recessed behind the picture plane. The existence of this plane as a material surface is now absolutely and completely denied.

One can, of course, apply the converse of this analysis and state that a convincing depiction of the heavenly locale, in which a detailed historical narrative is pervaded by an eternal atmosphere, was possible only in a truly perspective image. Indeed, the free application of the rules of perspective and the use of the Heavenly Jerusalem as a setting are genuine correlates in the art of Van Eyck and one cannot say which of these two factors is the primary and which the secondary one. While the concept of perspective presupposes the essential separation of the pictorial from the real space, this separation was afforded by a setting which signified the celestial realm. Repeating, as it does, the very idea of the Christian edifice, a setting connoting the Heavenly Jerusalem enabled the painted scene to become a self-contained entity independent of the surrounding church space.

[331] Cf. above Chapter 3, Part IV, the paragraphs supplied with notes 171-76.

By the use of these two correlates, Van Eyck had taken a decisive step, whose importance for his own art and for the general development of Northern fifteenth century painting can hardly be overestimated. Jan's seemingly reactionary device of placing his scene in an ideal non-specific setting, after the Master of Flémalle had painted his realistic domestic interior, was in actual fact one of the most significant pioneer steps ever made in the history of painting. By endowing this ideal setting with the explicit meaning of the Heavenly Jerusalem, Jan had found the means for restoring to the image the artistic unity which had been destroyed by the older master. The image was now both re-unified and self-contained. For with the Heavenly Jerusalem as a setting, Northern altar painting was liberated from its mediaeval subservience to architecture. Emancipated from its traditional tie to the church building, painting could now enter a glorious new development which led to the great illusionist art of the future.

The non-specific ideal setting as well as a systematically constructed perspective are both features characteristic of Italian art. With regard to perspective construction, I should like again to refer to my article, in which I suggested that Van Eyck may have known some of the most advanced Italian works of his time, and that he was perhaps familiar with an early Donatello relief or with the Annunciation fresco in San Clemente in Rome ascribed to Masolino (Figs. 124 and 125).[332] The wide empty space between the Angel and the Annunciate which characterizes the Ghent Annunciation, but which is otherwise found nowhere in the North, also occurs in the Masolino mural. Indeed, the large interval between the two figures is a very old, traditional feature in Italy, where the two persons of an Annunciation scene are often depicted widely separated from one another to the left and right of a window or doorway or on opposite ends of a polyptychal altarpiece (Fig. 95).

I explained in my article why I think that Jan's perspective construction could have been influenced by Italian works. At this point, I should like to add that Jan's re-introduction of a basically ideal setting in his Ghent Annunciation may also have resulted from an inspiration which he drew from Italian art. The setting in the Masolino composition is a sumptuous arcaded Renaissance hall certainly intended to present an ideal locale. In fact, the ideal, that is the non-specific and non-descriptive setting, has always been predominant in Italy. A personal contact and a rather intense one with Italian art has to be assumed for Jan van Eyck, not only because he apparently knew the latest works of the South but also because of his knowledge of Early Christian forms and iconography, which we have discussed in Chapter 3.[333]

The use of perspective and an ideal setting do not, however, occur for the first time in the Ghent Altarpiece. Both of these features already appear in an Eyckian work which

[332] Philip, *op.cit.*, 1967, pp. 67ff.
[333] Cf. above Chapter 3, Part VI, the paragraphs supplied with notes 218-23.

evidently is older than the Vijd polyptych and which, interestingly enough, shows a pronouncedly Italian character. I refer to the Friedsam Annunciation, a highly controversial work now in the Metropolitan Museum in New York (Fig. 179).[334] It has been ascribed to the early Eyckian period or to a follower of Van Eyck, usually to Petrus Christus, but it has also been regarded as a faithful copy of a genuine Eyckian invention. The painting is indeed difficult to evaluate not only because the paint surface, in the faces especially, is badly preserved but also because the panel is only a fragment. While it appears to have originally formed the left wing of a triptych, it can only have been part of this wing since the upper portion of the panel must have shown the horizon and at least some indication of a sky.[335]

Although we cannot really reconstruct the altarpiece to which the Friedsam panel originally belonged, we can say that this work must be visualized somewhat along the lines of the Prado Betrothal ascribed to the Master of Flémalle or the Tiefenbronn Altarpiece by Lucas Moser (Figs. 175 and 43). This would mean that the unit, though composed of individual scenes, not only was set in a continuous landscape ground but also showed its buildings combined in a fanciful architectural complex. The obliquely placed church edifice in the Friedsam panel corresponds, in a reversed direction, to the church building in the Flémalle altarpiece and in the Moser painting, and certainly continued into an adjoining architecture which spread over at least the central panel of the triptych.[336]

The scenery in the Friedsam painting is basically composed of two parts, the landscape and the church-like building. This building is set in a landscape which, though by and large persuasively receding, still has the somewhat archaic character of a sloping terrain.[337] In the manner in which landscape and architecture are combined, the composi-

---

[334] The literature containing the debate is listed in Panofsky 1953, I, p. 231, note 2, printed on p. 451. Later literature is cited in John L. Ward, "A New Look at the Friedsam Annunciation," *The Art Bulletin*, L, 2, June 1968, pp. 184-87. The most sensible evaluation of the panel seems to me the one by Wehle and Salinger, *op.cit.*, p. 15, with a tentative attribution to Jan's early period.

[335] For the cutting down of the panel, cf. Panofsky 1953, I, p. 231 and Baldass, *op.cit.*, p. 275.

[336] Two more panels preserved in Berlin show a similar type of architecture with an obliquely placed entrance front (and may ultimately derive from the type under discussion). These panels may have formed the wings of a large preserved Crucifixion and are attributed to the Master of the Darmstadt Passion, cf. Stange, *op.cit.*, III, figs. 198 and 199. These paintings belong to the very few German works that are strikingly Eyckian in style.

[337] Though it is true that the Angel's drapery takes this slope into consideration, as stated by Ward, *op.cit.*, p. 196, he is not correct when he remarks that, in contrast to this realistic relationship between figure and ground, early paintings always show the figures as viewed at eye level, even though the strongly tilted ground is seen from above. While the figures in the Mérode Altarpiece are, indeed, eye-level views in their entirety in spite of the tilted floor, even the earliest Eyckian designs that we know offer an interesting compromise solution. When we study the kneeling foreground figures of the Adoration of the Lamb and also the censer-swinging angels of the middle distance, we notice that the upper parts of the figures are seen in normal eye-level view, while their lower drapery sections, conforming to the slope of the ground, appear as though seen from a high view point (Figs. 62 and 53). Precisely the same can be observed

tion shows an obvious kinship to the Annunciation portion of Broederlam's altarpiece, in which the architecture surrounding the Annunciate is also placed on an angle (Fig. 177). It is, indeed, possible that the panel was originally even closer to Broederlam's scene, for the now missing upper section of the panel may not have been a blue sky but a gold ground which at one time had been intentionally removed to give a more thoroughly realistic appearance to the picture. We know that a gold ground could still occur at that time even behind a convincingly receding landscape, because we see it in several other paintings, among them the Descent from the Cross by the Master of Flémalle (Figs. 126 and 127).[338]

While the Eyckian composition is certainly similar to Broederlam's Annunciation, it radically differs from the older scene in one important respect. In the Broederlam altarpiece, each segment of the unified setting actually connotes only the one specific historical place which belongs to the biblical event shown in it. In the painting in New York, building and landscape obviously have a more general meaning as well. There can be no doubt that the edifice, brilliantly interpreted by Panofsky as a combination of the ideas of the New and the Old Testament, designates the architecture of the New Heaven, while the landscape now explicitly shown as a paradisaic garden in full bloom is the New Earth. The setting of the Friedsam Annunciation, in other words, already connotes the two parts of the Heavenly Jerusalem.

Nevertheless, even this idea was evidently inspired by Broederlam's composition. There the younger painter could find not only the continuous landscape which contained various buildings, but he could also see an architecture having a rather generalized, ideal meaning. The edifice into which Broederlam has placed his Annunciation scene certainly has the very specific historical connotation of the Jewish Temple. Simultaneously, however, this complex structure also shows certain overtones which gives it the quality of an ideal edifice. This ideal aspect may in itself have suggested a celestial connotation to the younger painter, especially since Broederlam's landscape, continuing as it does over the entire composition, intensified this suggestion.

The artist who invented the Friedsam composition has obviously used the idea of a much older work as the basis for an entirely new representation. Such a procedure would be much more in line with the mentality of a still youthful genius of the Founder Generation than with that of a mere follower of Jan van Eyck. It is very unlikely anyway that Petrus Christus, whose main concern was with the poetry of space and the method of its

---

in the case of the Friedsam figures. We can, therefore, by no means conclude from the figure design that the panel must be post-Eyckian. The characteristic treatment with the hemlines of the drapery following the sloping floor can also be seen in the German panels mentioned in the preceding note.

[338] The arrangement of placing a tooled gold ground behind a most realistic landscape remains popular in the German altarpiece production throughout the entire fifteenth century. In the various volumes by Stange, *op.cit.*, a very large number of pertinent examples can be found.

construction, should have been the inventor of such a highly original, elaborate, and ingenious iconography. Furthermore, while the harking back to a much older model would have no logical basis at all in the work of an artist like Petrus Christus, to the young Jan van Eyck it would have had a profound meaning. The painter would have returned to the use of the ideal elements of a fourteenth century composition in order to overcome the problem posed by the overly descriptive tendencies ruling the art of his own time.

Although the Friedsam composition follows Broederlam in the specific way of combining a landscape with a building, it greatly differs from the older scene in the posture and position of the Virgin and in the manner in which the building frames her figure. These features are not taken from Broederlam but stem from a still more remote model, for they follow a well-known Italian Trecento type of the Annunciation scene, which in turn ultimately derives from Byzantine representations. The Virgin, presented as the *porta coeli* and therefore directly placed into an *edicula* framing her, appears, for instance, in Maitani's famous relief in Orvieto (Fig. 180).[339] There, the Annunciate is rendered—just as in the Friedsam panel—in three-quarter profile and as a standing figure, while the Angel is depicted in full profile, kneeling outside the building and silhouetted against that part of the edifice which adjoins the doorway on the left side.

While a comparison with this work shows that Jan's model was this specific Trecento type, the relief itself was certainly not the actual source for the Friedsam design. The actual source was undoubtedly a painting coming from the Giotto tradition. The pronouncedly Giottesque form of the Friedsam Virgin with the monumental bell-like mass of her drapery makes this point perfectly clear. It could be that Van Eyck's direct model was a scene by Altichiero unknown to us today (Fig. 181).[340] The obvious Italian influence and, for that matter, the whole rather intricate derivation of the Friedsam composition considerably add to the doubts about Petrus Christus' authorship of the work, which is claimed by

[339] For the *porta coeli* (Genesis 28:17; not to be confused with the *porta clausa* of Ezechiel), cf. above note 192. The opened door to Heaven, a symbol that can already be found in the theme of the Annunciation in a very early period, occurs also as the attribute of the Madonna outside of the Annunciation context. Cf. the Metropolitan Museum Virgin and Child by Petrus Christus (No. 89.15.24, Wehle and Salinger, *op.cit.*, pp. 20ff) and the equally explicit representation by a German follower of Van Eyck showing the Madonna and Child in the open door of the seven-towered structure of Heaven (*Wallraf-Richartz-Museum der Hansestadt Köln, op.cit.*, I, 1939, p. 148).

[340] The same fresco cycle by Altichiero and Avanzo in the Oratoria di San Giorgio in Padua has already been pointed out by Baldass as the ultimate source of the space construction in Van Eyck's Madonna in a Church in Berlin. Baldass, *op.cit.*, p. 27. While Baldass may be right in assuming that this construction was already absorbed in the pre-Eyckian Northern tradition, the heavy form of the Giottesque figure was, as far as I know, imitated neither by the Limbourg brothers nor by the Boucicaut Master. It seems to me that the taking over of the Giottesque figure was a step personally taken by Van Eyck, perhaps as an early counter-measure against the gradually disintegrating unity in the Northern figure design. Cf. above Chapter 4, Part III, the paragraph to which note 271 belongs.

some writers. It is virtually unthinkable that Petrus Christus, ever reluctant to invent anything radically new in iconography or form, should have gone out of his way to revive a
composition as early as that of Broederlam or to have sought out an Italian Trecento
source.[341] The willingness to search among older and foreign forms for an adequate
expression for new iconographic content is an attitude, however, which would perfectly fit
the genius of the young Van Eyck.

Since we do not have the main representation of the altarpiece, of which the Friedsam scene was originally part, we do not know the basis for the artist's idea of making the
setting of his work the two-part representation of the Heavenly Jerusalem. But one point
is clear: in the Friedsam panel we see the concept in a still early stage of its development,
that is to say, in a form preceding that which it obtained in the Ghent Altarpiece. In fact,
both of the correlates which we have discussed as characteristic of the work of Van Eyck—
the use of the Heavenly Jerusalem as a setting and a systematic perspective construction—
are still in their infancy, so to speak, in the Friedsam Annunciation. If the panel should
have actually still shown a gold ground, as we have assumed, the representation of the
Heavenly Jerusalem would have occupied only part of the available picture surface. And
as to the perspective, detailed examination of the direction of the vanishing lines has demonstrated that it is still archaic for it employs a considerable number of vanishing points.

It is in the Ghent Altarpiece that the two great innovations of Van Eyck, the celestial
setting and systematic perspective, assumed the "canonical" form seen in all of his later
devotional paintings. There, the entire picture surface is covered by a representation of the
heavenly realm and there Van Eyck has used his new and convincing perspective construction. No matter whether the Friedsam Annunciation is an original by the hand of
Jan or merely the faithful copy of a follower, the painting clarifies two points. The idea
of making the Heavenly Jerusalem the setting of a painted scene as well as Jan's perspective attempts are both features which are, as such, older than the Ghent Altarpiece. But
the specific form which they have assumed in all of Jan's later works goes back to the
Ghent polyptych and not to anything earlier.

In the Ghent representations, the idea of shaping the painted settings into portrayals
of the Heavenly Jerusalem was the direct consequence of the connotation and the character of the altarpiece as a whole. The huge two-level architectural framework which surrounded the paintings of the Vijd retable signified in itself the New Earth and the New
Heaven. The paintings, pretending to be recessed compartments in this architectural structure, continued the connotation of the framework in settings designating the two parts of
the heavenly realm. The frame, as a sacred, objectively existing edifice in the chapel space,

---

[341] For the features apparently taken by Van Eyck directly from Italian art and for the strong possibility
of his personal sojourn in Italy, cf. the passages and notes given above in note 188.

has become a sort of consecrated peep-show box in which the images, having now assumed the character of a "panorama," could be painted with utter realism and could show a blue sky, the blue sky of the New Jerusalem.

We cannot assume a similar relationship between painting and frame in the Friedsam Annunciation, nor is it probable that the frame of the lost altarpiece to which this composition belonged was a symbolic object signifying the Heavenly City. No matter whether the frame consisted of simple moldings or was an elaborate carving of architectural details, its relationship to the painting was probably not very different from that which frame and paintings have in the Broederlam altarpiece. Thus the paradisaic landscape of the Friedsam panel with its obliquely placed building may well have appeared on the old gold ground to emphasize the objective existence of the celestial realm.

The frame of the Ghent Altarpiece and the intimate relationship which the paintings in the work had to this frame not only account for the fact that the images in their entirety were now a representation of the Heavenly Jerusalem, but also for the possibility for Jan to use his new and convincing perspective construction. The showcase character of these images, treated as compartments recessed in a sculptural edifice, called for a frontally oriented space which developed parallel to the picture plane. It was this type of box-shaped interior space running parallel to the panel surface which Jan needed to apply his systematically calculated perspective. The space of an obliquely set building presented enormous difficulties to a methodical perspective construction, and for this reason was never again used. All of Jan's later works show the frontally oriented space of the paintings in the Ghent retable.[342]

While it can hardly be doubted that it was the form and connotation of the sculptural frame and their continuation in the paintings which made the Ghent Altarpiece the springboard to the entire later Eyckian oeuvre, Jan's ingenious invention of this painting-sculpture combination was at the same time also a serious obstruction to the final breakthrough to a new completely nonmaterial image. The Vijd polyptych clearly paved the way to such an image. However, taken in itself, the great work may well be regarded as the termination and crowning point of the old era, rather than as a work already belonging to the new.

In our discussion in the previous chapter we have seen that the paintings of the Ghent retable are still set in "limited space." The "box" of the Annunciation room is a finite expanse having a view of infinite space only in the distance. While this box-shaped room provided Van Eyck with the perfect basis for developing his perspective, it was this very room, on the other hand, which was used by the artist to provide in a still somewhat archaic manner the link between the pictorial and the real space. Apparently, the rather advanced image achieved by the application of perspective did not appear to the painter to

---

[342] For "oblique" perspective's being the older form and outgrown by European painters around 1430, cf. Panofsky 1953, I, p. 166 and p. 166, notes 1 and 2, printed on p. 423.

be a satisfactory solution in itself. By applying a perspective method, the artist had auto-matically created a pictorial space distinct from the real one. But, evidently, he still con-sidered this "modern" separation as a kind of danger to the sacredness and validity of his painting.

By using his interesting *trompe l'œil* with the shadows of the carved columns appear-ing on the floor of the painted Annunciation room, Van Eyck has artificially relinked the pictorial with the real space. It seems that when the painter was working on the Ghent Altarpiece, he was not as yet able consciously to recognize the theoretical basis for the phenomenon which his own practice had entailed and thus to apply the consequence of the recognition.[343] Exploiting the idea of the retable's sculptural framework, he character-ized his painted figures as literally existing in it. This procedure turned, as we have seen, all the foreground representations into sculpture or at least into pseudo-sculpture. True, in the work of Van Eyck, this transformation is a deliberately used artistic device which shapes the figures into fully convincing "sculpture in the round."[344] But the phenomenon as such is still in a way similar to the earlier solutions of Broederlam and in the Annuncia-

[343] This statement does not, of course, contradict Panofsky's explanation of a "correct" perspective con-struction's presupposing, rather than engendering, the concept of space which it manifests (*ibid.*, I, pp. 5f). The point here in question is not the concept of space as such, but the concept of painted space in relation to the real space, a matter which concerns the nature and function of painting.

[344] The new conscious concentration on sculpture in the Ghent Altarpiece suggests that it may have been Van Eyck (not the Master of Flémalle) who invented the simulated stone-colored statue, a motif which was to become most popular in Netherlandish altar painting. The back of the Prado Betrothal, which shows two saints represented as statues in niches, has hitherto been regarded as the first example of this motif (*ibid.*, II, plate 87). Owing to the doubts about the early date of this panel and the conjecture that it may have followed, rather than preceded, the Ghent Altarpiece (cf. above note 303), the authorship of the famous device again becomes an open question. This question is intimately linked with an inquiry into the origin of the motif, a point which has not as yet found sufficient consideration. As has been explained before (*ibid.*, I, p. 162), Northern sculpture of the time was never left monochrome but was always adorned with painted colors. It was thus only in the unfinished statues as they were visible in the artist's workshop that monochrome sculpture could be observed. Though this observation of unfinished sculpture was cer-tainly of great importance for the form given to the new motif, it was hardly the occasion for its invention. The simulated statue had often appeared in the context of simulated architecture not only in Italian Trecento paintings but even in Northern art (Broederlam, cf. our Fig. 177). Moreover, painted saints in prominent positions have been rendered as statues on pedestals ever since the fourteenth century (most striking in the Crucifixion in Berlin, Stange, *op.cit.*, I, no. 136). The novelty of the motif under consideration consists, in the last analysis, only in its restriction to the stone color. But even the idea of the large *grisaille* figure (though not of the large simulated statue) already existed in Italian art, as it can be found in Giotto's dado frescoes of the Arena Chapel (Berenson, *op.cit.*, I, figs. 43 and 44). Since an enlarged architecture used as the framework was the *leitmotif* of the Ghent Altarpiece, with the large statues appearing as a logical companion motif, it seems rather probable to me that the representation of the full-sized monochrome statue was an invention which came in the wake of the great work. It is most likely, in any case, that it was Van Eyck who invented it, for it was he who had first-hand knowledge of Italian art. Moreover, his apparent fascination with antique statues (cf. our Excursus II), i.e., with works that time had turned into "mono-chromes," may have been the main impetus for the invention.

tion of the Master of Flémalle, where the three-dimensional treatment had automatically turned the representations into a layer of relief.

The old material connection in these works between the picture and the surrounding sanctuary space has been replaced by Van Eyck by an illusion of such a connection. But the very fact that he continued to feel the necessity to link his representation with the actual space makes the Ghent Altarpiece a work that is still somewhat archaic. There is no later painting by Van Eyck in which a *trompe l'œil* is used in the same manner, with the figures showing a strange ambiguity between sculpture and real life representations. In all his later works, the scene has become "painting pure and simple." It has been formed into a perfectly self-contained realm of illusion, a microcosm similar to the macrocosm of reality but radically distinct from the latter. And while this new illusionistic image now replaces rather than continues the sanctuary surrounding the devout, even its frame has become part of the new make-believe. In all of Jan's later paintings the frame consists of very simple moldings which are usually decorated with illusionistic painted details. It is the art of painting which has now completely taken over.

If we want to formulate the theoretic foundation of this new image, we have to state that painting has now become a purely human product, an entity created by the artist's mind and hand, and assuming the aspect of reality through the purely human act of vision on the part of the spectator. This strictly nonmaterial concept, humanized and perfectly subjective, is diametrically opposed to the mediaeval belief in the objective sacredness of ecclesiastical art derived from its essentially divine nature. Whether or not Van Eyck, in his later years, had ever consciously accepted the theoretical basis of his own illusionistic art is a question we cannot answer, for we have no writings by Jan van Eyck. One point, however, is clear: when he painted his Ghent Altarpiece, the described concept was still rather foreign to him. His aim was to create a visually convincing image, but he was not ready as yet to sacrifice the picture's time-honored connection with the sanctifying chapel space.

That this connection was actually no longer necessary in his new illusionistic image was not clear to him at that time. But the redundance may have struck him when the polyptych was completed and perhaps already at some point during his work on it. Studying the finished parts, he may have become aware of the fact that neither his characterization of the figures as semi-sculpture nor the huge sculptural framework was essentially needed for the illusion of reality.[345] He may, moreover, have realized that his panels, depicting as they do a heavenly realm, were perfectly sacred in themselves and did not actually require the additional sanctification of an architectural frame connecting them with the

---

[345] When the panels were in the hands of the painter, they were, of course, surrounded only by their simple wooden moldings, while their sumptuous architectural framework was still in the workshop of the sculptor. The painter thus had ample opportunity to study his "jewels" out of the "settings" that he had designed for them and to form an opinion about the panels' effect without the frame.

chapel architecture. It often takes a concretely existing form to enable an artist to recognize the full potentialities of his own artistic idea. It is obvious that Jan learned from his own completed Ghent Altarpiece a most important lesson, formidably fruitful for his entire subsequent work.

In comparison with the rest of Van Eyck's "canonical" oeuvre, the transitional character of the Ghent Altarpiece is perfectly clear. In all these other works, the painter freely admits the nonmaterial quality of the image and even underlines it by the new relationship between painting and frame which we have analyzed in our previous chapter through the example of the Dresden triptych. Though the Vijd altarpiece certainly stands at the beginning of these other works and had paved the way for them, it is distinctly and strikingly more archaic than the whole range of these other paintings. This fact, in itself, suggests that the polyptych may have been the achievement of a still youthful artist. Moreover, judging from the preserved examples of Jan's work, it seems that he dropped the leading idea of the Ghent retable, i.e., the specific painting-sculpture combination, immediately after its completion. All this in connection with the characteristic qualities of the Ghent paintings—their spectacular complexity, their lavishness, ambiguity, and the obvious indication that they were accomplished with considerable effort—speaks for the creation of a young man.

If we were to revise Jan's birth date to be more in line with Lukas de Heere's and Marcus van Vaernewyck's statement that Jan died young, the Ghent polyptych would, in fact, have been the work of a youthful painter.[346] The usual assumption is that Van Eyck was born between 1380 and 1390. According to this date, he would have been in his fifties when he died, an age which would have made him an old man in the opinion of his time. If instead he was born in 1401 or 1402, he would have only been thirty-nine or forty at the time of his death.[347]

[346] Cf. above note 254.

[347] This proposal of a birth date for Jan so much later than usually assumed makes one think also of the question of Rogier van der Weyden's birth date (cf. Panofsky 1953, I, pp. 154-58). The clash between the sources giving information about the latter has posed a serious problem. According to one set, the painter seems to have been born in 1399 or 1400; while an entry in the guild records of Tournai tells us that Rogier entered the workshop of Robert Campin as an apprentice on March 5, 1427. Since an apprenticeship was normally started at the age of fifteen or sixteen (sometimes even earlier), Rogier would have been over-age by more than ten years, according to the aforementioned sources, when he took this step. This all too mature age for an apprentice has caused considerable bewilderment to scholars, with various suggestions offered as to Rogier's studies or other activities before 1427. Perhaps the solution of the enigma is not to suppose that the painter at twenty-seven had already undergone a training in a different field elsewhere when he entered the workshop of Campin, but to assume that the other sources have been wrongly interpreted.

Since I have never seen the documents and even so would lack the training for their proper evaluation, I do not know which possible mistake might have caused an error of about ten years. Could it be that the main document in question, while offering all the correct numbers in its text, was filed under the wrong

If we assume this later birth date for Jan van Eyck, the entire life and career of the painter would take on a much more normal aspect than it has hitherto shown. According to this later date, Jan would have been about twenty when he became a master and entered the service of John of Bavaria. He would have married at the usual age and his wife would not have been sixteen to twenty-six years younger than he but only the customary four or five. Our information that his children (he had, by the way, only two and not ten) were small when he died would be understandable for a man of not quite forty.[348] According to these calculations, Jan was just past his mid-twenties when he designed the Ghent Altarpiece and about thirty when he finished it. This, indeed, seems to me to conform precisely with the particular character of the work.

The supposition that the work on the great altarpiece started in 1425—the year when Jan entered the service of Philip the Good—or even before this date was prompted by the Hubert theory and by the proposition that the first artist to work on the altarpiece had died in 1426. Having discarded this theory, we are free to suppose that Jan could have worked for quite a while for the Duke before he received Jodocus Vijd's commission. The triptych to which the Friedsam composition originally belonged, however, may have been a work painted by Jan in his earliest years with the Burgundian court. Just after entering the service of Philip the Good, the painter undertook a number of travels for his employer, one of which may have led him to Italy and may well explain the evidence of contact with Italian art so striking in the Friedsam Annunciation. But above all it is the paradisaic setting which links this painting to Jan's life with the household of the Burgundian Duke. The religio-political atmosphere of this court could in itself have suggested the representation of the Heavenly Jerusalem.

II. THE JERUSALEM IDEA AND THE COURT OF PHILIP THE GOOD

Of all the European princes of his time, Philip III of Burgundy was the one most ardently interested in the earthly kingdom of Jerusalem. During the entire course of his life, he was obsessed with the idea of a crusade.[349] Indeed, the idea, inherited from his

---

year so that the present date of the document itself is wrong? In any case, a renewed study of the sources with such a possibility in mind may be worthwhile, before one definitely accepts the advanced age for Rogier when he entered his apprenticeship. One has to take into consideration the nineteenth century tendency to place the birth dates for all the Northern artists, Netherlandish as well as German, far too early, a historical prejudice which may have caused a well-meaning archivist to "correct" a date or at least a filing. In short, we should keep in mind that Rogier may actually have been fifteen or sixteen when he entered Campin's shop. If this was so, his birth date was 1411 or 1412, a time well in line with a birth date of 1401 or 1402 which I have assumed for Jan.

[348] Weale and Brockwell, *op.cit.*, pp. XXXVIII-XXXIX.

[349] Philip's plans for the crusade are discussed in detail in J. D. Hintzen, *De kruistochtplannen van Philip den Goede*, Rotterdam 1918, *passim*. Cf. especially pp. 32f. Compare also A. G. Jongkees, *Staat en Kerk*

father, who had been defeated by the Turks at Nicopolis, preoccupied Philip from the very beginning of his rule. He pursued his plans with utmost zeal even though he was never able actually to realize his goal. Sources tell us of the delegations he dispatched to the Holy Land, and we have enough information to assume that he sent these embassies not only for reasons of prestige but also in order to study the conditions for conducting a war in the Near East.

In fact Philip's divers Palestinian activities were based on motives in which prestige and more directly practical aims were inextricably fused. He made substantial endowments to the sanctuaries of the Holy Land. The privileged position which the Western Christians enjoyed in Jerusalem during his rule was due to the Duke's generosity. The keys to the Holy Sepulcher were in his possession. The Church of the Coenaculum, where Philip willed his heart to be buried, was rebuilt by him, embellished, and furnished with his funds.[350] There was a lively interchange of travel between persons from the Holy Land and from Philip's court.

Monks from Palestine were received as guests in the Netherlands; the Bishop of Bethlehem visited in Hal in 1426. Numerous members of Philip's immediate entourage made the journey to Jerusalem. Not only Ghillebert de Lannois and the famous Bertrandon de la Brocquière went to the Holy Land, but the brothers Adornes of Bruges as well, for whom we know that Jan van Eyck painted a scene with St. Francis.[351] Coming from a wealthy Genoese family established in the Netherlands since the thirteenth century, the two brothers owned as their private sanctuary the Jerusalem Church in Bruges, which they

---

in Holland en Zeeland onder de Bourgondische Hertogen 1425-1477 (Bijdragen van het Instituut vor middeleeuwsche geschiedenis der Rijks-Universiteit te Utrecht), Groningen 1942, pp. 29-35.

[350] For this and all the following information on the Duke's connection with the Holy Land, cf. *Le Voyage d'Outremer de Bertrandon de la Broquière* (Recueil de Voyages et de Documents), ed. Charles Henri Auguste Schefer and Henri Cordia, Paris 1892, p. VI. A good English translation of Bertrandon's highly interesting account of his travels is found in *Early Travels in Palestine*, edited with notes by Thomas Wright, London 1848; Louis Bréhier, *L'église et l'orient au moyen âge. Les Croisades*, Paris 1911, pp. 327ff; H. Vincent and F. M. Abel, *Jérusalem. Recherches de topographie, d'archéologie et d'histoire*. II. *Jérusalem Nouvelle*, Paris 1914, pp. 292f; Aziz Suryal Atiya, *The Crusade of Nicopolis*, London 1934, pp. 19-37; Jean Ebersolt, *Orient et Occident. Recherches sur les influences byzantines et orientales en France avant et pendant les croisades*, 2nd ed., Paris 1954, pp. 106-10.

[351] For Jan van Eyck's work for the Adornes family, cf. Weale and Brockwell, *op.cit.*, p. 94; for the members of the family (also called Adorno) and their biographies, cf. F. Van Dycke, *Recueil heraldique de familles nobles et patriciennes de la ville et du franconat de Bruges*, Bruges 1851, pp. 104f; A. Couret, *L'ordre du Saint Sépulchre de Jérusalem depuis ses origines jusqu'à nos jours*, Orléans 1887, p. 887; for their church, cf. A. Duclos, *Bruges. Histoire et souvenirs*, Bruges 1910 (1913), pp. 559f and Henri Hymans, *Brügge und Ypern*, Leipzig/Berlin 1900, pp. 53f and figs. 49 and 50 (best reproduction of the interior in Edmond Pilon, *Bruges*, Paris 1939, p. 126). Compare also Roberto Weiss, "Jan van Eyck and the Italians," *Italian Studies, an Annual Review*, XI, 1956, p. 6, and the catalogue *Flanders in the Fifteenth Century: Art and Civilization, op.cit.*, pp. 304ff.

had remodeled. It still contains today a replica of Christ's tomb chamber, whose original in Jerusalem the Adornes brothers made several visits to see.

The Jerusalem idea, foremost in the life of the Burgundian court, even had a link with the Miraculous Host, the gift of the Pope to Philip which we have already discussed. Looked upon as a symbol of Christ's suffering at the hands of the unbelievers, it was used as a propaganda item for the proposed crusade.[352] Indeed, it is its relationship to the crusading idea which throws light on the reason for selecting the unusual central theme of the Resurrection for Philip's shrine for the Miraculous Host. The purpose of a crusade was to liberate the Tomb of Christ in Jerusalem, the Holy Sepulcher, from the possession of the infidels. The Resurrection scene, which we have postulated for the central representation of the shrine, presented the Tomb of Christ in a large and striking image (Fig. 153). In the hands of the Duke the crusading idea became a very specific political tool; he put everything to the service of this idea. He was a prince whose actual power by far exceeded his official rank. Among the most influential rulers of his time, Philip, nevertheless, lacked the title of king. The plan for a crusade was his means to overcome this disadvantage. By making himself their leader in a crusade, he sought to manifest his supremacy over the European monarchs.

Philip's religious ardor and his political zeal were one. In the fifteenth century, political and religious ideas were still completely inseparable. The concept of the Heavenly Jerusalem was intimately interlinked with that of the earthly city. So that when Philip's court painter, Jan van Eyck, made an unprecedented use of the Heavenly Jerusalem in his paintings, the Duke's religio-political Jerusalem idea had certainly not been without an influence on his artistic invention. Recalling the many examples in which the painter described the splendor of heaven by the splendor of an earthly court, we can safely assume that his life with Philip's princely household was a decisive factor in the genesis of Van Eyck's great idea.

Philip himself never traveled to the East. His life as a sovereign deeply engaged in a multitude of tasks connected with the politics of the day apparently left him no time for such a trip. Nevertheless, he may well have regarded a pilgrimage to the Holy Land a religious necessity and an obligation he would somehow have to fulfill at some time. Could it be that he undertook this pious voyage not *de facto* but *in nomine*, in other words that he appointed a substitute to make it for him? With this premise, the hitherto enigmatic notice of Jan's first journey for the Duke, which is mentioned in a Lille document of 1426 with the destination undisclosed, could take on a new aspect.[353] This trip, which, in contrast to all subsequent ones, is called a pilgrimage and is described as being performed not only "by the order" of Philip but also "in the name" of the Duke, could well have been a visit to the Holy Land.

[352] Cf. Pächt, *op.cit.*, 1955, p. 49, note 37.

[353] Léon Emmanuel Simon Joseph de Laborde, *Les Ducs de Bourgogne*, ii, Paris 1849, p. 225 (no. 741).

This surmise, which I submit only tentatively, seems to be supported by some further observations which are perhaps worth mentioning at this point. In the same year, 1426, Philip had dispatched an embassy to Jerusalem under the leadership of Guiot, Bastard of Burgundy.[354] Since in Van Eyck's time long and dangerous travels were usually done in groups, the painter may easily have joined this particular delegation. It would be most understandable if Philip had selected his newly appointed painter to act as his personal representative. For one thing, Jan would have been able not only to describe the religious monuments on his return, but also actually to portray them. Done in the realistic style for which the artist was known, these sketches could give Philip the feeling that he had seen everything with his own eyes. In addition, the Duke may have had a strictly utilitarian reason for sending his painter. Jan's art would have been precisely the means to an invaluable rendering of those places and objects which were of particular military importance. One of Jan's objectives, in other words, may have been comparable to the reconnaissance photography of modern army intelligence. It is by no means unthinkable that this kind of activity should be expected of a painter. Artists of the fifteenth and sixteenth centuries, when in the service of a sovereign, did not devote their entire time to aesthetic problems. As we know from the careers of Leonardo and Grünewald, their employers quite naturally expected them also to fulfill tasks of a utilitarian nature serving industrial or military purposes.[355]

With regard to Jan's life and art at the Burgundian court, we know from the text of Facio of at least one instance in which he painted a work of practical value for the Duke. The Italian writer gives high praise to a map of the world which he said was painted by Van Eyck for Philip and which is now unfortunately lost. One feature of the Eyckian map is especially acclaimed by the author, namely that the places shown on it were rendered in their correct distances one from another. Since the city of Jerusalem is usually placed in the center in the *mappa mundi* of this period, it is fairly safe to assume that the distances in the Eyckian map were all related to the Holy City and that the creation of that object was connected with Philip's crusading plan.[356] Indeed, it seems to me that we have still another record of the same kind of activity by Jan, this time handed down to us not in a description but in a painted copy.

[354] *Ibid.*, p. 234 (no. 772), p. 360 (no. 1249) and pp. 456f (no. 1746). Cf. also Hintzen, *op.cit.*, pp. 33f.

[355] One has only to recall the revolving stage which Leonardo built for the Duke of Milan, the maps and the military machines he drew for Cesare Borgia, or his work to make the Adda River navigable. Cf. Ludwig Heinrich Heydenreich, *Leonardo da Vinci the Scientist* (Catalogue of the IBM Exhibition), 1951, pp. 16ff. For Grünewald's commission to construct a mechanical fountain, cf. Walter Karl Zülch, *Der historische Grünewald, Mathis Gothardt Neithardt*, Munich 1938, p. 372. It is on the basis of contemporary sources that the spelling Matthäus Gotthart Neithart is used. Cf. Maria Lanckoronska, *Matthäus Gotthart Neithart*, Darmstadt 1963, especially p. 14.

[356] Cf. Michael Baxandall, "Bartholomaeus Facius on Painting: A Fifteenth Century Manuscript of the De Viris Illustribus," *Journal of the Warburg and Courtauld Institutes*, XXVII, 1964, pp. 102f. Cf. also Documenten, pp. 4-5.

It has often been assumed that the enchanting Jerusalem panorama which forms the background of the Rotterdam panel with the Three Marys at the Tomb may go back to a topographical sketch done on the spot (Fig. 182). This sketch, however, is usually presumed to be pre-Eyckian, whereas the painting itself is sometimes ascribed as an early work to one or the other Van Eyck.[357] In my opinion, the reverse could be true: that the painting itself is but a pastiche of an early follower of Van Eyck making use of very early but also of later Eyckian elements, while the author of the panoramic sketch was Jan van Eyck himself. The pastiche character of the composition, clearly noticeable in any case in the diverse style of the figures and the landscape elements, is strikingly shown in the combination of a biblical scene with a contemporary panoramic view. I believe that Van Eyck, who was a highly educated man of a most logical mind, was not capable of this kind of an anachronism. This combination, by which the artist apparently sought to heighten the realism of the scene by a "real" Jerusalem view, can, in my opinion, only be the invention of a follower. Van Eyck himself consistently renders a purely imaginary image in all of his other Jerusalem representations, no matter whether they depict the heavenly or the earthly city.[358]

The conjecture of an Eyckian trip to the Holy Land in 1426 would explain the Early Christian features that are so especially striking in the Ghent Altarpiece. Early Christian churches abounded in Palestine and seeing them he could have absorbed these elements. Moreover, the usual route to Jerusalem in that day would beautifully resolve the question of when and where Jan received his strong exposure to Italian art.[359] Travelers generally reached the Palestine coast by boat embarking from Venice. Had he followed this usual course, Jan could have seen at least the northern part of Italy. However, he may even have been to Rome as well, because pilgrims of the period as a rule included a visit to the papal capital of Italy in their voyage to the Holy Land.[360] Jan's presence in any one of these

---

[357] Cf. Panofsky 1953, I, p. 231 and p. 231, note 1, printed on p. 451.

[358] Compare above note 317. There is a striking difference in the Rotterdam painting between the foreground and the background of the scene as far as the spectator's view point is concerned. While the foreground is seen at eye level, the cityscape in the rear is a bird's-eye view. This clash could perhaps be interpreted as an early stylistic feature because a similar dichotomy of views occurs rather often in popular archaistic representations, for instance, in the engravings of the Master of the Garden of Love or in those of the Master E.S. But in the leading art, mirrored in Early Netherlandish miniatures, the bird's-eye view, while rather usual in the foreground, is used only rarely in the background. Moreover, the view point from which the Rotterdam cityscape is taken so strongly suggests a map-maker's panorama taken from a hill that we might be tempted to conclude that it is a copy of a portrait of the Holy City painted by Van Eyck and here utilized in a context for which it was not originally intended.

[359] Cf. *Le Livre de la Description des Pays de Gilles Le Bouvier dit Berry* (Recueil de Voyages et de Documents) ed. E.-T. Hamy, Paris 1908, pp. 197f, *Early Travels in Palestine, op.cit.*, p. xxviii and Geck, *op.cit.*, pp. 45f.

[360] It was on their way to Palestine that the pilgrims used to go to Rome. An exception was Jan van Scorel, who went there on his way back. For this painter's pilgrimage in 1520/21, cf. G. J. Hoogewerff, in the catalogue *Jan van Scorel*, Utrecht 1955, pp. 12f.

regions, Rome, northern Italy, or Palestine, as early as 1426 would account for the general Italian elements as well as the Early Christian features to be found throughout his art, and particularly in the Ghent Altarpiece.

Even though Jan's trip to the Holy Land of course remains a hypothesis despite the foregoing considerations, the influence of Philip's Jerusalem idea on the art of the great painter may be assumed as fact. Indeed, in my opinion, the importance of this influence cannot be overrated. In the Ghent Altarpiece, interestingly enough, not only the concept of the Heavenly Jerusalem plays a prominent part, but also the crusading idea as such. The five panels of the lower zone showing the Adoration of the Lamb with the Heavenly City as a background are tinged by this idea (Fig. 1).

The reader may recall that some scholars have taken this lower level for an altarpiece unit originally planned to stand by itself and to form a complete work. Panofsky has even seen traces of a former donor panel in the left wing of this unit. According to him, the group at the extreme left depicting the Just Judges was originally intended to portray the magistrates of Ghent, the *schepenen*, as the people who gave the commission of this penta-tych to Hubert (Fig. 173).[361] To Panofsky, this assumption was a welcome solution to a problem seemingly posed by the panel of the Judges. Since he took the five-part Adoration scene for an All Saints picture, the representation of the Just Judges, who are obviously not saints, did not fit the presumed scene and required a special explanation.

On the basis of our assumption that the Adoration of the Lamb depicts the congrega-tion of Christ, which is comprised not only of the saints but of the entire circle of the blessed, this whole problem disappears. A special explanation of the depiction of the Judges is no longer necessary. In any case, needless to say, Panofsky's explanation is unacceptable once the Hubert theory is abandoned and the whole polyptych is considered as having been designed for Jodocus Vijd from the outset. Nevertheless, that great scholar's adher-ence to the traditional notion that among the Just Judges are portraits of Vijd's contempo-raries is certainly correct. This assumption is not only based on a tradition repeated again and again in many written texts but is also strongly suggested by the painting itself, which gives highly individual features to the horsemen in the foreground.

The portrait character of these figures is so outspoken and compelling to the spectator that many generations saw the likenesses of the two painters Hubert and Jan among the mounted rulers, a supposition long since rejected by modern art historians, even by schol-ars who accept the Hubert theory. Van Mander, whose text was one of those which spread the story of Jan's and Hubert's portrait in the panel of the Judges, also mentions at the same time what seems to me to be the remainder of a different tradition of thought on these portrait heads. He says that Philip the Good is depicted among the Judges in his

[361] Panofsky 1953, I, p. 217.

position as the Count of Flanders.[362] This remark merits serious consideration. We have to keep in mind that donors of fifteenth century altarpieces not only specified that their own portrait be included in the work but often also wanted to have the likeness of their sovereign or of some other high officials whom they particularly meant to honor. Such an "honor portrait," as I should like to call it in counterdistinction to the actual donor portrait, appears, for instance, in Rogier's famous Columba Altarpiece, where Charles the Bold is depicted as the youngest of the three kings adoring the Christ Child (Fig. 183).[363]

I am, in fact, absolutely convinced that Paul Post has correctly identified the horsemen in the Ghent Altarpiece panel as the likenesses of the Counts of Flanders. At least the identity of three of them seems to me certain on the basis of their striking similarity in facial feature and attire to the official portraits of these personages (Fig. 184).[364] No doubt,

[362] Edition Jacobus de Jongh, *op.cit.*, pp. 18ff; ed. Constant van de Wall, *op.cit.*, pp. 6ff.

[363] As the face of Charles is well known from his many authentic portraits, it is not difficult to recognize it in the Munich painting. Even Johanna Henriette Schopenhauer (the mother of the philosopher), who was, as far as I know, the first author ever to write a monograph on Jan van Eyck (*Johann van Eyck und seine Nachfolger*, Weimar 1821—Sämmtliche Schriften, Leipzig/Frankfort-on-the-Main 1830, I, p. 41) and who still took the Columba Altarpiece for a work by Jan, even she knew that Charles the Bold was there depicted as the adorer of the Christ Child. No one, in fact, has ever doubted the identification, despite the fact that there is an actual donor portrait on the left side of the same composition. However, other "honor" portraits, although in my opinion equally obvious, have been doubted even in their quality of being portraits, especially when the "sitters" could less easily be identified. This is the case, for instance, in Memling's Lübeck Crucifixion (Fig. 155), which shows three gentlemen of rather outspoken portrait character (indeed, they all seem to me to be Italian) standing below the left-hand cross. In Carl Georg Heise, *Der Lübecker Passionsaltar von Hans Memling*, Hamburg 1950, p. xiii, the possibility that they are portraits is emphatically denied. I side with those who take them for portraits. Moreover, I am also convinced that the controversial female figure in the lower right-hand corner of the New York Crucifixion by Jan van Eyck is a portrait as well (Fig. 168). Pointing to this figure's posture, which is different from that of the usual donor, Panofsky objects to Julius Held's suggestion that the figure portrays the Duchess Isabella, wife of Philip the Good, and sees in it instead the representation of the Erythrean Sibyl (Panofsky 1953, I, p. 238, note 2, printed on p. 454). Our discussion above explains why one of these possibilities does not necessarily exclude the other. Yet, in view of the strictly "historical," non-symbolical character of the scene, I am rather inclined to believe that Isabella is here portrayed simply as one of the women under the cross. Her figure is, so to speak, the reverse counterpart of the corresponding female at the left margin who is seen from the back. In the scenes of the Resurrection and the Crucifixion, the holy women often include figures in oriental dress. The similarity that Panofsky has observed between the female apparel in the New York Crucifixion and that of the Sibyl in the Ghent Altarpiece only proves, in my opinion, that this colorful attire belonged to Jan's workshop collection of costumes. Neither as the Sibyl nor as one of the holy women could Isabella be depicted at the side of her husband, whose portrait, as explained above (cf. note 299), may have been included among the mounted riders beneath the Cross. Scenes of the Crucifixion traditionally separate the sexes (with the exception, of course, of St. John's being depicted in the group of the holy women). Though appearing in a picture section different from the one showing Philip, the presumed figure of Isabella is at least visible in an almost direct line below the presumed portrait of her husband.

[364] Paul Post, "Wen stellen die vier ersten Reiter auf dem Flügel der gerechten Richter am Genter Altar dar?," *Jahrbuch der preussischen Kunstsammlungen*, XLII, Berlin 1921, pp. 67ff.

the elderly horseman, who is the main figure in the foreground of the panel and appears on a splendid white mount (the Hubert of the old tradition), is Philip the Bold, founder of the Burgundian dynasty and Count of Flanders through his marriage (Fig. 186). It seems equally certain to me that the younger rider farther back, who is deliberately shown turning his head in order to face the spectator (the presumed likeness of Jan), is his grandson Philip the Good, sovereign of Jan van Eyck and of Jodocus Vijd (Fig. 185). Finally, the portrait between these two, a face only partly visible and crowned by a bulky and towering hat characteristic of the likenesses of John the Fearless, obviously presents this ruler who was the son of Philip the Bold and the father of Philip the Good (Fig. 188).[365]

The rulers whom we see in the wing of the Judges signify the universal concept of the civilian power of Christendom, as opposed to the military power shown in the next panel. Their characterization as portraits of the Counts of Flanders is certainly only a sub-connotation of this universal meaning. Indeed, this subconnotation may have been introduced by way of giving a specific biblical reference to the figures. Even though they do not show their attributes, they may have been intended as the rulers of the Old Testament impersonated by the Counts of Flanders. For instance, it is possible that the foreground figure on the white horse is Philip the Bold in the disguise of the most famous of all Judges, the Old Testament King Solomon. If this is so, the likenesses in the Ghent Altarpiece are of the same kind as that of Charles the Bold in Rogier's Columba Altarpiece where Charles appears as the youngest king. Here, too, the biblical figure impersonated by a contemporary ruler has a wider and more universal connotation, which transcends the biblical one. He is one of three monarchs who together signify the world which pays homage to Christ.[366] In any case, Old Testament figures or not, the Judges in the Ghent Altarpiece symbolize the civilian power of Christendom and it is this very broad and universal connotation which suggests to us that Post's identification of the fourth horseman should perhaps be revised.

Post's reasoning for the profile face behind the foreground figure of Philip the Bold to be Louis de Mâle, Count of Flanders and father-in-law of the first Burgundian Duke, seems basically sound. In the only likeness of Louis which is known, and which is a rather late drawing, he is actually depicted with a beard, as is the figure in the Ghent Altarpiece. Moreover, the inclusion of Louis in the Ghent scene would, by and large, fit the Eyckian

[365] While the lower part of the face is overlapped by another rider's hat in Jan's original painting (the present one in the altarpiece is a copy, the original having been stolen in April 1934 and never returned), many of the copyists have corrected this feature, showing the face in its entirety by reducing the form of the hat. It apparently was the unappealing area around his mouth which gave John the Fearless the unattractive look which struck his contemporaries. It seems to me that Post may be right in suggesting that Van Eyck had intentionally concealed this least comely feature of John's face.

[366] For the universal symbolism of the three kings as represented in the Adoration scenes, cf. my article "The Prado *Epiphany* by Jerome Bosch," *Art Bulletin*, xxxv, 4, December 1953, p. 279 and note 55.

context. However, we do not have a portrait of Louis de Mâle which is either detailed enough or near enough in pose to the portrait by Van Eyck really to ascertain whether the delicate and noble profile in the Ghent Altarpiece, showing as it does a strikingly brunette and non-Germanic face, is actually that of the old Count of Flanders. On the other hand, we have a profile portrait of a famous ruler of Van Eyck's time which bears an unequivocal resemblance to this particular profile in the Ghent Altarpiece. Thus we may feel inclined to contest Post's identification of it as Louis de Mâle.[367]

The famous medal of the Byzantine Emperor John Paleaologus VIII created by Pisanello in 1438 could well show the same man approximately ten years later than in the Ghent portrait in question (Fig. 187). Born in 1392, and thus only four years older than Philip the Good, John Paleaologus became co-emperor in 1421 and then ruled by himself from 1425 to 1448. He was a troubled ruler of an empire virtually restricted within the walls of the city of Constantinople and constantly threatened with the danger of the advancing Ottoman Turks. He had toured Western Europe as early as 1423 seeking the help of the Western princes and offering to submit the Greek Church to the papacy.[368] At the same time, he attempted to persuade the rulers of the West to join him in a crusade against the infidels. Thus, if it in fact should be his portrait which appears in the Ghent Altarpiece, the panel of the Judges would present a train of horsemen showing the Western and Eastern Christian rulers united, an idea most pertinent to the universal meaning of the representation. A kind of "retroactive" proof for the assumption that it is John Paleaologus whose portrait appears in the Ghent Altarpiece and that the idea of the union of Christian East and West was one of the concepts in the retable may be found in a famous Italian work painted approximately thirty years later. In Benozzo Gozzoli's fresco of the Adoration of the Kings in the Florentine Palace Medici Riccardi, apparently influenced by the Ghent Altarpiece, one of the mounted kings bears the features of the younger Paleaologus, Michael (Fig. 191).[369]

In the Ghent Altarpiece, the very presence of the portrait of the Byzantine king would

---

[367] When I wrote the present paragraph, I was not aware of the fact that an identification of this figure different from that of Post's had been put forward as early as 1910. Nor did I suspect that the earlier identification could be precisely the one that I was going to propose. In his article "Jean VI Paléologue et Hubert van Eyck," *Revue Archéologique*, XVI, 1910, pp. 369-77, S. Reinach had already pointed to the same Byzantine ruler (usually called John VIII Paleaologus, not John VI Paleaologus) as the one whom I have in mind and for the very same reasons which I am going to set forth.

[368] Cf. George Ostrogorsky, *History of the Byzantine State* (translated from the German), New Brunswick, New Jersey 1957, pp. 496ff and Joseph Gill, *The Council of Florence*, Cambridge 1959, *passim*.

[369] The cavalcade of Christian rulers in the Ghent Altarpiece undoubtedly held a strong fascination, especially for the Italian artist of the time. It was often imitated in Italian works and in contexts rather different from the Eyckian one. In the famous frescoes of the Schifanoia Palace in Ferrara, for instance, the Eyckian group reappears in the representation of March, with the most literal repetitions to be noted in the rear figures of the cavalcade. Cf. Paolo d'Ancona, *The Schifanoia Months at Ferrara* (translated from the Italian), Milan *s.d.*, plate 9.

strongly imply the concept of a crusade. This concept, while possibly implied in the panel of the Judges if this portrait identification is correct, is strikingly explicit in the panel of the Knights of Christ (Fig. 174). Three youthful heroes, wreath-crowned and in full armor, are the leaders not only of the military kings and emperors shown in their own panel but also of the train of the Judges in the adjoining one, whose representation continues the cavalcade. The three banners carried by these youths are certainly meant to be seen as leading all of the members of the two-fold train. The first of these banners appearing to the right, nearest to the middle panel, presents a symbol well known from numerous other representations (Fig. 189). The large golden cross accompanied by four smaller ones and placed on a red-colored ground is the coat of arms of the Christian Kingdom of Jerusalem, familiar especially from the miniatures in the books of René of Anjou, who had the title of King of Jerusalem (Fig. 190). Indeed, it was on the basis of these three banners that the group was identified as crusaders in the pioneer article written by Waagen in 1824.[370] But, curiously enough, this identification, though reasonable and very close at hand, has never, so far as I know, been taken seriously in later history of art.

True, in his direct application of the crusading idea to an identification of the three youthful leaders as Godfrey of Bouillon, Tancred, and Robert of Flanders, Waagen may have gone too far. The three horsemen are certainly three knightly saints who connect the representation of the wings to the groups of saints in the middle panel. Therefore, James Weale's identification of the three knights as St. Martin, St. George, and St. Sebastian should certainly be preferred.[371] But, undoubtedly, these saints are presented as the early proponents of the crusading idea. Indeed, their banners, as De Bast has shown in his footnotes to Waagen's text, are those of the local military confraternities of Ghent, which, according to the custom of the time, each supplied a contingent of soldiers to the military expeditions of the Counts of Flanders and thus had also accompanied them to the Holy Land during the crusades.[372]

The faces of the leading knights are strongly individualized, especially the two foremost ones (Fig. 189). Probably here too, just as in the panel of the Judges, the features of famous contemporaries are used to depict the protagonists of the sacred story. Perhaps St. Martin and St. George bear the faces of Ghillebert and Bertrandon, the great adventurers and Jerusalem-farers of the time.[373] In any case, we can safely assume that in both the panels of the Judges and of the Knights contemporary personages and ideas appear in the framework of Christian history and hagiography—or better that the historical and the hagiographical are presented in the light of their own contemporary manifestation. Philip

---

[370] Cf. Waagen and De Bast, op.cit., pp. 16f.   [371] Cf. Weale and Brockwell, op.cit., pp. 46f.

[372] Waagen and De Bast, op.cit., note on p. 17; compare also Dhanens, Inventaris, VI, pp. 54f, and the literature given in the footnotes of these pages.

[373] See the literature cited above in notes 350 and 359. For the portrait character of the Eyckian horsemen, cf. also above note 210.

the Good and his ancestors are shown as the representatives of the Christian civilian government of the West and as following the path of the crusaders. That this is the idea of the two combined left-hand wings of the Adoration of the Lamb is further corroborated by the fact that the towers of Jerusalem, which are depicted in the background of the middle panel but which are not shown in the wings of the Hermits and the Pilgrims, are continued behind the two groups of the Judges and the Knights.

While Philip's crusading obsession has certainly made its impress on the representation of the great polyptych, the idea is still more obvious and more important in Jan van Eyck's small panel of the Madonna of Autun, which is usually called the Rolin Madonna after the donor Nicolas Rolin, who was the chancellor of Philip the Good (Fig. 192). This undated work is often attributed to the time immediately following the completion of the Ghent Altarpiece, an assumption which I wholeheartedly share. The elevated room in which the two protagonists are placed certainly belongs to the structure of the New Heaven, while the landscape below with its phantastic fairy-tale city composed mainly of Christian churches unquestionably signifies the New Earth. The upper and the lower part of the Heavenly Jerusalem are here combined in a perspective representation in which the New Earth is seen as the background of the New Heaven, a combination still constructed in essentially the same way as are the foreground and background of the Ghent Annunciation (Fig. 81).[374] Indeed, just as in this Annunciation scene of the large altarpiece, in the Rolin Madonna too, the continuity of the two picture parts is still secured by a linking zone. We have seen that two annex rooms were used in the Ghent Annunciation to form such an intermediate level. In the Rolin Madonna, it is provided by the garden of the fortress, which here too is located on the same high plane as is the celestial structure of the foreground.

The splendor of this heavenly hall surrounds a figure combination whose unusual tenor is unique even in the art of Jan van Eyck. Because of the seated posture of the Madonna and the kneeling one of the donor, the two figures are of equal height. And since a book and a prie-dieu are enclosed in the representation of the donor, the bulk of this left-side representation almost equals that of the right and forms an almost perfectly equivalent picture component to the group of the Madonna and the Child. Thus, despite the praying gesture of the donor and the angel holding the crown of the Madonna, we receive the impression of an almost familiar relationship between the donor and the holy figures. The two parties, in other words, appear as though "socially" on equal footing.[375]

[374] Cf. above note 172 and the literature cited there.

[375] This impression is so strong that Richard Hamann in his widely read book *Geschichte der Kunst von der altchristlichen Zeit bis zur Gegenwart*, Berlin 1933, pp. 396-97, could give a description of the Rolin Madonna which, with a sly wink, reverses the comparative status of the figures (the mortal donor before the heavenly Queen). Hamann compares the scene with a visit paid by a moderately attractive woman of

This peculiarity may find its explanation if we consider the donor's position in the government of his country. He was chancellor to a ruler whose political ambitions were, as we know, intimately linked with a plan for a crusade. According to the explanation of John Gower, an English poet (c. 1330-1408), a crusade had a very particular religious purpose.[376] Its aim was to reconquer the lost Kingdom of Jerusalem and to restore to it its rightful King, Christ, Who, as the "Son" and legitimate successor of David, was entitled to rule the Holy Land. Certainly this idea formed the basis of the elaborate pictorial metaphor that Van Eyck has created in the Rolin Madonna.

The phantastic cityscape shown in this painting at the foot of the celestial castle, though certainly connoting the Heavenly City of the Apocalypse, points also to the earthly Jerusalem, which is and has always been the symbol *par excellence* of the celestial one. The glorious buildings to the right in Van Eyck's background representation encircle the head of the Christ Child like a crown. While the Child is characterized as a ruler by the orb which he holds, the majestic circle of buildings signifies Him as the uncrowned King of Jerusalem. This idea explains the strange exaltation of the donor in Van Eyck's painting. Rolin, as the chancellor of a sovereign who was planning a crusade, is the very man to help the Holy Child and His mother resume possession of their rightful heritage, the Holy Land. The donor, to be more precise, is here portrayed as the chancellor of Christ.

The unusually informal relationship between donor and holy figures is based on a metaphor in which the two parties appear in the pursuit of a common goal. The Queen Mother is shown in an informal conversation, as it were, with her highest court official and most trusted adviser. The hall in which this conversation takes place, and which in form and splendor is reminiscent of the open room in the palatinate buildings of the German emperors, may have been intended, in this instance, to depict the hall in a crusader's castle.[377] In any event, while the painting is, of course, meant as a prayer for the

---

the lower classes to the house of a doctor, to whom she rather timidly presents her clumsy baby with swollen limbs. Dr. Deinhard has kindly drawn my attention to this highly interesting passage. Hamann's somewhat blasphemous comparison, here summarized and quoted out of context, may fill the reader with more indignation than it deserves. In its own context it was rather skillfully, though unceremoniously, used to make a valid point.

[376] Gower, *Vox Clamantis*, Lib. III, pp. 651f, G. C. Macaulay, *John Gower. The Complete Works*, Oxford 1899-1902, Vol. IV, pp. 124-25, cf. also the note on p. 384. For a summary of the passage in English, see Aziz Suryal Atiya, *op.cit.*, pp. 19ff.

[377] Aware of the artist's intention to convey the impression of oriental splendor, art historians have suggested divers models for the palaces depicted in the Rolin Madonna. Among the exotic sources, the Spanish palaces (among them the Alhambra) with their dainty forms and their vast views have been pointed out—in my opinion correctly. Like the background city, Jan's foreground architecture is composed of details based on the various impressions which the painter received on his many travels. But all of these impressions were ultimately cast into indigenous forms which, in the case of the foreground architecture, are those of Northern Romanesque buildings. For Early Christian architecture being another of the "exotic" sources for the castle, cf. above note 222 and the text to which it belongs.

redemption of the donor's soul, Rolin's help in the pious venture of a crusade is referred to in this context, so to speak, as a plea to accept this help as the expiation of his sins.[378]

III. THE EYCKIAN DONOR PORTRAITS

THE painting itself is obviously an *ex voto*, as are, of course, all the religious scenes by Van Eyck in which the donor portrait is prominent. And it is the *ex voto* meaning of a painted altarpiece which is clearly brought out by the use of a setting connoting the Heavenly Jerusalem. In order to explain this point, it is necessary briefly to summarize the ramifications of the concept and its various shades of meaning and to become aware of the fact that the characteristic polarity which we as moderns see in the paintings of Van Eyck is essentially inherent in the universal character of the idea as such. The symbolic imagery used to express the concept is manifold. Since the Heavenly Jerusalem encompasses a wide variety of ideas found in the Bible and in the writings of the Church Fathers which overlap each other as "almost identical"—for example, the *civitas dei*, Paradise, the Church, the Bride, or the Virgin—the Heavenly Jerusalem can be depicted in the guise of an object as well as a person. The former is used when the idea appears as a city, a single building, a landscape, or a garden; the latter when it is embodied as the Ecclesia or as Mary, the mother of Christ.[379]

What we see as a curious ambiguity between heavenly and earthly values in the art of Van Eyck is rooted in the mediaeval concept of reality. While to modern man "reality" consists of the sum total of the objects and forces which visibly or tangibly surround him, these are "unreal" to mediaeval man, to whom the true reality can be found in ideas alone. The transitory earthly things are but the shadows of their divine models in Heaven. The tangible altar in an earthly church building is the "image" of the invisible Heavenly Altar, the earthly celebration of the Eucharistic rite is the imitation of the Heavenly Mass and the earthly Jerusalem is but the symbol of the Heavenly City.[380] In art, the heavenly concept can always be expressed through the image of its earthly equivalent. And since neither the Middle Ages nor the Early Renaissance are ever interested in "reality" in our modern sense and are profoundly unconcerned with what we would call secular "values," our

---

[378] Jan van Eyck's Rolin Madonna is the subject of a number of very recent scholarly articles, all of them published after the text part of the present book was completed (James Snyder, *Oud-Holland*, 1967; Emil Kieser, *Städel Jahrbuch*, 1967; Marvin Felheim and F. W. Brownlow, *Art Journal*, 1968). Some of them (especially Snyder's essay) raise a few interesting points whose validity and importance for the painting I do not deny. However, I still believe that the Jerusalem metaphor discussed in my text above is the foundation of the iconography in Van Eyck's composition, with some of the ideas proposed in the recent articles perhaps used as secondary points to elaborate the fundamental concept.

[379] For the literature on the various aspects of the idea, cf. above note 110.

[380] The Neo-Platonic and the Augustinian tradition which were the basis of this concept were accepted even by the most outspoken Aristotelians, such as, for instance, St. Thomas Aquinas. Cf. Anne Fremantle, *The Age of Belief*, New York 1954, p. 149.

interpretation of Eyckian forms, if based only on our spontaneous impression, is often bound to go wrong.

Van Eyck's intense observation of natural forms and his almost miraculous ability to imitate them enchants and edifies the modern viewer, mainly because he delights in Van Eyck's convincing imitation of the things which to us moderns are "reality." The origin of the new trend, which has been called the fifteenth century realism, has usually been discussed with an eye to the beginning of the Renaissance and of modern secular culture.[381] It is futile, I think, to delve into the origin itself, for the origin of any historical trend is always ultimately unexplainable. However, this much at least is certain: the "new realism" as we see it in Van Eyck's art did not serve secular ends. Van Eyck's visually convincing images were not intended to appeal to an audience which had the taste and experience of modern man. His contemporaries expected a spiritual elation from ecclesiastical art, and it is this task which the Eyckian realism could fulfill much more effectively than any previous type of painting.

Panofsky, in his beautiful summary of Van Eyck's art published in his book on Early Netherlandish painting, clearly implies that to the master the act of painting was a religious activity and that the painter's subject was not earth but Heaven. In his later book on tomb sculpture, Panofsky was even more explicit on this point.[382] We find there a statement that the Early Netherlandish artists, through the miraculous touch of their art, defy the distinction between heavenly and earthly things, thus transforming the vision of a distant beatitude into the experience of a world which mortals are permitted to share with the Deity. To this masterly formulation of a profound insight, a few qualifications have to be added. First of all: if these painters defy a distinction between Heaven and earth, it is a distinction which we make and not a distinction made by their predecessors. In other words, it is the intrinsic unity of the two realms which is characteristic of mediaeval thinking and it is only in the modern thought that Heaven and earth are clearly separated categories. If we are surprised not to find this distinction in Early Netherlandish painting, this has to do with our mistaking the so-called Early Netherlandish realism for "reality" in the modern sense.

Secondly, no artist, ancient or modern, has any other way of depicting a supernatural realm but to show it in the guise of natural forms. Heaven itself is invisible; and in his endeavor to make the invisible seen, every artist depends on the colors and forms which an earthly environment presents to his eyes. Even the seemingly "abstract" gold ground

---

[381] Riding in the wake of Jacob Burckhardt's great book *The Civilization of the Renaissance in Italy,* published in 1860, in which the author discussed the age as the birth hour of the modern world, later scholarship has shown the tendency to stress those features which the era has in common with our own. This view tempts us to see the Renaissance phenomena too naively with our own eyes and to mistake them for being identical to trends which we find in nineteenth and twentieth century art.

[382] Erwin Panofsky, *Tomb Sculpture,* New York 1964, p. 59.

is, in the last analysis, based on the appearance of an earthly substance, the metal gold, regarded as precious and therefore as suitable for a symbol of Eternity, but it is actually just as much an element of our world as all the other substances surrounding us. And when the Eyckian depiction of the heavenly realm strikes us as particularly earthly, this is so because the artistic means of the painter for presenting Heaven does not conform with our preconceived notion of how Heaven should look. He uses neither a gold ground nor the Raphaelic concept of Heaven familiar to us from the Sistine Madonna and from countless images of the Renaissance and the Baroque in which a blue sky with fluffy clouds is populated by hovering or reclining angels. This latter concept which, by the way, is no less based on an earthly observation than all the others, namely on the notion of a bird-filled natural sky, has so strongly influenced our idea of the beyond that the Eyckian representation of the heavenly realm does not really appear very celestial to us.

Van Eyck sees the eternal region as the splendor of a great city, as the glory of an ecclesiastical or princely building, as the grandeur of a park-like landscape or the sweetness of a garden. And when he clothes these symbols in a form enchantingly similar to that which our eye perceives in our own surrounding, this is because he uses the beauty of God's nature to depict the beauty of God's Heaven. The eternal appears in the form of the transitory. It can do so because the Lord created every mortal or perishable earthly substance after the model of its immortal and imperishable heavenly equivalent. To Van Eyck, therefore, his study of physical nature was an important religious task. The natural forms were to him the mirrors of a divine truth.

The forms of Van Eyck thus assume a characteristic polarity whereby Heaven is glorified by the beauty seen in God's earthly creation, and earthly creation is glorified by proclaiming it the direct reflection of God's eternal thought. Despite this polarity, however, we have to keep in mind that it is the heavenly model and not the earthly copy which is the subject matter proper in the art of Van Eyck. To do so is often difficult for the modern spectator, especially when he is confronted with images which are sometimes actually used as the symbols of our world by other artists, such as, for example, the view of a city. It has, therefore, by no means surprised me that my interpretation of the city view in the Ghent Annunciation as the New Earth, which I have previously published in a separate article, has met with some contradiction. I still believe, however, that the interpretation of this view as basically celestial, though not exclusively celestial, is correct.[383]

Even if De Bast's claim that this view is the faithful portrait of a street corner in the city of Ghent, a text which has come to my attention only recently, should be valid, the view nevertheless has to have a celestial meaning (Figs. 81 and 88).[384] We have literary as

[383] Cf. above notes 172-75, and the paragraphs of Chapter 3 to which these notes belong.

[384] Waagen and De Bast, *op.cit.*, pp. 26-27, note 2. Identifying houses, street corners, city gate and church, De Bast comes to the conclusion that the view from the Annunciation room was taken from a house on the corner of the "koey-straet" in Ghent. This house, the number 26 of "koey-straet" in De Bast's time,

well as pictorial proof that an actually existing earthly city can function as the symbol of the Eternal City of God. It is clearly affirmed by a thirteenth century source that the inhabitants of the city of Brescia saw their own man-made earthly town as the symbol of the Heavenly Jerusalem. The site is sacred "*quod civitates facte sunt ad similitudinem paradisi.*"[385] It is, of course, the same idea that accounts for the numerous city portraits which are used again and again in the religious paintings of the time around 1500. When the city of Cologne or of Bruges appears behind the figures of saints or the Madonna, this background is certainly meant to indicate that the scene is set in a celestial realm. The painting in Detroit by the Master of the St. Lucy Legend, which shows the Virgin among the Virgins in an enchanting garden foiled by the view of Bruges, is clearly a portrayal of Paradise (Fig. 193).

Simultaneously, however, the painting is also a pious prayer by the citizens of Bruges for the sacred presence of the Virgin and her saints in their own earthly town. If Jan's view through the windows of the Ghent Annunciation was actually meant as a portrait of Ghent, his painting may have set the pace for a large following of pious city portraits in the later art.[386] As a portrait of Ghent, the city view in Jan's altarpiece, appearing as it does above the portraits of the Ghent donors, would have had a similar meaning in the

occupies in his opinion the site of Hubert van Eyck's house, where the painter took the view from his own window. Although I was unable to check on De Bast's topographical information, I am convinced that he is right in one respect: The view (if, in fact, it should be a "portrait" at all) can only show a district in Ghent, not in Bruges, as some later writers believe. It was the home town of the donor, not the city of the painter, which was important in the context of the altarpiece. The little research I could do on this matter for the time being was restricted to material available in New York libraries. My limited inquiries, however, did bring to light one piece of information which may be interesting in the event that De Bast's identification of the view should turn out to be correct. The neighborhood which he describes was distinguished by an important building which had the name "Hôpital de Sainte Barbe dans Jérusalem" and was called "Jérusalem" for short. Cf. Charles-Louis Dierix, *Mémoires sur la Ville de Gand*, Ghent 1815, pp. 277-80, for a description of the district and of the founding of this institution (dating from around 1420). If Jan had painted the city view in imitation of a view from a window of a building called Jerusalem, this idea would have been well in line with the over-all meaning of the altarpiece. Perhaps this problem may prompt a scholar more conversant than I with the Ghentian topography to do further research on the points in question.

[385] Cf. Hermann Bauer, *Kunst und Utopie*, Berlin 1965, pp. 1-2.

[386] In the second half of the fifteenth century and in the early sixteenth, we find city portraits in numerous Flemish paintings. There is a beautiful view of Saint Gudule in Brussels in a panel showing a scene from the life of a saint (Louvre No. 2198). City views are especially frequent in German and Austrian paintings of the period. Cf., for instance, the Flight into Egypt by the Master of the Schottenstift (Stange, *op.cit.*, xi, fig. 91), which presents a city view of Vienna, and the panel with Saints, the Virgin, St. Anne, and the Christ Child by the Master of the Glorification of Mary, which shows a panorama of Cologne (Wallraf-Richartz-Museum no. 120). The specific connotation of the cityscape portraits may vary from case to case. It is to be hoped that a scholarly investigation will soon be devoted to this material with the intention of clarifying the relationship of the city portraits to the scenes or stories they adorn, to the donors who dedicated the painting, and to the concept of the Heavenly Jerusalem.

context of the Vijd retable as has the view of Bruges in the painting of the St. Lucy Master (Fig. 2). In fact, the city portrait occurring in connection with the donor portraits would greatly have strengthened the *ex voto* meaning of the Ghent Altarpiece.

It is the intrinsic polarity of the Eyckian image which helped to establish a most effective *ex voto* meaning in the paintings of the master. In the Ghent Altarpiece, for instance, Jodocus Vijd and his wife are kneeling in a region which is both the Heavenly Jerusalem and the earthly domain of the Ghent church (Fig. 42). This is evident even without assuming that the city view above the donors shows the same duality. Since the statues of the two SS. John, which are the immediate and particular recipients of the donors' devotion, simulate sacred objects directly belonging to the holy furnishings of the Ghent altar, it is clear that the donors are conceived as actually kneeling in the Ghent church. However, since the place in which they appear is the New Earth, according to the two-level division of Van Eyck's painted structure, Jodocus Vijd and his wife are, at the same time, also shown as kneeling in Paradise. The portraits, indeed, have an intrinsic polarity not only with regard to place but also with regard to time. The donor images belong to both the present and the future. They are shown in the "here and now" of the earthly sanctuary in the city of Ghent, but they are also depicted in the future bliss of an eternal adoration, of which the earthly sanctuary and its ritual is but a sacred symbol.

Though Panofsky's identification of the concept under which Van Eyck has introduced the donors into his paintings is basically correct, he did not explain the dual polarity of the Eyckian image (in place and in time) which is anchored in the dual polarity of the Christian concept of the Heavenly Jerusalem and which made the *ex voto* meaning of an Eyckian altarpiece so formidably effective. When the great scholar in his book on Early Netherlandish painting describes the Eyckian donor as being included in the work of art by way of "anticipation," he saw only one of the two poles characterizing the underlying concept of time and place, namely that of a future time and a faraway Paradise. According to him, Van Eyck has depicted the mortal donor meeting the sacred personages after his death in a domain of eternal bliss.[387] While this explanation is unquestionably valid, it gives us the meaning of only one side of the Eyckian concept. For the praying mortal is also depicted as offering his devotion here and now in the present time and in the present sanctuary.

To be precise, the donor is worshiping while the rite of the Eucharist is being celebrated over the very altar above which his portrait appears. It is through this rite that the Christian believer hopes to become worthy of Redemption. The idea that the Eucharistic act is the reflection of the Heavenly Mass and that the sanctuary in which this earthly rite is being celebrated is the reflection of Heavenly Paradise, means that the mortal donor is at the same time praying in the faraway time and place where all Christian hope will find its ultimate fulfillment. Keeping in mind that this faraway time and place is only

[387] Panofsky 1953, I, p. 139.

part of the Eyckian concept and that its immediate here and now is of equal importance—in fact, still inseparably connected with the former—Panofsky's formulation that the donor is included by way of "anticipation" should perhaps be replaced by the statement that the donor is included by way of "participation," that is to say by virtue of his taking part in the solemn act of the Eucharist.

In the donor portraits of the Ghent Altarpiece, the duality of the idea is clearly evident, for the painter not only depicted Vijd and his wife kneeling in the region of the future New Earth. Van Eyck also made it clear that the two donors, shown as they are as worshiping stone-colored statues, are kneeling in the present time in their own earthly chapel (Fig. 2).[388] Their mortal appearance as they pray in the earthly sanctuary is used to depict their immortal image as they will look after the resurrection of the body on the day of Christ's Second Coming, which is at the same time the day of the Last Judgment, of the Celestial Wedding, and of the Heavenly Mass. While all this is clearly evident in the Ghent Altarpiece, the same idea, though less obvious in them is certainly also the basis of Van Eyck's later donor portraits.

The reader may recall that the concept of the Heavenly Jerusalem found a two-fold expression in the retable of Jodocus Vijd. There, Van Eyck's huge sculptural structure signified the celestial place because it was conceived as being a physical part of the Vijd chapel. This side of the concept was expressed in the paintings through the master's ingenious *trompe l'œil* which made them appear to be part of the structure and the factual continuation of the physically real chapel space. On the other hand, however, the idea of the celestial place is also expressed in the very iconography of the settings. They signify a paradisaic realm, characterized as the room in a sumptuous palace or as the delightful landscape of a park. As already mentioned in the beginning of this chapter, this dual characterization never again appeared in the work of the master. In the last analysis, the iconographic connotations of the settings were in themselves perfectly sufficient for the basic sanctification of the painted scenes. Having realized this point, Van Eyck never again used an elaborate sculptural frame and the idea of the *trompe l'œil* in his later works.

[388] The donors while kneeling in front of their altarpiece in their own private chapel are looking at their own likenesses. Here again, we have the same strange confrontation of a human with a portrait of himself which we have mentioned above in the examples given in our note 315. The meaning of this confrontation is perfectly clear in an altarpiece: The painting makes the invisible content of the donor's devotion visible. He sees himself kneeling in his own sanctuary whose identity with the celestial sanctuary is made fully explicit in the painting. All human devotion, if sincere, is offered not only to Heaven but *in* Heaven, that means that the prayer during Mass transports the soul into Paradise. Far from being only the place to which the soul is carried after death, the Heavenly City is the spiritual realm of the devout here on earth. The donor portrait heightens the donor's awareness of this fact. This, in my opinion, is its prime aim, while the other, namely to remind the relatives of the donor to pray for his soul after his death, is but a secondary purpose.

The elimination of these features, which was, as we have seen, the final step toward the emancipation of the painted scene from the church architecture, had an important effect on the image of the donor. From this point on, it is less clear that the donor is worshiping here and now in the present sanctuary surrounding his portrait. Nevertheless, it is absolutely certain that this idea still plays a decisively important part in the over-all concept. The Heavenly Jerusalem, though now functioning as a painted setting only, is itself a timeless universal concept, encompassing the present time as well as the past and the future. And when the donor in the Rolin Madonna is shown as praying before the Virgin and the Child, his image expresses not only the idea of his future hope but also—and especially—his present pious attitude (Fig. 192). Just as it is depicted in the donor portraits of the Ghent Altarpiece, his is a prayer offered here and now during the very mass which is celebrated by the earthly institution of the Church.

Our realization of this point makes all the donor figures rendered in the art of Van Eyck appear in a new light. Panofsky's interpretation of them could still raise a question such as that of Julius Held, who expressed his doubt as to the validity of Panofsky's opinion that it is Rolin who came to visit the Heavenly Queen.[389] Professor Held correctly observed that the Virgin in Van Eyck's painting is rather casually seated on a small taboret, while Rolin's prie-dieu looks like an object permanently installed in the exalted place. Held therefore concluded that the situation could just as well suggest that it is the Madonna who visits the Chancellor. If we keep in mind that the place of action is the Heavenly Jerusalem and that it thus connotes the Christian Church in the most general form of the concept, which of course includes the present earthly institution, this whole question as to who is visiting whom dissolves. Both the Madonna and Rolin are legitimately as well as permanently at home in the locale which Van Eyck has depicted: the Madonna because she is the Queen of the heavenly palace, the Chancellor because he is the faithful son of the Church.

The old concept of the intrinsic unity of Heaven and earth and of the essential oneness of the past, present, and future of God's cosmos is still intact and valid in all of Van Eyck's paintings. In the age of the master, Western man still firmly adhered to the idea of the divine origin and destination of the universe. The fate of this universe was established in the past when, after the Fall of Man, Christ's sacrifice had offered the possibility of the world's Redemption. That its destiny will ultimately be fulfilled on the day of the last Judgment is but the final consummation of things inherent in the present state and already recognizable to man because of the divine revelation of them given to him in the New Testament. The eschatological idea of the Middle Ages found a new and powerful

[389] Held, op.cit., p. 213. The setting had already been interpreted by Hamann, op.cit., p. 396, as the castle of Rolin, an opinion which—after Panofsky—is again stated in Snyder, op.cit., p. 165, whose findings seemingly confirm Held's opinion.

expression in the art of Van Eyck. This art did not really show the future things as seemingly occurring here and now (this concept which Panofsky had in mind is intrinsically modern since it presupposes the artist's freedom to indulge in a personal "make-believe"). Instead Van Eyck shows a factually present earthly reality in the light of its true meaning and ultimate consummation in the future. Though this is clearly not the beginning of our modern secular thinking, it is certainly the beginning of the era which we call the Renaissance.

The study of the natural appearance of the things that surround us in our earthly life was a pious activity, as we have seen. It was certainly based, however, on a new evaluation of the realm which we today are used to call "reality." And when, in his Rolin Madonna, Van Eyck finally has separated the pictorial space from the real space and has eliminated even the last remainder of its connection, the famous *trompe l'œil* still used in the Ghent Altarpiece, this is the moment when his painting becomes a "picture" in the modern sense. No longer conceived as physically part of the surrounding sanctuary space, the work of art is now an entity which is entirely nonmaterial, a vision of the creating mind of the artist which comes to life in the receiving mind of the spectator. Though the material vehicle used in this process, the work of art itself, was certainly still considered a sacred object, its sacredness is now no longer of the austerely material kind as in the old icon. In the new art of Van Eyck, the iconic quality of "being" is now converted into the modern property of "representing." This is the process of humanizing and dematerializing the work of art which, in the last analysis, constitutes the essence of the Renaissance.[390]

[390] It is this process, in my opinion, not the imitation of classical antiquity, which characterizes Renaissance art. Even the fact that, in Italian paintings, the antique content is again expressed in its own antique form, a phenomenon so well described by Panofsky, is only a symptom but not the essence of the art in the new age. Certainly, in the late phase of classical antiquity (and this is the period from which the antique models of the Renaissance artists came), the works were humanized as well as dematerialized. But it was not from his antique model that the Italian Renaissance artist drew these qualities. On the contrary, he could see and use these models only because his own art had entered a similar phase. It is clear that Italian art had entered this phase by the logic of its own evolution. This fact is all the more evident, as Northern art by the same logic had entered the same phase without a decisive influence from antique works.

Another and distinctly different matter is Italy's relationship to classical antiquity as the factor responsible for the striking differences between Northern and Italian Renaissance art. These differences, which concern the handling of light and the construction of space, are masterfully described in a short passage in Panofsky 1953, I, p. 7. The Northern artist's intense observation of sunlight and its use "as a qualitative and connective principle," his depiction "in terms of defraction, reflection and diffused reflection," and conversely, his relatively small concern with the clear distinction between plastic shapes in mathematically constructed space, are both tendencies which derived in my opinion from the mediaeval past of Northern art as distinct from the mediaeval past of Italy. As already mentioned above in note 327, it was the Gothic cathedral (the great symbolic structure in which light had become prominent as the prime expression of divinity) which was the basis of the tradition in the wake of which the Northern Renaissance artist came to his loving observation of both natural and artificial light. The existence or the absence of the Gothic cathedral building had determined the character of Northern and Italian mediaeval art respectively. And

It was perhaps in the Rolin Madonna that the modern concept of a picture as mere "representation" appears for the first time fully matured in the art of Van Eyck. In any case, the painting seems to be one of the earliest Northern examples of the new form which is preserved today. The work, nonetheless, still shows a rather complex composition which was certainly directly developed on the basis of the Ghent Annunciation (Fig. 81). As we have observed, the Rolin Madonna also presents the two parts of the Heavenly Jerusalem as foreground and background and they are characterized by the predominance of the solid foreground architecture of the New Heaven. True, this architecture is more radically opened in the Rolin Madonna than is the room in the Annunciation. But nevertheless it still occupies a large area when compared with that of the landscape and it is still definitely the architectural foreground space alone which surrounds the protagonists of the painting. Furthermore, as already mentioned, we have the intermediate zone of the fortress garden, which links foreground and background much as do the annex rooms of the Annunciation. This garden area in fact carries the same symbolism as one of these annex rooms. For, just as the right one of these rooms signifies the closed tower, a symbol of Mary's Virginity, the garden of the Rolin Madonna is also a Marian symbol. It certainly connotes the *hortus conclusus* as we can see from its solid enclosure by a crenelated wall.

But two features have changed when compared with corresponding parts of the Ghent Annunciation. In contrast to the two annex rooms in the earlier painting, the intermediate level in the Rolin picture is now really a continuous zone stretching uninterruptedly from one side to the other. Moreover, the garden, though actually belonging to the foreground structure, has a landscape character and thus really shows a greater affinity to the cosmic view offered by the background than it does to the foreground architecture. In fact, it is, quite generally speaking, the greater emphasis on God's nature which distinguishes the Rolin Madonna from the Ghent Annunciation, where the background is but a rather close view of a certain part of a city.

---

it is precisely on this point that the relationship to classical antiquity was the decisive factor. It was the uninterrupted contact with the art of the antique past which prevented the Italian artist of the Middle Ages, working as he did on antique soil, from ever completely abandoning the antique concept of the basic distinction between the pictorial and the real space. Thus, in Italy, the painted or sculptured work powerfully maintained its own sphere of existence asserting itself against the sacred architecture surrounding it. In the North, however, this sacred structure, the Gothic cathedral, had long since completely absorbed the painted and the sculptural art, which had lost their own realm of existence and had become entities directly connected with the architecture and with the space of actual reality. Italy, therefore, still possessing a concept of space not too different from that of antiquity, was able to develop in her paintings a new rationally founded space construction which the North was subsequently only gradually able to take from Italian art (cf. above note 327). The North, on the other hand, developed during the same time a most admirable way of depicting surface values based on the different reaction of the various portrayed substances to the illumination in the painting. It was the North which created—among other enchanting light phenomena—that sweet and mysterious diffusion of light and atmosphere which was so greatly admired by Fra Filippo and by Leonardo da Vinci, and which was imitated in Italian art as the well-known *sfumato* not before the second half of the fifteenth century.

IV. THE MADONNA OF NICHOLAS VAN MAELBEKE

THE trend which we notice when studying the development from the Ghent Annunciation to the Rolin painting is logically continued in Van Eyck's famous unfinished Madonna of Nicholas van Maelbeke, Provost of St. Martin's Abbey in Ypres, a work which may well have been one of the last designed by the master (Figs. 194 and 195). In the center panel of this rather large triptych, we see the donor kneeling before the Madonna and the Child, and again, just as in the Rolin Madonna, an architectural setting which permits a view of an enchanting landscape background. However, in the Madonna of Nicholas van Maelbeke, both picture sections now differ in nature from those found in the Rolin Madonna. In the Maelbeke painting, the foreground is no longer a castle referring to the environment of a chancellor. It is a portico made up of ecclesiastical forms, quite suitable to a donor who was the provost of an abbey. The landscape now lacks the representation of the large city, which in the Rolin Madonna had stressed, as we have seen, the idea of the Jerusalem of the crusaders. In the later work, the landscape is merely a stretch of superb countryside with level land, background mountains, a watercourse, castles, and hamlets. Despite these differences, however, it is obvious that we are again confronted with a representation of the New Heaven and the New Earth, which together form the celestial Jerusalem. It is also clear that the details of the setting are symbols both of the Church and of the Virgin, who herself signifies the Church.

Indeed, there are two Marian symbols in the triptych, which in their outstanding beauty and explicitness have always attracted the attention of scholars. I refer to the Burning Bush and to the Closed Door of Ezechiel—here presented as part of a tower—which are shown in the two upper sections of the interior wings. Since the unfinished middle panel shows the traces of several post-Eyckian attempts to complete the work, the wings have been regarded as being in their entirety the results of these attempts. In other words, scholars have always been inclined to consider the wings as totally non-Eyckian; they have taken them not only for the work of later hands but also for the invention of later minds. Indeed, some parts of the two panels so distinctly show areas which are badly preserved, and continuously reworked and overpainted, that this opinion is not really surprising. Even Panofsky, who pointed to the great iconographic interest of the wing representations, sees in them merely the achievement of a follower.[391] It is, however, a grave mistake to reject the wing designs wholesale. For in so doing we deprive ourselves not only of the knowledge of some interesting Eyckian elements but also of the opportunity to see the center composition in its proper iconographic focus and in its original formal environment.

There can be hardly any doubt that the two Marian symbols of the upper zone set in their beautiful landscapes are Eyckian, at least in their basic design. For, when we lower the reproductions of the two wings to the point where the horizon lines of these land-

[391] "The wings were never touched by Van Eyck . . . ," Panofsky 1953, I, p. 190.

scapes run flush with the horizon of the middle panel, we make the surprising and fascinating discovery that the landscape details in the shutters align perfectly with the elements in the center landscape. The building to the left behind the donor is continued in the composition of the Burning Bush, and the land as well as the river behind the Madonna extend in their precise design into the panel of the Closed Door. The two representations of the wings, which, in contrast to the other wing parts, are in a more or less satisfactory condition, show a Van Eyck-like style and technique. This very fact strongly points to the possibility that the paint surface was technically and artistically prepared by the master himself. This observation, together with the discovery that the landscape as today seen in the middle panel and the shutters must originally have been continuous, gives us a firm basis for the assumption that the existing shutters are the original Eyckian wings which at one time were cut and shifted into the present awkward position.

In the usual mediaeval or Renaissance triptych, the wings cover nothing but the middle panel and have, therefore, exactly the same height as the latter. If we suppose that the Maelbeke triptych had this form, we would have to assume that the later craftsman who tampered with the wings not only cut their tops but also added some wood sections at the bottom to make up for the reduction in height. But there seems to be no evidence that the lower parts of the present wings were added in post-Eyckian times. At my recent examination of the shutter panels, I gained the impression that they consist of a perfectly continuous original board. Supposing that an X-ray test will verify this impression, we would have to conclude that the shutters had formerly reached farther down than the middle panel. That means that they would have been intended to protect not only this middle panel but also a narrow predella-like section which must have originally appeared below it.

Before discussing the reasons for the alteration, which must have taken place if our observation is correct, and before offering a suggestion as to the original appearance of the Maelbeke triptych, it is necessary to make at least some qualification of what has been described as "several attempts" to complete the unfinished work. As far as the later work on the triptych is concerned, I think that basically we have to distinguish two successive procedures. The first seems to have taken place around 1500 and was obviously done by a master still conversant with the Eyckian technique and excellent enough in his art to be able to duplicate the refinement of the Eyckian surface treatment.[392] Some parts of the

[392] It may be worthwhile to take this occasion to mention a recent and highly interesting book on Van Eyck's technique, which was published by the heirs of a deceased Israeli painter from the notes left by the artist. Emanuel Emanuel (Luftglass), *Van Eyck und Vasari im Lichte neuer Tatsachen*, Maor-Verlag, Tel-Aviv 1965. Mr. Luftglass' discovery resulting from many painstaking experiments in conjunction with a new and rather brilliant interpretation of Vasari's text on Van Eyck, contradicts all our seeming knowledge on the working process used by the Netherlandish painters of the fifteenth century. His findings (accompanied by detailed recipes and charts) can be summed up as follows: Van Eyck painted with pure water color on a base of pure (transparent) oil which was the first coat applied to the smooth white ground of the prepared wooden panel. Since the water color dried much quicker than the oil base and was, after

central panel seem to have been worked by this hand as well as large sections of the interior wings, at least their best-preserved parts showing the Marian symbols in the delectable landscape.

The other hand apparently worked toward the end of the sixteenth century. This later master, though painting in a mode that is rather expressive and unmistakably characteristic, employed an art infinitely cruder than that of the earlier artist and without his Van Eyck-like sophistication. This latest hand seems to have been responsible for the execution of all the representations today visible on the exterior wings (Fig. 195), but merely for their execution. For, interestingly enough, it is not only the early sixteenth century work in the interior wings but also the late sixteenth century painting on their exteriors which seem to have been, at least in part, determined by an Eyckian design already existing on the surfaces in varying stages of Eyckian execution.

On the exterior faces of the wings, it is obvious that the two lower representations, showing the Sibyl and the Emperor Octavianus, were painted on top of Van Eyck's preparatory silverpoint drawings. The late and rather crude manner of the artist responsible for the present appearance of these two standing figures, makes them look Flémallesque rather than Eyckian. It is clear, however, that it must have been Van Eyck who invented these two lower representations. Not only is the idea of inserting a couple of shadow-throwing *grisaille* figures into the shallow niche compartments familiar to us from a number of Eyckian Annunciation scenes which appear on exterior wings, it is also the specific design of these figures which betrays the Eyckian invention. An unquestionably Eyckian feature is the inimitable gentleness and sophistication of the Sibyl's gesture as she points with her right hand, while supporting her beautifully flowing drapery with her left. This is strongly reminiscent of the Angel in the Ghent Annunciation, and even the strangely distorted three-quarter profile of the figure has a counterpart in the Ghent Altarpiece (Figs. 62 and 196).[393]

---

having dried, absorbed by the latter, the process of applying water color layers could often be repeated on the same oil coat. When this coat finally dried before the area in question was completed by the painter, another transparent oil coat could be applied to take still more layers of water color. No egg or any animal glue was used; no pigments were ever mixed with oil. The oil was always applied clear, and all pigments were mixed only with water. This process did not require a final application of a coat of varnish.

Without being able to test the correctness of Mr. Luftglass' sensational discovery, I am rather inclined to believe him. The procedure of applying water color to moist oil is strange enough to have been kept a workshop secret. It also explains the detailed preparatory drawings in Early Netherlandish paintings: They remained visible almost to the very end of the painting process, because of the transparency of the pure oil. It is to be hoped that Mr. Luftglass' book will be carefully studied by laboratory authorities here and abroad, not only to verify or reject his findings but also because there could be a chance that even the most knowledgeable restorer might profitably apply some of the findings of the essay in his practice of restoring.

[393] This kind of a three-quarter profile with the lower part in the distant half of a face more strongly foreshortened than the upper part of that half, is an archaic type which was nevertheless used until approxi-

While these two figures still convey to us the "ghost" of an Eyckian design and the beautiful landscapes with the Burning Bush and Ezechiel's Door on the interior wing faces convey to us much more of Van Eyck than a mere ghost, the rest of the wing representations, front as well as back, have apparently nothing or very little to do with the Eyckian style. To be precise, they were hardly painted in execution of an Eyckian sketch which had existed on the panel surface. Indeed, the angel group and the Madonna as they appear in their oval mandorlas in the upper part of the wing exteriors are obviously the personal "invention" of the late sixteenth century painter who finished these exteriors (Fig. 195). The style of these two upper sections is late sixteenth century pure and simple. Moreover, it is rather unlikely that Van Eyck himself should have repeated the representation of the Madonna and Child in the exterior view of a work which showed this very same representation in its interior. Indeed, on closer comparison of the two Madonnas as they appear in the middle panel and in the exterior wing, we notice that the latter is but a slightly changed copy of the former, an observation which excludes Van Eyck's authorship of this wing representation.

The upper part of Van Eyck's projected wing exteriors must have shown, or at least implied, the apparition which the Sibyl points out to the Emperor. According to the legend, this apparition is the *ara coeli*, the Heavenly Altar, which can be depicted as the Madonna and Child, because the Madonna when carrying the Christ Child is the *ara coeli*. But it can also be shown simply as the symbolic object of an altar. It is possible that in the Eyckian wings the latter form was used, rather than the figures of the Madonna and Child. There is, however, another possibility for this upper section of the exterior wings. Perhaps it was simply covered by the brocade pattern of a curtain which was shown as closed, but about to be drawn by angels.

If this was the case, it would be the standing Madonna of the central panel who functioned as the *ara coeli* to which the Sibyl refers. As the Sibyl points, the Madonna would still be invisible to the Emperor and to the spectator. But the apparition is ready to become visible to the viewer (and to them) when the wings are opened. Such an idea would have been well in line with Van Eyck's artistic thinking. We have seen a similar use of this same time element in the succession of the painted views in the Ghent Altarpiece, where the empty foreground in the Annunciation between the Angel and the Virgin indicates the coming of the Lord, Whose painted image was shown on the interior directly behind this empty space.[394]

No matter which of these two suggestions comes closer to the truth, in either case, the upper part of the exteriors of the Maelbeke wings would have been covered by painted

---

mately 1500 in the North, at least in German painting. In the time around 1400, the type was frequent even in the great centers of art. Cf., for instance, the Adoration of the Magi in the so-called small Bargello Diptych (Ring, *op.cit.*, cat. no. 15, fig. 16).

[394] Cf. above Chapter 3, Part IV, the paragraph to which note 185 belongs.

details which were not of overwhelming interest, since they would mainly have consisted of the patterns of inanimate forms. In the upper section of the interiors of the wings, the situation was similar, for, as we shall presently see, they mainly showed architectural details. These observations provide a clue to the reason why the wings were cut at the top rather than at the bottom. Once one had decided to re-use them to cover a middle panel whose predella-like socle was never executed, their height had naturally to be reduced. Since the bottom section of the wings showed an important Eyckian figure drawing, at least on their exterior faces, the people of the time would, of course, have been reluctant to sacrifice this part. The tops, however, showed only patterns and no figures. Hence, the decision to lift the wings to a new position and to do the cutting at the top.

But what sort of representation could have adorned the predella-like socle below the middle panel, and why does this section no longer exist, or why was it perhaps never actually designed? The particular shape of the missing part, a long but low horizontal stretch, in itself suggests a motif which rather frequently occurs in paintings in which the portraits of donors play a leading part. The space would be perfectly suitable for the representation of a stretched-out skeleton of a human being or of his dead body (the latter called the *gisant* and shown either as lying in state or in a frightening condition of advanced decay). A skeleton occurs, for instance, in Masaccio's famous fresco of the Trinity in the corresponding section of the composition (Fig. 197).[395]

With this possibility in mind, we recall a well-known piece of information, often cited in discussions of Jan's Maelbeke Madonna, namely that the painting was hung in its unfinished condition over the tomb of the donor, who was buried in the chevet of his abbey church, St. Martin in Ypres.[396] This procedure is usually taken as a touching but rather odd way of honoring the uncompleted work of a great painter and its dead donor. Actually, however, the thought may not have been so strange at all. We have to ask ourselves whether the Maelbeke painting may not from the outset have been intended to form the tomb monument of the Provost. It had been usual throughout the course of all previous centuries for a tomb monument to be ordered during the lifetime of the person for whom it was meant. Thus, the only unforeseen event as far as Maelbeke's commission is concerned, may have been the fact that the artist died before his donor.

In all likelihood, Jan's triptych had been intended from the start to be attached to the wall above Maelbeke's *tumba* and to crown the image of his *gisant*, which was either meant to appear as a sculptured relief above the sarcophagus or as a *grisaille* fresco directly applied to the wall as a simulation of such a relief.[397] In either case, the augmentation of

---

[395] For the meaning of the skeleton, cf. Ursula Schlegel, "Observations on Masaccio's Trinity Fresco in Santa Maria Novella," *Art Bulletin*, XLV, 1, March 1963, pp. 25ff.

[396] Cf. Waagen and De Bast, *op.cit.*, pp. 64-65, note 2. Compare also Weale and Brockwell, *op.cit.*, pp. 139f.

[397] The bas-relief portrait of a dead person was not unknown in the North. It appeared, for instance, in the monument to Jacques Germain (died 1424), datable between 1436 and 1443, which comes from a church

the wings at the bottom would have been quite a practical device for protecting the image added below the center panel. Their lower extensions, in fact, offered a most welcome opportunity for the painter to insert architectural representations which could link the pictorial space of the triptych to the space of the *gisant* and thereby bridge the gap between their divergent techniques.

The combination of painting and sculpture was most familiar in funerary monuments. Indeed, one Italian Trecento type, discussed in Panofsky's book on tomb sculpture, well illustrates a monument based on this combination. This type, which is familiar from numerous tombs in the city of Rome, shows a sarcophagus topped by a sculptured *gisant*, and this *gisant* is crowned by a painted representation, usually done in the technique of mosaic. Giovanni Cosmati's tomb of Guglielmo Durandus in Sta. Maria sopra Minerva is a particularly good example (Fig. 200).[398] While the dead body of the Bishop is presented in a sculptured image above the sarcophagus, he is depicted again in the crowning mosaic, this time as a living person venerating the Madonna in a celestial zone of heavenly bliss. A similar arrangement is found in the now destroyed tomb of Boniface VIII, formerly in the crypt of St. Peter and today preserved only in a drawing (Fig. 198). There we see that an altar was connected with the tomb, a combination also found in Masaccio's Trinity fresco and certainly to be postulated for the presumed Maelbeke monument.[399] Most likely, Jan van Eyck's Madonna of Ypres had thus been both an altarpiece and a funerary image as well.

If the Maelbeke triptych had actually been an altarpiece and a tomb monument, it would not be surprising if the exterior wings had in fact shown, as surmised above, a curtain which was drawn by angels. In early Italian Quattrocento tombs this motif appears

---

in Dijon and is today in the Dijon Museum. Cf. *Musée des Beaux-Arts de Dijon, Catalogue des Sculptures, Palais des Etats de Bourgogne*, 1960, p. 14 and plate XVI, and Panofsky, *op.cit.*, 1964, no. 256. The sculptured effigy in the North can even be combined with a wall painting appearing above it. Cf. the tomb in the church of St. Castor in Koblenz of Archbishop Kuno von Falkenstein who died in 1388. Illustrated in Stange, *op.cit.*, II, no. 154, with discussion and further literature on p. 120.

[398] For this and the following example, cf. Panofsky, *op.cit.*, 1964, p. 77.

[399] No matter whether the mensa stood directly in front of the Masaccio painting or was placed at some distance from it, the fresco was in any case part of an altar arrangement. The reasons which to Dr. Schlegel speak against a direct connection of the mensa with the painting are, in my opinion, not actually valid. Cf. Schlegel, *op.cit.*, 1963, p. 21. Without entering the discussion of the reconstruction of the artistic unit to which Masaccio's fresco belonged, I should like, nevertheless, to take this occasion to define my position on some important points which were raised in Dr. Schlegel's essay and answered by her in the negative. Keeping the arrangement of the Ghent Altarpiece in mind, the question as to whether a blending of real and painted architecture of a large size was possible in the Quattrocento, should, in my opinion, be answered in the affirmative. Cf. Dr. Schlegel's own note 24 dutifully citing Hans Kauffmann's correct information that this blending was already possible in the Trecento. The other point denied in the article is the possibility for life-size donors to appear kneeling in the region immediately above the altar. Considering the arrangement in the Ghent Altarpiece, this question, too, should emphatically be answered in the affirmative.

again and again, and always with the figures of the Madonna and Child to be revealed behind the curtain. As one example among many, I illustrate the Brancacci monument in Naples by Michelozzo and Donatello, which was begun by 1427 at the latest (Fig. 199). There we see not only a curtain revealing the figures of the Madonna and the Child as it may have occurred in the Eyckian triptych but also the semicircular upper confine of the frame as it can still actually be seen in the painting by Van Eyck.

While my reconstruction of the exterior view of the Maelbeke triptych is only a suggestion, we are on much firmer ground when trying to visualize the interior. It is clear that the architectural structure which we see in the middle panel must originally have been continued on the two wings. The foremost vaults of this structure with their Romanesque piers and the low dado-like parapet must have been formerly visible also in the lateral panels. With the total composition thus determined by three large arched openings of equal size, the view as a whole would have been rather similar to the one offered in the small painting of the Frick Collection which presents the Madonna of Jan Vos (Fig. 203). In the Maelbeke triptych, the lateral openings would have shown the representations of the Burning Bush and of Ezechiel's Closed Door immediately behind the low parapet; overlapped by the latter, they would have functioned as elements of a middle distance. In fact, the tower which contains the Closed Door would thus have appeared in a position and environment resembling St. Barbara's tower, as it is depicted in the Frick painting. Since Van Eyck, as the Ghent Annunciation proves, was not afraid of showing an empty foreground, I am inclined to believe that the sumptuous tile floor of the middle panel which must have been continued at the sides, had remained empty in the wings.

The tomb chamber of the lower part, which contained the *gisant*, was most likely made to appear as a crypt structure carrying the celestial edifice which appeared above it. The architecture of this chamber was probably, as already mentioned, continued in the lower sections of the shutter panels. Perhaps Van Eyck had designed two empty vaulted compartments for these two areas. Their present scenes, which depict Gideon with an Angel and Aaron standing before an altar with the budding rod, are, in my opinion, entirely unconvincing as Eyckian inventions. But the excellent artist who worked around 1500, who completed the upper wing scenes, and who may have invented the lower ones, was very likely influenced by the original Eyckian sketch when he placed his two scenes in vaulted compartments.[400]

[400] Actually there was no reason to place the Gideon scene—whose story really requires an open air setting—in an architectural space. If, in spite of this requirement, the later painter chose an indoor setting, this very fact speaks for an architectural design's having existed on the panels before he began his remodeling work. Whether an Eyckian silver-point drawing of the original architecture can still be found under the present paint coat or whether it was removed by the later painter could only be revealed in an X-ray examination. In any event, however, the Eyckian preparation of the paint ground can hardly have exceeded the drawing stage in these lower parts of the wing panels. That these are the least attractive parts of the wings today has to do with the present condition of the paint coat applied by the late fifteenth or early

If the original Eyckian composition included two empty side chambers, the configuration would not only have been reminiscent of the two annex rooms in the Ghent Annunciation but it would again bring to mind the two empty chambers painted by Giotto on the lower east wall of the Arena Chapel in Padua (Fig. 99). As previously explained, I am inclined to see in the two Giotto compartments mainly a Eucharistic meaning since, in my opinion, they point to the pastophories of the early churches. Ursula Schlegel, however, has regarded them as chiefly connoting two funerary chambers. If Van Eyck had, in fact, depicted the two empty low-vaulted rooms in his Maelbeke triptych, their meaning may have combined both connotations.[401] Stressing the funerary use as well as the sanctuary nature of the lower zone, the two vaulted rooms would have characterized the cryptlike structure as the earthly sanctuary which carries the heavenly one. Actually the cryptlike part with the *gisant* and the two empty chambers would have been seen not only as representing any earthly sanctuary but as the direct continuation of the specific sanctuary space which housed this particular tomb.[402]

While my reconstruction of the lower section of the Maelbeke triptych is admittedly conjectural, I do not think we can doubt that the main part had shown one continuous landscape and that large sections of this landscape, including parts of the sacred symbols appearing in it, were in fact executed by Van Eyck's own hand. In order to help the reader in his visualization of the Eyckian work as it may have been planned by the master himself, I have added a photomontage reconstruction of the triptych with the missing parts filled in by a water-color sketch (Fig. 201). The considerations on which my reconstruction is based automatically gave the triptych an over-all appearance that is rather tall and slender. The elongated proportions are those of familiar headpieces used in the North since the late fourteenth century to crown altar retables of monumental size.[403] Usually

---

sixteenth century artist whom we have mentioned. It seems that he too never finished his work, or that a later decision to remove his over-paint led to its ruin but did not remove it completely. As to the original architectural design by Van Eyck which I have postulated for the sections in question, they must have shown rather short columns which would carry the low vaults of the funerary structure. I am inclined to believe that the short columns in the Madonna of Jan Vos in the Frick Collection (Fig. 203), rather than preceding the Maelbeke composition, were influenced by the now lost architecture which had occurred in the lower wings of the Ypres Madonna.

[401] As, for that matter, do the chambers depicted by Giotto. Cf. above note 189 and the text of Chapter 3, Part IV belonging to it.

[402] Since it was important to the believer to be buried in a consecrated place and as near as possible to the relic of a saint or to another element of particular sanctity, it was usual to emphasize the sacred vicinity in funerary monuments. Thus Giotto's painted chambers are the illusionistic continuation of the real sanctuary and the niche in which Masaccio's Trinity is set acts as an actual recess in the church wall (Figs. 99 and 197).

[403] It seems to me that most of the small tabernacle shrines showing a sculptured Madonna in the center and movable wings adorned by paintings had originally not been self-contained holy objects but had crowned large altar retables. Cf., for instance, the small shrine from the Dijon Chartreuse now in the

THE MADONNA OF NICHOLAS VAN MAELBEKE

showing a sculptured Madonna and Child protected by painted shutters, they appear high above eye level and are topped by a slim tracery tower adding still further to their height. In Rogier van der Weyden's panel of the Seven Sacraments, we see their typical form in the top-piece of the choir-screen altar (Fig. 202). Although the Maelbeke Madonna by Van Eyck crowned a tomb with an altar, rather than just an altarpiece, we can still visualize the total arrangement on the basis of Rogier's representation. Even a towering tracery top projecting from behind the structure into the space of the spectator may have been part of the Eyckian structure. We have to bear in mind that the painted architecture which encloses the painted figures of Maelbeke and the Madonna is constructed so as to appear to be reaching into the believer's space, an impression which would have been greatly intensified by a crowning tracery tower.

The great probability that it was the motif of the *gisant* which had appeared below the middle panel of the Maelbeke triptych brings to mind the close connection which had always existed between the ordinary altarpiece with a full scale donor kneeling before the Madonna and the retable-like image which functioned as a tomb monument. In the North around 1400, we have many impressive tomb reliefs which show the large-sized figure of the dead being introduced by saints to the Madonna enthroned. In his discussion of these reliefs, Panofsky seems to intuit the basic connection between the two types when he uses Van Eyck's Van der Paele Madonna in his book on tomb monuments to illustrate the "ordinary" donor portrait appearing in a similar pictorial context (Fig. 139).[404]

I have not delved very deeply into the problem of the relationship between these two categories of works. But it seems to me that the altarpiece with the new type of donor appears in the North at approximately the same time as the funerary reliefs with the kneeling dead. Offhand I am inclined to believe that it was the former that was derived from the latter and not vice versa. In any case, we must realize that there is no essential difference between an altarpiece showing a large-scale donor in a prominent position and a funerary image which appears in connection with an altar and which depicts the deceased as a kneeling figure. An altarpiece is created for the devotion of the believer as well as for the memory of the donor for whose soul the believer is exhorted to pray. The funerary image when connected with an altar serves essentially the same dual purpose, no matter whether it is only a cenotaph erected as a memorial or a tomb monument proper with the deceased actually buried below or near it.

No doubt, Jodocus Vijd and his wife built the famous chapel in the Ghent church to serve as their own memorial sanctuary. The anniversary of the death of Jodocus as well as of his wife Elisabeth were both commemorated in a mass for their souls celebrated in

---

Collection Mayer van den Bergh in Antwerp, *Catalogue du Musée Mayer van den Bergh*, Antwerp/Brussels 1933, no. 359, pp. 35f with (unnumbered) illustrations in the plates.

[404] Panofsky, *op.cit.*, 1964, pp. 58f.

this chapel, his on June 18 and hers on June 24.[405] It is, therefore, quite legitimate to regard the Ghent Altarpiece as a memorial monument. Indeed, it may actually have been a tomb monument proper. For it seems to me that it was this very purpose which could have determined the unusual shape which Van Eyck selected for his elaborate structure and which required a very substantial socle zone. Most likely, the thought behind this structure was to install the two sarcophagi of the donors behind the altar table with the head ends visible to the left and right of the mensa (Figs. 41 and 42). It is also possible that the stone slabs which must have appeared in these two places in the socle were to carry the donor's memorial inscriptions, even if their bodies were to have been buried in the corresponding sites in that part of the crypt which they had also built. The tomb of Jodocus Vijd is unknown today. His wife is buried with her own family.[406] I do not know whether this was her original burial place or only the plot where her body was finally interred. But it seems possible that the couple, or at least Jodocus himself, was actually buried in the chapel and the tombs were destroyed in the same riots that so cruelly fragmented their altarpiece.

The Maelbeke triptych, though most probably also meant to serve as an altar retable and a memorial image combined, shows neither the huge scale nor the elaborate complexity of the Vijd polyptych. Its protagonists are somewhat under life size and its composition, as already mentioned, follows the ideas which had been developed in the Rolin Madonna. The great wealth of motifs, which the Ghent Altarpiece unfolds in their immediate and eschatological implications, are now expressed in the simple and concise image of the donor kneeling before the Madonna. The Madonna is the Church; she is the Bride in the Holy Wedding, the Deacon in the Eternal Mass, and mankind's intercessor in the Last Judgment. The paradisaic setting of the scene is her attribute adorned with the symbols of her virginity.

While all this is basically derived from the Rolin painting, the ideas as well as the form have greatly matured in the triptych of Nicholas van Maelbeke (Figs. 192 and 201). As far as the middle panel is concerned, foreground and background are now no longer connected by an intermediate zone. The level of the Marian symbols, which still functions as a linking middle ground in the Rolin painting, is now restricted to the wings, where a middle distance containing the Burning Bush and the Closed Door has become the area of the chief representation. The elimination of the middle ground in the main panel adds both to the austere simplicity and to the emphasis on two-dimensional values which characterize this last work of Van Eyck. The foreground architecture has the basic form of an ecclesiastical chevet reaching beyond the area of a transept shown in the wings.

[405] Cf. Dhanens, Inventaris VI, p. 95 and 96. Compare also the interesting discussion on tombs and funerary monuments, *ibid.*, p. 20.

[406] Cf. *ibid.*, p. 96.

But the painter has shaped the structure into a building without walls and windows. This strange portico-like architecture depicts the New Heaven as radically opened as it could be without destroying the iconographic identity of the edifice.

The New Earth, too, is now greatly reduced in its wealth of form and in the area which it occupies on the picture surface. The landscape is abbreviated to a narrow strip which rather unassumingly fills the space between the parapet of the building and the now very low horizon line of the scene. In the general reduction of the elements of the setting, through which Van Eyck has placed a new and forceful emphasis on the figures, only one area is not diminished, namely the ceiling of the building. This part of the setting is never particularly emphasized in other Eyckian works. Indeed, it is not shown at all in the Madonna of the Chancellor Rolin. But, in the Maelbeke painting, it is just this part of the setting which carries the greatest importance.

The ceiling is made up of a system of vaults formed by a magnificent array of round and pointed arches. It creates a canopy over the figures. This vault area, as the symbol of Heaven *par excellence*, was indeed the only architectural motif actually needed to bring out the meaning of the structure. The building, crowning the two protagonists with its vaults and anchoring the two figures in the picture space through the sturdy vertical forms of its piers, is, in the last analysis, mainly a network of lines to be seen as a flat configuration on the picture plane. This network acts as a linear grid giving accents to the places where the voluminous forms of the protagonists are set against the neutral foil of the blue sky. Nothing is easier than to re-translate this Eyckian composition into the idiom of early fourteenth century art to which this late work has such a strong affinity. Two figures, crowned and connected by a canopy architecture, and the whole outlined against a neutral background had then been a popular picture type. In its concealed two-dimensionality, the Maelbeke Madonna directly continues the trend which can already be witnessed in Van Eyck's Antwerp Madonna of 1439 (Fig. 129). In this small painting, too, the two-dimensional tendency is striking and has always greatly astonished critics of Jan's art.

The new trend amounts to the "re-gothicization" of the devotional image. It presents that particular reaction against the previous wealth of pulsating life and strong three-dimensionality which marks the next phase of Northern fifteenth century painting. Precisely this trend was to determine the whole work of Rogier van der Weyden. In the Maelbeke Madonna by Jan van Eyck, the reduction of the setting and the new emphasis on the figures does not result in the aridity which sometimes can be noted in the paintings of Rogier. It only gives to the work a new hieratic power and a new genuine monumentality which matches its still forceful visual persuasion. In fact, the new formal restrictions which we have described were instrumental in bringing out a new and overwhelmingly beautiful version of Jan's great idea of the Heavenly Jerusalem.

Heaven has become transparent. We are not only permitted to see the New Earth through this edifice, we actually feel the atmosphere of the heavenly landscape which has now "tangibly" invaded the structure from all sides. The luminous air of God's divine nature not only pervades the background view but the foreground structure as well. It converts it into a garden pavilion of Paradise. The protagonists of the scene, enveloped by the paradisial air, exist in a blissful realm which is now the true union of the New Heaven with the New Earth. This is the triumphal culmination of the entire Eyckian art: the painting symbolizes man's Salvation by presenting the donor united with the Deity in a setting in which the earthly part, the attribute of a mankind redeemed, and the heavenly part, the realm of the redeeming Deity, fuse in a miraculous embrace.

The skeleton structure of a portico, to which Jan has reduced the building of the New Heaven, is a dematerialized and, as it were, an "abstract" architectural unity. As such, it brings to mind the skeleton work we have postulated for the lost frame of Van Eyck's Ghent Altarpiece (Figs. 41 and 42). Indeed, the Maelbeke Madonna is Jan's final return to the Heavenly Jerusalem in its traditional architectural abstraction, after he had presented the idea in so many "concrete" realistic guises. Although the structure is now completely rendered in the technique of painting, in its quality of being a rigid architectural abstraction it clearly links the Maelbeke triptych to the great altarpiece of Jodocus Vijd. With this observation the circle of Jan's artistic development is closed. At the end of his life, drawing the conclusions from a decade of work dedicated to the same idea, the painter returns, on a new basis, to his initial form of the Heavenly Jerusalem. This form, the most abstract expression of the idea, was able not only to present the most perfect unification of its two parts but to convey to the viewer in an instantaneous flash the most comprehensive and universal meaning of the concept as a whole.

V. THE AFTERLIFE OF JAN'S JERUSALEM IDEA

JAN's idea of making the image of the Heavenly Jerusalem the setting of a painted work had a considerable afterlife. Our brief discussion of the Detroit painting by the Master of the St. Lucy Legend has already indicated how familiar the concept must still have been in Bruges around 1500 (Fig. 193). This late period, however, rather than showing the results of an uninterrupted line of Eyckian ideas and forms, is in actual fact a deliberate revival of them after they had been modified by the generations immediately following Jan van Eyck.

The conventionalization of Van Eyck's scenery which took place in the art of Rogier van der Weyden was the first step towards a modified meaning of the setting. It has long been known that Rogier's work, though basically derived from the form arsenal of his teacher, the Master of Flémalle, also reflects from the very start the direct influence of the art of Van Eyck. However, that many of Rogier's ideas so far considered to be his own are those of the Ghent Altarpiece and were thus actually Eyckian becomes evident only now after the reconstruction of the great retable and the analysis of its basic pictorial concepts. Rogier's famous Prado painting of the Descent from the Cross, for instance, is clearly a modernized version of his teacher's triptych of the same theme (Figs. 204, 126 and 127). The pupil "corrected" the traditional historical Calvary landscape of his master by placing his own figures as pseudo-sculpture into an ideal shrine-like compartment. Attempts have been made to explain Rogier's method as the result of his presumed early training as a sculptor. Actually, however, his "correction" was based on Jan van Eyck's idea of pseudo-sculpture placed into a shrine-like recess, a concept ingeniously evolved in the Ghent Altarpiece. And when Rogier, in two of his later works, in the St. John Altarpiece as well as in the Granada-Miraflores retable, frames his sacred scenes with a number of elaborately historiated arches, this too is but the idea of the Ghent polyptych, whose sculptural frame is translated by Rogier into the medium of painting (Fig. 205).[407]

Even assuming that Rogier still understood Jan's idea of the Heavenly Jerusalem, it is evident that he took no special interest in the essence of the concept. What he did was simply to use Jan's celestial sceneries as conveniently precoined types of ideal settings. This is obvious even from the very fact that the vivid portrayal of human motion and emotions is the trademark of Rogier's art, while such an emotional display would have been impossible for Rogier had he penetrated the depths of Jan's idea. As we have seen in Jan's own art, the setting, if fully understood as the realm of a celestial nirvana, precluded the dramatic outburst of the human temperament. To Rogier it was sufficient that these settings have the general aspect of a sacred locale and thus are able to surround his figures with the atmosphere of an ideal environment.

The change in the basic character of the setting which has taken place in the work of Rogier becomes evident when we compare his Madonna of St. Luke with the Rolin Madonna by Jan van Eyck (Figs. 206 and 192). The derivation of Rogier's scene from the composition by Van Eyck has often been mentioned. The later painting retains the characteristic two-part setting of the earlier and even imitates the linking zone of the garden tract. But it is rather doubtful that the setting's original meaning as the two parts of the apocalyptic realm had any importance to Rogier. He takes it for granted that both parts are symbols of the Virgin and he does not even take pains particularly to characterize the linking garden tract as the *hortus conclusus*, as Jan had done by placing the Marian lilies in it.

Rogier's background landscape is no longer Jan's distant and comprehensive panorama, nor does he fill it with an Eyckian wealth of minute details. The forms are few and

---

[407] The St. John Altarpiece is illustrated in Panofsky 1953, II, plate 202. It is interesting that Rogier makes use of the Eyckian "threshold" idea in both of these retables. In both cases, the architecture establishes a portal zone rather similar to that of a rood-screen. But Rogier's architectural forms have in themselves no similarity to the Eyckian classicizing structure as it must have appeared in front of the Adoration landscape in the lower zone of the Ghent Altarpiece. While Van Eyck there uses the antique combination of tall columns carrying a straight entablature (cf. above the end of note 222), Rogier depicts a familiar Gothic architecture, as the Ghent Altarpiece had only shown in the upper section of its sculptural framework (Fig. 41).

nearby, with the city indicated by a limited number of streets and houses, and the river so close that a schematic ripple of the water was needed to indicate its motion. The terrain of the foreground architecture is not raised to any significant height when compared with the landscape view. This view, of an empty crystalline nearness, is certainly still an ideal landscape but hardly intended to be the New Earth of the apocalyptic vision. Indeed, its specific connotation was made perfectly clear by the painter by means of a symbol which he placed, as it were, as a pictorial type of inscription above his city view. The foreground hall shows in the upper part of its rear wall and directly crowning this view a circular window which is crossed by the tie-beam and the king-post of the roof in such a manner that the lighted disc forms the familiar sign of the world (Figs. 207 and 208). This standard symbol is constituted by a globe or round disc divided into three segments, two quarter circles and one half circle, which usually signify the three continents but which can also simply connote the cities, the land, and the water of the world.[408]

Rogier's background landscape was no doubt meant to be the world redeemed. Although this is certainly also the basic meaning of the term "the New Earth," there is, nevertheless, a subtle but important difference between the two concepts. While the concept of the New Earth is used in the biblical text as the complement to the New Heaven, the word "world" is always employed to denote the opposite of the divine realm. Indeed, the word is frequently used not only for the more or less neutral domain which we today call the world, but also to signify the sinfulness of this domain. This latter meaning is intended when St. John warns his congregation of the "world."[409] Rogier's symbol of the world as we see it in his painting of St. Luke Drawing the Madonna is therefore strangely prophetic of the things that were to come. In the art of the later fifteenth century, the landscapes and buildings of a setting can start to mean our own unredeemed earthly world; and they can even be used to signify the world in its radically negative sense.

The shift in meaning was gradual, with strange ambiguities and overlapping of concepts marking the process of transition. The Eyckian natural unity of the ideal and the historical aspect of a biblical scene more and more falls apart to give way to a new awareness of a distinction between the historical occurrence as such and its doctrinal meaning. At the beginning of the separation process, the new awareness caused indecision, perhaps

[408] While our illustration shows the three parts of the disc inscribed with the names of the three continents, the other possibility can be found in the woodcut world map by Hanns Rüst (fifteenth century) which is illustrated in Leo Bagrow, *History of Cartography* (translation from the German), Cambridge 1964, plate LI.

[409] "Do not bestow your love on the world, and what the world has to offer; the lover of this world has no love for the Father. What does the world offer? Only gratification of corrupt nature. . . ." I John 2:15-17. Cf. also I John 5:19, I Corinthians 11:32 and II Corinthians 4:4. In the paintings of Hieronymus Bosch, it is this concept of the world that is the basis for the whole realm of evil contrivances depicted by this fifteenth century painter. Cf. Philip, *op.cit.*, 1953, pp. 291f and especially note 105.

even anguish. This, however, is not the occasion for the difficult analysis of the pictorial concepts of place and time as they appear in the paintings of the later fifteenth century. Suffice it now only to point to the problem-filled art of Hugo van der Goes, whose scenes, though set in an earthly scenery, still seek to establish a direct connection with the surrounding sanctuary space.

There can be no doubt, for instance, that the setting in Hugo's Portinari Altarpiece depicts our own earthly world, or that it is, at least basically, a historical place of action, with the background landscape showing, in the manner of Rogier's art, a number of scenes preceding that of the Nativity (Fig. 209). The traditional stagelike foreground has been abandoned in favor of a large stretch of uninterrupted space, which as a single expanse reaches into a very far distance. This for the first time is a dynamic moving space spiraling around the Madonna and the Child and in no way similar to Van Eyck's and Rogier's static succession of planar space levels. The new quality in Hugo's art is connected with the new meaning of his scenery, which is no longer the hieratic realm of a sanctuary. The very appearance of the strikingly earthly shepherds, touchingly emphasizing the imperfection of our earthly existence and thus stressing the human need for Salvation rather than a Redemption already consummated, proves that Hugo had the old earth and not the New Earth in mind when he painted his Nativity scene. Furthermore, the sinfulness of the place is clearly indicated by the figure of a demon who dwells in the dark recess of the ruin to the left, directly above the two animals.[410]

Nevertheless, in spite of the distinctly earthly nature of his place of action, Hugo admirably succeeded in making the doctrinal meaning of his Nativity perfectly clear. As pointed out in an excellent article, recently published, the painter shaped the scene into an image of the first Mass celebrated by the newly born Saviour of the World. The particular ecclesiastical vestments of the angels distinctly indicate that the nude Christ Child (clad in the new garb of His human body) is the young Priest for the first time celebrating the Sacrament over the altar.[411] Here, however, the Christ Child is not only the Priest in the holy act, He is also the Victim of the Sacrifice. The Host has turned, as it were, into the radiant body of the sacred Child, a vision which is described over and over in legends of the Middle Ages.[412] Hugo's Nativity picture is thus based on an idea which is in essence the same as that of the Ghent Altarpiece. There too Christ is both the Priest and the Sacrifice in a miraculous Mass.[413] But it is not just the idea as such which links Hugo's paint-

[410] Cf. Robert M. Walker, "The Demon of the Portinari Altarpiece," Art Bulletin, XVII, 3, September 1960, pp. 218-19.

[411] Cf. M. B. McNamee, "Further Symbolism in the Portinari Altarpiece," Art Bulletin, XLV, 2, June 1963, pp. 142-43.

[412] Cf. above note 191 (second part), and the literature cited there.

[413] Cf. above note 123, the literature cited in this note and the text to which this note belongs.

ing to the great polyptych by Jan. The particular treatment of the lowermost picture level also connects this later Nativity to the retable in Ghent.

The Eucharistic meaning of the nude Christ Child is distinctly underlined by the sheaf of wheat, part of a delightful still life placed in the center of the composition's lowest zone and clearly repeating the shape and position of the Child's body. We are thus given both the true form of the sacred Host and its symbolic form. And it is the latter which the artist used to connect his work with the sanctuary space surrounding it, for the symbolic wheat appears directly above the altar table and thus is to be seen in relation both to this table and to the painted composition. The figures of the adoring angels serve to make this dual connection perfectly clear. These angels, kneeling on either side of the foreground, are rather equivocal in the direction of their devotion. They can be interpreted as adoring the Christ Child and also as worshiping the Eucharistic species symbolized in the sheaf of wheat.[414] Indeed, their strange in-between scale, which matches neither that of the other figures in the painting nor is as distinctly small as that of Van Eyck's flying heavenly spirits, makes them appear to belong to a realm of reality different from the one which surrounds the other figures.[415] They stand out from the composition as a paste-up from a different snapshot stands out in a commercial photograph. There can be no doubt that this awkward impression is deliberately achieved: the foreground angels only partly belong to the painted historical scene; they were also intended to exist directly in the space of the spectator and thus to extend this sanctuary space into the realm of the historical scene.

While this method is basically the same as the one used by Jan van Eyck in the lower region of the middle panel of the Adoration of the Lamb, it has an entirely different effect in a painting that is basically earthly and "historical" than it has in Jan's composition, where the setting is in its entirety a sanctuary space (Figs. 62, 41). In Hugo's painting, the sudden shift in picture reality produces an almost weird effect. In a composition in which the specific and the earthly outweigh the general and the heavenly, and in which Jan's hieratic symmetry has been loosened by forms encompassing diagonal movement and foreshadowing the Baroque, this shift not only appears incongruous but it also has a depressing effect. In a space which is no longer eternal and which thus merely depicts the sacred past and the sacred present but not the sacred future, the glorious certainty of a future Redemption is not shown and therefore the tension remains unresolved.

We can safely assume that Hugo was fully aware of this predicament. We may perhaps even surmise that it was this predicament which was principally responsible for his agony as an artist. A contemporary source explicitly tells us of the painter's despair due to

---

[414] As observed by Margaret L. Sprague in a term paper written for a course I gave at the University of Pennsylvania, Philadelphia, the angels' adoration is directed toward the sheaf of wheat rather than toward the holy Child.

[415] Hugo's angels show the same strange in-between size as do the music-making angels in the Ghent Altarpiece.

his inability to duplicate the art of Jan van Eyck.[416] Since, as a craftsman, Hugo was certainly Jan's equal and must have been conscious of this fact, it is highly probable that his sufferings resulted from the shift in pictorial concept, fatal but unavoidable in his time. It would seem that Hugo was crushed by the realization that Jan's Paradise was lost and that no genius on earth could regain it.

The loss of the "Eyckian Paradise" involved not only the artists' loss of a convenient formal device successfully used by their predecessors. Its roots reach deeply into the fundamental outlook of man toward human life and religion at that time. The firm and triumphal belief in man's final Salvation was slowly shaken by a new and desperate doubt which eventually was to bring about the age of the Reformation. And when Hieronymus Bosch, whose art marks the very eve of this age, uses as the setting of all his paintings the image of our own evil world which is possessed by the Devil, this direct reversal of the Eyckian device is the painter's ironic expression of his own period's tragic lack of religious security.

In the work of Bosch, Christ, the Madonna, and the saints appear as helpless figures in a setting of huge landscapes whose rather high horizon permits the artist to populate his world with a multitude of demons and monsters. Even in his famous Epiphany in the Prado, where the demonic contrivances are relatively sober and the demons look relatively human, the very setting of the foreground, the dilapidated hut, clearly conveys the pessimistic spirit of the painting (Fig. 210). Unlike the hut in the Dijon Nativity by the Master of Flémalle, from which Bosch's structure is basically derived, the ruin in the Prado Epiphany is not the remainder of a real building but only the shrewdly arranged makeshift of a stage prop. A closer observation shows us that Bosch's hut simply consists of a cardboard-like plane slightly folded on the right side to make it stand up. Otherwise, it is supported only by a frontal "foot" consisting of the thatched roof with its assemblage of carrying sticks. The nail connecting this front support with the basic folded "wall" is plainly visible in the pointed top of the roof.

Bosch's statement is clear: a shabby and wicked world cannot afford anything better for the holy figures than this cheap and shaky setting like those used in pageants performed at a village fair. The Madonna is no longer the splendidly adorned Queen of Heaven, the Child no longer the young, self-confident ruler of the universe. The princely attire of the Virgin as seen in the paintings of Jan has been reduced to the utmost simplicity in dress. Clad in modest garb, adorned only by the purity of her divine virtue, the Madonna faces the hollow pomp of the wicked world. This is how the three kings, who are the representatives of this world, would have seen her, an idea made all the more distinct because Bosch has taken the basic form of his Madonna and Child in a flush of cun-

---

[416] Hieronymus Münzer, cf. Documenten, p. 10. Compare also Panofsky 1953, I, p. 331 and p. 331, note 2 printed on p. 499.

ning irony from Jan's famous panel of the Madonna and Chancellor Rolin (Fig. 192).[417]

The contrast, however, between the Van Eyck and the Bosch concept, though out-spoken, is a contrast not in kind but in viewpoint. Bosch's paintings are not "historical" images in counterdistinction to Jan's superhistorical scenes. The art of both of these great painters is metaphorical. Bosch's art, especially, far from rendering a historical reality, is the image of a spiritual truth. Through his trick of the hut as a stage prop, his intention is made patently clear: since the Holy Family would hardly have sought shelter in what is nothing more than thin sheets of board, Bosch's scene can only have been meant as a metaphor.

His is the metaphor of the evil world, not of the merciful Heaven. As I showed many years ago in an article on Bosch's Epiphany, the Wicked in the form of Antichrist and his cortege populate the area behind and around the hut wall.[418] The landscape too, as already mentioned, is filled with demonic contrivances. Instead of the powerful reassurance which Jan offers to the devout, Bosch demands from him a decision between good and evil. His paintings have ceased to be religious images in the proper sense of the word. Instead, they are a rather didactic moralizing lesson, exhorting and threatening the believer. Though most effective in fulfilling this purpose and, in so doing, taking an important step toward the later strictly secular art, they are intrinsically unsuitable for ecclesiastical devotion. It is thus not surprising that the majority of ecclesiastical works of the time stays conventional; it remains determined by Rogier's powerful formulations and never ceases to depict the sacred figures reassuringly in an ideal space. Indeed, in the first two decades of the sixteenth century, precisely at the time when Bosch was at the peak of his fame, a younger generation started systematically to revive the art of the founders, especially that of Jan van Eyck and his Jerusalem idea in particular.[419]

In their desire to renew the great era, gifted artists like Gerard David and Jan Gossart often became the copyists of Eyckian models. The impressive architectural structures of Gossart have the tendency to run wild with profuse and ornate Gothic lacework in order to convince us that we are confronted with the edifice of the New Heaven.[420] The landscapes become overly sweet and paradisial. This conscious renewal has a rather artificial look: the artists are ultimately unable to conceal the bitter truth that their time is no longer really convinced of the validity of the religious statement. The paintings of Gossart and

[417] Charles de Tolnay was the first to notice the reflection of the Rolin Madonna in the painting by Bosch. Cf. Charles de Tolnay, *Hieronymus Bosch*, Basel 1937, p. 43. For the concept of the "world" as illustrated in the art of Bosch, cf. above note 409.

[418] Philip, *op.cit.*, 1953, pp. 267ff.

[419] The revival of the art of the "Founders" is discussed in Panofsky 1953, I, pp. 350-58.

[420] Sculptural forms of a richly flourishing Gothic style are most strikingly used as a paradisaic symbol in Gossart's Madonna Enthroned of the Malvagna Triptych in the Museum in Palermo, cf. *Jan Gossart genaamd Mabuse*, Exhibition Rotterdam/Bruges/1965, plates following p. 18.

the Antwerp Mannerists, lacking an intrinsic religious conviction, have now for the first time become "art" in the modern sense, in the sense implied in the term "Mannerism," which has long been used to describe them.

In Germany, which was, so far as painting was concerned, still rather provincial in the time of Van Eyck and Rogier and which came artistically into its own only in the last decades of the fifteenth century, the general revival of the Jerusalem idea, falling so to speak on virgin soil, assumed a much greater intellectual and spiritual depth than it did in the Netherlands around 1500. But in Germany too the idea lacked the quality of being natural to the work as it was for Van Eyck. The Heavenly Jerusalem now becomes an image for religious poetry. When, in Albrecht Altdorfer's panel of the Birth of the Virgin now in Munich, the lying-in room of Saint Anne is placed in the aisle of an elaborate Renaissance cathedral, it is with the air of idyllic phantasy that the artist used a symbolic setting signifying the Heavenly Jerusalem and as such the person of Maria-Ecclesia herself (Fig. 211).

In using the Jerusalem idea, Altdorfer had perhaps been inspired by the Isenheim Altarpiece of his famous contemporary Matthäus Gotthart (called Grünewald). The two-part center representation of one of the various views of this retable is obviously based on the old apocalyptic concept (Fig. 212). Although the general theological content of the two-fold image with Mary as the Celestial Bride in the mystical bridal chamber to the left, and the Nativity of Christ in the mystical landscape to the right, is usually correctly interpreted, its specific apocalyptic meaning has, so far as I know, never been pointed out. But it is evident, in my opinion, that the left part signifies Mary-Ecclesia as the New Heaven and the right one Mary-Ecclesia as the New Earth—the first set in the traditional celestial architecture, the second in the traditional celestial landscape.[421] The very fact that this two-part painting appears as one of the images in the interior of the polyptych and is preceded by an exterior representation depicting the Crucifixion, speaks for the strong eschatological meaning of the former. From the strictly narrative point of view, the two-part image should precede the Crucifixion. But the artist made not the Crucifixion but the two mystical images the climax of his series. He could do this only because the emphasis in the meaning of these images is on the future, rather than on the strictly historical past. It is in them that the blissful fulfillment of the New Covenant is shown.

While the Ghent Altarpiece is one of the first of the giant Northern altarpieces with a multitude of movable wings, Master Matthäus' retable in Isenheim is one of the last of

---

[421] For the more general apocalyptic meaning of the Isenheim scenes in question, cf. Günther, *op.cit.*, *passim* and von Einem, *op.cit.*, *passim*. The unique feature, that the Isenheim Nativity surrounds its protagonists with furnishings belonging to an indoor scene—the cradle, the wooden tub, and the chamber pot— but is as a whole rather "illogically" set into a landscape, so strongly characterizes this landscape as a symbol that there can be hardly any doubt that it was intended to signify the New Earth. For the correct first name of the so-called Grünewald, see above note 355.

these huge and complicated "religious machines." In comparing the artistic mood of the two, a definition comes to mind which Panofsky once used, not in comparing Van Eyck and Grünewald but in his comparison of Van Eyck and Bosch. In contrast to an image by Bosch, Panofsky asserts, the Eyckian representation is not dreamt but seen; it is supremely real.[422] The "supreme reality" of the Eyckian image is striking also when it is compared with Grünewald's ecstatic art. The images of the Isenheim Altarpiece show the Heavenly Jerusalem as the vision of an enraptured mind. In a perfectly "modern" way, they depict a religious truth as the experience of the human psyche but not as an objective reality. This was the only form in which the great Apocalyptic idea could manifest itself once again in this rather late time. In the art of Van Eyck, however, reality and truth had still been one. Seen by a sober mind clearly awake in the broad light of day, the Eyckian image possesses all the power of religious reassurance. It still states a spiritual truth as a fact of a tangible objective reality.

[422] Cf. Panofsky 1953, I, p. 239.

APPENDICES

EXCURSUS I

THE DATE OF THE "EYCKIAN PART" OF THE
TURIN-MILAN BOOK OF HOURS

THE chief basis for an early dating of this portion of the Hours is the miniature depicting a Caval-cade by the Seashore (Fig. 133, cf. Panofsky 1953, I, p. 234), which is believed to show the coat of arms of William VI, Count of Holland, Zeeland, and Hainault, and to present his personal portrait in the rider on the white horse. On the assumption that the portion of the book which shows this miniature was painted for the Count, the date of this portion was fixed before 1417, which is the death date for that prince. This hypothesis, which had already been rejected by Dvořák, De Tolnay, Duverger, and others, and was most convincingly contested on stylistic grounds by Ludwig Baldass (*op.cit.*, pp. 91ff), was again accepted by Panofsky. After having submitted to his readers the history of the famous book and the history of its evaluation by modern writers, Panofsky indulges in a scholastic game of *pro* and *contra* for the early date, which leaves the problem unresolved but has the advantage of making the reader familiar, in a most entertaining way, with all of its ramifications. However, when in the end Panofsky attempts to cut the Gordian Knot by disproving his opponents' alternative theory, namely, that the miniatures are the creation of a Dutch artist of the thirties, he still has not proved his own point that the paintings must then be early. His final argument, that the miniatures are a miracle no matter whether they were painted in the second or the fourth decade, and that, as the works of a genius, they can only be attributed to Jan, is based on a debatable assumption. It is, in my opinion, by no means certain, that these illuminations are the work of a genius. Perhaps, in their own time, they were much less miraculous than they appear to us, who are left with but a few sad remnants of a once glorious tradition largely unknown today.

A comparatively recent article (Kurz, *op.cit.*, pp. 117-31) tries to strengthen the old theory on the early date of the miniatures with two new observations. Attention is drawn in this article to the fact that a prayer which appears together with the miniature of the Cavalcade in the book uses the masculine gender, a fact from which Dr. Kurz concludes that this portion of the Hours can have been painted neither for William's widow nor for his daughter, as some of the advocates of the later date had assumed. The second observation concerns an interesting drawing in the Louvre which shows a group portrait that includes a figure identified by Dr. Kurz as William VI. According-ing to him, this figure is the likeness of the same person who appears on the white horse in the miniature.

Though it may well be correct that the owner of the book was a man and that the portrait in the Louvre drawing depicts William VI, there is still no compelling reason to assume that the rider on the white horse is also a portrait of the same prince and that this and the other miniatures of the same group were painted before 1417. The identity of the coat of arms in the Cavalcade minia-ture is far from certain, so that the male owner of the hour book must not necessarily have been of the house and generation of William. Moreover, the tiny and rather generalized faces in the drawing and in the miniature show only a vague similarity to each other. And since the face in the Louvre drawing is even distorted by later over-painting, and the face in the miniature is not necessarily a portrait at all, the identification and subsequent conclusion as to date rest on rather shaky grounds. I side with the scholars who reject the early date because I am convinced of the derivative character of all of the miniatures and do not believe that there is any reason to attribute them to a Dutch artist of the thirties. The pastiche-like nature of these little paintings, often hinted at and even implied in Panofsky's own description, makes it impossible, in my opinion, that they present the *juvenilia* of Jan.

There is one remark which I should like to add to Baldass' excellent observation that the figures in these miniatures show a rather early design but are placed in landscape and interior settings of a most mature type. The small male figure which is depicted in the Cavalcade miniature as kneeling before the rider on the white horse literally repeats the design of the kneeling king whom we find in the frequently discussed Berlin drawing of the Adoration of the Magi (Figs. 133 and 134). This figure, which by the way rather often appears in subsequent book illumination, is most typical of the International Style. In the Berlin drawing this figure conforms with the style of the total composition, with its archaic landscape of a ravine-split plateau and with its trees and buildings out of scale with the foreground. It is obvious that the rock plateau is used to hide the difficult point of transition from foreground to background and to make the sudden appearance of the kings' train in the foreground more convincing. These features still bear a pronounced affinity to the landscapes of the Brussels Hours (cf., for instance, Panofsky 1953, II, fig. 44 on plate 19). The drawing is certainly an authentic and most faithful reproduction of one single Netherlandish composition which may have been the center panel of a rather famous altarpiece. It is highly probable that this composition is even pre-Eyckian rather than early Eyckian. While the kneeling male figure is well in keeping with the archaic design of the landscape in the Berlin drawing, in the miniature of the Cavalcade the figure is an obvious intrusion. We therefore have to conclude that the Cavalcade miniature is a pastiche.

This observation disqualifies, I think, the entire miniature group attributed to the "Hand G" as original inventions and puts them into more or less the same class as all of the others, whose derivative character is too striking to be denied. For Panofsky's attempt to deny this character in another miniature of the "Hand G" group, cf. above note 264. It seems to me that the highly skilled miniature painters whose combined efforts are seen throughout the Turin-Milan Hours have followed the well-known method of placing figures of an early design into landscape settings of contemporary taste. As Dr. Kurz has himself correctly mentioned, it is this method which characterizes many examples of sixteenth century imitations.

EXCURSUS II

THE NEW TYPE FOR CHRIST'S RESURRECTION
AS FOUND IN THE ALTARPIECES OF BRUGES AND IN OTHER
NORTHERN WORKS AROUND AND BEFORE 1500

IN A NUMBER of early Netherlandish altarpieces which show the Crucifixion in the center panel and the Resurrection in the right wing, the figure of the resurrected Christ is depicted as rising from a cave tomb and as elevated in the air. In all of them, the Crucifixion scene is placed against a landscape background with a city, while the foreground shows a large crowd of people which includes mounted soldiers, a group of women surrounding the fainting Madonna, and an elegant figure of the Magdalene who wrings her hands as she turns toward the Cross. This is the same type as Van Eyck's New York Calvary (Fig. 140) and, indeed, all of the altarpieces in question are painted by artists who lived in Bruges, which was Jan's residence during his later years, and thus continued his tradition. The earliest of the retables is Memling's large work in Lübeck which dates from 1491 (Fig. 155). The Resurrection scene of this retable, employing a type then still unique in Northern painting, has caused some perplexity to Schrade (cf. Schrade, *op.cit.*, p. 304). Certainly Memling was not a painter inventive enough to have introduced into the art of his region a completely new iconographic type taken from a foreign tradition. When we realize, however, that his Resurrection scene may have been derived from a work by Van Eyck now lost, the enigma begins to explain itself.

There are two other altarpieces following Memling which show the same type of a Resurrection, one of them is Gerard David's small triptych in the Frans Hals Museum in Haarlem (Fig. 158), the other is a work of a follower who commingles elements from Memling's polyptych with those from David's retable (reproduced in Karl Voll, *Memling, des Meisters Gemälde*, Klassiker der Kunst, Berlin/Leipzig *s.d.*, pp. 146-49). While the latter is thus of no particular interest for our problem, the triptych by Gerard David is well worth consideration. Though it basically operates with the same troupe of actors, so to speak, as does the altarpiece by Memling, it bears witness to its painter's wish to make in all of the details as many small changes as possible. In order to achieve this aim, Gerard David has obviously "corrected Memling with Van Eyck," that is to say, he has again used the same set of Eyckian drawings which had also been the models for Memling. The David triptych is, in fact, in some respects closer to the designs of Van Eyck than is the retable by Memling. In his Magdalene, for instance, David has abandoned the profile view of Memling's figure and has resumed the back view in which the Magdalene is rendered by Van Eyck (Figs. 159 and 160). Thus, when the Christ figure in David's Resurrection scene has the appearance of a heavenly apparition and is, at least in that respect, similar to the figure by Bruegel, this resemblance is not surprising. Obviously David, though basically imitating Memling, has kept closer than Memling to the Resurrection by Van Eyck.

David's imitation of Eyckian forms, and especially of those in the New York Calvary, has been suspected in Martin Davies, "A Reminiscence of Van Eyck by Gerard David?," *Miscellanea Erwin Panofsky, op.cit.*, pp. 173-75. In the Resurrection of his triptych in Haarlem, David's close imitation of Van Eyck links his Resurrection to the composition by Bruegel and provides us with a valid proof for our assumption that the Bruegel scene is a reflection of an Eyckian scene. In the center of the Bruegel Resurrection, we see a pair of guards who appear in front of the stone that had closed the tomb of Christ. The foremost one of the two is depicted in a kneeling position forming a beautifully complex *contrapposto* (Fig. 164). This figure, being the obvious imitation of an antique statue, seems to have been inspired by the back view of the same piece of Roman sculpture (Fig. 166) whose front view was used in a miniature by the Limbourg brothers (for the miniature, cf. Panofsky 1953, II, fig. 82 on plate 37; for the antique statue, cf. Jean Adhemar, *Influences antiques dans l'art du moyen âge français*, London 1939, Studies of the Warburg Institute, 7, p. 301). Considering Jan van Eyck's predilection for Classical Antiquity, so prominent in the Murder of Abel from the Ghent Altarpiece where Cain is ostentatiously depicted in a Greek chiton (Fig. 109), the antique *contrapposto* of the Resurrection guard speaks in itself for the Eyckian origin of the figure. The reappearance of this same figure (characteristically changed in many details) in the Resurrection by Gerard David disperses all our doubts about the Eyckian derivation of the Bruegel design (Figs. 164 and 165).

It is, in fact, clear that this figure of a kneeling guard, the motif of the cave, and the raised figure of Christ, are not the only elements which Bruegel took from Van Eyck. The entire scene in the foreground with its lively description of the sleeping and awakening guards, as rendered in the Bruegel composition is obviously also an older invention. Bruegel's soldiers are assembled around a dead fire, of which the burned-out branches placed on stones are the telling remains, and which, in conjunction with the jugs standing near it, characterize the foreground scene as the "morning after" of the guards. This foreground, in its negative connotations of a dead fire and sleeping humans arranged around the dark mouth of a cave, is, of course, pointedly contrasted to the triumphal figure of Christ and the rising sun. One may think at first glance that the unusually graphic description of the foreground is typical of Bruegel's realism. But a look at a German Resurrection scene painted a hundred years earlier tells us that this is not so (Fig. 148).

The Westphalian Master of the Schöppingen Altarpiece depicts the guard scene in his Resurrection in a very similar manner. The men are arranged around a fire (this time still burning) with jugs placed nearby in a manner very similar to Bruegel's still life. The Schöppingen Master, an imitator mainly of the Master of Flémalle and apparently belonging to a generation too early to be influenced by Rogier, evidently knew a drawing after the Eyckian Resurrection scene. When he changed the heavenly figure of Christ back to the familiar type on earth and the dead fire to a burning one, he had every right to do so in the entirely different context in which his Resurrection scene appears. But it seems that he retained some features of the basic arrangement of Christ's mantle as it was rendered in the Eyckian model. Christ's mantle is similarly arranged in the miniature of the Resurrection in the Vienna *Hortulus Animae*, a work of the Gerard David era in which Christ is raised rather high above his rock tomb (Fig. 156). It seems to me that the figure of Christ in this miniature is the most Eyck-like one of all the Christ figures appearing in the Resurrection scenes of the Bruges tradition around 1500. It is for this reason that I have used it in addition to the Bruegel figure (Fig. 149) as the basis of my reconstruction (Fig. 153).

BIBLIOGRAPHY

I. AUTHORS

Adhemar, Jean, *Influences antiques dans l'art du moyen âge français* (Studies of the Warburg Institute, 7), London, 1939.

Ampe, A., s.j., "De metamorfozen van het authentieke Van-Eyck-Katrijn op het Lam Gods," *Jaarboek van het Museum voor schone Kunsten*, Antwerp, 1969, pp. 7-60.

Ancona, Paolo d', *The Schifanoia Months at Ferrara*, Milan, s.d.

Appuhn, Horst, "Der Auferstandene und das Heilige Blut zu Weinhausen," *Niederdeutsche Beiträge zur Kunstgeschichte*, I, Cologne, 1961, pp. 73-138.

Aquinas, Thomas, cf. below IV. Sources.

Atiya, Aziz Suryal, *The Crusade of Nicolopolis*, London, 1934.

Augustine, cf. below IV. Sources.

Bagrow, Leo, *History of Cartography*, Cambridge, 1964.

Baets, J. de, O.P., "De Gewijde teksten van 'het Lam Gods,'" *Koninklijke Vlammse Academie voor Taal-en Letterkunde*, Verslagen en Mededelingen, 1961, pp. 532-614.

Baldass, Ludwig, *Jan van Eyck*, New York, 1952.

Bandmann, Günter, *Mittelalterliche Architektur als Bedeutungsträger*, Berlin, 1951.

——, "Ein Fassadenprogramm des 12. Jahrhunderts und seine Stellung in der christlichen Ikonographie," *Das Münster*, v, 1/2, 1952, pp. 1-31.

——, "Über Pastophorien und verwandte Nebenräume im mittelalterlichen Kirchenbau," *Kunstgeschichtliche Studien für Hans Kauffmann*, Berlin, 1956, pp. 19-58.

Bassermann-Jordan, Ernst, *Die Geschichte der Räderuhr*, Frankfort-on-the-Main, 1905.

Bast, L. de, cf. Waagen.

Bauer, Hermann, *Kunst und Utopie*, Berlin, 1965.

Baxandall, Michael, "Bartholomaeus Facius on Painting: A Fifteenth Century Manuscript of the De Viris Illustribus," *Journal of the Warburg and Courtauld Institutes*, xxvii, 1964, pp. 90-107.

Beatis, Don Antonio de, cf. below IV. Sources.

Beenken, Hermann, "Zur Entstehungsgeschichte des Genter Altares: Hubert und Jan van Eyck," *Wallraf-Richartz Jahrbuch*, new series, ii/iii, 1933/34, pp. 176-232.

——, *Hubert und Jan van Eyck*, Munich, 1941.

Begemann, E. Haverkamp, "De Meester van de Godelieve-Legende, een Brugs schilder uit het einde van de XVᵉ eeuw," *Miscellanea Erwin Panofsky: Musées Royaux des Beaux-Arts Bruxelles Bulletin*, 1-3, 1955, pp. 185-98.

Berry, Gilles le Bouvier, cf. below IV. Sources.

Bertrandon de la Broquière, cf. below IV. Sources.

Brand and Brand Philip, cf. Philip.

Braude, Pearl F., "'Cokel in oure Clene Corn': Some Implications of Cain's Sacrifice," *Gesta*, vii, 1968, pp. 15-28.

Braun, Joseph, *Die liturgische Gewandung im Occident und Orient nach Ursprung und Entwicklung, Verwendung und Symbolik*, Freiburg-im-Breisgau, 1907.

——, *Der christliche Altar in seiner geschichtlichen Entwicklung*, ii, Munich, 1924.

Bréhier, Louis, *L'église et l'orient au moyen âge. Les Croisades*, Paris, 1911.

Breydenbach, Bernhard, cf. below IV. Sources.

Brockmann, Joseph, "Der Reliquien-Hochaltar des Paderborner Domes, ein Nachtrag," *Alte und neue Kunst im Erzbistum Paderborn*, XIII, 1963, pp. 27-30.

Browe, Peter, *Die eucharistischen Wunder des Mittelalters*, Breslau, 1938.

Bruyn, Josua, *Van Eyck Problemen*, Utrecht, 1957.

Burckhardt, Jacob, *The Civilization of the Renaissance in Italy* (translated by S.G.C. Middlemore), I and II, New York, 1952.

Cämmerer, Monika, *Die Rahmungen der toskanischen Altarbilder im Trecento*, Strasbourg, 1966.

Chapuis, Alfred and Edmond Droz, *Automata*, London, 1958.

Chapuis, A. and Edouard Gélis, *Le monde des automates*, I, Paris, 1928.

Chydenius, Johan, *The Typological Problem in Dante, A Study in the History of Medieval Ideas*, Helsingfors, 1958.

———, *The Theory of Medieval Symbolism* (Societas Scientiarum Fennica, Commentationes Humanarum Litterarum, XXVII, 2), Helsingfors, 1960.

Clemen, Paul, *Der Dom zu Köln* (Die Kunstdenkmäler der Rheinprovinz, Vol. 6, Part III), Düsseldorf, 1937.

Corblet, Jules, *Histoire dogmatique, liturgique et archéologique du Sacrement de l'Eucharistie*, I, Paris, 1885.

Coremans, Paul, *L'Agneau Mystique au Laboratoire* (Les Primitifs Flamands, III, 2), Antwerp, 1953.

Couret, A., *L'ordre du Saint Sépulchre de Jérusalem depuis ses origines jusqu'à nos jours*, Orleans, 1887.

Davies, Martin, "A reminiscence of Van Eyck by Gerard David?," *Miscellanea Erwin Panofsky: Musées Royaux des Beaux-Arts Bruxelles Bulletin*, 1-3, pp. 173-75.

Debouxhtay, Pierre, "A propos de l'Agneau Mystique," *Revue Belge d'Archéologie et d'Histoire de l'Art*, XIII, 2/3, 1943, pp. 149-50.

Dhanens, Elisabeth, *Sint-Baafskathedraal Gent*, Inventaris van het Kuntspatrimonium van Oostvlaanderen, V, Ghent, 1965.

———, *Het Retabel van het Lam Gods in de Sint-Baafskathedraal te Gent*, Inventaris van het Kunstpatrimonium van Oostvlaanderen, VI, Ghent, 1965.

Didron, A., *Annales archéologiques*, VIII, Paris, 1857-81.

Dierix, Charles-Louis, *Mémoires sur la Ville de Gand*, Ghent, 1815.

Dijk, S.J.P. van and J. Hazelden Walker, *The Origins of the Modern Roman Liturgy*, London, 1960.

Duclos, A., *Bruges. Histoire et souvenirs*, Bruges, 1910.

Durandus, William, cf. below IV. Sources.

Dürer, Albrecht, cf. below IV. Sources.

Duverger, Jozef, *Het grafschrift van Hubrecht van Eyck*, Antwerp/Utrecht, 1945.

———, "Kopieën van het 'Lam-Gods'-retabel van Hubrecht en Jan van Eyck," *Musées Royaux des Beaux-Arts Bruxelles Bulletin*, new series, III, 2, June, 1954, pp. 51-68.

———, "Brugse Schilders ten tijde van Jan van Eyck," *Miscellanea Erwin Panofsky: Musées Royaux des Beaux-Arts Bruxelles Bulletin*, 1-3, pp. 83-120.

Dvořák, Max, "Das Rätsel der Kunst der Brüder van Eyck," *Jahrbuch der Kunsthistorischen Sammlungen des Allerhöchsten Kaiserhauses*, XXIV, 1904, pp. 161-317, reprinted in *Das Rätsel der Kunst der Brüder van Eyck*, Munich, 1925.

Dycke, F. van, *Recueil heraldique de familles nobles et patriciennes de la ville et du franconat de Bruges*, Bruges, 1851.

Ebersolt, Jean, *Orient et Occident, Recherches sur les influences byzantines et orientales en France avant et pendant les croisades*, 2nd edition, Paris, 1954.

Einem, Herbert von, "Die 'Menschwerdung Christi' des Isenheimer Altares," *Kunstgeschichtliche Studien für Hans Kauffmann*, Berlin, 1956, pp. 152-71.

Emanuel Emanuel (Luftglass), *Van Eyck und Vasari im Lichte neuer Tatsachen*, Tel-Aviv, 1965.

Engl, Joh. Ev., *Das Hornwerk auf Hohensalzburg, dessen Geschichte und Musikstücke*, 2nd edition, Salzburg, 1909.

Facio, Bartolomeo, cf. below IV. Sources.

Feldhusen, Ruth, *Ikonologische Studien zu Michaelangelos Jüngsten Gericht*, Diss., Hamburg, 1953 (typescript).

Felheim, Marvin and F. W. Brownlow, "Jan van Eyck's 'Chancellor Rolin and the Blessed Virgin,'" *Art Journal*, XXVIII, 1, Fall, 1968, pp. 22-26.

Fleury, Charles Rohault de, *La Messe*, v, Paris, 1887.

Folie, Jacqueline, "Les œuvres authentifiées des primitifs Flamands," *Bulletin de l'Institut royal du Patrimoine artistique*, VI, 1963, pp. 183-256.

Formigé, Jules, *L'abbaye royale de Saint-Denis*, Paris, 1960.

Förster, Otto H., *Stefan Lochner*, Frankfort-on-the-Main, 1938.

Frankl, Paul, *Gothic Architecture* (Pelican History of Art), Baltimore, 1962.

Freeman, Margaret B., "The Annunciation from a Book of Hours for Charles of France," *Metropolitan Museum of Art Bulletin*, XIX, 4, December 1960, pp. 105-18.

Freemantle, Anne, *The Age of Belief*, New York, 1964.

Friedländer, Max J., *Die altniederländische Malerei*, I and II, Berlin/Leiden, English edition: *Early Netherlandish Painting*, comments and notes by Nicole Veronee-Verhaegen, I, *The Van Eycks and Petrus Christus* and II, *Rogier van der Weyden and the Master of Flémalle*, New York/Washington, 1967.

Geck, cf. below IV. Sources, Breydenbach.

Gill, Joseph, *The Council of Florence*, Cambridge, 1959.

Goldschmidt, Adolph and L. Giese, *Die Skulpturen von Freiberg und Wechselburg* (Denkmäler der deutschen Kunst, II, Sektion: Plastik), Berlin, 1924.

Goldstein, Carl, "Studies in Seventeenth Century French Art Theory and Ceiling Painting," *The Art Bulletin*, XLVII, 2, June, 1965, pp. 231-56.

Gower, John, cf. below IV. Sources.

Grabar, A. and C. Nordenfalk, *Early Medieval Painting*, London, 1957.

Graeve, Mary Anne, "The Stone of Unction in Caravaggio's Painting for Chiesa Nuova," *The Art Bulletin*, XL, 3, September, 1958, pp. 223-38.

Granvella, Cardinal of, cf. below IV. Sources.

Gregory of Tours, cf. below IV. Sources.

Grossmann, F., "The Drawings of Pieter Bruegel the Elder in the Museum Boymans and Some Problems of Attribution," *Bulletin Museum Boymans Rotterdam*, Part v, 2, July 1954, pp. 41-63.

———, *Bruegel, The Paintings*, London, 1955.

Günther, Rudolph, *Die Bilder des Genter und Isenheimer Altars* (Studien über christliche Denkmäler, 15-16), Leipzig, 1923.

Hamann, Richard, *Geschichte der Kunst von der altchristlichen Zeit bis zur Gegenwart*, Berlin, 1933.

Heckscher, William S., "The Annunciation of the Mérode Altarpiece, an Iconographic Study," *Miscellanea Jozef Duverger*, I, Ghent, 1968, pp. 37-65.

Heere, Lucas de, cf. below IV. Sources.

Heise, Carl Georg, *Der Lübecker Passionsaltar von Hans Memling*, Hamburg, 1950.

Held, Julius S., "Erwin Panofsky, *Early Netherlandish Painting, Its Origin and Character*," review in *The Art Bulletin*, XXXVII, 3, September 1955, pp. 205-34.

Heydenreich, Ludwig Heinrich, cf. below III. Catalogues.

Hintzen, J. D., *De kruistochtplannen van Philip den Goede*, Rotterdam, 1918.

Hirn, Yrjö, *The Sacred Shrine*, 2nd English edition, Boston, 1957.

Hirsch, Alfred, "Zur Datierung des Genter Altars von St. Bavo," *Repertorium für Kunstwissenschaft*, XLII, Berlin/Leipzig, 1920, pp. 77-82.

Honorius Augustodunensis, cf. below IV. Sources.

Hoogewerff, G. J., cf. below III. Catalogues.

Huerne, Christopher von, cf. below IV. Sources.

Huizinga, Johan, *The Waning of the Middle Ages*, London, 1952.

Hulin de Loo, Georges, *Heures de Milan*, Brussels/Paris, 1911.

Hymans, Henri, *Brügge und Ypern*, Leipzig/Berlin, 1900.

Jacques, Charles, *La peinture française. Les peintres du moyen-âge*, Paris, 1941.

Janson, H. W., *The Sculpture of Donatello*, Princeton, 1963.

Jongkees, A. G., *Staat en Kerk in Holland en Zeeland onder de Bourgondische Hertogen 1425-1477* (Bijdragen van het Instituut vor middeleewsche geschiedenis der Rijks-Universiteit te Utrecht), Groningen, 1942.

Jungmann, J. A., The Mass of the Roman Rite (English translation of *Missarum Solemnia*, Vienna, 1949), I and II, New York, 1955.

Katzenellenbogen, Adolf, *The Sculptural Programs of Chartres Cathedral*, Baltimore, 1959.

Kauffmann, Hans, "Über 'rinascere', 'Rinascita' und einige Stilmerkmale der Quattrocentobaukunst," *Concordia Decennalis. Festschrift der Universität Köln zum 10 jährigen Bestehen des Deutsch-Italienischen Kulturinstitutes Petrarcahaus*, Cologne, 1951, pp. 123-46.

Keller, Harald, "Der Flügelaltar als Reliquienschrein," *Studien zur Geschichte der europäischen Plastik, Festschrift Theodor Müller*, Munich, 1965, pp. 125-44.

Kieser, Emil, "Zur Deutung und Datierung der Rolin-Madonna des Jan van Eyck," *Städel-Jahrbuch*, new series, I, 1967, pp. 73-95.

Kirchner-Doberer, Erika, *Die deutschen Lettner bis 1300*, Diss., Vienna, 1946 (microfilm of typescript).

——, "Der Lettner, Bedeutung und Geschichte," *Mitteilungen der Gesellschaft für vergleichende Kunstforschung*, Vienna, 1956, pp. 117-22.

——, cf. below II. Dictionary Articles.

Koch, Robert A., *Joachim Patinir*, Princeton, 1968.

Konrad, Martin, *Meisterwerke der Skulptur in Flandern und Brabant*, Berlin, 1929-34.

Kurz, Otto, "A Fishing Party at the Court of William VI, Count of Holland, Zeeland and Hainault," *Oud-Holland*, LXXI, i-iv, 1956, pp. 117-31.

Laborde, Léon E.S.J. de, *Les Ducs de Bourgogne*, II, Paris, 1849.

Lanckorońska, Maria, *Matthäus Gotthart Neithart*, Darmstadt, 1963.

Lande-Nash, Irene, *3000 Jahre Jerusalem*, Tübingen, 1964.

Liebeschütz, Hans, *Das allegorische Weltbild der heiligen Hildegard von Bingen* (Studien der Bibliothek Warburg, XVI), Leipzig/Berlin, 1930.

Ludolf of Saxony, cf. below IV. Sources.

Mander, Karel van, cf. below IV. Sources.

Martinsdale, Andrew, *Gothic Art*, New York/Washington, 1967.

McNamee, M. B., "Further Symbolism in the Portinari Altarpiece," *The Art Bulletin*, XLV, 2, June, 1963, pp. 142-43.

Meiss, Millard, "Jan van Eyck and the Italian Renaissance," *Venezia e l'Europa, Atti del XVIII Congresso Internazionale di Storia dell'Arte* (1955), Venice, 1956, pp. 64-68.

——, " 'Highlands' in the Lowlands," *Gazette des Beaux-Arts*, series 6, LVII, June, 1961, pp. 272-314.

Menz, Henner, "Zur Freilegung einer Inschrift auf dem Eyck-Altar der Dresdener Gemäldegalerie," *Jahrbuch 1959, Staatliche Kunstsammlungen Dresden*, pp. 28-29.

Morand, Kathleen, *Jean Pucelle*, Oxford, 1962.

Müller, Theodor, *Deutsche Plastik der Renaissance*, Königstein, 1963.

Münzer, Hieronymus, cf. below IV. Sources.

Musper, T., *Untersuchungen zu Rogier van der Weyden und Jan van Eyck*, Stuttgart, 1948.

Nilgen, Ursula, "The Epiphany and the Eucharist: On the Interpretation of Eucharistic Motifs in Mediaeval Epiphany Scenes," *The Art Bulletin*, xlix, 4, December 1967, pp. 311-16.

Ostrogorsky, George, *History of the Byzantine State* (translated from the German), New Brunswick, New Jersey, 1957.

Paatz, Walter and Elisabeth, *Die Kirchen von Florenz*, iv, Frankfort-on-the-Main, 1952.

Pächt, Otto, "René d'Anjou et les Van Eyck," *Cahiers de l'association internationale des études françaises*, 1956, pp. 41-51.

——, "Panofsky's 'Early Netherlandish Painting,' " review in *The Burlington Magazine*, xcviii, Part i in 637, April, 1956, pp. 110-16, and Part ii in 641, August, 1956, pp. 267-79.

——, "Josua Bruyn, *Van Eyck Problemen*," review in *Kunstchronik*, xii, 9, September 1959, pp. 254-58.

Panofsky, Erwin, *Abbot Suger on the Abbey Church of St.-Denis and Its Art Treasures*, Princeton, 1946.

——, *Albrecht Dürer*, 3rd edition, i and ii, Princeton, 1948.

——, *Early Netherlandish Painting, Its Origin and Character*, i and ii, Cambridge, 1953.

——, *Tomb Sculpture*, New York, 1964.

Peters, Heinz, "Die Anbetung des Lammes, ein Beitrag zum Problem des Genter Altars," *Das Münster*, iii, 3/4, March-April, 1950, pp. 65-77.

——, "Zum New Yorker 'Diptychon' der 'Hand G'," *Munuscula Discipulorum* (Kunsthistorische Studien Hans Kauffmann zum 70. Geburtstag 1966), Berlin, 1968, pp. 235-46.

(Philip) Brand, Lotte, *Stephan Lochners Hochaltar von St. Katharinen zu Köln*, Hamburg, 1938.

Philip, Lotte Brand, "The Prado *Epiphany* by Jerome Bosch," *The Art Bulletin*, xxxv, 4, December 1953, pp. 279-93.

——, "The *Peddler* by Hieronymus Bosch, A Study in Detection," *Nederlands Kunsthistorisch Jaarboek*, ix, 1958, pp. 1-81.

——, "Raum und Zeit in der Verkündigung des Genter Altares," *Wallraf-Richartz Jahrbuch*, xxix, 1967, pp. 62-104.

Philo, cf. below IV. Sources.

Pilon, Edmond, *Bruges*, Paris, 1939.

Pope-Hennessy, John, *Fra Angelico*, London, 1952.

Post, Paul, "Wen stellen die vier ersten Reiter auf dem Flügel der gerechten Richter am Genter Altar dar?," *Jahrbuch der preussischen Kunstsammlungen*, xlii, Berlin, 1921, pp. 67-81.

Puyvelde, L. van, *La Peinture Flamande au siècle de Bosch et Brueghel*, ed. Meddens, Paris, *s.d.*

Réau, Louis, *Iconographie de l'art chrétien*, ii, Paris, 1957.

Reinach, Salomon, "Jean VI Paléologue et Hubert van Eyck," *Revue archéologique*, 4th series, xvi, July-December 1910, pp. 369-77.

Renders, Emile, *Hubert van Eyck, personnage de legende*, Paris/Brussels, 1933.

Ress, Anton, *Studien zur Plastik der Martinskirche in Landshut* (Verhandlungen des Historischen Vereins für Niederbayern, 81), Landshut, 1955.

Ring, Grete, *A Century of French Painting 1400-1500*, New York, 1949.

Rorimer, James J., *The Hours of Jeanne d'Evreux*, New York, 1957.

Roth, E., *Der volkreiche Kalvarienberg in Literatur und Kunst des Spätmittelalters*, Berlin, 1958.

Rousseau, Theodore, Jr., "The Mérode Altarpiece," *Metropolitan Museum of Art Bulletin*, xvi, 4, December 1957, pp. 117-29.

Salmi, M., *La pittura e la miniatura gotica in Lombardia* (Storia di Milano), vi, 1956.

Scharfenberg, Albrecht von, cf. below IV. Sources.

Schlegel, Ursula, "Zum Bildprogramm der Arenakapelle," *Zeitschrift für Kunstgeschichte*, xx, 2, 1957, pp. 125-246.

——, "Observations on Masaccio's Trinity Fresco in Santa Maria Novella," *The Art Bulletin*, xlv, 1, March 1963, pp. 19-33.

Schneider, Constantin, "Die Musikstücke des Orgelwerkes im mechanischen Theater zu Hellbrunn," *Mitteilungen der Gesellschaft für Salzburger Landeskunde*, LXII, 1927, pp. 169-75.

Schnitzler, Hermann, "Das Kuppelmosaik der Aachener Pfalzkapelle," *Aachener Kunstblätter*, 29, 1964, pp. 17-44.

Schöne, Wolfgang, *Über das Licht in der Malerei*, Berlin, 1954.

Schopenhauer, Johanna Henriette, *Johann van Eyck und seine Nachfolger*, Weimar, 1821 (Sämmtliche Schriften, Leipzig/Frankfort-on-the-Main, 1830).

Schramm, Percy Ernst, *Herrschaftszeichen und Staatssymbolik; Beiträge zu ihrer Geschichte vom 3. bis zum 16. Jahrhundert* (Schriften der Monumenta Germaniae historica), I, II, and III, Stuttgart, 1954-56.

Schrade, Hubert, *Ikonographie der Christlichen Kunst, I, Die Auferstehung Christi*, Berlin/Leipzig, 1932.

Schryver, A. P. de and R. H. Marijnissen, *De oorspronkelijke plaats van het Lam Gods-retabel* (Les Primitifs Flamands, III, 1), Antwerp, 1952.

Sedlmayr, Hans, *Die Entstehung der Kathedrale*, Zurich, 1950.

Seiferth, Wolfgang, *Synagoge und Kirche im Mittelalter*, Munich 1964.

Simson, Otto G. von, "*Compassio* and *Co-Redemptio* in Roger van der Weyden's *Descent from the Cross*," *The Art Bulletin*, XXV, 1, March, 1953, pp. 10-16.

Snyder, James, "Jan van Eyck and the Madonna of Chancellor Nicolas Rolin," *Oud-Holland*, LXXXII, 4, 1967, pp. 163-71.

Stange, Alfred, *Deutsche Malerei der Gotik*, 11 vols., Munich/Berlin, 1934-61.

Stephany, E., *Wunderwelt der Schreine* (ed. H. Busch and B. Lohse), Frankfort-on-the-Main, 1959.

Stones, Alison, "An Italian Miniature in the Gambier-Parry Collection," *The Burlington Magazine*, CXI, 790, January, 1969, pp. 7-12.

Strabo, Walafrid, cf. below IV. Sources.

Suhr, William, "The Restoration of the Mérode Altarpiece," *Metropolitan Museum of Art Bulletin*, XVI, 4, December 1957, pp. 140-44.

Summonte, Pietro, cf. below IV. Sources.

Tack, Wilhelm, "Der Reliquien-Hochaltar des Paderborner Domes," *Alte und neue Kunst im Erzbistum Paderborn*, VII, 1957, pp. 5-32.

Tolnay, Charles de, *Hieronymus Bosch*, Basel, 1937.

———, *Le Retable de l'Agneau Mystique des Frères van Eyck*, Brussels, 1938.

Tourneur, Victor, "Un Second Quatrain sur l'Agneau Mystique," *Académie Royale de Belgique, Bulletin de la Classe des Lettres et des Sciences Morales et Politiques*, series 5, XXIX, 1943, pp. 57-65.

Troescher, Georg, *Burgundische Malerei, Maler und Malwerke um 1400 in Burgund, dem Berry mit der Auvergne und in Savoyen mit ihren Quellen und Ausstrahlungen*, Berlin, 1966.

Ungerer, Alfred, *Les horloges d'édifices*, Paris, 1926.

———, *Les horloges astronomiques et monumentales les plus remarquables de l'Antiquité jusqu'à nos jours*, Strasbourg, 1931.

Vaernewyck, Marcus van, cf. below IV. Sources.

Vincent, H. and F. M. Abel, *Jérusalem Recherches de topographie, d'archéologie et d'histoire*, II, *Jérusalem Nouvelle*, Paris, 1914.

Vincent, L. H., *Jérusalem de l'Ancien Testament*, I, Paris, 1954.

Viollet-Le-Duc, E., *Dictionnaire raisonné de l'architecture française du XIe au VXIe siècle*, II, Paris, 1875.

Volbach, Wolfgang Fritz, *Early Christian Art*, New York, *s.d.*

Voll, Karl, *Memling, des Meisters Gemälde* (Klassiker der Kunst), Berlin/Leipzig, *s.d.*

Vriendt, Maximilian de, cf. below IV. Sources.

Waagen, G. F. and L. de Bast, *Notice sur le chef-d'œuvre des frères van Eyck*, Ghent, 1825.

Walker, Robert M., "The Demon of the Portinari Altarpiece," *The Art Bulletin*, XLII, 3, September 1960, pp. 218-19.

Wall, Constant van de, cf. below IV. Sources Mander, Karel van.

Ward, John, "A New Look at the Friedsam Annunciation," *The Art Bulletin*, L, 2, June, 1968, pp. 184-87.

Weale, W. H. James and Maurice W. Brockwell, *The Van Eycks and their Art*, London, 1912.

Wehle, Harry B. and Margaretta Salinger, cf. below III. Catalogues.

Weiss, Roberto, "Jan van Eyck and the Italians," *Italian Studies, An Annual Review*, XI, 1956, pp. 1-15 and
    XII, 1957, pp. 7-21.

White, John, *Art and Architecture in Italy, 1250 to 1400* (Pelican History of Art), Baltimore, 1966.

Wilhelm, Pia, *Die Marienkrönung am Westportal der Kathedrale von Senlis*, Hamburg, 1941.

——, cf. below II. Dictionary Articles.

Winkler, Friedrich, "Die Stifter des Lebensbrunnens und andere Van-Eyck-Fragen," *Pantheon*, IV, 5, May
    1931, pp. 188-93.

——, "Die Wiener Kreuztragung," *Nederlands Kunsthistorisch Jaarboek*, IX, 1958, pp. 83-108.

Zülch, Walter Karl, *Der historische Grünewald, Mathis Gothardt Neithardt*, Munich, 1938.

II. DICTIONARY ARTICLES

Lexikon der christlichen Ikonographie, Freiburg-im-Breisgau, 1968. Pia Wilhelm, "Auferstehung Christi,"
    letter e, cols. 215-16.

Lexikon für Theologie und Kirche, 2nd edition, Freiburg-im-Breisgau, 1961. Erika Kirchner-Doberer,
    "Lettner," VI, pp. 987-88.

Oxford Dictionary of the Christian Church, London/New York/Toronto, 1966. "Requiem," p. 1155.

New Catholic Encyclopedia, New York, 1967. "Tiara," XIV, pp. 148-50.

Reallexikon zur deutschen Kunstgeschichte, Stuttgart, 1937. "Altarciborium," I, cols. 473-85. "Altarretabel,"
    I, cols. 529-64.

III. CATALOGUES

ANTWERP. *Catalogue du Musée Mayer van den Bergh*, Antwerp/Brussels, 1933.

BALTIMORE. *The International Style, The Arts of Europe around 1400*, Walters Art Gallery, Baltimore, 1962.

CHATSWORTH. *Old Masters Drawings from Chatsworth, a Loan Exhibition from the Devonshire Collection.*
    1969-70.

COLOGNE. *Die Sammlungen des Baron von Hüpsch*, Exhibition Catalogue, Cologne, 1964.
    Wallraf-Richartz-Museum der Hansestadt Köln, I, *Die Gemälde altdeutscher Meister*, Cologne, 1939.
    Wallraf-Richartz-Museum Köln, Führer durch die Gemäldegalerie, Cologne, 1957.

DETROIT. *Flanders in the Fifteenth Century: Art and Civilization*, Detroit, 1960.

DIJON. *Musée des Beaux-Arts de Dijon, Catalogue des Sculptures*, Palais des Etats de Bourgogne, 1960.
    La Sainte-Chapelle de Dijon, Siège de l'Ordre de la Toison d'Or, Dijon, 1962.

HAMBURG. *Katalog der alten Meister der Hamburger Kunsthalle*, Hamburg, 1956.

NEW YORK. Ludwig Heinrich Heydenreich, *Leonardo da Vinci, the Scientist*, Catalogue of the IBM Exhibi-
    tion, 1951.
    Harry B. Wehle and Margaretta Salinger, *The Metropolitan Museum of Art, A Catalogue of Early
    Flemish, Dutch and German Paintings*, New York, 1947.

OBERLIN. *Allen Memorial Art Museum Bulletin*, Oberlin, Ohio, XI, 2, Winter, 1954.

ROTTERDAM. *Jan Gossart genaamd Mabuse*, Exhibition Rotterdam/Bruges, 1965.

UTRECHT. G. J. Hoogewerff, *Jan van Scorel*, Utrecht, 1955.

VIENNA. *Europäische Kunst um 1400*, Vienna, 1962, Exhibition in the Museum of Art History in Vienna.

IV. SOURCES

AQUINAS, THOMAS. *Summa Theologiae*, Latin text and English translation, London/New York, 1964.

AUGUSTINE. *De civitate Dei*, 10, 20 and 10, 16, *Corpus Scriptorum Ecclesiasticorum Latinorum*, XL, I.

BEATIS, DON ANTONIO DE. August 1, 1517—Description of visit of Cardinal Louis of Aragon in Ghent. Cf. Dhanens, Inventaris VI, p. 102, and *Jan en Hubert van Eyck, Documenten*, Utrecht, 1954, p. 12.

BERRY, GILLES LE BOUVIER. *Le Livre de la Description des Pays de Gilles le Bouvier dit Berry* (Recueil de Voyages et de Documents), ed. E.-T. Hamy, Paris, 1908.

BERTRANDON DE LA BROQUIÈRE. *Early Travels in Palestine*, edited with notes by Thomas Wright, London, 1848.

  Le Voyage d'Outremer de Bertrandon de la Broquière (Recueil de Voyages et de Documents), ed. Charles Henri Auguste Schefer and Henri Cordia, Paris, 1892.

BREYDENBACH, BERNHARD. *Bernhard von Breydenbach, Die Reise ins Heilige Land; Ein Reisebericht aus dem Jahre 1483*, translation and afterword by Elisabeth Geck, Wiesbaden, 1961.

CHRONICLE OF FLANDERS (Kronyk van Vlaenderen). Entry for April 23, 1458. Cf. Dhanens, Inventaris VI, pp. 96-99; Documenten, pp. 7-9; De Baets, pp. 612-14.

DURANDUS, WILLIAM (Guglielmus). *Rationale Divinorum*, Liber I, ed. Rousselet, Leyden, 1612.

DÜRER, ALBRECHT. *Albrecht Dürers schriftlicher Nachlass*, ed. Ernst Heidrich, preface by Heinrich Wölfflin, Berlin, 1910, p. 90 (reference to Ghent Altarpiece, April 10, 1521). Cf. also Documenten, p. 13 and Dhanens, Inventaris VI, p. 103.

FACIO, BARTOLOMEO. Michael Baxandall, "Bartholomaeus Facius on Painting: A Fifteenth Century Manuscript of the De Viris Illustribus," *Journal of the Warburg and Courtauld Institutes*, XXVII, 1964, pp. 90-107. Cf. also Documenten, pp. 4-5.

GOWER, JOHN. *Vox Clamantis*, Liber III, in G. C. Macaulay, *John Gower, The Complete Works*, Oxford, 1899-1902.

GRANVELLA, CARDINAL. Letter of Provost Morillon to Cardinal Granvella, Louvain, August 31, 1566, cf. Edmond Poullet, *Correspondance du Cardinal de Granvelle*, 1565-1586, I, Bruxelles, 1877, CVIII, pp. 443-44. Cf. also Coremans, p. 37, no. 13.

GREGORY OF TOURS (Gregorius Turonensis). *Libri Miraculorum*, I, *De Gloria Beatorum Martyrum*, ed. J. P. Migne, *Patrologia Latina*, LXXI.

HEERE, LUCAS DE. *Den Hof en Boomgaerd der Poësien*, Ghent, 1565, pp. 35-38 (dated July 23-25, 1559), cf. Dhanens, Inventaris VI, pp. 104-7 and Documenten (van Mander), pp. 34-36.

HONORIUS AUGUSTODUNENSIS (Honorius of Autun). *Elucidarium*, ed. J. P. Migne, *Patrologia Latina*, CLXXII.

HUERNE, CHRISTOPHER VAN. Cf. Emile Renders, *Hubert van Eyck, personnage de legende*, Paris/Brussels, 1933, p. 39.

JONGHE, B. DE. *Ghendtsche geschiedenissen*, Bibl. Univ. Gand, ms. 159, II, Ghent, 1752. Cf. Coremans, p. 37, no. 15 (end).

LUDOLF OF SAXONY (Ludolphus de Saxonia). *Vita Christi*, ed. Bertrand Etienne, Paris, 1497.

MANDER, KAREL VAN. *Het Leven der Doorluchtige Nederlandsche en eenige Hoogduitsche Schilders (Het Schilder-Boek)*, Haarlem/Alkmaar, 1604, Amsterdam, 1618, edition of Jacobus de Jongh, Amsterdam, 1764, English translation: Wall, Constant van de, *Dutch and Flemish Painters*, New York, 1936.

MÜNZER, HIERONYMUS. Document of 1495. Cf. Dhanens, Inventaris VI, p. 102, and Documenten, p. 10.

PHILO (Judaeus). *Who is the Heir (Quis Rerum Divinarum Heres)*, *Loeb Classical Library* (translation by F. H. Colson and G. H. Whitaker), XIV, Harvard, 1958.

SCHARFENBERG, ALBRECHT VON. *Jüngerer Titurel*, notes by Werner Wolf (*Deutsche Texte des Mittelalters*, 45, 55), Berlin, 1955-64.

STRABO, WALAFRID. *Glossa Ordinaria, Liber Genesis*, ed. J. P. Migne, *Patrologia Latina*, CXIII.

SUMMONTE, PIETRO. *Lettera a Marcantonio Michiel*, March 20, 1524, in Fausto Nicolini, *L'Arte Napoletana del Rinascimento e la Lettera di Pietro Summonte a Marcantonio Michiel*, Naples, 1925. Cf. also Documenten, p. 15.

TITUREL, THE YOUNGER. Cf. Scharfenberg.

VAERNEWYCK, MARCUS VAN. *Van de beroerlicke Tijden in die Nederlanden en voornamelijk in Ghendt*, 1566-1568, Ghent University Library, Hs. G 2469. Cf. Dhanens, Inventaris VI, pp. 108-10, Documenten, p. 22, and Coremans, p. 37, no. 13.

Den Spieghel der Nederlandscher audtheyt, Ghent, 1568 Cf. Dhanens, Inventaris VI, pp. 110-15 and Documenten, pp. 16-21.

VRIENDT, MAXIMILIAN DE. Cf. Victor Tourneur, "Un Second Quatrain sur l'Agneau Mystique," *Académie Royale de Belgique, Bulletin de la Classe des Lettres et des Sciences Morales et Politique*, series 5, XXIX, 1943, pp. 57f.

INDEX

A

96, 97, 116, 175, 178, 179, 209, 210, **2**, **3**, **46**, **47**, **48**, **52**, notes *27, 52, 70, 79, 173, 202, 254*; Tomb of and wife, 210, note *203*

Viollet-Le-Duc, 16, **25**, notes *30, 32*

Virgin, 63, 80, 95, 96, notes *129, 159, 183, 195*; among Virgins, 195; as Altar, cf. *Ara Coeli*; as Bride, cf. Bride and Bridegroom; as Host vessel, 93, 95, notes *133, 191*; as *Fenestra Coeli*, cf. Window; as *Porta Coeli*, cf. Door; as Queen of Heaven, 80, 83, 191, 198, 217, note *375*; as symbol of Church, 79, 88-90, 93, 95, 113, 136, 137, 192, 201, 210, 219, notes *25, 110, 112, 182*, cf. also Church, self-oblation of; Ascension of, 80; *Compassio* of, note *164*; Coronation or Triumph of, cf. Coronation; Immaculate Conception of Christ, 87, 90, 136; Nativity of, cf. Birth of Virgin; pre-figured in Eve, 59; in Van Eyck's New York Calvary, 159, note *283*; Virgin with the Ears of Corn, 93, note *191*; Surrounded by her symbols, 83, 84, note *171*; cf. also Annunciation, Crucifixion, Deësis, Intercessors, Holy Wedding, Mystic Marriage, *Vierge Ouvrante*; Virgins (saints), cf. Holy Virgins; cf. Wise and Foolish Virgins

Vischer, Peter the Elder, 52, note *99*

Vriendt, Maximilian de, 47, 48, notes *70, 88, 89, 91, 93*

W

Warwick Castle
  Van Eyck, Madonna of Nicholas van Maelbeke, Chapter 5, Section IV, **194**, **195**

Washington, D.C., National Gallery
  Van Eyck, Annunciation, 87, 139, 140, 163, **138**, notes *177, 272, 321*

Water color painting, 32, 100, 208, notes *202, 392*

Water, stream of, 11, 13, 66, 67, 77, 109, 201, note *211*; Well of Living Water, cf. Fountain of Life

Wechselburg, Church
  Choir Screen, 101, 102, **104**, **105**, notes *196, 205, 206*

Wedding (Mystical and Eternal), cf. Holy Wedding

Westphalia (Westphalian), 15, note *29, Excursus II*

Weyden, Rogier van der, 134, 211, 212, 215, 218, 219, notes *291, 303, 347, Excursus II*
  Antwerp, Musée Royal des Beaux-Arts
    Altarpiece of the Seven Sacraments, 209, **202**
  Beaune, Hôtel-Dieu
    Last Judgment, notes *112, 157*
  Berlin, Staatliche Museen (Gemäldegalerie)
    Bladelin Altarpiece, note *192*
    Granada-Miraflores Altarpiece (second version), 9, 24, 213, **205**, notes *246, 407*
  Boston, Museum of Fine Arts
    St. Luke Portraying the Madonna, 213, 214, **206**
  Frankfort-on-the-Main, Städelsches Kunstinstitut
    St. John Altarpiece, 213, note *407*
  Madrid, Prado
    Descent from the Cross, 212, **204**, note *164*
  Munich, Bayerische Staatsgemäldesammlungen
    Columba Altarpiece, 186, 187, **183**, note *363*

Wienhausen, Convent of
  Altarpiece, note *136*

William VI, Count of Holland, Zeeland and Hainault, *Excursus I*

Wilten, Paten, note *210*; cf. also Innsbruck (Triptych Schloss Tirol near Meran)

Window (stained glass), in actual architecture, 84, 171, 173, note *384*; in painting: Annunciation chambers, 87; Mérode Annunciation, 126, notes *177, 247*; in Ghent Annunciation, 83, 88, 123, 195, notes *175, 178, 180, 183, 236* (foreground); in Berlin Madonna, 137, 138; in Dresden triptych, 129; in Maelbeke Madonna, 211; in Lorenzetti, 122, note *243*; in Boucicaut Miniature, 124; in Rogier's St. Luke, 214; stained glass, 165, note *173*

Wisdom of Solomon, note *142*

Wise and Foolish Virgins, note *134*

World (our), 214, 215, notes *408, 409*; world redeemed, 214; Van Eyck *Mappa Mundi*, 217, 218, note *417*

Y

Ypres, St. Martin's Abbey, 201, 205, 206, note *400*; Tomb of Maelbeke, 205, 208, 209

Plates

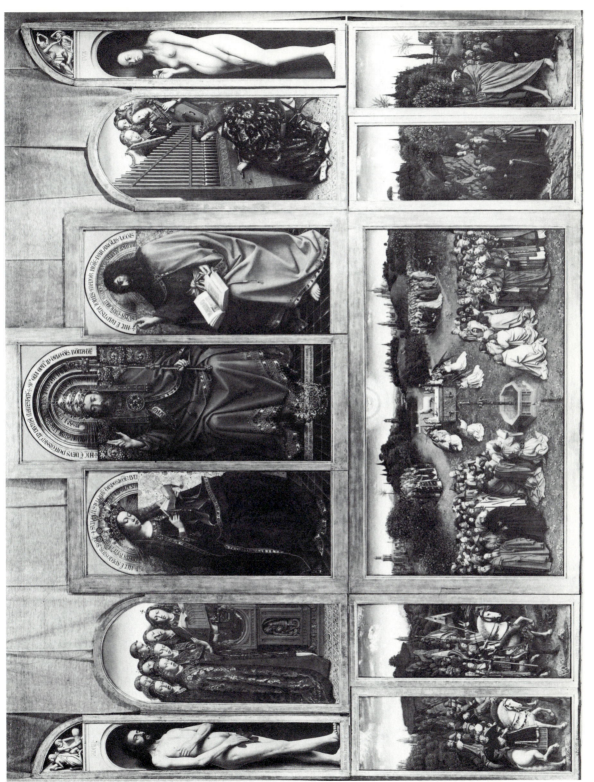

1. Ghent Altarpiece, Interior View; St. Bavo, Ghent

2. Ghent Altarpiece, Exterior View

3. Ghent Altarpiece,
Exterior View, untrimmed

4. Ghent Altarpiece,
Singing Angels (detail)

5. Ghent Altarpiece,
St. John of the Deësis (detail)

6. Shrine of Three Kings (detail);
Cathedral Treasury, Cologne

7. Shrine of St. Elizabeth;
Church of St. Elizabeth, Marburg

8. Shrine of Charlemagne (detail);
Cathedral Treasury, Aix-la-Chapelle

9. Ghent Altarpiece,
Virgin of the Deësis (detail)

10. Shrine of St. Anno; Abbey Church
of St. Michael, Siegburg

11. Jan Gossart, Deësis; Prado, Madrid

12. Dirc Bouts, Ordeal of the Countess;
Musée Royal, Brussels

13. Isenheim Altarpiece; Musée Unterlinden,
Colmar, Reconstruction

14. Altarpiece of c. 1370/72 from Schloss Tirol near Meran;
Ferdinandeum, Innsbruck

16. Main Altar of St. Martin, Landshut; Reconstruction of Rear View

15. Main Altar (stone, 1424), Front View; Church of St. Martin, Landshut

18. Ciborium Altar (stone, mid-15th century); Cathedral, Regensburg

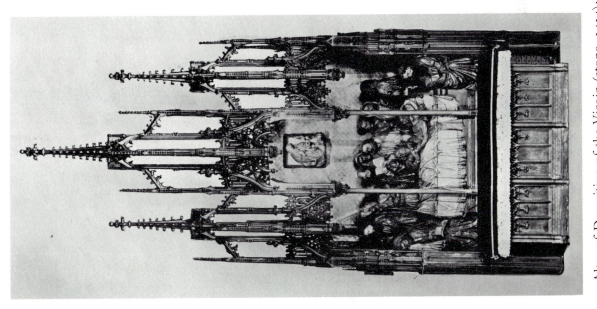

17. Altar of Dormition of the Virgin (stone, 1434); Cathedral, Frankfort-on-the-Main

19. Petrus Christus (copy), Fountain of Life; Prado, Madrid

20. Fountain of Life (detail: watercourse, fountain, and wafers)

22. Tabernacle of Holy Sacrament; Church of St. Peter, Louvain

21. Jean Fouquet, Annunciation, *Livre d'Heures d'Etienne Chevalier*; Musée Condé, Chantilly

24. Ambulatory; Abbey Church, St. Denis

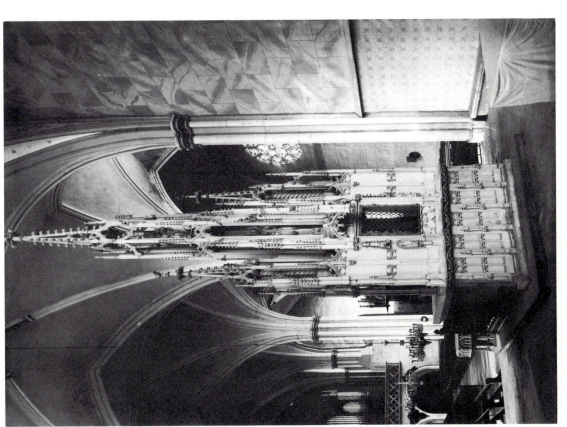

23. Reliquary Altar; Church of Our Lady, Herford (Westphalia)

9

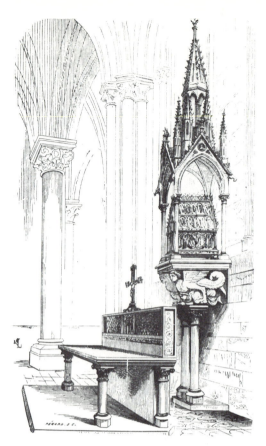

25. Reliquary Altars in Notre-Dame, Paris (left) and St. Denis, Reconstruction
Drawings (after Viollet-Le-Duc)

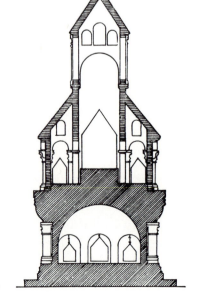

26. Tomb of St. Denis and His Companions;
Abbey Church, St. Denis, Reconstruction Drawing
(after Panofsky)

27. Follower of Van Eyck, The Lord Enthroned, *Très Belles Heures;* Formerly Royal Library, Turin

28. Reliquary Structure; Cathedral, Arras, Reconstruction

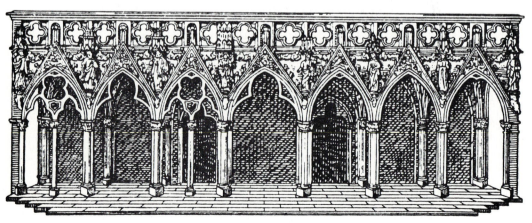

29. Rood Screen; Cathedral, Strasbourg, Reconstruction

30. Reliquary Structure;
Ste. Chapelle, Paris

31. Rood Screen; Cathedral, Halberstadt

32. Copy after Ghent Altarpiece; Musée Royal des Beaux-Arts, Antwerp

33. Copy after Ghent Altarpiece, lower left wing

34. Copy after Ghent Altarpiece, lower right wing

35. Circle of Jan Gossart, Drawing for Altar Wing;
Kupferstichkabinett, Berlin

36. Desiderio da Settignano,
Tabernacle of the Sacrament (detail);
San Lorenzo, Florence

37. Hans Memling,
Altarpiece of Jan Floreins, Exterior View
(detail); St. John's Hospital, Bruges

38. Albert Bouts,
Triptych in "standard" frame;
New York Historical Society

39. Hans Memling,
Shrine of St. Ursula (detail);
St. John's Hospital, Bruges

40. Lancelot Blondeel, Life of the Virgin; Cathedral, Tournai

41. Author's Reconstruction of Ghent Altarpiece in its Framework, View with Wings Partially Open

42. Author's Reconstruction of Ghent Altarpiece in its Framework, View with Wings Closed

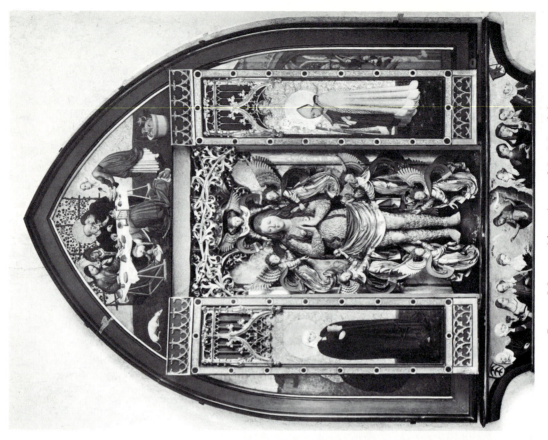

44. Lucas Moser, Altarpiece of St. Magdalene,
View with Wings Open;
Parish Church, Tiefenbronn

43. Lucas Moser, Altarpiece of St. Magdalene,
View with Wings Closed;
Parish Church, Tiefenbronn

45. Reliquary Altar, Rear View; Cathedral, Arezzo

46. Chapel of Jodocus Vijd;
St. Bavo, Ghent

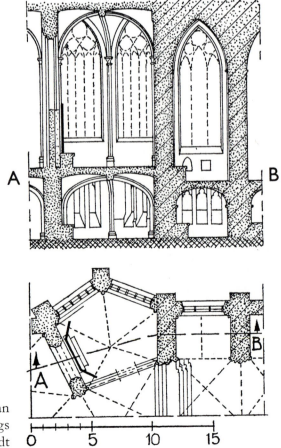

47. Chapel of Jodocus Vijd, Groundplan
and Elevation, Drawings
by Professor F. De Smidt

48. Pierre François de Noter, Chapel of Jodocus Vijd (painting, 1829);
Rijksmuseum, Amsterdam

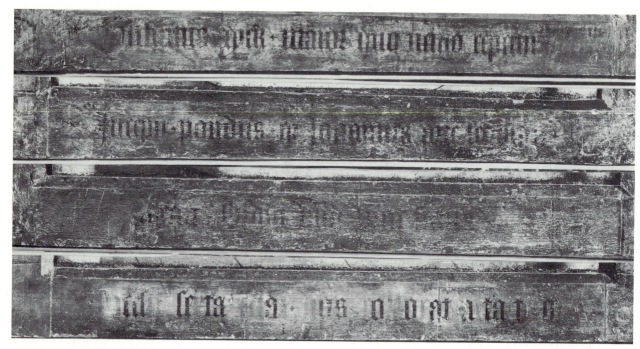

49. Ghent Altarpiece, Quatrain (details of exterior wings)

50. Fra Angelico, Madonna of the Linaiuoli
(frame design by Ghiberti);
Museo di San Marco, Florence

51. Andrea Orcagna, Tabernacle; Orsanmichele, Florence

52. Pierre François de Noter, Chapel of Jodocus Vijd (detail of Fig. 48)

54. Fountain of Life (detail of Fig. 19: Synagogue group)

53. Ghent Altarpiece, Adoration of the Lamb (detail)

55. Engraving after Hieronymus Bosch, Triptych of Last Judgment

57. Ghent Altarpiece, St. John of the Deësis

56. Ghent Altarpiece, Lord of the Deësis

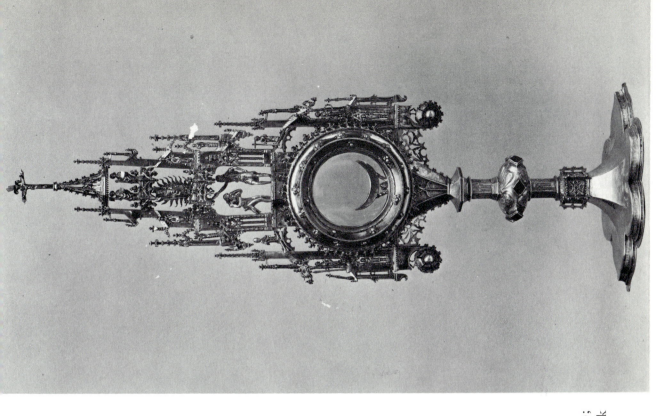

58. Sedilia (first half 15th century); Musée de la Ville, Dijon

59. Monstrance, Flemish or German (15th or early 16th century);
The Metropolitan Museum of Art, New York

60. Sacrament of the Holy Mass, German *Biblia Pauperum* of 1414/15; Staatsbibliothek, Munich. Clm 826

61. Hans Brüggemann, Bordesholm Altarpiece;
Cathedral, Schleswig

62. Ghent Altarpiece, Adoration of the Lamb

65. Dove-shaped Eucharistic Vessel
of Laguenne,
Reconstruction Drawing (E. Rupin)

64. Dove-shaped Eucharistic *Vessel*;
The Metropolitan Museum of Art, New York

66. Crown Suspended from Dove, *Pontifical*;
Biblioteca Casanatense, Rome. Ms. 724

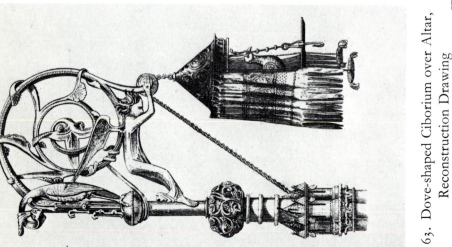

63. Dove-shaped Ciborium over Altar,
Reconstruction Drawing
(Viollet-Le-Duc)

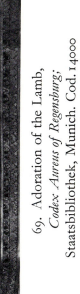

69. Adoration of the Lamb,
Codex Aureus of Regensburg;
Staatsbibliothek, Munich. Cod. 14000

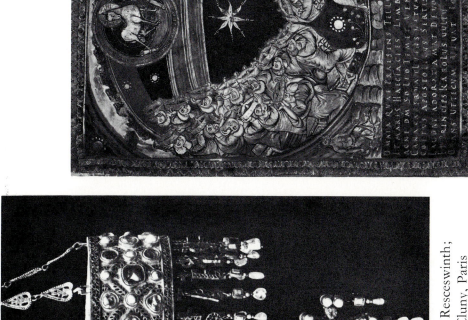

68. Crown of Resceswinth;
Musée de Cluny, Paris

67. Votive Crown over Altar (detail);
Bibl. Nat., Paris.
Ms. Lat. 8846, fol. 75

70. Dome Mosaic; Imperial Chapel, Aix-la-Chapelle (engraving of 1690)

71. Ghent Altarpiece, Lord of the Deësis (detail: crown)

72. Ghent Altarpiece, Annunciation
(Panel of the Virgin)

73. Annunciation, *Belles Heures of Jean, Duc de Berry;*
The Metropolitan Museum of Art,
The Cloisters Collection, New York

75. Attributed to the Master of Flémalle, Betrothal of the Virgin (detail of Fig. 175)

74. Ghent Altarpiece, Virgin of the Deësis (detail)

76. Mosan Master of c. 1415, Altarpiece; Museum Boymans Van Beuningen, Rotterdam

78. Giovanni del Biondo, Christ and the Virgin in Paradise;
Yale University Art College, Jarves Collection, New Haven

77. Nardo di Cione, Christ and the Virgin Enthroned in Paradise;
Santa Maria Novella, Florence

80. Mosan Master of c. 1415, Christ and the Virgin Enthroned (detail of Fig. 76)

79. Boucciaut Master, Christ and the Virgin Enthroned, *Cité de Dieu;* Walters Art Gallery, Baltimore, Ms. 770

81. Ghent Altarpiece, Annunciation

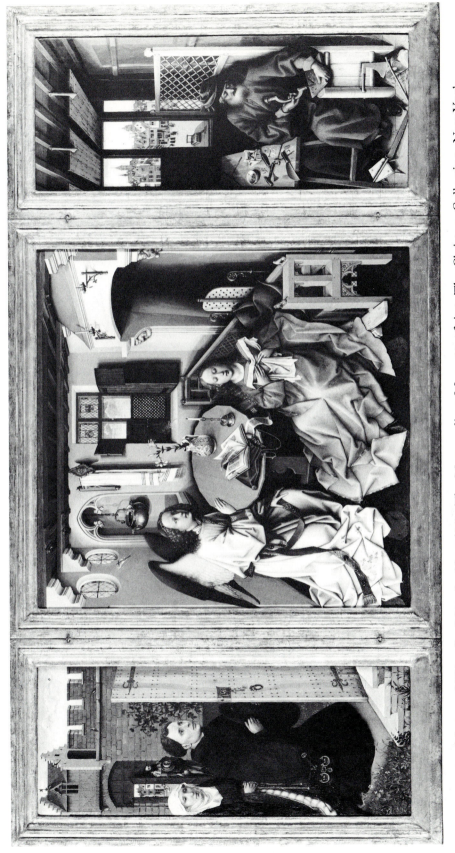

82. Master of Flémalle, Mérode Altarpiece; The Metropolitan Museum of Art, The Cloisters Collection, New York

83. Ghent Altarpiece, Annunciation (detail of panel of the Virgin)

84. Master of Flémalle, Mérode Altarpiece (detail: center panel)

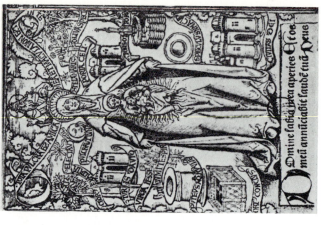

87. St. Anne, the Virgin and Child with Marian Symbols, metalcut from French book of hours

86. The Virgin Surrounded by Her Symbols, metalcut from a book of hours; Paris

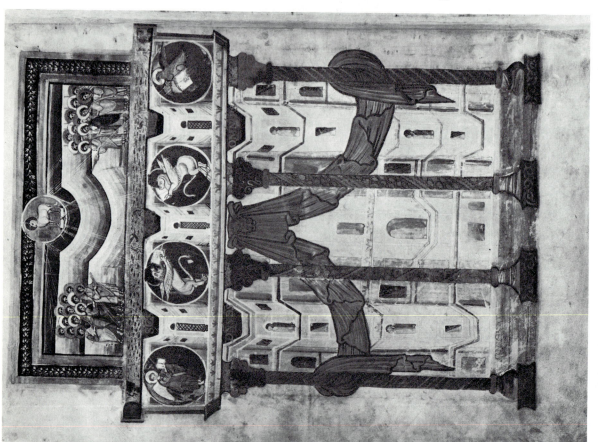

85. Adoration of the Lamb, *Gospels from St. Médard, Soissons;* Bib. Nat. Paris. Ms. Lat. 8850, fol. 1 v°

90. Mystic Marriage of Christ and the Virgin, Styria (c. 1420); The Metropolitan Museum of Art, The Cloisters Collection, New York

89. Ghent Altarpiece, Annunciation (detail of right center panel)

88. Ghent Altarpiece, Annunciation (detail of left center panel)

91. Empty Seats and Offering of Crowns, Dome Mosaic (detail); Orthodox Baptistery, Ravenna

92. Empty Throne of Christ with SS. Peter and Paul, Dome Mosaic (detail); Arian Baptistery, Ravenna

93. Apse Mosaic; Santa Pudenziana, Rome

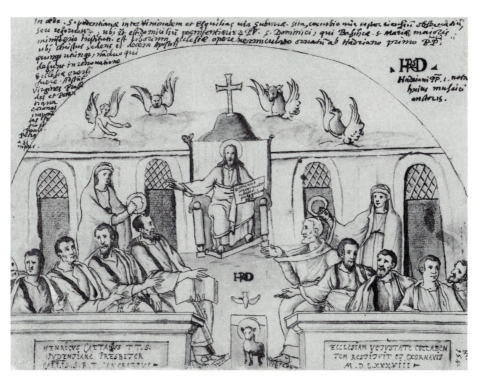

94. Apse Mosaic, Santa Pudenziana, Drawing after original condition, including Dove and Lamb; Vatican Library, Rome

95. Lorenzo di Niccolò, Annunciation and Throne
of Grace (details of polyptych of the Coronation of
the Virgin); San Domenico, Cortona

96. Hans von Reutlingen, Cover, *Gospels
the Holy Roman Empire;* Treasury, Vien

97. Priest Washing His Hands, *Pontifical* (1455);
University Library, Utrecht. Ms. 400

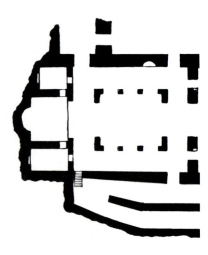

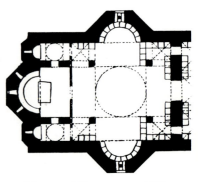

98. Plans of Eastern and Western
Churches (with pastophories facing
east), after Bandmann

99. Giotto, Arena Chapel, East Wall; Padua

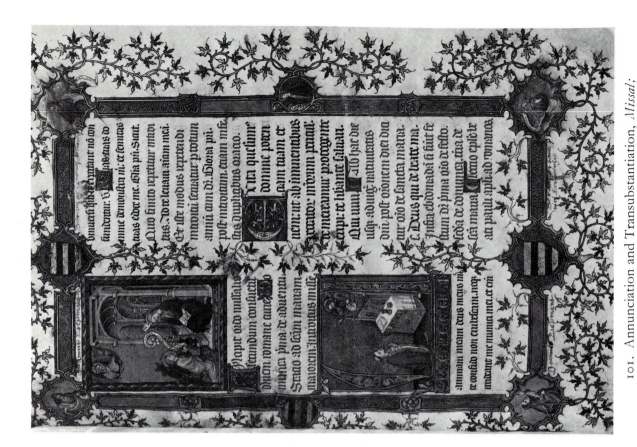

101. Annunciation and Transubstantiation, *Missal*; Bibl. Nat., Paris. Lat. 848

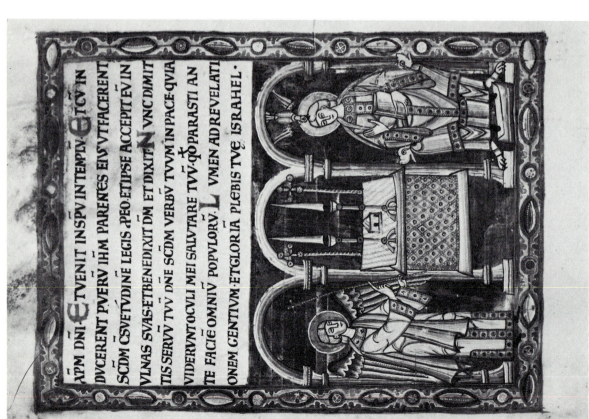

100. Annunciation Flanking Christian Altar, *Pericope of Vyšehrad*; University Library, Prague

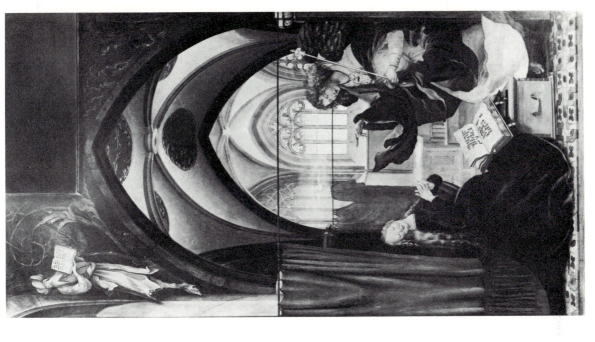

103. Matthäus Gotthart Neithart (Grünewald), Isenheim
Altarpiece, Annunciation; Musée Unterlinden, Colmar

102. Annunciation (detail of right side), *Book of Hours for Charles of France,
Duke of Normandy*; The Metropolitan Museum of Art,
The Cloisters Collection, New York

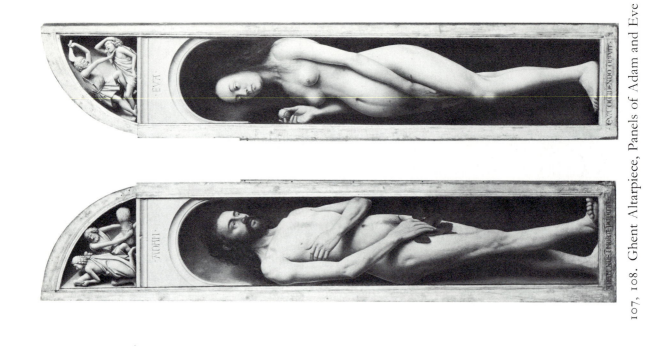

107, 108. Ghent Altarpiece, Panels of Adam and Eve

104. Abel Offering Lamb,
relief from choir screen; Wechselburg

105. Cain with Sheaf of Wheat and Club,
relief from choir screen; Wechselburg

106. Murder of Abel, *Psalter*; British Museum, London.
Ms. Add. 38116, fol. 9 rº

110. Master of the Gathering of Manna, Jews Sacrificing; Museum Boymans Van Beuningen, Rotterdam

109. Ghent Altarpiece, Murder of Abel (detail of panel of Eve)

112. Adventures of Odysseus, wall painting from a house on the Esquiline;
Museo Profano, Vatican, Rome

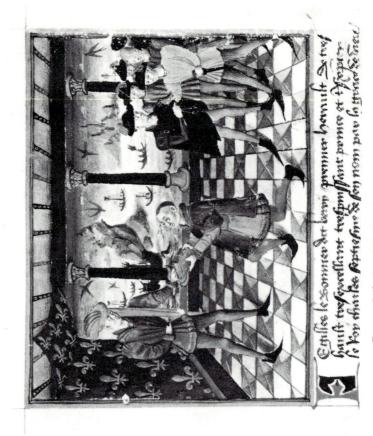

113. Berry Offering His Book to King Charles VII;
Bibl. Nat., Paris. Ms. fr. 2985

111. Fountain of Living Water, *Gospels from St. Médard, Soissons;*
Bibl. Nat., Paris. Ms. Lat. 8850, fol. 6 v°

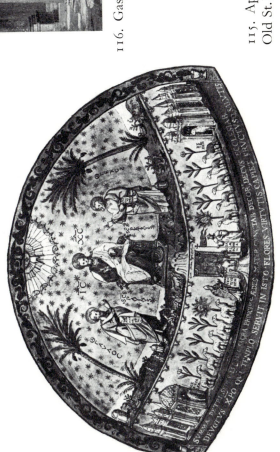

116. Gaspar Dughet, Lateran Basilica, fresco; San Martino ai Monti, Rome

115. Apse Mosaic;
Old St. Peter's, Rome

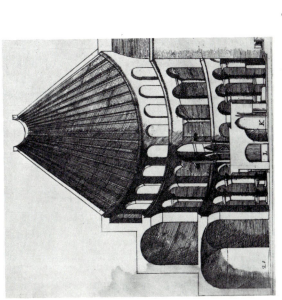

114. Jacques Callot, Anastasis Rotunda, Jerusalem, as of 1609 (engraving from Amico, *Trattato della Piante et Imagini*, pl. 12)

117. Ghent Altarpiece, Singing Angels (detail)

118. Ghent Altarpiece, Music-making Angels (detail)

121. Pietro Lorenzetti, Birth of the Virgin Altarpiece; Museo del Duomo, Siena

119. Giotto, Birth of the Virgin, fresco; Arena Chapel, Padua

120. Workshop of Boucicaut Master, Female Donor Venerating Madonna; Bibl. Nat., Paris. Ms. Lat. 1161, fol. 290

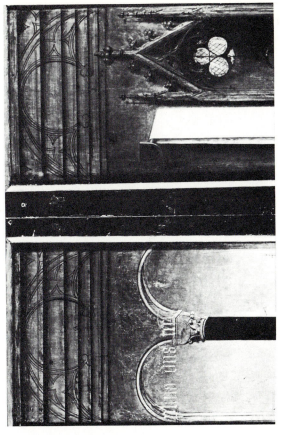

123. Ghent Altarpiece, Annunciation (detail: two center panels), infra-red photo

122. Ghent Altarpiece, Annunciation (detail: Angel panel), infra-red photo

124. Masolino (?), Annunciation, fresco; San Clemente, Rome

125. Donatello, Feast of Herod; Baptistery, Siena

126. Master of Flémalle, The Good Thief; Städelsches Kunstinstitut, Frankfort-on-the-Main

127. Master of Flémalle (copy), Descent from the Cross; Walker Art Gallery, Liverpool

128. Jan van Eyck, Small Altarpiece of the Madonna; Staatliche Kunstsammlungen, Dresden

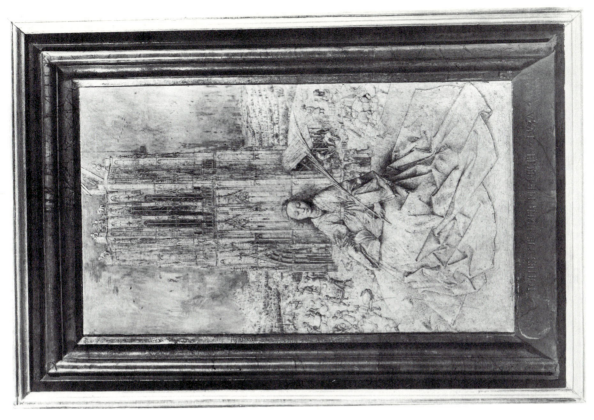

130. Jan van Eyck, St. Barbara; Musée Royal des Beaux-Arts, Antwerp

129. Jan van Eyck, Madonna at the Fountain; Musée Royal des Beaux-Arts, Antwerp

132. Jan van Eyck, St. Barbara (detail of Fig. 130: background figures)

131. Follower of Van Eyck (?), Ceremony in a Churchyard, *Très-Belles Heures*; Museo Civico, Turin

134. Anonymous Drawing, Adoration of the Magi; Kupferstichkabinett, Berlin

133. Follower of Van Eyck, Cavalcade by the Seashore, *Très-Belles Heures*; Formerly Royal Library, Turin

135. Jan van Eyck, Madonna in a Church; Staatliche Museen, Berlin (Gemäldegalerie)

136. Master of Flémalle, Madonna and Child; Städelsches Kunstinstitut, Frankfort-on-the-Main

137. Jan van Eyck, "Lucca Madonna";
Städelsches Kunstinstitut, Frankfort-on-the-Main

138. Jan van Eyck, Annunciation;
National Gallery of Art, Washington

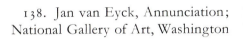

139. Jan van Eyck,
Madonna of Canon van der Paele;
Musée Communal, Bruges

140. Jan van Eyck, Calvary;
The Metropolitan Museum of Art, New York

141. Jan van Eyck, Last Judgment;
The Metropolitan Museum of Art, New York

142. Miraculous Host of Philip the Good, *Hours of René d'Anjou;*
British Museum, London. Egerton Ms. 1070, fol. 110 v°.

143. Miraculous Host in Monstrance;
British Museum, London. Ms. 31240, fol. 21

144. House-shaped Tabernacle (13th century);
The Metropolitan Museum of Art, New York

145. Wall Tabernacle Shaped Like
Monstrance; Church, Gernsbach

146. Wall Tabernacle; Church of the Holy Spirit, Rothenburg ob der Tauber

147. Wall Tabernacle with Doors Open; Church of the Holy Spirit, Rothenburg ob der Tauber

148. Master of the Schöppingen Altarpiece, Resurrection of Christ (detail); Parish Church, Schöppingen

149. Engraving after Pieter Bruegel the Elder, Resurrection of Christ

150. Andrea da Firenze, Resurrection of Christ, fresco; Spanish Chapel, Santa Maria Novella, Florence

151. Andrea di Bartolo, Resurrection of Christ;
Walters Art Gallery, Baltimore;

152. Sano di Pietro, Resurrection of Christ;
Wallraf-Richartz-Museum, Cologne

153. Jan van Eyck, Painted Tabernacle, Author's Reconstruction

154. Jan van Eyck, Painted Tabernacle, Three Symbolic
Configurations (schematic drawing)

155. Hans Memling, Altarpiece of the Crucifixion; Cathedral, Lübeck

156. Resurrection of Christ, *Hortulus Animae;*
Österreichische Nationalbibliothek,
Vienna. Cod. 2706, fol. 319 v°

157. Hans Memling, Altarpiece of the Crucifixion
(detail of Resurrection panel: rising sun)

158. Gerard David, Altarpiece of the Crucifixion; Frans Hals Museum, Haarlem

159. Gerard David, Altarpiece of the Crucifixion
(detail of Crucifixion panel: Magdalene)

160. Jan van Eyck, Calvary
(detail of Fig. 140: Magdalene)

161. Master of Schloss Lichtenstein, The Meeting at the Golden Gate (detail); Philadelphia Museum of Art

162. Master of the Karlsruhe Passion, Arrest of Christ (detail); Wallraf-Richartz-Museum, Cologne

163. Wooden Mesusa with Letter "Shin"; Collection Dr. Bruno Kirschner, Jerusalem, Israel

164. Engraving after Pieter Bruegel the Elder, Resurrection of Christ (detail: guard awakening)

165. Gerard David, Altarpiece of the Crucifixion (detail of Resurrection panel: guard awakening); Frans Hals Museum, Haarlem

166. Wounded Gaul, Roman sculpture; Museum, Aix-en-Provence

168. Jan van Eyck, Calvary (detail of Fig. 140)

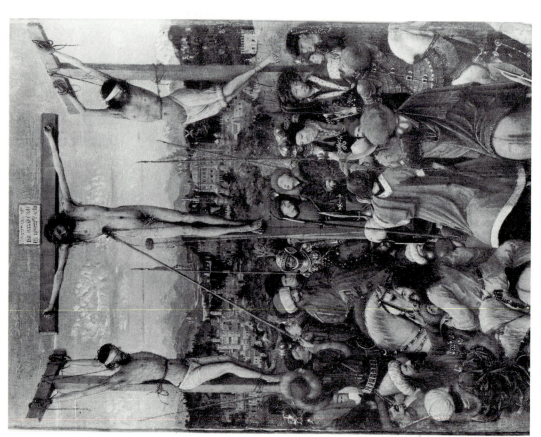

167. Jan van Eyck, Calvary (detail of Fig. 140)

169. "Large Calvary"; Wallraf-Richartz-Museum, Cologne

170. Jan van Eyck, Last Judgment (detail of Fig. 141: Archangel Michael)

171. Ghent Altarpiece, Adoration of the Lamb (detail: group of virgins)

172. Master of the Garden of Paradise, The Garden of Paradise;
Städelsches Kunstinstitut, Frankfort-on-the-Main

173. Ghent Altarpiece, Panel of Judges   174. Ghent Altarpiece, Panel of Knights

176. Cologne Master of c. 1325, Annunciation; Wallraf-Richartz-Museum, Cologne

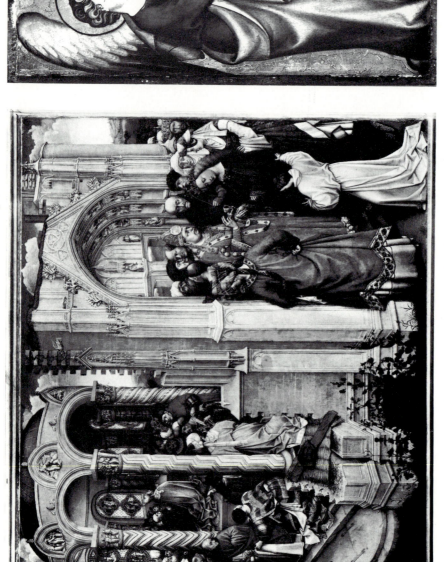

175. Attributed to the Master of Flémalle, Betrothal of the Virgin; Prado, Madrid

177. Melchior Broederlam, Annunciation and Visitation, Dijon Altarpiece (left wing, exterior); Musée de la Ville, Dijon

178. Melchior Broederlam, Presentation in the Temple and Flight into Egypt, Dijon Altarpiece (right wing exterior); Musée de la Ville, Dijon

179. Jan van Eyck (copy), Annunciation; The Metropolitan Museum of Art, New York

180. Lorenzo Maitani (?), Annunciation, façade relief (detail of third pilaster); Cathedral, Orvieto

181. Altichiero and Avanzo, St. Lucy before the Judge (detail), fresco; Oratorio di San Giorgio, Padua

182. Follower of Van Eyck. The Three Marys at the Tomb;
Museum Boymans Van Beuningen, Rotterdam

183. Rogier van der Weyden, Columba Altarpiece, Adoration of the Magi (central panel);
Bayerische Staatsgemäldesammlungen, Munich

184. Ghent Altarpiece, Panel of Judges (detail: portrait heads)

185. Philip the Good of Burgundy
(reproduced in reverse);
Musée de la Ville, Dijon

186. Philip the Bold of Burgundy
(reproduced in reverse);
Musée de la Ville, Dijon

187. Pisanello, John VIII
Paleologus, medal; Victoria
and Albert Museum, London

188. John the Fearless of
Burgundy (detail);
Musée Royal des Beaux-Arts,
Antwerp

189. Ghent Altarpiece, Panel of Knights (detail: banners)

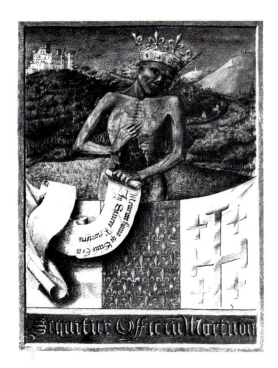

190. King René d'Anjou as Skeleton (Le Roi Mort),
Hours of René d'Anjou;
British Museum, London. Ms. Egerton 1070

191. Benozzo Gozzoli,
Journey of the Magi
(detail: Michael Paleologus), fresco;
Palazzo Medici Riccardi, Florence

192. Jan van Eyck, Madonna of Chancellor Rolin; Louvre, Paris

193. Master of the St. Lucy Legend, Virgin of the Rose Garden; Detroit Institute of Arts

194. Jan van Eyck, Madonna of Provost Nicholas van Maelbeke, Interior View; Warwick Castle

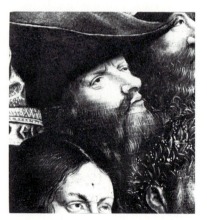

196. Ghent Altarpiece, Adoration of the Lamb (detail: lower left)

195. Jan van Eyck, Madonna of Provost Nicholas van Maelbeke, Exterior View; Warwick Castle

197. Masaccio, The Trinity, fresco; Santa Maria Novella, Florence

198. Drawing after Tomb of Boniface VIII (destroyed); Vatican Library, Rome

199. Donatello and Michelozzo, Monument of Cardinal Rinaldo Brancacci; Sant'Angelo a Nilo, Naples

200. Giovanni Cosmati, Tomb of William Durandus; Santa Maria sopra Minerva, Rome

201. Jan van Eyck, Madonna of Provost Nicholas van Maelbeke, Author's Reconstruction

202. Rogier van der Weyden, Altarpiece of the Seven Sacraments
(detail); Musée Royal des Beaux-Arts, Antwerp

203. Jan van Eyck and Petrus Christus, Madonna of Jan Vos;
The Frick Collection, New York

204. Rogier van der Weyden, Descent from the Cross; Prado, Madrid

205. Rogier van der Weyden, Granada-Miraflores Altarpiece (second version);
Staatliche Museen, Berlin (Gemäldegalerie)

206. Rogier van der Weyden, St. Luke Portraying the Madonna; Museum of Fine Arts, Boston

207. Master of the Mansi Magdalene, Salvator Mundi (detail);
John G. Johnson Collection, Philadelphia Museum of Art

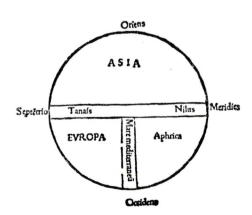

208. World Map in "Orbis Breviarum," Printed
Edition by Zacharias, Florence, 1493

209. Hugo van der Goes, Portinari Altarpiece, Adoration of the Shepherds
(central panel); Uffizi, Florence

210. Hieronymus Bosch, Adoration of the Magi; Prado, Madrid

211. Albrecht Altdorfer, Birth of the Virgin; Bayerische
Staatsgemäldesammlungen, Munich

212. Matthäus Gotthart Neithart (Grünewald), Isenheim Altarpiece, Mary as the
New Heaven and the New Earth; Musée Unterlinden, Colmar